PARENTING
FOR A
PEACEFUL WORLD

Author's note

This book is not intended to be a parenting manual. The material contained in this book is intended as general information about research in the areas of developmental psychology, social psychology, biology and psychohistory. None of the material contained in this book is intended as the definitive source of information on the sciences relating to child development and the care of children, or as a source or substitute for professional advice.

The author, editor, endorser or publisher of this publication exclude any liability suffered by any person, corporation or other entity for any loss, damage or injury caused by or arising from reliance upon any statement made or information contained in this publication.

You are urged to always obtain professional advice relating to your particular situation, in relation to parenting, childcare or child education, from a qualified child health practitioner.

Your use of any of the information contained or referred to in this publication is your confirmation that you do not rely upon same as, or as a substitute for, professional advice.

PARENTING
FOR A
PEACEFUL WORLD

Robin Grille

The Children's Project
Richmond

For Yaramin

First published in 2005 in Australia by Longueville Media, PO Box 7143
Alexandria, NSW 2015, Australia

This revised edition published in the UK in 2008 by The Children's Project
PO Box 2, Richmond, TW10 7FL, United Kingdom
www.socialbaby.com

UK edition edited by Heather Welford
Cover designed by Clive Dorman
Cover photograph © 2005 Helen Dorman

A CIP catalogue record for this book is available from
the British Library

Mixed Sources
Product group from well-managed
forests and other controlled sources
www.fsc.org Cert no. TT-COC-002227
© 1996 Forest Stewardship Council
FSC

Printed in the UK by CPI Bookmarque, Croydon, CR0 4TD

Permissions

Contents

Foreword

I wish this scholarly and passionately argued book had existed when I first became a parent and when the parenting sector embarked on a mission to persuade policy makers to invest in support for parenting.

"Man hands on misery to man," said Philip Larkin: Robin Grille would agree. He brings together insights from recent and established research to make a compelling case for new ways of relating to children to enable them to be happy, fulfilled and productive. He takes us through a hell of abusive child-rearing practices throughout history and brings us to a vision of the possibility of Utopia, a world of happiness and inner peace with detailed suggestions for how this might be achieved.

But this book is no flight of fancy: facts and suggestions are all based on solid, carefully documented research. The UK publication is timely, coming as it does during a period of rapid growth in provision to enable parents to do a better job when parenting service providers and students are hungry for information and ideas.

The author argues convincingly for changes in how we bring up the next generation. What is at stake is not simply the happiness of children, though the UK certainly cannot be complacent about its place at the bottom of the UNICEF list of child-friendly nations. What the book makes clear is that by avoiding cruel and manipulative parenting practices we stand to gain adult happiness, fulfillment, ultimately world peace and a deepening respect for the planet and our fellow human beings.

Though he strongly recommends universal provision of education for parenting, Robin Grille does not think all the burden should fall on parents; it is the business of the whole community to ensure children are brought up in accordance with their needs and that parents are supported. Grandparents and other adults also have an important role in supporting parenting.

In their 2002 report *Helpful Parenting*, the Royal College

of Paediatrics and Child Health suggested that "our familiar assumptions about bringing up children are not always correct." *Parenting for a Peaceful World* provides an analysis of what is going wrong and clear suggestions for how to create a world where children and adults can fulfill their potential and lead happier lives.

Mary Crowley OBE
Stakeholder Adviser
National Academy for Parenting Practitioners

Preface

The key to world peace and sustainability lies in the way we collectively relate to our children. I am aware, of course, that this has been said before. Until recently however, whenever this idea has been expressed, it has been either downplayed or resisted. Perhaps we are afraid of the responsibility it entails. Today however, groundbreaking research has brought new confirmation to this ancient idea. Our understanding of early childhood development has grown so rapidly in recent years, that we can now say the following with unprecedented confidence: *the human brain and heart that are met primarily with empathy in the critical early years cannot and will not grow to choose a violent or selfish life.*

The fact that scientists and politicians have so easily dismissed the importance of childhood as sentimentality, has enabled them to sideline some of the most critical reforms that are needed to improve children's emotional lives. This is costly for all of society. Early childhood emotional development does not matter too much, the hardliners reason, for children are 'resilient' and their characters are built-in at birth. This grim, genetic-deterministic view of human relations has historically underwritten societies lacking in compassion.

But science has opened up new vistas. New technologies have unlocked many secrets about how early life experiences direct the course of the growing brain. We have witnessed an explosion of interest in 'emotional intelligence' as we begin to recognise the critical role it plays in all levels of human relations. International research has shed new light on infant bonding and attachment. For the first time in history, the idea that a society's destiny rests on how it treats its children has concrete foundations, and the implications demand our attention. As this portentous new knowledge begins to burst its banks, I cannot imagine that society will remain unchanged. What developmental psychologists are telling us today is going to revolutionise our approaches to child rearing and education – in fact, a quiet revolution has been taking place already – with far-reaching social results.

These new discoveries have opened up a realm of possibility beyond what many of us may have imagined. Modern wisdom increasingly begs us to look at, for instance, the growing incidence of knife-violence in the UK in a whole new light. Those who understand the implications of the new research will know that if we are to reduce social violence, we must begin by reducing our violence against, and neglect of, babies and children. It is time that this kind of information became far more widely available.

If you are a parent, carer, health professional or educator, I have designed this book to help you to tune in to the emotional needs of children in your care, in order to support their developing emotional intelligence. However, I would also invite you to use this book to gain insights into the origins of your own unique emotional make-up, and thus illuminate your own path of healing and growth. (Parts IV, V and VI are particularly geared towards the latter purpose.)

It is my hope that this book will also be used as a resource for policy makers whose decisions chart the course of families' lives and social destiny.

I do have some concerns about how the information contained in this book and others like it might be used. There is a risk that the kind of knowledge we have gained about the links between child rearing and society will result in the politicising of childhood. The idea of manipulating children for the purpose of creating little 'pacifists' bothers me a great deal. Whenever we impose our own purpose on our children, our plans tend to backfire. Children want to be seen for the totality of their being — they resist (and rightly so) our fervent hopes that they become good doctors, lawyers, humanitarians, or nice people. We smother them with our expectations. Our children do not want to be our 'projects'. They want to be enjoyed and related to for who they are at any given moment, as if who they are now, and who they are becoming in this instant, is all they will ever be. They want to get to know us as real people. And they need us to remain open to whom they are as individuals: almost always, they will surprise us, and confound our expectations. Children are not adults-in-the-making; they are not clay to be moulded. They are children, and that is that. Our task is to wonder at them, to learn about ourselves through our relationships with them. It is also important to remind ourselves that children are not 'them' – they are 'us'. We have felt what they feel, yearned for what they yearn for – and if we are honest with ourselves . . . we still do.

So, the purpose of this book is not to list what we 'should' do for children. This book is my way of arguing that *all of us are parents to society's children*, and that societies must, as a matter of top priority, support parents so that they can fulfil their nurturing potential.

I would caution that no text dealing with child development should replace consultation with well-researched, trained child health professionals. As Parts VI and VII do not cover medical or nutritional issues, or norms of physical or intellectual development, I recommend that they be used in conjunction with other relevant books, and the advice of sympathetic child health practitioners. This book should not be thought of as a child-rearing manual.

While making some suggestions, this book does not tell parents how to be parents. It tells parents and health professionals what science and clinical experience have taught us about what babies and children need for optimal emotional development. Parents are free to adapt their own abilities and resourcefulness to meeting these needs to the best of their ability and based on the support available.

My perspectives on early-childhood emotional development have been gained from 20 years of personal experience as a psychotherapist, and from countless hours as a client of psychotherapists. Beyond my own, personal observations I draw upon the collective wisdom of clinicians from a range of psychotherapeutic modalities. I also rely on research findings in areas including (but not limited to) prenatal and perinatal psychology, mother-infant attachment and early brain development. My views have been strongly influenced through several years' of training with psychologist Chris Campbell PhD, and his unique and innovative insights into childhood and human relations.

Some readers may wonder why I have included recently uncovered accounts of child rearing through history, and across many cultures (Parts II and III). Reading the history of childhood has been life-changing for me, and has, I believe, helped to make me a better parent. This history offers us all immense understanding and compassion, while providing new-found and tangible causes for optimism regarding our future.

To compile this book I have ventured beyond my own field of expertise and drawn upon findings from a variety of fields of study, including psychohistory and neuropsychology. Though I have taken every care in collecting my research, I may be found wrong on some details and specifics. However, I am confident in my central message: that healthy emotional development for children is critical for a peaceful and sustainable world.

Since we have each travelled such unique and different life-paths, I suspect that this book will evoke quite different feelings and thoughts in each reader. Whatever your personal experience is when you embark on your course through these pages, I thank you for taking this journey with me.

FROM VIOLENCE TO HARMONY: CHILD REARING AND SOCIAL EVOLUTION

To look into some aspects of the future, we do not need projections by supercomputers. Much of the next millennium can be seen in how we care for our children today. Tomorrow's world may be influenced by science and technology, but more than anything, it is already taking shape in the bodies and minds of our children.

Kofi Annan[1]

1

HOW PARENTING
CHANGES THE WORLD

Violence is in large measure a result of culture, and to reduce violence one must reduce all of the contributing causes. This cannot be achieved by decree, treaty or imposition.

Rodrigo Carazo[2]

war ought to be a psychiatric health program. A solution to this problem may still be a long time in the future, but this is no reason why we should continue to ignore it, or leave it only to politicians ... war behaviour results basically from emotional disturbance.

George Stevenson[3]

What if war was not inevitable? What if tyranny, human rights abuses and ecological destruction were not inescapable? And what if the means to prevent them were in the hands of ordinary mums and dads, and all those involved in the care and education of children? Are these idealistic or utopian flights of fancy? Not at all, if we consider some of the most valuable insights gained in recent years.

Childhood and world affairs
Explanations for major societal ills have traditionally been economic, historic, religious, or moral, and few authors have addressed the psychological when trying to understand war and tyranny. Since it is well established that delinquency is the

product of violence or neglect experienced in childhood, is it not logical to suspect the same to be true of large-scale violence?

If war is a psychological problem, the most effective solutions are psychological rather than political. The implication is clear: we should be directing far more of our resources to psychological solutions and preventions. This entails re-evaluation of the way that we, as a global community, rear our children.

Childhood and social evolution

It is only recently that researchers have begun to piece together a tableau of the quality of children's lives throughout the ages. What has surfaced stands in stark contrast to what most of us might have imagined. Much of the history of childhood in the west is a hellish tale of widespread neglect and abuse, and the further back into history we look, the more brutally we see children treated, with abusive practices institutionalised or embedded in cultural and religious rites.

Fortunately, child-rearing practices have been slowly evolving towards more nurturance. As a result, we have taken momentous strides toward greater democracy, justice and equality. Social evolution has been the product of child-rearing evolution: one cannot happen without the other.

As we keep learning about the conditions that are most conducive to healthy emotional development, we can look forward to a wide range of social dividends. Each incremental step toward the mass betterment of children's lives hastens the democratisation process. The evolution in child rearing is helping to create societies that are more harmonious, just and compassionate, and can mitigate social ills such as crime, substance addiction and 'mental' illness. Anyone involved in the care of children – parents, carers, teachers and policy makers – can consciously play a significant role in accelerating this evolution.

Psychological roots of social ills

The worst extremes of human suffering have often been at the hands of humans through the abuse of power. Globally, human rights and environmental abuses are committed by governments and corporations – sometimes with considerable public support. At the community level, crime, delinquency, domestic violence, and the self-abuse of substance addiction

3

and workaholism abound. These social ills are all distortions of human relations; the adult product of early injuries to children's emotional development. Ultimately, most social ills can be better understood in terms of their psychological roots.

War is increasingly recognised to be a symptom of psychological injury. Alice Miller (renowned psychologist and writer on issues of childhood trauma) is one of the most passionate advocates of this idea, and she is far from alone. Robert Scharf, contributing editor to the *Journal of Psychohistory*, recognises that "the threat to the very existence of the human species which is posed by ecological mismanagement and nuclear weapons underscores the irrational nature of human society".[4] In 1984, the Board of Social and Ethical Responsibility of the American Psychological Association sponsored a meeting of research psychologists to discuss the psychology of war, and how organised psychology might assist in its prevention. The results of these discussions were published in 1986, titled *Psychology and the Prevention of Nuclear War.*

A popular myth contends that social afflictions – such as addictions to substances or to gambling – pertain to people who are weak, or feeble-minded in some way. Another idea is that crime and violence exist because there are 'bad' people who are born that way. Explanations such as these will never lead to useful solutions. In fact, they usually bring about disastrous consequences.[5]

We should be paying more attention to the psychological basis for social and global problems. The way we bring up our children is what determines the kind of society we live in. Since the health of any society is dependent upon the emotional health of its children, children's wellbeing should be our top priority.

A question of relationship
The collective changes urgently needed are more fundamental and profound than can be wrought through the crude tools of politics. Changes are needed on the level of 'relationship' – core changes in the way we relate to each other as families, communities, organisations, cultures and nations. We need to transform the way we relate to our environment; the way we perceive our place in the cycle of biological life. Our interactions are guided by forces that spring from deep in our psyches; too deep for a set of rules or behavioural codes to change them.

4

For all our human efforts to define 'right' and 'wrong' and punish the 'bad', we are still tearing each other and our planet to pieces. It's not that rules of behaviour aren't important, but fundamental changes don't come from adherence to rules, or from the formulation of better codes of conduct. The capacity for deep and abiding change in the way we interact with one another springs from childhood. As we will see in Parts II and III, the most positive social changes around the world have followed mass improvements in the way in which children are treated.

We are only at the foetal stage of the change in consciousness required to preserve the ecological viability of our planet. Our survival depends on our learning more emotionally intelligent ways to relate to each other and to our planet. This is the cultural change, more effective than political and legislative manoeuvres, that former Costa Rican president Carazo suggested above.

Aren't humans inherently violent?

Aren't war, crime and violence just facts of life, natural and intrinsic parts of the human condition? Fatalistic ideas about the destructiveness inherent in human nature may not be as silly as they sound. The science of evolutionary biology suggests that behaviour patterns we commonly regard as 'evil' are integral to most species. There is reason to believe that 'evil' is a basic biological imperative. 'Evil' may have even played an important role in the evolution of humanity, but this point of view is not as bleak as it first appears.

In his book *The Rise and Fall of the Third Chimpanzee*,[6] zoologist Jared Diamond states that we humans share 98 per cent of our genes with chimpanzees. It is said that we are one of three species of chimp – the upright and technological one. Based on thousands of hours of painstaking observation in the field, primatologists have only recently (and reluctantly!) been forced to accept some unpalatable truths about our chimp cousins. In their natural habitat, chimpanzees (not the 'bonobo' or 'pygmy' chimpanzees) are genocidal and infanticidal. One group methodically decimates another by picking-off and killing them, one at a time. In fact, in most species of primates, both males and females frequently abduct and kill each other's children. We share so much of our biology with chimps, why would we be any different in our behaviour? Biologists argue that human 'evil' has brought survival advantages to our species, as it has done to other species.

Biologist Lyall Watson demonstrates that the capacity for destructiveness and violence has an evolutionary and genetic purpose. In his book *Dark Nature*[7] he offers countless examples of the 'usefulness' of cruelty. Fratricide is common in the animal kingdom, as is infanticide. Gorillas and lions kill the offspring of rival males after successful challenges for supremacy. Even females, usually seen as victims of violence, contribute to it by becoming attracted to the most aggressive males – as Warren Farrell PhD argues in *The Myth of Male Power*.[8] The image of the warrior has been cloaked in romance, the soldier in uniform is quintessential attractiveness. One of the most hawkish of US politicians, Donald Rumsfeld, was nominated among the 'sexiest men alive' by a leading American magazine.[9] This combination of male and female instincts, which favours violence, secures the viability of each species via the propagation of the 'strongest' genes. For similar reasons to those of our animal cousins, we humans are intrinsically violent. Or is it rather that we have an innate *capacity* for violence, dependent on what is triggered in childhood?

Humans have thrived with remarkable success, colonised every continent, and bumped off countless other species. If our history is fraught with war, genocide and ecological destruction, it is because our belligerence is grounded in biological reality – our chimp-like or animalistic substance compels us.

On the other hand dogs, elephants, cetaceans and many other kinds of animals have demonstrated a capacity for 'altruistic' behaviours by risking grave danger to rescue non-kin and even members of other species.[10] Watson tells of wild orca (killer whales) that gently buoyed him out of the water and pushed him to shore when, with the aid of a snorkel, he feigned sounds of distressed breathing. Though all too often we attack each other, history is also full of examples of kindness, of individuals going to great lengths, and even giving their lives, to protect and care for others.

Altruistic and nurturant behaviours make just as much 'survival' sense as cruel ones. The impulse to bond and create friendship is the glue of *community,* and it helps to create a safer world. In the grand scheme of evolution, love exists alongside violence – both are vital cogs in the wheel of Life. Capacities for viciousness and love inhabit every one of us. If original sin exists at our core, then so does original love. Whether we enact the violent chimp, or the compassionate orca, depends to a large extent on how we were nurtured as children.

For humans, the bridge between instinct and behaviour is built by our learning experiences. Early life experiences mould our raw aggression, determining whether it will manifest as rage and hostility; or as creativity, innovation, industriousness and leadership. The environment we grow up in decides how our so-called 'instincts' are expressed.

At this point in history, violence has ceased to offer a survival advantage. We have populated our planet to capacity, and are dangerously close to wiping out the human race – and perhaps most life on earth. The new survival imperative entails a radical evolution in the dimension of relationship.

Is such social change conceivable, or is it mere new age fantasy? As psychohistorian Lloyd de Mause suggests, we are moving from a climate of "survival of the fittest – children of the most ruthless parents", towards "survival of the most innovative and co-operative – children of the most loving parents".[11]

Violence as a learned response

The behavioural repertoire of creatures that have simpler nervous systems is narrow and determined.[12] 'Higher' animals on the other hand, though born with some in-built programs, have a capacity – and a need – to *learn* social behaviours from each other. Our 'instincts' don't set our behavioural patterns in stone. In humans, what we call 'instinctual behaviour' does not always manifest unless modelled by more experienced individuals, and it varies dramatically based on how it is role-modelled. Few 'instinctual' behaviours – like the sucking reflex, for instance – are a complete package at birth. Most human 'instinctual' behaviour has to be learned in a social context. That is why there is more variation in the way humans parent their young, than in any other animal.[13] As anthropologist, Sarah Blaffer Hrdy's review of research into human social behaviour confirms, there has always been huge diversity in parenting styles.[14]

Human behaviour is more free and changeable by far than that of any other animal, and to a large extent violence is a learned response passed down from generation to generation. We are demonstrably capable of creating an infinitely broad and variable range of cultures. Our enormous ability to choose and evolve distinguishes us from other animals. The way is open for us to create the kind of societies we want, once we understand how relationship styles emerge from emotional development in childhood.

Can societies evolve?

The experiences we have in infancy have been shown to have permanent effects on brain development. Some of the deepest, pattern-like aspects of our personality, and our fundamental dispositions regarding relationships, are shaped in childhood, babyhood and possibly even in the womb. More than any other animal, the human infant is dependent on abiding care and education from family and community in order to thrive. This reliance on prolonged nurturance grants humanity the scope for a much more rapid form of evolution: a *social* evolution, which operates independently of biological evolution.

One recent example of social evolution, which was particularly striking for its velocity and scope, took place during the 1960s. This period ushered in some far-reaching changes to the nature of gender relations; upheavals that were permanently to alter the rules of marriage, family dynamics, sexual relations and industrial relations. Social changes wrought since the 1960s have radically transformed the face of modern society, beyond the point of no return. In modern times, it is possible for positive social changes to happen very quickly.

Unlike biological evolution, social evolution can progress quite rapidly. What's more, we each have the power to influence its speed and direction. The knowledge we have amassed through the development of social and behavioural sciences brings within our grasp the ability to accelerate the collective advance towards more loving and peaceful communities.

Although many people have suspected that parenting determines society, we have not realised until recently how profoundly true this is. When we parent a child, we are parenting the world and its future.

Current dilemmas

Two things threaten all our lives: high-tech warfare and indus- trially driven ecological disaster. Both are a kind of madness; born of emotional injury. Both are the result of arrests in emo- tional development. Both are problems of relationship. Both will be mitigated as we raise children with better attention to their emotional development.

At millennium's end, up to 40 countries are believed to be capable of manufacturing nuclear weapons.[15] The Comprehensive Nuclear Test Ban Treaty has not been ratified by the USA, Pakistan, India, China or Israel, and more recently, it has been flouted by North Korea.[16] Crude nuclear explosives in all probability are already in the hands of terrorist groups. Sophisticated biological and chemical weaponry is proliferating and, as missile technology improves, it threatens more distant targets. Between wars, we shoot each other down in the streets (and in the USA, among others, at school too), with the support of an international small-arms trade that has reached an annual worth of US$10 billion. In the USA, it was recently estimated that the military spends in just one-and-a-half weeks what the government spends on the management of fisheries and wildlife, national parks, and public lands over a whole year.[17] In other words, war was over 30 times more important than preserving the environment.

It is now indisputable that our contempt for natural resources, our thoughtless exploitation and our pollution, are wreaking worldwide havoc. We are warned of increasingly unseasonal weather patterns that will multiply crop failures, disease, natural disasters and wildlife extinctions beyond anything civilisation has ever experienced.[18] This will occur within the lifetime of most readers. In fact, it has already begun. Since the 1950s, there has been more than a doubling in the global cost of natural cataclysms. Natural disasters caused by climate change have multiplied five-fold in two decades.[19] Over two million people die each year around the world as a direct result of air pollution,[20] which is more than are killed through war, terrorism and homicide.[21] Our violence towards our natural environment has become an even more pressing problem than our violence towards each other.

The trite but popular rationale for our global dilemma is 'overpopulation'. Although there is no doubt that our planet is overpopulated, this is a very narrow analysis of the problem. Historians and anthropologists have tended to blame human violence on dwindling resources, and the resulting competition for survival – as if the causal relationship was a simple, one-way ticket.[22] However, as we will see in later chapters, the tendency towards violence is not spontaneous for any social or ethnic group, and it must be mediated through harsh and authoritarian child-rearing practices. In other words, we are not necessarily born to choose violence as if it is the only solution to territorial or resource disputes. Furthermore, it is often the case that human violence – towards each other and towards nature – is what creates resource scarcity in the first place.

At the very core, our dilemma is a problem of relationship – that is, we have been driven to fight against nature, to dominate it, exploit it, instead of learning how to live harmoniously as part of it. The excessive and unsustainable plunder of the environment could be treated, to borrow from George Stevenson's vernacular, as a 'psychiatric health' problem.

Given that we are at – if not beyond – the eleventh hour, it is bewildering what few resources are devoted to researching and developing sustainable energy technologies,[23] while astronomical sums are spent by fossil fuel companies to secure and prolong their overwhelming market dominance,[24] with copious and unwavering backing from global financiers.[25] Meanwhile, vast sums – that could be diverted towards research and development of clean energy – are used to fund public relations campaigns to deny scientific opinion on climate change.[26]

Just half of one per cent of the US$89 billion spent globally in 1998 exploring for and producing more oil, if invested on research and development, would suffice to make solar energy commercially viable.[27] It may be argued that lack of clean energy sources reveal society's addiction to short-term profits, with its willingness to overlook the consequences. Our existence is not threatened by our numbers, but by our way of relating.

It is also popular to blame overpopulation for the fact that 815 million people do not have enough to eat,[28] and for the fact that around half of the world's population ekes out an existence at less than US$2 per day. This rationale is evaporated when we examine the obscene disparities in the way the world's bountiful resources are consumed.[29] World hunger is not caused by 'too many people', but – to a significant degree – by an absurd and spectacularly inequitable distribution of wealth.

Meanwhile, mountains of perfectly edible produce are warehoused and destroyed annually in wealthy nations because 'market forces' dictate that some produce is the 'wrong size' or the 'wrong shape' for the shelves. We produce unimaginable amounts of waste,[30] while our overfed populations binge their way to obesity.[31] Far from the situation of scarcity promoted by vested interests (businesses promoting genetically modified foods), there is actually enough food around the world to provide two kilos worth of balanced nutrition a day for every individual on earth.[32]

In *Reworking Success* economist Robert Theobald[33] demonstrates that the idea that demand exceeds supply is a fallacy. At this moment in our history, and for some time now, industrial and technological advances have created hyper-productive societies in which supply has outstripped demand. The world makes more than it uses, developed nations use more than they need, and unimaginable resources are wasted. The problem faced by over-efficient producers today is in finding or creating new markets – there are not enough people to buy the goods!

This is a far cry from the idea that we are victims of overpopulation. Like war, environmental degradation and world hunger are the results of dysfunctional human relations and incompletely developed emotional intelligence. The current global dilemma arises from exploitative relationships towards others, and towards the environment. It is a predicament of psychological origins.

The question is: Can we evolve socially fast enough to avert ecological, social, or nuclear cataclysm? Everything that we do at family and social levels to attend to children's emotional wellbeing, will help to pull us back from the brink.

Whose responsibility? Community as parent
Investment in child and family wellbeing has passed, with flying colours, rigorous tests of cost-benefit analysis. For every $1 spent on supporting children, much more is saved down the track in areas of crime and health. Any concerted effort to protect and improve the lives of children benefits society as a whole.

The better we understand the critical role that childhood plays in the functioning of society, the more the issue of child rearing becomes a matter of international concern. The United Nations Convention on the Universal Rights of the Child (established in 1989, and ratified by every country except the

USA and Somalia) was the first product of this recognition. (This is progress, since in the 18th century declarations of human rights by the USA, Britain and France children were omitted, because they were considered to be the property of their parents.) We are likely to see an increasing number of attempts to globalise children's rights, such as the April 2001 initiative, through the United Nations Human Rights Commission, to put an end to the corporal punishment of children (supported by UNICEF (United Nations Children's Fund), EPOCH (End Physical Punishment of Children),[34] and the United Nations Human Rights Commission).

Since the idea of universal and free education has taken hold during the last 200 or so years, the trend has been for government and industry to increasingly sponsor all that is important for the welfare of children. As governments took on an increasingly active role, modern innovations have included maternity leave, baby-health centres, bans on corporal punishment, and child protection laws, to mention just a few. This sense of community and global responsibility for the care of and respect for children will hopefully continue to expand.

It makes sense for governments, and other community organisations, to take an active role in supporting and educating parents. The buck certainly does not stop with parents, though they may be the first port of call for their children. Both parents are responsible, but parents are only as good as the support they get from their extended family and community. Children's emotional make-up is also influenced by the quality of relationships provided by siblings, other family members and by their teachers at school. Finally, parents' capacity to give of their best is dependent on government and industrial provisions that enable them to devote enough time to their kids without risking financial ruin. A progressive community hinges on parents having access to quality parenting education, and support services such as home visitation programs by health professionals and volunteers where needed.

I hold that responsibility for each child's wellbeing rests with the entire community. So, although this book can be a valuable resource for parents, it can also be more. It addresses educators and anyone involved in social policy making, in government and the private sector. I wish to demonstrate that funding good parenting and education is the most effective way to reduce violence, crime, substance addiction and a host of other social problems. Industry support such as paid maternity and paternity leave and provisions for nursing mothers creates greater staff loyalty as well as contributing enormously to the health of society. Universal care for children's emotional health is the key to creating a more peaceful and just global community that lives sustainably, in harmony with its environment.

My cautious optimism about our future comes from my conviction that most social maladies, including war, are symptoms of emotional injury. Therefore, if we continue to improve child rearing, we are likely to enjoy continued progress towards more harmonious societies. I wrote this book because I think it is possible – and urgent – for us to accelerate the natural social-evolutionary process that is already under way.

For centuries, child rearing has evolved away from violence towards more intimate and empathic personal involvement with children. Part II examines the distinct stages of this continuum along which child-rearing evolution has progressed.

This book speaks of great hope for humanity. However, it begins by examining the suffering of children through the ages. Before we can adequately move forward, we need to come to terms with the existence of the monstrous in humanity. Carl Jung called this the 'shadow', and he said most of us strive to disavow its presence. But it is only once we have the courage to fully acknowledge the 'monster' that is born of the battered and neglected child that we are truly free to move on and express the best of what is in the human heart. I do not intend to catalogue the horrors of the history of childhood for the sake of telling the tale – that would be tedious and gratuitously violent. My purpose is to offer a small but evocative cross-section of this history, in order to convey a sense of how far we have evolved in the care of children, and what heartening outcomes this heralds for our future.

Endnotes

[1] Secretary-General of the United Nations in United Nations Children's Fund (1998).

[2] Former president of Costa Rica: Bounds (2000).

[3] Stevenson (1967) pp 166–167.

[4] Scharf (2001) p 281.

[5] For example, the belief in a 'criminal class' led 18th century British authorities to think that by deporting outcasts to penal colonies, their society would become more harmonious. Not

only was this experiment a prodigious failure, it involved human rights abuses on a grand scale.

6 Diamond (1991).

7 Watson (1995).

8 Farrell (1994).

9 See Scheer, Scheer and Chaudry (2003) p 125.

10 Masson and McCarthy (1996).

11 De Mause (1999) p 649.

12 For example, caterpillars are born knowing how to spin cocoons, and spiders need no education to build their webs.

13 Masson (1999).

14 Hrdy (2000).

15 According to Mohamed ElBaradei (2004), chief of the International Atomic Energy Agency (IAEA). Search 'List of countries with nuclear weapons' in Wikipedia http://en.wikipedia.org/ (last accessed 1 December 2004).

16 See Preparatory Commission for the Comprehensive Nuclear-Test-Ban Treaty Organization http://www.ctbto.org/ (last accessed 1 December 2004).

17 Personal correspondence and conversation with a USA National Parks' officer in 2001.

18 The 'International report on climate change' (prepared by 700 international scientists), and the Intergovernmental Panel on Climate Change (informed by over 2000 scientists from around 100 countries) have declared that human industrial activity is producing catastrophic climate changes globally: Baird (2003) p 10.

19 Baird (2003).

20 Personal correspondence from Gregory Hartl of the World Health Organisation, 23 March 2004. By itself, the Greenhouse Effect kills around 160,000 people annually:Vincent (2003).

21 See the World Health Organization, *World Report on Violence and Health* e-book – search http://www.who.int/ (last accessed 1 December 2004).

22 LeBlanc SA (2003).

23 By its own admission, as recently as in 2001, one of the largest oil corporations on earth was spending only US$12 million a year on finding ways to reduce greenhouse-gas emissions: see 'The good oil for Exxon is having a buddy in the White House' *The Sydney Morning Herald* 18 April 2001 p 10.

24 In the same year, this company put $8 *billion* into further oil exploration, and millions on its PR campaign to discredit the

scientific consensus on climate change, and to support the
politicians who opposed the Kyoto climate change treaty: see
Baird (2003).

[25] Hertsgaard (2004).

[26] Milburn and Conrad (1996) pp 216–217, and Rampton and
Stauber (2001), chapter 10

[27] Greenpeace estimate, search, 'Oil, the facts' *New Internationalist*,
June 2001 Vol 335 p 19 in http://www.findarticles.com/ (last
accessed 1 December 2004).

[28] Search 'Food and farming – the facts' *New Internationalist*
January/February 2003 Vol 353 p 20 in http://www.findarticles.
com/ (last accessed 1 December 2004).

[29] In 1998, the world's 225 richest individuals enjoyed an income
equal to that of the world's poorest 2.5 *billion*. It would take
no more than an annual levy of four per cent on the same 225
mega-wealthy individuals to provide sufficient food, sanitation,
safe drinking water, basic education and health care *for all
developing countries*. See 'Wealth distribution statistics' as reported
by the United Nations Development Program (UNDP) http://
www.cooperativeindividualism.org (last accessed 1 December
2004). A UNDP Human Development Report in 1992 found
that the wealthiest fifth of the world's population receives 150
times the income of the poorest fifth. Search 'Development and
poverty' in http://www.worldrevolution.org/ (last accessed
1 December 2004). The three richest individuals on earth
enjoy wealth that exceeds the combined GDP of the 48 least
developed countries, or put another way, they have as much
money as every person and every government in Africa put
together: see Kielburger (2001).

[30] What a waste: Britain throws away £10bn of food every year.
Independent, May 8, 2008. Report from the UK Government's
waste campaign Wrap (Waste & Resources Action Programme)
Americans waste 28 billion pounds of food every year:
Hawken (1997). Australians are the world's second most
prolific generators of garbage: see Hodge (2003).

[31] Over 65 per cent of Americans are overweight, and 31 per cent
are obese – at an annual cost of US$123 billion to the economy:
see The Sydney Morning Herald, 21 January 2004, p 10. In the
UK, Health Survey for England (HSE) data revealed that in
2006, 38% of adults in England were overweight and 24% were
classified as obese. 67% of men and 56% of women were either
overweight or obese in 2006.

32 'Ten myths about world hunger' *New Internationalist* January/February 2003 in http://www.newint.org/issue151/myths.htm (last accessed 1 December 2004).

33 Theobald (1997).

34 See EPOCH USA http://www.stophitting.com/disathome/ and End All Corporal Punishment of Children http://www.endcorporalpunishment.org/ (last accessed 1 December 2004).

CHILDHOOD THROUGH THE AGES

The history of childhood is a nightmare from which we have only recently begun to awaken. The further back in history one goes, the lower the level of childcare, and the more likely children are to be killed, abandoned, terrorised, and sexually abused.

Lloyd de Mause[1]

2

FROM HORROR TO HOPE

The history of childhood is frightfully difficult to come to terms with, and at the same time, enormously reassuring. On the one hand, a look at this history confronts us with some shocking truths about what we humans are capable of as parents. Since childhood shapes society – as we will see through the remainder of this book – little wonder humanity has been so war-like. On the other hand, the clear evidence that parenting has been evolving towards greater nurturance and empathy can give us great cause for hope. Part II traces this historical and ongoing evolution towards more empathic child rearing.

Are humans naturally 'good' parents?
No other phenomenon challenges our ideals about parental love like the historical tendency for humans to kill or abandon our own, and each other's children. Infanticide is not uncommon among other animals, and has been observed in at least 50 species. Amongst our cousins, the chimpanzees, females sometimes kill and cannibalise others' young. Ape mothers sometimes abandon their young under extremely unfavourable circumstances, although they never directly kill them. Humans, however, are the only primates who kill their own young – alas, not infrequently. We share this trait with a few other species, including wolves, bears and lions.

The discovery of the sheer magnitude and recurrence of human infanticide, is such an assault to our senses that it takes most people some time to let it sink in. One historian had this to say: "Many millions of infant deaths can be attributed directly or indirectly to maternal tactics to mitigate the high cost of rearing them."[2] Psychohistorian Lloyd de Mause's more assiduous estimate puts this death-toll in the *billions*.

Following a massive cross-cultural analysis, psychologist

Gwen Broude concluded that "infanticide is virtually universal".[3] The fact that children from most cultures have been killed off by their own parents in immense numbers has only recently begun to dawn on the scientific community. In 1990, a World Conference on Infanticide was convened in Sicily in order to discuss the implications. The attendees were not only dismayed at how common infanticide has been, but also how much of it has been culturally condoned, even among contemporary traditional societies. It was agreed that its existence had been too long suppressed or ignored, and needed to be openly discussed.

Around the world, and through the ages, child battery has hardly been the rare occurrence we would like to think. De Mause has made it his life's work to scrutinise as many historical documents, biographies, and other literature depicting parent–child relations as he could lay his hands on. In over three decades of exhaustive and meticulous research, he has not found evidence of a single pre-20th century parent–child relationship that did not include at least some measure of child abuse.[4] By today's standards, no pre-20th century parent reviewed by de Mause would escape prosecution for abuse or neglect.

How many of our social and political problems can be explained by this near-universal history of childhood trauma? For much of our history, children have been mistreated, despised and exploited more often than they have been nurtured. Is it any wonder that war, social violence and tyranny have been so prevalent?

Parenting 'instinct': myth or reality?

Many people speak nostalgically about a lost time, when there was supposedly more family love. We are told that children were once happier and more respectful. Modern lore weaves tales of an idyllic bygone existence; when parents were closer to their kids, when dads joyfully took their sons to work with them each day. For the most part, this is Hollywood romance. Anthropologist Robert Edgerton sums it up this way: "Until quite recently, all societies placed the well-being of adults above that of children, especially the very young."[5]

Edgerton's view may be a little extreme. There have been a handful of exceptions to this norm, such as the Cheyenne of North America, the Mbuti pygmies of Zaire, the Senoi of Malaysia,[6] the Yequana of Venezuela,[7] and the Tasaday of the Philippines.[8] These societies have genuinely raised their children non-violently and serve as an example of what is possible. Their remarkably peaceful existence also serves as a reminder of the rewards that await any culture that rejects violence towards children.

Alas, societies such as these have been extremely rare, and there appears to be little doubt that most traditional societies were violently patriarchal and misogynous. Almost all hunter-gatherer societies have regularly engaged in warfare,[9] losing around 25 per cent of men in battle.[10] If inter-group violence reflects violence in the family, our bellicose pre-history should come as no surprise. For the bulk of human history, mothers' lives were full of suffering since "[m]en have approved wife beating in virtually every folk society".[11] With few exceptions, women and children in traditional or 'folk' societies were given less food, and food of inferior quality to that given to the men.[12]

Reality bites, sometimes very hard. The history of children shows abandonment and abuse of such immensity that one historian refers to it as "a wide scale demographic catastrophe".[13] Others, such as Elizabeth Badinter, refuted the idea of a "maternal instinct" altogether.[14]

What we have been taught to think of as 'maternal instinct' or 'paternal instinct' does not always manifest automatically, in every parent. Good parenting depends on our circumstances, both material and emotional. Animal mothers constantly make compromises between their own survival and the quality of nurturing they offer their young. In a similar way, human parents limit the energies devoted to each child according to their available emotional and physical resources. The history of parenting reveals the presence of forces opposing the parental imperative to nurture. There is reason to believe in the existence of an impulse to push away our children, to reject them and refuse them care. This phenomenon has been studiously avoided and denied, simply because it offends. The idea of a common anti-parenting impulse flies in the face of our society's 'wishful thinking', as Sarah Blaffer Hrdy calls it, about instinctive maternal commitment.[15] But we ignore this understanding at our own peril.

Parenting styles tend to evolve over generations. During each progressive stage of evolution, parents used slightly less violent means to distance themselves from their children. Many historians (of western civilisations, at least) agree that the ideal of a doting, loving and self-sacrificing mother was invented late in the 18th century, and that this was a major deviation from the norm at the time. The kind and gentle father came later still. In many parts of the world, loving relationships between parents, and between parents and their children, are newcomers to the human story.

Since the original publication of Parenting for a Peaceful World, I have found further evidence that the quality of environment that parents find themselves in can powerfully influence parenting behaviour and hence social behaviour. In other words, when parents feel safe, supported and nourished, they tend towards more expression of nurturing instincts, and when parents are severely stressed, over time the quality of parenting behaviour is likely to suffer. Over a few generations, if environmental conditions change significantly this can radically alter cultural behaviour, first by changing the way parents raise their children.

In his book Saharasia – *The 4000BCE Origins of Child Abuse, Sex-Repression, Warfare and Social Violence in the Deserts of the Old World*,[16] James De Meo examines evidence from ethnographic, archaeological, anthropological, climatological and palaeoclimatic field studies to uncover an distinct pattern of increased social violence as a response to sharp deteriorations in food supply.

De Meo gives several examples of ancient cultures that did not subordinate women, and who left behind little or no evidence of social violence or warfare. He speaks of an era, at the dawn of settled, agricultural society, when herders, agriculturalists and hunters traded with each other and tended to live peacefully, in an atmosphere of abundance and resource security.

The period spanning from 6,000BCE to 4,000 BCE, saw catastrophic changes in climate that led to severe desiccation, and hyper-aridity expanded rapidly throughout previously moist and fertile regions of 'Saharasia'. A huge belt of desert developed and spread across northern Africa, the Middle East, Central Asia and north-western China. This vast expanse of arid and inhospitable country had once teemed with life; it had been wet, lush and green. Human inhabitants of these once fertile regions had once benefited from an abundance of arable wild grains and domesticated animals.

The possibility of surplus production in these regions had, before the onset of these climate changes, enabled the first agricultural settlements to emerge. The devastating deterioration in climate and the resulting desertification precipitated widespread and chronic famine and malnutrition.

Over centuries, societies in these regions adapted to these changes by becoming more competitive and aggressive in nature and organization. Violently patriarchal societies may have always existed here and there, but according to De Meo's survey they made their first large scale and lasting appearance from around 4000BCE to 3500BCE.

Many of these severely drought-affected civilizations were forced to abandon agriculture and return to a nomadic, but militaristic way of life. Permanent settlements remained only in areas adjacent to secure water sources. As these more aggressive peoples, the product of despair, scarcity and malnutrition, became increasingly competitive and aggressive through the generations, they began to migrate outward to colonize moister and more fertile territories. Warring tribes fanned out in all directions, everywhere displacing, subjugating, exterminating and subsuming gentler peoples as they advanced. Their readiness for violence, as well as their horsemanship and metallurgy tended to give them a devastating military superiority. For example, De Meo suggests that the military use of cavalry and battle chariots were developed among nomadic tribes from the drought affected Asian steppes.

Neolithic farming and trading communities of North Africa and the Middle East from 10500 BCE to 4000BCE were generally cooperative and peaceful in social behaviour, according to De Meo; there was little significant social stratification among them and 'strongman rule' was unknown. They left behind no war weaponry and an abundance of sophisticated art.

De Meo tells how, from around 4000BCE onward, regions east of the Nile endured waves of violent intrusions from mounted nomadic warriors who came from beyond the Iranian plateau. Whereas prior to this era local cultures tended to be relatively gender-balanced, the status of women was hence reduced to servitude and concubinage following these invasions.

These Eastern invaders brought with them their harsh child-rearing practices, including circumcision, swaddling and infant cranial deformation (see chapter 3, section on 'child mutilation'). De Meo traces migratory routes that radiated from these unfriendly desert regions of the world, and shows us how over the centuries, through progressive migration and military conquest these patriarchal, infanticidal and warlike societies spread throughout much of the globe, taking their harsh customs with them and assimilating or destroying gentler cultures in their path.

Migration and conquest extended violent patriarchy through much of Africa, into Western and Northern Europe, east into Asia, across Polynesia and Oceania, and through the Bering Strait into the Americas. Harsh parenting styles produced more war-capable cultures, and so the cultural honouring of battle and martial arts has predominated for millennia, through much of the world, up to this day.

Peaceful and egalitarian societies in all continents would either learn to adopt more violent ways, or face being overrun or marginalized. To De Meo, this explains why excavations of the earliest known fortifications in Europe are dated to around 3500BCE. Each wave of patriarchal/warrior migration and invasion brought with it the characteristic, traumatic child-rearing modes. De Meo methodically makes the case that infant swaddling, genital circumcision, cranial deformation and child sacrifice existed first among warrior-nomad people from this band of desert he calls 'Saharasia' (there is also evidence of harsh parenting practices independently emerging from the most inhospitable desert areas of Australia and the Americas).Over centuries, groups of relatively peaceful, child-nurturing people were eventually annihilated, enslaved, assimilated, or forced to retreat into fringes and forests.The desertification of these vast 'Saharasian' regions has triggered a demographic catastrophe of global proportions, which over the centuries rippled into every continent. Humanity is only now beginning to heal from this millennia-old social devolution.

Over generations, overwhelming stress on parents will skew any society towards violence. Our history indicates that humans are not inherently ruthless or uncaring towards children. In fact, we are capable of an extremely broad range of behaviours. As parents, we seem to exceed every other animal in both viciousness and enduring tenderness.

I believe we do all have the biological hard-wiring for a parenting instinct, and this instinct comes through in flying colours when we feel well supported and nurtured by our families and communities. On the other hand, this instinct fails us, and is overcome by our instinct for self-preservation, when overwhelming life-stress combines with unhealed trauma from our childhood. Additionally, good parenting behaviour is highly dependent on role models. By itself, the parenting instinct does not guarantee good parenting behaviour.

More than any other animal, our social behaviour, including

parenting, is shaped by our circumstances, our role models, and our life experiences. That's why it is especially important to learn about the conditions that undermine our ability to parent – and those that support us in expressing the best potential parent in each of us.

Childhood and society

'Emotional intelligence'[17] is what enables good relationships. It is the essential ingredient that individuals need in order to create, maintain and participate meaningfully in democratic, peaceful, and effective institutions. Since the foundations of emotional intelligence develop in childhood, cultural attitudes towards children determine the kind of society we have. A violent or non-nurturing upbringing stumps the development of 'emotional intelligence'. En masse, this leads to violent and unjust societies and institutions. On the other hand, the more empathic the upbringing, the more emotional intelligence develops, which in turn moves us toward fairer and more democratic societies. That is why all major social changes have followed mass improvements in parenting. Childhood shapes society, and impacts on world affairs. When you consider the torments suffered by children throughout history, you will understand the violence and inequality besetting our world. On the other hand, what we now know about the continuing evolution of parenting enables us to envisage wonderful new possibilities for the future. Parenting evolution drives social evolution, and appreciating this shows us the steps needed to make this world a better place.

What is psychohistory?

The new field of psychohistory analyses the way in which childhood experiences and emotional development influence social changes and world events. Lloyd de Mause kicked off this new field of study with his groundbreaking essay, 'The evolution of childhood'.[18] Since then, many historians of childhood have unearthed unthinkable horrors that were the norms accepted and perpetrated by our forebears. What is also coming to light, however, is an evolutionary pattern involving a gradual decline of violence towards and exploitation of children.

Most people think of current trends in parenting simply as 'the way it has always been done', in accordance with an innate 'parenting instinct'. In fact, today's parenting trends are no more than a point on an evolutionary scale. Over the centuries, parenting styles have undergone a number of drastic changes, and these changes continue to accelerate.

De Mause found that child rearing has tended to evolve through six distinct stages or 'modes'. Most societies contain all six modes in varying proportions. However, through consecutive epochs, and across the world's many cultures, specific child-rearing modes have predominated.

The six child-rearing modes

Child-rearing attitudes have evolved at very different rates across cultures. This means that some of the world's myriad communities still retain practices from early parenting modes, while others have progressed to the most advanced.

The early stages represent a radical rejection of parenting en masse; an unqualified rejection of the child as a person. Practices common to the first four stages would warrant government intervention in most modern societies.

Each chapter in Part II gives an account of parenting practices belonging to one of the six modes and their salient characteristics. Unless otherwise stated, the parenting modes will be examined as they have manifested in 'western' cultures. We will look at what was considered normal and acceptable throughout history, rather than what was considered criminal, pathological or rare. It is not possible to perfectly define the periods of western history during which the diverse parenting modes predominated, since there was considerable overlap in the evolution from one mode to another, and all six modes have tended to co-exist in varying proportions.

I should warn readers that some of the passages that follow are quite disturbing. I appreciate the courage it may require of you to explore the early part of childhood history, and hopefully to feel moved by it. But from the depths of horror will come more than a glimmer of hope. Both relief, and cause for optimism, are generated by the evidence of a distinct evolution in parenting, an improvement in child-rearing practices that has driven humanity forward for centuries. If this evolution continues along the same path, there are some marvellous possibilities in store.

My presentation of the history of child rearing is less a commentary on parents' motivations, and more an exploration of children's experiences; how it felt to be a child under each of the evolving child-rearing modes. I invite the reader to ponder upon the psychological and emotional effects upon children wrought by each parenting mode. Subsequent chapters will provide many additional insights into the psychological impact of early childhood experiences.

Endnotes

[1] De Mause (1982) p 1.

[2] Hrdy (2000) p 297.

[3] Broude (1995) p 166.

[4] Child abuse is a broad and general term used to encompass sexual, physical, emotional or verbal abuse of children by their carers. All historical accounts of childhood studied by de Mause exemplified one or more of these kinds of abuse, and severe physical punishment was a particularly salient and near-universal feature. See for example de Mause (1974), (1981), (1982), (1990), (1991), (1997), (1998), (1999), (2000), (2001), (2002a), (2002b) and (2002c).

[5] Edgerton (1992) p 75.

[6] Pearce (2002).

[7] Liedloff (1986).

[8] See Home for the Friends of the Tasaday http://www.tasaday.com/ (last accessed 1 December 2004).

[9] Keeley (1996).

[10] LeBlanc (2003) p 8.

[11] Edgerton (1992) p 81.

[12] Edgerton (1992) p 81.

[13] Hrdy (2000) p 303.

[14] Badinter (1981).

[15] Hrdy (2000) p 79.

[16] De Meo (2006) p 424

[17] An in-depth discussion about emotional intelligence appears in Chapter 22.

[18] This article appeared as Chapter 1 in de Mause (1982).

3

THE INFANTICIDAL MODE

The most primal means of lessening the load of parenting is to murder the child. In infanticidal societies, the burden of parenting was (and in some places still is) frequently resolved in this way. Most readers will be shocked to learn how commonly children in ancient times were allowed to live only in so far as they served the needs of their parents. To a great extent, children were not seen as persons; they were no more than nuisances, unless they could satisfy adult needs for labour, sexual gratification, or the release of sadistic urges. Infanticidal societies were (and are) characterised by high rates of socially condoned infanticide, incest, ritualised mutilation of children, and large-scale use of children as slaves and sexual objects. In much of western civilisation, this mode predominated until approximately the 4th century AD, and only began to abate during the Middle Ages.

In many parts of the world, infanticide was the family planning method *de rigueur*. For example, Ancient Roman parents were not legally required to keep any of their children. The law upheld and safeguarded fathers' absolute authority, explicitly including the right to execute their own children. Small children and babies were routinely thrown into rivers, flung into cesspits, or simply left to die on the street or in the wilderness. Greek and Roman infants – mostly daughters – were 'exposed' on hills and roadsides, left to fall prey to wild beasts and birds.[1] Their fate was to be devoured, or captured and reared as slaves and prostitutes.[2]

Across the Mediterranean Sea, some ancient Egyptians dumped their unwanted children as waste on garbage heaps. Though infanticide was officially illegal in Egypt, it was nevertheless common.[3] The ancient Hebrews were probably the first civilisation to put a stop to this practice, although at first they rejected many of their newborn girls in much the same way as the cultures that surrounded them.[4]

Girls were almost universally thought less worthy, and hence were more frequently disposed of than boys. As a result, throughout much of early civilisation, population ratios were dramatically skewed in favour of men.

The ancients had little regard for children and there are few writings expressing delight in them. Aristotle described them as "dwarfs with bad memories".[5] Babies were exposed if they were illegitimate, the wrong gender, if parents simply couldn't be bothered with them, or if they seemed weak, sickly or malformed. In his book *Gynaecology,* the Greek physician Soranus gave instructions on how to recognise the "child worth rearing".[6] This text was widely consulted, and infants who did not meet its standards were often discarded. Even the much-revered Plato advocated the rearing of only the "best men and women", and the disposal of "defective" children or those born to "inferior" parents. Any children born to women over 40 or men over 55, Plato advised, should be violently disposed of, and every family should raise only one son, while other viable sons should be adopted out to others.

Members of every social class 'exposed' their babies, which demonstrates that infanticide was not simply motivated by material hardship, but also by emotional impoverishment. In fact, the rich were more prone to 'exposing' their children. The majority of women living in Rome between 0 and 300 BC who had over one child, had 'exposed' at least one of their babies. Somewhere between 20 and 40 per cent of newborns were dumped by their parents.[7] It would be several centuries before any institutions were set up to care for discarded children, so all either died or were doomed to a life of slavery.

Infanticide is known to some degree in most pre-modern cultures. As far back as the Great Ice Age, primitive societies killed between 15 and 50 per cent of their own children.[8]

Since the 1970s, field workers have encountered rates of infanticide as high as 40 per cent in contemporary traditional patriarchal societies that strongly favour sons. Between 1974 and 1978, anthropologists studying the Eipo on the northern slopes of Papua New Guinea, found an infanticide rate of 41 per cent of all children born. De Mause's review of anthropological studies of tribal Papua New Guinea concludes that mothers generally killed "a third or more of their newborn".[9] Cannibalising of infants, a tribally sanctioned custom, has also been widely documented in PNG – just as it was in Rome in the first century BC.[10]

Even among the supposedly peaceful Kung of the Kalahari Desert, infanticide is sanctioned under certain circumstances, at a rate of one per cent of births. Well into colonial times, the Ijaw of Nigeria killed all twins at birth – their only explanation for this custom being that their ancestors had always done it. Infanticide is accepted among many traditional South American societies, including the Ache forest dwellers of Paraguay. The inter-tribal skirmishes among the Yanomamo of Brazil are brutally infanticidal. The children of rival tribesmen are especially singled out for some of the most atrocious attacks. Among Polynesian and South Pacific societies, which we have come to associate with idyllic and carefree lifestyles, ritual infanticide has been widely observed – in Hawaii, Tahiti and Bali among others. Just as in ancient Greece or Rome, infanticide in tribal cultures is prevalent in situations of plenty, and so it cannot be said to be a response to drought or other harsh circumstances.[11]

Among pre-Islamic Arabs, infanticide was also common. The Koran spoke out against this practice, but as daughters were undesirable, their abandonment continued unabated. In response to the unstoppable reality of the exposure of children, the Prophet Mohammed decreed that one fifth of all war booty should be distributed among abandoned children.[12]

During the reign of the Ching dynasty in 18th century China, daughters who brought dishonour to their family could be strangled or hacked to death, and, as in ancient Rome, this was considered the father's right. Throughout the 18th and 19th centuries in China, there were 154 boys to every 100 girls. Since the natural ratio is 104 to 106 boys for every 100 girls, this indicates an enormous rate of infanticide, with girls being preferentially killed. In Beijing, where newborn baby girls were killed by drowning, special wagons toured the streets in the early mornings to collect the corpses.[13] The Chinese infanticide rate was dwarfed by that of India, where child sacrifice persisted into the 19th century, and where the boy: girl ratio was an appalling 300:100.[14] In order to reduce the number of inheritors, Indian military officials would kill their own daughters, even though they could easily afford to feed them. In Britain, both the Celts and the Irish – irrespective of social status or wealth – exposed illegitimate children.

As Christianity spread throughout Europe, early church fathers attempted to ban infanticide, but it continued to rage around the world. In Germanic lands, illegitimate children were killed rather than abandoned as late as the 8th century. A 9th century Germanic law specifically exempted from prosecution mothers who killed their babies. As late as the 16th century, church reformer Martin Luther reversed the Christian sanction against infanticide by ordering that mentally defective children should be drowned. Luther maintained that these children were "instruments of the devil".[15]

Not until the period between the Middle Ages and the French Revolution did the church really begin to intervene and prohibit parents from killing, abandoning or severely abusing their children. By the 12th century AD, the church in France explicitly forbade infanticide, though it continued illicitly. In France and England, throughout the Middle Ages, it was not unusual to see unwanted infants in street gutters.

It continues to baffle historians how such wholesale indifference toward infants could be possible. Since infanticide was so ordinary and quotidian, should we conclude that people then did not feel for children as most of us do today? When rifling through documents recording child deaths in pre-revolution France, historian Elizabeth Badinter was struck by the remarkable absence of sorrow or grief. In fact, she found that grieving for the loss of a child was considered strange at the time. Family records of child death seemed blunt and matter-of-fact. Across the Channel, mourning was not expected for children under seven.[16] Infanticide is facilitated by an emotional atrophy or detachment; a severe injury to the human faculties of feeling and empathy.

Parental attitudes to children have evolved at different rates throughout the world's many cultures. Although most people find the idea unthinkable, nine per cent of cultures today are still infanticidal. Female infanticide continues in the Indian states of Tamil Nadu and Rajasthan, either by denying breastmilk to girls, by smearing opium on mothers' nipples, or by poisoning baby girls with plant extracts. In 1995, the male–female ratio was 106.9 boys to 100 girls.[17]

Every year large numbers of widowed Hindu women are still burnt alive in a practice known as 'sati'. This is most often seen in the province of Bengal. Since the practice of child marriage was still common during British occupation, girls as young as four were known to meet this fate. In 1987, an 18-year-old jumped into the flames before an admiring crowd of thousands.[18]

Some women (and girls) have been burned alive simply because their fathers have fallen behind in dowry payments, or offered a dowry not pleasing to the in-laws.[19]

Infanticide is also suspected to persist in certain parts of rural China, where recent census figures show significant imbalances in boy: girl ratios.[20] This is at least in part due to the Chinese government's 'one child policy', which it thoroughly enforces.

Traditionally infanticide is seen as an act committed by parents on their own children. Infanticide in this sense shocks us, is inconceivable to most parents today, and is severely punished. However, what we refer to as 'collateral' damage in warfare could partly be seen as a legitimised version of infanticide, so it has not altogether disappeared even from the modern world.

In infanticidal times, those children who survived alongside their infanticidal parents would have been witness to the horror of child murder going on around them. We can barely imagine how this trauma would have impacted upon surviving siblings; how it felt to grow up with death as a real and present danger for any who displeased their parents. When grown into adulthood, surviving siblings all too often re-enacted the atrocity upon their own children.

Child sacrifice
Humans the world over have tended to attribute the urge to kill children to the will of capricious deities. Child sacrifice was common throughout antiquity and is well documented in many Mediterranean cultures. Early Hebrews, Moabites, Ammonites, Phoenicians, and many others practiced child sacrifice. The charred remains of tens of thousands of ritually slaughtered children have been found around Carthage, Knossos, and many other Mediterranean archaeological sites. In Carthage, childless parents would buy children from the poor and cut their throats to gain favour from their gods. In Sparta, a council of elders would preside over sacrificial ceremonies that included hurling newborn babies from the top of Mount Taggetus, or flogging youths to death on the altar of Artemisia. In the British Isles, the skulls of sacrificed children have been found at Stonehenge. Anglo-Saxons considered it a virtue to kill babies who cried when they came into the world.[21]

31

In the Americas, child sacrifice was central to the Aztec, Mayan and Inca cultures, among the Natchez of the lower Mississippi and nearby Pawnee nations, and even until modern times among the Mapuche of Chile. The Pawnee ritually tortured their child victims before sacrificing them. The Aztecs were the supreme sacrificers of children, and perhaps the most sadistic of parents. Aztec children suffered a living hell; they were regularly beaten, cut, bled, bound, burned, drugged, or otherwise tortured.[22]

Child sacrifice persisted into the 20th century amongst many African cultures, such as the Tiv of Nigeria and the Mtwara of Zimbabwe. An age-old convention in India, child sacrifice is still seen in more traditional pockets of this complex society. In China, the practice was common until the 6th century BC. If we include the sacrifice of adults, human sacrifice has been almost universal throughout the world's traditional societies and early civilisations.[23]

The Old Testament depicts a very matter-of-fact attitude to the sacrifice of children (for example, in Exodus 22:29, God is said to have ordered the sacrifice of first-born sons). The Israelites were the first to abolish child sacrifice in the time of Abraham, while the surrounding cultures were heavily involved in child sacrifice.

Child mutilation
The disregard for children's pain among parents of this mode was evidenced in the ritual mutilation of children's bodies. Mutilation was perhaps even more widespread than child sacrifice. Children have been cut, burnt, castrated, circumcised and infibulated, forced to endure severe pain, and often permanently disabled. Finger amputation rituals, for instance, were common in Oceania, Polynesia, and among native North Americans.

Although the practice of male circumcision has been popularly associated with the Jewish faith, penile mutilation, in one form or another, was widely practised throughout the Middle East, Africa, Peru, Polynesia, Australia, and Ancient Greece. The Hebrews differed by circumcising males at infancy, rather than at puberty. The Jewish rite required the circumciser (mohel) to suck the blood from the boy's penis and spit it out. This aspect of the ritual was rejected by Reformists in the middle of the 19th century.[24]

Today, it is estimated that there are over 130 million women around the world – more than twice the population of the UK – who have had their clitorises cut out. Girls were once infibulated also in Russia and South America.[25]

Castration of boys was 'big business' in early empires, says historian John Boswell.[26] It was a common practice to castrate boys in ancient Egypt, in Byzantium, throughout the Middle East, in mediaeval Italy, China, India, and among some Native Americans. Aztec parents repeatedly cut both boys' and girls' genitals.

In ancient Rome, it was a commonly accepted practice for boys to be castrated for use in brothels. Children of impoverished parents were deliberately blinded or otherwise mutilated, and forced to work as beggars. One popular form of entertainment regularly enjoyed by thousands of spectators at the Colosseum was to watch live children being torn to pieces and devoured by hyenas.

Well-to-do Chinese parents would bind their daughters' feet until the bones were crushed, repeating this treatment over and over again. The object was to progressively reduce the feet in size, and shape them into a fine pointed cone, with the toes wrapped under the ball of the foot. This grotesque malformation was sometimes utilised as a sex aid for men. It was a sign of status that spread through all social classes until the 1930s.[27]

Throughout much of Europe, until the 19th century, babies' heads were tightly wrapped into wooden boards to alter their shape, and the ligament under the newborn's tongue (frenulum) was cut with a thumbnail.[28]

In Papua New Guinea, examples of mutilation include initiation rites that involve introducing sharp leaves into the initiates' nostrils, and pumping these in and out until blood gushes out. In some tribes, barbed grasses are introduced into boys' urethras until they bleed. During this ritual many of the boys are said to involuntarily urinate and defecate from the fear and shock. In Papua New Guinea, as among some Australian Aborigines, circumcision involves deep incisions along the entire length of the underside of the penis.

A further form of customary child mutilation existed among numerous cultures, in every continent. Infant cranial deformation (ICD) was an excruciating procedure that involved binding infants' skulls in extremely tight bands, or trussing them tightly between two flat wooden boards. The bands and boards were applied through the day and night, and removed only for occasional bathing.

This resulted in chronic, splitting headache, and sometimes bleeding through the nostrils. The crushing pressure led to grotesquely flattened or weirdly elongated skulls.

ICD was common among Central Asian warrior nomad societies; evidence of ICD has also been found in the Eastern Mediterranean, Egypt, Northwest China, in Nth America's Pacific Northwest, in Inca Peru and Mesoamerica. ICD skulls have been unearthed in Australia's south east, together with archaeological evidence of tribal violence against women, dating back to a period between 11,000BCE to 7,000BCE. This coincided with a period of extreme aridity in this area, adding weight to James De Meo's theory (see chapter 2, section: 'Parenting instinct: myth or reality?' that cultural violence arises as a result of chronic environmental harshness.

We can see that the practice of mutilating children's bodies has been almost universal. If mutilation is more a rule than an exception in human history, it is a social phenomenon that needs to be understood as intrinsically human in some way. What underlies this urge to disfigure, and to inflict intolerable pain on children? Around the world, mutilation has been justified as a sacrificial ritual to gain the favour of gods, a way of 'making men of boys', a means of subjugation, or in order to turn children into submissive sex-objects. One form of male circumcision was once rationalised as a preventive health measure, but this idea has fallen out of favour with modern medical thought. Fortunately, the most excessive of folkloric child-mutilation rituals tend to disappear as cultures progress to the next parenting mode.

Child slavery and physical abuse

Amongst the early western and Middle-Eastern civilisations, the ancient Hebrews were perhaps the most doting and affectionate parents of their era. Although, as in all contemporary cultures, family and civic life was male dominated, women enjoyed considerably more respect and equality amongst the Hebrews. But even among these comparatively compassionate people the chastisement of children could be severe. While their scriptures urged them to beat their children,[29] they also proclaimed that a child who struck or cursed his parents should be put to death.[30] One ancient Hebrew edict stated "a man who loves his son will whip him often".[31] A father or teacher who flogged a child to death was not to be held liable.[32] Neighbouring civilisations exceeded the Hebrews in brutality towards children.

Child slavery was also known among the Hebrews (as it was throughout the major civilisations around the world, even as far east as China). It was common for impoverished fathers to sell their daughters into slavery. Ancient scriptures contained explicit guidelines for the sale of children into servitude. In Genesis 19:8, Lot offers his two virginal daughters to an angry crowd in order to appease them, urging the crowd to do with them as they please.

For a child to escape infanticide was a mixed blessing. Many of those permitted to live were destined to be used as servants and sexual playthings. Sexual use of children seems to be a recurring theme in infanticidal cultures. Both child labour and paedophilia were condoned and encouraged in antiquity, and sex with children was openly depicted in both art and literature.

Pederasty (sodomy with a boy) bears a special mention as an aspect of this parenting mode, since it was (and still is) at its zenith in infanticidal cultures. Adults whose attitudes to children belong in the 'infanticidal mode' see nothing wrong with child rape. That is because the 'infanticidal mode' adult does not see a child as a person.

In ancient Greece and Rome, boys were sexual playthings, and pederasty was condoned and openly practiced. Hairless, pre-pubescent boys were preferred. Greek boys were frowned upon if they had not attached themselves to a pederast. Even married men were expected to have sex with boys. Physicians were on call to provide lubricating ointments to ease the difficulty of anally penetrating little boys, and regularly had to repair boys' rectal tears. Sexual use of boys was sadistic, pleasure was derived from their cries of pain. The fact that pederasty was the norm did nothing to make anal rape any less traumatic for the young victims.[33]

Philosophers who are venerated to this day, such as Plato and Aristotle, were ardent advocates of the sexual use of pre-pubescent boys and they glorified and promoted this practice. Pederastic marriages and honeymoons were common in Crete and Boetia. Greek and Roman literature, drama and poetry are loaded with the theme of pederasty. It was not unusual for fathers to approve of the sexual abuse of their sons and in fact to feel offended if other men showed no lust for them. Across the sea, Egyptian men kept up their supply of soft, hairless youths by castrating boys. Meanwhile, Egyptian nurses would customarily

35

fondle and suck little boys' penises, reasoning that this would 'strengthen their erections' and 'prepare them for sexual activity later in life'.[34]

Many early civilisations were pederastic and used boys as temple prostitutes: this includes the ancient Hebrews, Sumerians, Persians, Mesopotamians, Celts, Egyptians, Etruscans, Carthaginians, Chinese, Japanese, Indians, Aztecs, Greeks and Romans.[35]

China shares a pederastic history with its Western counterparts. Boys here were castrated for use as eunuchs, child servants, slaves, or prostitutes. Among the Aztecs, pederasty was universal and boy rape was expected to be violent.

Girls were by no means exempt from exploitation. The rape of young girls was so common that doctors commented that an intact hymen was a rare abnormality. Many classical Greek comedies contained scenes depicting the rape of young girls. In Athens, Sparta, Corinth and Crete, barely pubescent girls were compelled to marry men 15 to 20 years their senior.[36]

Among the ancient Hebrews, betrothal by sexual intercourse was permitted with girls aged three years and a day,[37] and marriage for girls was actually recommended at 12 years of age. The Biblical woman and child were property, not persons. For the right to marry a pre-pubescent girl, one simply had to pay an agreed sum to her father. A convicted child rapist was expected to pay reparations to the girl's father for having taken her virginity. The psychological damage to the girl was not considered; rape was merely a matter of devaluing the father's property.[38] In India, child marriage was not condemned by law until 1929, although around 80 per cent of the population was still practising it.[39]

Parents who wished to cast off unwanted children often chose to sell them into prostitution, and children were easily bought and sold as slaves. In ancient Rome, child prostitution was institutionalised, and the government went so far as to tax child prostitutes.

Children were also sex objects in many tribal societies. Young boys called *berdaches* were dressed as girls and used sexually by men in many North and Central American tribes. Ethnographers and anthropologists have documented frequent fondling and kissing of babies' and children's genitals among tribes of Papua New Guinea, in traditional Manchu China and among the Banoi in Thailand. In Papua New Guinea, Sambian initiation rites involved fellatio of older men by boys. When infants became boys, they were anally raped and or forced into fellatio by the men of the village, until they reached puberty. Both maternal and paternal incest were common among such tribes. Ritual stimulation of children's genitals by mothers has been documented in Hawaii, the Marquesas and many other Pacific islands.

The earliest recorded explicit prohibitions against sexual abuse of children seem to have appeared amongst the ancient Hebrews. Anyone who raped a boy over nine years of age would be stoned to death, but those caught copulating with boys under nine would receive only a whipping. Evidently, rape of smaller boys was seen as a lesser crime.[40]

For centuries, European children were sexual playthings until the age of seven. De Mause has unearthed many illustrations of European mothers and grandmothers fondling their infants' genitals. In England, incest was only made a criminal offence in 1908. Until the 18th century, rape of girls was rarely noticed nor punished, being largely regarded as a trivial issue. As it was widely believed that sex with a virgin would cure venereal disease, those tried for rape would be released if they used this excuse. Public advertisements in most European cities offered children as young as six for sale and sexual use.

Although Christianity slowed the rate of infanticide, it did little to reduce the rape of children. What the church did achieve was to propagate the idea that child rape and infanticide of unwanted children is not a good thing. The early church fathers combated these two evils by introducing rigid sexual mores dictating that non-procreative sexual relations were sinful. All that this accomplished was to drive people to commit the same crimes against children in more covert ways. A new guilt denied child rape its image of acceptability, but its incidence did not decline. In fact, historically, nunneries and monasteries were places where the sexual abuse of children was rife. In Europe, it was not until the 15th century that cases of violent sexual abuse of children were brought to court. In late 15th century Florence the majority of males were prosecuted at least once for raping boys. Only in recent times has the rate of sexual child abuse dropped to less than half of all children.

In modern times, the incidence of child sexual abuse remains extremely high. While most research in the western world estimates the molestation rate at around a quarter of all children, some indicates a figure of 60 per cent of girls and 45 per cent of boys, or even higher.[41] There are still millions of child slaves, sexual or otherwise, around the world. In other words, to this day there remain many cultures and sub-cultures worldwide that fit into de Mause's 'infanticidal' category. In areas of northern Thailand, for instance, child prostitution is culturally condoned, and encouraged by some parents.

In the present day, the sexual abuse of children is more frowned upon than any other time in history. More importantly, there are more adults today who are psychologically healthy enough to find the idea of sex with a child abhorrent – irrespective of legal or social sanctions against it. Pederasty as a sexual deviation is much less prevalent, but remains alarmingly high.

ECPAT (End Child Prostitution, Child Pornography and Trafficking of children for sexual exploitation)[42] is an international network of organisations fighting the colossal global use of children as sex objects. Although countries such as Thailand and the Philippines are notorious for their flourishing child sex industry, the practice is still rife in all continents.

The rate of sexual exploitation of children seems to remain high for all but the most advanced child-rearing modes. However, the next child-rearing mode brings with it some minor changes in societies' commitment to children's survival.

Endnotes

1. De Mause (1974) p 25.
2. Boswell (1988).
3. Radbill in Helfer and Kempe (eds) (1974).
4. Cooper (1996) pp 35–37; Boswell (1988) p 149.
5. Greenleaf (1978) p 23.
6. De Mause (2001) p 381.
7. Hrdy (2000) p 298.
8. Breiner (1990).
9. De Mause (1999) p 675.
10. De Mause (1999) p 675.
11. Detailed accounts can be found in Hrdy (2000); Edgerton (1992); Piers (1978); Breiner (1990).
12. Boswell (1988).
13. Hrdy (2000).
14. Pakrasi in de Mause (2002c) p 301.
15. Radbill in Helfer and Kempe (eds) (1974).
16. Gathorne-Hardy (1972).

[17] See Rajan (2004).

[18] Edgerton (1992).

[19] Sharma (2002).

[20] See 'Case study: female infanticide, India, China' Gendercide
      Watch http://www.gendercide.org/case_infanticide.html (last
      accessed 1 December 2004).

[21] De Mause (2001) p 373; Newton (1996) p 104; Kahr (1991) p
      197; Greenleaf (1978); also mentioned in Boswell (1988).

[22] De Mause (2001); Newton (1996); Kahr (1991); Greenleaf
      (1978).

[23] Newton (1996).

[24] Cooper (1996).

[25] De Mause (2002b) p 341, (2001) p 384.

[26] Boswell (1988).

[27] De Mause (1991) pp 151–152.

[28] De Mause (2001) p 388.

[29] Cooper (1996) p 23.

[30] Exodus 21:15–17 in Cooper (1996) p 23.

[31] Ecclesiasticus 2:2 in Cooper (1996) p 91.

[32] Makkot 2:2 in Cooper (1996) p 91.

[33] Kahr (1991).

[34] Kahr (1991) p 191; Breiner (1990).

[35] De Mause (2001).

[36] Rush (1980).

[37] Rush (1980).

[38] Atlas (2001).

[39] Rush (1980); de Mause (1991) p 145.

[40] Cooper (1996).

[41] De Mause (1991); Kahr (1991).

[42] See Child Wise http://www.ecpat.orgl and http://www.
      childwise.net (last accessed 1 December 2004), its Australian
      representative.

4

THE ABANDONING MODE

As infanticide began to be increasingly frowned upon, other alternatives for getting rid of children began to take its place. People in vast numbers still wanted to offload their children. Just as before, many parents chose abandonment when, as historian John Boswell puts it "they simply could not be bothered with parenthood".[1] In her study of abandonment throughout history, Sarah Blaffer Hrdy calls it the "default mode for a mother terminating investment".[2] Abandonment was often no more than a sanitised form of infanticide, and a ruthless form of family planning. This new parenting mode appeared to be predominant in western cultures roughly between the 4th and 14th centuries AD, although there was considerable overlap with other parenting modes.

In Europe, the first legislation forbidding parents from exposing or abandoning their children was introduced by the Christian emperor Valentinian in AD 374. It was the first time infanticide was officially branded as murder; a development that reflected the influence of both Christian and Jewish ideals.[3]

Sadly, this piece of legislation was utterly ineffective, and the abandonment of children continued unabated for the next millennium. All that can be said is that this law represented the beginnings of disapproval of abandonment and infanticide. The first legislation to have any real impact on infanticide throughout Europe came in the shape of the Canonical Decrees of AD 906, which imposed severe penalties for infanticide or allowing a child to die through neglect.

As legislation stifled opportunities for infanticide, parents sought to dump their children where they had a slightly better chance of survival, or to delegate the task of parenting to someone else – usually a stranger.

Child abandonment became so common, that the early

Christian warnings against sex with prostitutes were motivated by the very real possibility that one could unwittingly be copulating with a sister or a daughter (who had been abandoned and eventually sold into prostitution).

Through the European Middle Ages, the boy:girl ratio spanned from 140:100 to 400:100, indicating a strong cultural preference for boys. For the most part, abandonment – like infanticide – had little or nothing to do with material hardship. The wealthy or elite were just as prone to abandoning their children as their poorer counterparts. The urban poor abandoned children due to extreme economic hardship while the well-off abandoned them due to indifference, or in order to reduce excessive division of inheritance. The rates of child abandonment seemed to be lower among minority Jewish communities in Mediaeval Europe.[4]

As recently as the 18th century in Paris, an average of 20 to 25 per cent of babies were dumped. One third of abandoned babies were middle class and one quarter were the offspring of master artisans and merchants. Between 1879 and 1881, 69,000 babies were abandoned in Sicily. In Sardinia, which was much poorer, only 15 were abandoned. This different capacity for care existed in Sardinia because it was customary for women to stay together in kinship groups to help each other rear the children.[5]

What was done by European forebears is dubbed by Sarah Blaffer Hrdy as a "wide-scale demographic catastrophe of unprecedented dimensions".[6] In 1995, a conference on anthropological and historical studies of child abandonment was held in Durham, England. It was agreed at this conference that abandonment had been routine all across Europe. More infants died from abandonment in Europe than from all the plague epidemics combined! It strains our capacity to comprehend, but parental indifference was a greater killer than the worst infectious disease ever to have ravaged civilisation.

James De Meo's collection of evidence (see chapter 2, section: 'Parenting instinct: myth or reality?') seems to call for a slight adjustment to De Mause's telling of the evolutionary tale. There is some powerful evidence that a great number of relatively peaceful, socially just and child-nurturing societies prevailed for long periods in pre-history. Ultimately, De Meo's evidence adds to De Mause's psycho-historical model, strongly confirming that cultures that subordinate women and inflict trauma on their children produce more violent and warlike societies. So, whereas De Mause draws a picture of originally infanticidal human societies that tended to use competition and violence as predominant survival strategies, De Meo argues for a rapid social decline towards harsh parenting and violent societies – the result of catastrophic climactic factors, around six thousand years ago. In De Meo's assessment of the evidence, human societies that arise in areas of friendly climate and   abundant resources will evolve towards social harmony and empathic child-rearing styles, provided that they remain free from invasion by patriarchal, warlike neighbours.

Both accounts place child-rearing styles at the very centre of how a society's behaviour is shaped. De Meo's account has one advantage, however. He has, I believe, demonstrated that the quality of parenting behaviour depends on the support offered to parents by their social and natural environment. Our ability to be tender towards our children rests on how well nourished and cared for we are. The parenting instinct is vulnerable, and if life is a struggle, it can suffer.

De Meo shares the recognition of all psycho-historians that social violence has its roots in childhood: 'Human violence and warfare were the products of social institutions which inflicted great pain and trauma upon children . . .'. By implication, a return to peaceful society will be possible if child-rearing reforms aimed at healthy attachment and non-violent parenting are enacted – and if parents receive more social, educational and financial support.

The rise of foundling homes

Although the abandonment of children left them with some small chance of life, it was more often than not a death sentence. What distinguished this stage from the last, is that government and religious authorities began making some efforts, albeit half-hearted and inadequate, to save the lives of discarded infants. Parents, on the other hand, generally showed little increase in commitment to their children's wellbeing.

The earliest attempts to rescue discarded infants came in the 13th century, when they began to be accepted, along with the sick, the old and the disabled, into regular hospitals. The first 'foundling' hospitals for the care of abandoned babies emerged in Florence in the early 14th century. Foundling hospitals filled quickly, and possibly encouraged an increase in abandonment.

One 14th century Florentine hospital reported receiving 900 outcast infants annually. While the proportion of Florentine babies who were foundlings rose from 20 per cent to 40 per cent between 1640 and 1840, foundling hospitals barely coped with the tide. Between 20 to 40 per cent of babies taken in did not survive and hospital staff were notorious for their neglect. In late 18th century Sicily, of 70,000 babies abandoned in 26 years, only 20 per cent survived.[7]

In 1638, St Vincent de Paul established the first foundling hospital in France, to cope with the tide of abandoned babies there. In an attempt to stem an appalling infant mortality rate, London opened its first foundling hospital in 1741. By 1753, this hospital was receiving over 100 infants per day.[8]

Urged by reformist politicians, Catherine II of Russia opened the first foundling homes in Moscow and St Petersburg in 1764, in order to remove the accumulations of dying babies from the streets. However, the appalling conditions in these homes did little to improve the babies' fate and in 1767, 99 per cent of those admitted died within a year. High rates of abandonment persisted in Russia until the end of the 19th century. From 1880–1889, about 25,000 babies were dumped in Moscow and St Petersburg. Foundlings fared no better in 18th century Dublin, where just 45 of 10,272 foundlings survived the foundling hospital.

The lamentable quality of care in most foundling homes suggests that they were no more than warehouses for human detritus; a means of sanitising society's disdain for dependents by keeping the dead and dying from public view. Historian John Boswell sums it up as a rubber stamp for guilt-free abandonment, whereby professionals were paid to cleanly dispose of unwanted babies.

Even as child rearing continued to improve, foundling homes were busy almost until modern times. As recently as 1873, there were 1392 infants abandoned at the New York Foundling Asylum, in Randall's Island, USA. In the same year, 122 infants found dead in New York streets, alleys and rivers.[9]

Abandonment did not necessarily reflect more compassion than infanticide, but rather collective guilt or squeamishness about the more directly brutal means of dispatching children. In order to shield parents from guilt feelings, foundling hospitals were equipped with a revolving door in which to deposit the infant. This device enabled the parent to slip away undetected.

Wet-nursing

For those babies who remained under their own parents' custodianship, quality of life was not necessarily better. It was rare for mothers to nurse their own babies not only among the wealthy, but also among many who could ill afford 'wet-nurse' services. All over the world, since time immemorial, mothers have rejected the intimacy and commitment that breastfeeding entails. 'Wet-nursing' was the earliest means available to keep babies away from their mother's bosom. Professional 'wet-nurses' breastfed others' babies for a fee, but some wet-nurses were slaves.

The use of wet-nurses was common practice in societies all over the world, from Europe to Asia. In Rome, professional wet-nurses gathered daily around the designated 'Colonna Lactaria' to sell their services. In ancient Greece, well-born sons were not suckled by their own mothers, but by servants. The practice was present throughout ancient civilisations; in China, Japan, India, the Near East, and Arab cultures. It was commercialised as early as 300 BC in Egypt, where servants would be contracted to suckle their master's babies for two to three years each. The ancient Babylonian 'Code of Hammurabi' (around 1750 BC) even allowed wet-nurses to sell their charges if the parents failed to pay the contractual amount.[10]

The addiction to wet-nursing was so great that it survived despite advice to the contrary from all the major religions. Both Buddhism and Hinduism stress the benefits of maternal nursing. Judaism enjoins mothers to breastfeed for at least two years, or more if the child does not feel ready to be weaned. The Koran advised mothers to suckle their young for two full years, only permitting the use of wet-nurses when maternal nursing was impossible. Christianity also honours breastfeeding: "Blessed is the womb that bore you, and the breasts which nursed you!",[11] even if it does not prescribe a particular length of time.

The abandonment of children to the care (or more often neglect) of wet-nurses, seemed to increase as infanticide waned. Vast numbers of city dwellers would allow their babies to remain with their assigned wet-nurses in the country until weaning. Immediately after birth, babies were farmed out to wet-nurses who usually lived in far away villages. The parents would not see the child again until he or she was returned at two to four years of age. A survey conducted as late as 1780 by the police chief of Paris found that of the 21,000 children born in the city, 17,000 were sent out to the country. Of the 1400 lucky enough to stay at home with their parents, only 700 were nursed by their own mothers, the rest were fed by in-house hired wet-nurses.[12]

Since babies of all social classes were sent to wet-nurses, this practice was not motivated by material poverty but by emotional poverty; that is, the psychological inability to nurture. Reasons given for sending newborns to wet-nurses included: mothers' fear of "loss of beauty" or "misshapen breasts", "breastfeeding is boring", and "the child's cries are upsetting". Husbands of breastfeeding mothers complained of losing their wives' sexual attention. In fact, babies were generally regarded as distasteful and disgusting. French Doctor Moreau de St Elier publicly asserted that childcare was an "embarrassing burden".[13]

While there was far less wet-nursing in Holland and Scandinavia, it was huge in Germany, Italy, England and France. In Germany, breastfeeding was shunned and replaced with artificial feeding from the 15th century. Those who did not send their infants out for wet-nursing fed them instead on meal-pap, a mixture of flour and water, and/or animal milk. This varied from region to region, but those German mothers who did breastfeed were openly called swinish and filthy by others. Infant mortality rates of 50 per cent prevailed, dropping to 40 per cent by 1889, four times the Norwegian rate where breastfeeding was more common. Artificial teats were made from actual cow teats, with horns used as a bottle.[14]

During the Renaissance, two out of three Italian families sent their newborns to the country to be brought up by the *balia* (wet-nurse), with whom they would remain for an average of two years. The rest tended to employ a wet-nurse at home. In Finland, babies were left in specially designed cradles with a holder for an artificial feeding device. The Finnish infant mortality rate halved from 40 per cent to around 20 per cent by the 1850s, when mothers were gradually returning to breastfeeding. In Eastern Europe, the Romanian wet-nurse (*doica*) was employed by the wealthy well into the 20th century.

It was well known to parents that wet-nurses offered care of the poorest quality, and that to leave babies with them was to place them in danger. Grossly underpaid wet-nurses in country towns took on many babies at once in order to make ends meet. Many children returned from wet-nurses sickly, malnourished, crippled, dying, or dead. In France, five to 15 per cent died in transit. The coach trip to the wet-nurse's village was often bumpy, long and perilous, and it was common for babies to be jolted off the carriage en route. As wet-nurses came mostly from the most impoverished classes, the homes to which they took their charges were usually extremely unsanitary hovels.[15]

Little care was taken in selecting wet-nurses, who were procured or recommended by *meneurs* (agents) for a fee. Most parents never met the nurse, and made no effort to do so. Life at the wet-nurse's home was infernal and the treatment of the infants can only be described as abominable. Throughout the day, babies were tightly swaddled and hung up on a hook, un-washed, totally immobilized, and deprived of contact or the warmth of human touch. The impoverished wet-nurses were otherwise occupied, and this is how they minimized the effort required for their pay. To further cut corners, many wet-nurses fed the babies pap, gruel, or diluted cow's milk instead of breastmilk— a certain recipe for agonising colic and malnourishment.

So poor were conditions that in Lyons, toward the end of the 18th century, two-thirds of wet-nursed babies died. This mortality rate was similar in many areas of Europe, even into the 19th century. The general public was fully aware that wet-nursing doubled the infant mortality rate and jokes and satire about the subject were commonplace. Each time church bells tolled in Lyons, townsfolk would quip: 'there goes another little Parisian!' The French nickname for wet-nurses was *faiseuse d'anges*, angel maker in England, and in Germany *engelmacherin*. Yet this did nothing to deter their clients: if anything, it seemed to encourage them. Children born to wet-nurses fared no better. Many of these impoverished women would become pregnant in order to produce breastmilk, then immediately abandon their own infants to feed others' for a fee. In France, infant mortality caused by wet-nursing was so high that at its peak the population went into decline.[16]

For historian Maria Piers, this is clear evidence that in many cases, the wet-nurse was a "professional killer", whose unspoken social contract was to surreptitiously dispose of the unwanted.[17] In Italy, where infanticidal mothers were punished by death, *balias* who killed their charges were only given a fine, or a whipping. French reformers such as Dr Alexander Mayer condemned wet-nursing as "barbaric", and since the death rate was widely known, stressed the murderous intent of abandoning parents. A present-day commentator agrees, calling wet-nurses "surrogates upon whom parents could depend for a swift demise for unwanted children".[18]

European–Jewish families tended to either avoid wet-nursing, or to invite Christian wet-nurses into their own homes, where they could be supervised. As a result, infant survival rates were higher among Jewish communities.[19]

There is nothing 'natural' about wet-nursing as it was done in Europe. Among primates, mothers only allow direct kin to briefly nurse their infants when the most difficult circumstances demand it. Ethnographers have found numerous examples of traditional societies in which allo-maternal (surrogate mothering) suckling takes place, but only when difficult circumstances require it. As with other primates, it is only done by close and trusted friends or kin, among co-resident women so the mother is never far away, and only for brief periods.[20] European wet-nursing reflected a widespread and emphatic rejection of, perhaps revulsion towards, the baby.

The early rejection of the mother–child bond at the breast has been so commonplace that we could surmise it to be an intrinsic human impulse, a stage of human evolution. One study of 57 societies[21] showed that only in nine of these societies mothers breastfed their infants immediately after birth. The rest waited between three to seven days after birth, thus customarily denying babies the essential immunological nutrients found in colostrum. Even today, the medically recommended return to 'demand' breastfeeding is baulked at by many women around the world.

The first sign of improvement took place in the 17th century, when wet-nurses started to be brought into the home, mainly in England, Holland and America. Much to the revulsion of European mothers, England took the lead in slowly re-introducing the mother–child breastfeeding bond. Dr William Cadogan had observed that mothers who were too poor to afford wet-nurses tended to have much healthier children, and thus became the first English advocate of maternal nursing. Following Cadogan, during the 18th century, a proliferation of literature advocated that mothers should feed their own babies, and hence the English infant mortality rate began to drop. Wet-nursing did not disappear altogether until the late 18th century in England and America, the 19th century in France and Italy, and the 20th century in Germany. By the end of the 19th century, most European mothers had returned to breastfeeding.

Fosterage

Most children of this period were sent into the service of distant friends or relatives, often not to be seen by their parents until adolescence. Children were educated by foster carers, who also benefited from the children's labour until they reached young adulthood. They spent barely a few nights under their parents' roof during their growing years.

Mediaeval Germanic and Celtic writings are full of references to parents sending children into servile 'fosterage'. Amongst all classes of the Welsh, Anglo Saxons and Scandinavians, it was common for parents to send their children away to be reared until around 17 years of age. The customary farming out of children that prevailed throughout Britain resulted in an appalling death rate, prompting historian Jonathan Gathorne-Hardy to describe it unreservedly as "mass murder".[22] Well into the 19th century, advertisements offering to take other people's children appeared every day in *The Times* in London.[23]

The deportation of children for their labour lasted for centuries. Half of all migrants to the colonies in the American south were indentured children. England sent hundreds of thousands of children into fosterage in Canada and Australia well into the 20th century, and not all were orphans.[24]

Unlike modern fosterage, which is mediated and supervised by government, and exists solely for children of severely disadvantaged backgrounds, fosterage was once the customary way of banishing the unwanted from their family home. It was practised in most civilisations until modern times. It is difficult to distinguish the early model for fosterage from slavery, as children had no rights or choices about their destiny. Working conditions tended to be appalling, and provisions for occupational health and safety non-existent.

Apprenticeship

In the Middle Ages, all children were sent into service or apprenticeship, usually far from home. It was also common for children to be sent into service by indebted parents, as hostages in lieu of debt repayments.

Apprenticeship differed from fosterage only in that it enabled children to learn a trade. Unlike modern apprentices though, children resided with and were the full-time servants of their masters. Many were sent out to full-time apprenticeship at the age of four. Not only were they given no choice about the kind of trade they were to learn, their everyday existence was subject to the master's whim – which was often brutally imposed. In 1630, a master from Salem, Massachusetts, USA, was tried for the murder of his apprentice after bashing him and cracking his skull. The jury acquitted him, because the apprentice was found to be "ill-disposed" (misbehaved).[25]

Historian Barbara Kaye Greenleaf concluded that "mediaeval parents seemed to neglect their babies to an appalling degree", and she describes the treatment of children as "uniformly brutal".[26]

Oblation

Another standard means of relief from the burden of parenting was to hand children over to monasteries or nunneries as a permanent bequest. This practice – called 'oblation' – was common throughout Western and Eastern Europe. Oblation to a monastery or nunnery was, in many ways, as oppressive as slavery. In 6th century France, for instance, oblates were imprisoned in monastic duties for life.[27]

During the 11th and 12th centuries Europe saw a period of unprecedented prosperity and expansion. Nevertheless, parents still found reasons to separate themselves from their children. Those who did not place their children into apprenticeship or fosterage, opted for oblation. While outright abandonment declined in Europe between 1000 and 1200, this did not persuade parents to be close to their children, and instead oblation increased. Oblation was a form of abandonment that gave children a better chance of survival – though not necessarily a better quality of life.

Thus the majority of Mediaeval clerics had been abandoned to their fate, with no choice in the matter. For instance, it was estimated that between 1030 and 1070, 85 per cent of new monks at Winchester were oblates. The oblation rates were not much different for the rest of Europe.[28]

Through the Middle Ages, oblates were effectively slaves of the church, and were permanently forbidden sexual relations or marriage. Few children chose oblation, for most this fate was imposed on them by parents who could not – or would not – raise them. Many tried to escape as soon as they could, but people who harboured fugitive oblates were imprisoned. The life of an oblate was materially austere and emotionally destitute. They were subjected to rigid daily regimens consisting of hours of liturgy, labour and study. Affection, physical or otherwise, was strictly denied, and discipline was meted out with stunning brutality. An oblate's daily grind, behind the monastery walls, was bleak and full of anguish.[29]

Not until the 13th century were oblates given the choice to reconfirm their vows, or leave.[30] Since education had by then become available without commitment to a monastery, oblation declined from this point. Consequently, more perilous forms of abandonment resumed. Meanwhile, the sale of children into slavery continued unabated.

Child slavery

The sale of one's children into slavery, a practice embraced in many ancient cultures, dates back into the times of the Old Testament, which contains numerous references to this practice among the Hebrews. Those particular Biblical passages were quoted as scriptural authorisation to sell one's children, well into the Middle Ages, when children constituted a substantial part of the slave trade. Since the Bible does not contain a substantial and explicit condemnation of slavery, abandoned children provided most of the slave-labour force for early Christians.[31]

That children were seen as sources of labour, is reflected in the language of the times. The terms for 'boy', 'girl' or 'child' were frequently employed to mean 'slave' or 'servant', in Greek, Latin, Arabic, Syriac, Hebrew and many Mediaeval languages.

Public auctions of children were common throughout Europe and Asia well into modern times. In Russia, child sale was only outlawed as late as the 19th century. In late 18th century England, one could buy the service of an illegitimate child for seven years, at 20 to 30 shillings – less than people would pay to buy a terrier. Even children from the British upper classes were bought and sold in order to garner advantageous family alliances.

The trafficking of child slaves has persisted into the new millennium. Although this is a worldwide phenomenon, it tends to be more pervasive on the African continent. Millions of children are believed to have been abducted, trafficked across borders, and used as labourers, soldiers and sex slaves.[32]

Sexual abuse

Children continued to be widely used as sex-objects through the 'abandoning mode' era, and the buggering of boys was commonplace in monasteries. Clerical molestation and rape was rife, and even the confessional was known as a place of sexual abuse. Stories of clerical abuse and illegitimate children born to the clergy are legion. In order to evade scandal for the church, conviction of clerical sex offenders was made extremely difficult. It was very rare, and punishments were light.[33]

American social worker and writer Florence Rush states that the 12th century Jewish philosopher Moses Maimonides re-affirmed this ancient edict: that intercourse with a girl as young as three and a day was acceptable, as long as her father permitted it.[34] Maimonides is also credited with the declaration that if a Jew rapes a three-year-old non-Jewish girl, she must be killed for she has defiled the Jewish man.[35] According to Rush, Maimonides reasoned that intercourse with girls younger than three was not to be worried about since they would soon recover their virginity and be like other virgins.[36] The victim's virginity was only considered of value in terms of her future bride-price.[37] In this regard, girls were not persons, they were property.

Early Christian Canon Law permitted the marriage of girls as young as 12, and boys as young as 14. Infractions were rarely punished, however, and a simple act of church 'convalidation' could legitimise any union. Any girls illegally given in marriage were by church law bound to their husbands once intercourse had taken place and thus rape, even of young girls, validated marriage. Meanwhile, the rape of girls under seven was ignored by the legal system.

Something we now expect and take for granted – the raising and loving of our own children – was an oddity through antiquity and the Middle Ages. Wet-nursing and all other forms of abandonment represented a large-scale lack of emotional capacity for parenting, a global impoverishment in emotional intelligence.

Endnotes

1. Boswell (1988) p 429.
2. Hrdy (2000) p 297.
3. Cooper (1996).
4. Cooper (1996).
5. Hrdy (2000).
6. Hrdy (2000) p 303.
7. Boswell (1988); Hrdy (2000).
8. Boswell (1988).
9. Radbill in Helfer and Kempe (eds) (1974).

[10] De Mause (2001) p 398.

[11] Luke 11:27.

[12] Badinter (1981).

[13] Badinter (1981).

[14] De Mause (1982), (2001) p 390, (2000) p 411.

[15] Badinter (1981).

[16] Hrdy (2000).

[17] Piers (1978).

[18] Hrdy (2000).

[19] Cooper (1996).

[20] Hrdy (2000).

[21] Study by Dana Raphael in Edgerton (1992) p 117.

[22] Gathorne-Hardy (1972) p 35.

[23] Gathorne-Hardy (1972).

[24] Humphreys (1994).

[25] Radbill in Helfer and Kempe (eds) (1974).

[26] Greenleaf (1978).

[27] Boswell (1988).

[28] Boswell (1988).

[29] Boswell (1988).

[30] Boswell (1988).

[31] Boswell (1988).

[32] See Human Rights Watch (2004); Relief Web (2004); 'Scale of African slavery revealed' 23 April 2004 BBC News – search http://news.bbc.co.uk/; Villanueva Siasoco (2001).

[33] Rush (1980).

[34] See references to Maimonides *The Book of Women – Book Four* in Rush (1980) pp 16–22.

[35] Maimonides *Laws of Prohibited Intercourse* Chapter 12 rule 10 in Shahak (1994).

[36] Rush (1980) p 27.

[37] Atlas (2001); Radbill in Helfer and Kempe (eds) (1974).

5

THE AMBIVALENT MODE

A new parenting style – dubbed the 'ambivalent mode' by Lloyd de Mause – began to emerge in Europe around the 14th century. In the western world, this stage of evolution overlapped with the 'abandoning mode'. The changeover from one mode to the next was slow and gradual, taking hundreds of years. Abandoning practices continued in Europe well into the 18th century and beyond. The boarding-school is, in many cases, a modern (though less extreme) vestige of earlier and more radical abandonment.

Although ambivalent mode parenting was an incremental step forward from abandonment, it may have only been a small improvement for children. Parents began attempting to keep their children close, but under conditions of strict control. It is as if parents were collectively saying to their children, 'I'll keep you if I can mould you, or thrash you into shape.' The child was increasingly allowed to stay at home, but he or she was still not accepted as a child.

This new era ushered the beginning of child protection laws, including punishment for child rape. Sex with children began to be publicly disapproved of in Europe, and church moralists began to speak out against sexual molestation. There developed for the first time an interest in children's welfare, but this was a kind of interest mainly preoccupied with control – often brutal. Hence there appeared the first child-rearing instruction manuals, which multiplied in 14th century Europe. The guidebooks that emerged at this time were devoted to the strict and punitive control of children's behaviour. Having been treated as non-entities in previous modes, children were increasingly seen as little 'devils' who needed to be whipped into human form.

Centuries of Christian theological 'wisdom' about the nature of children were guided by St Augustine. Educational and pedagogical theory was dominated by Augustine thought until the end of 17th century, and until then his edicts were invoked around Europe. St Augustine was responsible for ideas about children such as: "If let do what he wants, there is no crime he will not plunge into", and, "Is it not a sin to lust after the breast and wail".[1] Children were believed to be born evil, and the purpose of parenting was thought to be the correction of this evil.

St Augustine was not alone in finding children loathsome and malevolent – this seemed to be the dominant attitude throughout Christendom. Spanish preacher and educator Juan Luis Vives (1492–1540), severely denounced maternal affection, preached coldness toward children, and his anti-child tirades were much quoted and translated. "Mothers damn their children when they nurse them voluptuously." His prescription for children was "castigations and tears".[2] All manuals recommended punishment and denounced love, while tenderness was believed to 'spoil' children. Seventeenth century educationist Pierre de Berulle said "Childhood is the vilest and most abject condition of human nature".[3]

What kind of childhood was created by Augustine and Christian pedagogical thought? The new parenting style emphasised the need to beat children, often severely, and mould their behaviour. De Mause's examination of over 200 pre-18th century statements on child-rearing advice found that the overwhelming majority expressed approval of severe beatings, whereas only three discouraged child beating of any kind. One 13th century article of law begins with: "If one beats a child until it bleeds, then it will remember."[4]

Obedience was the be-all and end-all – parenting relations were based on authority and control, rather than affection. The word 'love' is almost never mentioned, in reference to children, in surviving documents from this era. Literature produced before the late 18th century tended to refer to children with annoyance. Few violent means were spared in extracting obedience from the 'little devils'.

Punishment and child battery

Viewed from a modern perspective, almost all children before the 18th century could be classed as 'battered children'. Instruments such as whips, canes, birches and shackles for feet were commonplace, both at school and at home. Since education for children had begun to spread, flogging became a regular teachers' aid. Other tools of punishment commonly used included the cat-o'-nine-tails, bundles of sticks, the *discipline* (a whip made of small chains), the goad (a knife made for pricking the child on the head or hands), or the flapper (which had a small round hole in one end designed to raise blisters). It was not unusual for children to be restrained with stocks around their feet during study, tied to chairs, wrapped in restrictive corsets, made to wear iron collars for 'posture', or forced into standing stools to prevent crawling. This onslaught was not linked to social class or family income, rich and poor alike would thrash their children with impunity, and it was not uncommon for beatings to go on until bruising or bleeding appeared.[5]

In 1646, the American colonies of Massachusetts and Connecticut adopted Mosaic Law, which prescribed the death penalty for unruly children. A public flogging was usually substituted.[6]

Having examined hundreds of memoirs of mothers from this period, de Mause found that they were 'endlessly beating their children'.[7] Those who felt unfit for the task would hire a professional flagellant. In Victorian England, professional beaters would visit homes with their sophisticated bondage equipment, using systems of straps to immobilise children for their whippings. Screams and struggles only served to attract increased beatings.

In the time of the Renaissance, it was customary in most Christian countries for children to be ritually whipped on 'Innocents' Day', to make them remember the massacre of innocents by King Herod. In his *Advice to Christian Parents* (1839), John Hersey urged parents to "let the child from a year old be taught to fear the rod, and cry softly…make him do as he is bid, if you whip him ten times running to do it".[8] Beatings received at home were repeated at school, often ferociously. As exemplified by this one Medieval German manual, terror was considered to be the very basis for learning: "fear is good for putting the child in the mood to hear and to understand. A child cannot quickly forget what he has learned in fear".[9] Around the world, educational institutions from antiquity to the Middle Ages carried instruments of child beating.

If the child-rearing practices of Christians and Jews differed in many key areas they seemed, during this era, to be in agreement with regard to child battery. Jewish ethical tracts abounded with the counsel to "strike their sons even if they scream", and to "show no softness in the matter".[10] It seems that punishment in Jewish schools (heder) was every bit as cruel as it was in Christian institutions.

In all of de Mause's investigations, he is unable to find a single child of Antiquity or the Middle Ages who escaped "severe physical abuse".[11] Certain Judeo-Christian scriptures demand the beating of children, the Old Testament even contains a requirement that stubborn or defiant children should be put to death by public stoning.[12]

John Locke, writer on education, was among the first to advise against the use of the rod – in a world that thought flagellation totally natural. The old fashioned whippings only started going out of style in Europe and the USA around mid-19th century, continuing longer in Germany. Many countries around the world still tolerate corporal punishment in schools, and almost all still allow it in the home, though in less extreme form. The 'cane' or 'strap' used until quite recently in Australian schools is a vestige of this and earlier child-rearing modes.

When punishment was psychological, it attained the absolutely grotesque. Well into the 18th century, regular public hangings in England attracted eager crowds of up to 80,000. Some parents would force their children to watch the execution, then take them home and flog them to reinforce the disciplining example.[13]

Children were not exempt from the monstrous and draconian penal system of the day. It was not unheard of for unruly children to be thrown in jail. In fact, English children of parents who were sent to prison were frequently sent along with them. Their only crime was to belong to parents who were apprehended for crimes that were often petty. Jail conditions were abominable, the demented were intermingled with the sane, prisoners of all ages and both genders were shoved together in group cells. Jails were acutely overcrowded, Dante-like infernos where sexual abuse, violence and disease were rampant, and where sanitation was non-existent. Authorities thought nothing of tossing children in for years, whether or not they had broken the law. In English and Australian penal institutions children were subjected to floggings – an horrifically damaging form of torture according to historian Robert Hughes's uncensored account.[14]

The First Fleet, which brought the first settlers to establish the penal colony in Sydney in 1788, included three convict children sentenced to transportation. As late as 1837, five children between eight and 11 were transported as convicts to Australia. Not until 1818 were boys accommodated separately from men in Australian penal institutions and until then, minors were often the sexual playthings of male convicts. In the infamous penal settlement of Norfolk Island, for instance, boys were referred to as 'colonial women'. In England, children under 14 could still be sentenced to death. As late as 1831, a nine-year-old boy was hung for arson in England.[15]

Child labour

The beginning of the industrial revolution saw the proliferation of child labour, under the most inhumane conditions. Chimney sweeps as young as four were forced up chimneys for hours at time, in total darkness and in a suffocating and toxic environment. Only little boys were used because they were small enough to squeeze up into the narrow chimney flues. Reluctant new recruits were persuaded to climb into flues through the use of beatings, or by pricking or scorching their bare feet. Apprentices were confined in flues for hours to accustom them to the stifling conditions. Sweeps were either orphaned or abandoned. They had no medical attention, and grew up with severe deformities of the legs and spine as a result of their work. As soon as these boys became too big to navigate the narrow flues, they were cast aside, uneducated, unwanted and unemployed. Many chimney sweeps died of pulmonary disease or cancer of the scrotum – the so-called 'chimney-sweep's cancer'.[16]

Some survivors who weren't too crippled by their trade took to street crime. The most notorious case is that of chimney sweep John Hudson, who was transported to the Australian penal colony for theft at nine years of age.

A 1788 Act against the use of little boys as sweeps proved unenforceable. Over time, the groundswell of public agitation against this kind of exploitation resulted in the abolition of the chimneysweep trade, but not until 1875 – 67 years after adult slavery was abolished.[17]

Starting at four years of age, children worked 16-hour days in coal mines or textile mills. As there were no safety regulations, they suffered frequent accidents and amputations, but were often denied medical attention except under the most severe or life-threatening circumstances. It was not unusual for child workers to be kept in chains to prevent escape. Inefficiency or idleness were punished with whippings. The monstrously long hours meant that children had to have their heads regularly dunked in buckets of cold water, to keep them awake and productive.[18]

The first piece of legislation written specifically to protect children was passed in England. This was the *Factory Act* of 1802, which limited children's work hours to 12 per day. Not only was this legislation pitifully insufficient – according to historian Barbara Kaye Greenleaf – it was probably never enforced.[19]

Swaddling

A particularly bizarre, yet universal, fashion was the excessively tight and prolonged swaddling of babies. Bandages were used to completely immobilise babies into rigid cocoon shapes. Designed as inescapable bonds, swaddling could be so tight and complex as to require over an hour to apply. Tight swaddling was employed by the ancient Jews, Greeks and Romans, and persisted in Europe through the Middle Ages. Various styles of restrictive and immobilising swaddling are also seen among many indigenous North and South American groups, in contemporary Eastern Europe, some parts of the Middle East, and rural Japan.[20]

Doubtless this practice rendered the unfortunate infant more manageable. With a minimum-maintenance, controlled child being the goal, it is little wonder that this kind of swaddling continued in England and America until the 18th century, and in France and Germany until the 19th century. German babies were swaddled tighter and longer than the French, and were called *Wickelkinder*. One observer described them as piteous objects who were changed once or twice a day, rarely bathed, bound like mummies in yards of bandages.

Swaddled babies were tied to wooden boards, hung up on hooks, and left unattended while carers went about their business. They were left to stew in their own excrement and urine for hours, and were covered in hideous and excruciating skin irritations. The worst effect of swaddling is that it made fondling or caressing, something vital to healthy emotional development, impossible.[21]

Swaddling was given some bizarre justifications, based on irrational ideas about the nature of babies. People were gripped by fear that the un-swaddled baby would crawl like an animal, scratch out its eyes, break its limbs, or (God forbid!) touch its genitals. More to the point, complete immobilisation made babies less troublesome, quieter, and generally more convenient for the carer. Often, as they hung from wall-hooks, rags soaked in gruel were left stuffed in their mouths to stifle their annoying cries. Swaddling has been shown to calm babies, which explains why this practice persists into the new millennium in many parts of the world. The much sought-after 'calm' of the swaddled baby is in fact a listless and withdrawn stupor induced by bondage. Swaddled babies are more passive, and sleep longer and more readily. The heart rate of a swaddled infant is lower, and they tend to cry less. Doubtless this makes babies less of a nuisance, but their enforced passivity comes at a grave cost.

Researchers have found that when animals are immobilised they develop lesions such as peptic ulcers.[22] When animals are immobilised for as little as two hours a day, their brain chemistry is altered. The resulting increases in terror, rage, and violence last long beyond the treatment.[23] In clinical studies, babies have been observed to struggle immediately after the swaddling, and then to give up. This is commonly mistaken for restfulness. Prolonged swaddling has been associated with retarded social and motor development, and impaired emotional development due to the sensory deprivation.[24]

Touch deprivation, a product of swaddling, results in a depletion of oxytocin (a hormone associated with wellbeing or pleasure), and oversupplies of the stress hormone cortisol. When such upsets in hormonal balance occur at a time critical to brain development, the effects are long-term. Excessive and prolonged swaddling can lead to a lifetime of elevated irritability and anxiety.[25]

Swaddling was first spoken against by the 18th century English doctor William Cadogan, the same individual who first discredited the practice of wet-nursing. He noticed that the children of impoverished women who couldn't afford to buy swaddling clothes tended to be more robust and healthy.

Sexual abuse

Sexual abuse of children was still rampant throughout this period, and the next. In 15th century France, for instance, the legal 'age of consent' was six. Throughout Europe, little had changed in this regard since the 'infanticidal' period, except that child molesters felt guilty for this sin owing to the efforts of the church. The use of children did not abate but became covert, and a way was found to blame the child for the improper sexual encounter. Europeans en masse were somehow persuaded that girls, when possessed by the Devil, were wont to seducing adults – and thus superstition expiated perpetrators' guilt. Thus, in the late Renaissance, and during the 16th and 17th centuries, girls as young as three were burnt at the stake: under charges of seducing 'innocent' and 'unsuspecting' men.

Christian guilt about sex with minors did little to protect

children from wholesale exploitation as sex objects, and in fact, it only made matters worse for them. The witch-hunts of 14th to 16th century Europe targeted thousands of children who were accused of being possessed by demons. They were subjected to harrowing trials in court, tortured and put to death. The signs of 'demonic possession' that seemed to be in epidemic proportions are now known to be symptoms of dissociative disorders, caused by severe trauma, sexual or physical abuse. The psychological symptoms displayed by the most abused children became the evidence used against them. Children were massacred in order to cleanse the guilt of the perpetrators who lusted after them.[26]

Endnotes

[1]   Badinter (1981) pp 30–31.

[2]   Badinter (1981) pp 33–34.

[3]   Badinter (1981) p 36.

[4]   De Mause (1982) p 49.

[5]   De Mause (1998) p 228, (2001) pp 404–415, (1982) p 47.

[6]   Radbill in Helfer and Kempe (eds) (1974).

[7]   De Mause (2001).

[8]   Hersey (1839) p 83 in de Mause (2001) p 405.

[9]   De Mause (2001) p 409.

[10]   Cooper (1996) p 224.

[11]   De Mause (2001) p 410.

[12]   Deuteronomy 21:21.

[13]   Holden (1999).

[14]   Hughes (1996); Holden (1999).

[15]   Holden (1999).

[16]   Holden (1999).

[17]   Holden (1999); Greenleaf (1978). See the UK National Archives in the 'Citizenship' and 'Child labour' sections http://www.nationalarchives.gov.uk/ (last accessed 1 December 2004).

[18]   Greenleaf (1978).

[19]   Greenleaf (1978).

[20]   Lipton and Steinschneider (1965)

[21]   De Mause (2001) pp 396, 399–403.

[22]   Lipton and Steinschneider (1965).

[23]   Lamprecht (1990).

[24]   Lipton and Steinschneider (1965).

[25]   De Mause (2001) p 403.

[26]   Rush (1980).

6

THE INTRUSIVE MODE

The notion of a loving family, revolving around a presumed 'maternal' instinct, was first envisioned in the 18th century. Despite exhaustive research, Lloyd de Mause found no references to the cherishing of children in European literature predating this era. Nor was there a clear and distinct concept of childhood, prior to this time.

In this era of 'intrusive mode' parenting, children began to be seen (but not yet heard!) as children, rather than as faulty miniature adults. The 'Age of Reason' and the 'Industrial Revolution' were powerful social forces that freed peoples' minds from some of the darker superstitions of Mediaeval times. Children were still largely viewed as bothersome, but at least they ceased to be branded as malevolent or demonic. This permitted some affection, and the first signs of empathy, to creep into the parent–child relationship.

The beginning of the end of arranged marriages in Europe brought more love into some family homes. Mothers had fewer births, and so more care was available for each child. Parental displays of tenderness were likely, though not freely given. Perhaps because it was a newcomer to human relations, emotional intimacy was strictly controlled.

As child battery and abandonment receded, this led to a reduction in infant mortality and increased health. The added freedom and vitality of children posed new challenges which parents met by becoming intrusively over-controlling. Thus, increased emotional bonds were coupled with an obsessive urge to control the child's innermost thoughts and desires. The objectives of parents were to conquer the child's will, emotions, impulses and needs. They sought to gain dominion over children's minds, their every urge, their physical and emotional insides. Many parents became fixated on applying strict discipline, repressive codes of 'good manners', early toilet training, regular enemas, and the prohibition of masturbation.

The sea-change in attitudes was embodied in the 'Romantic' movement, and spearheaded by philosophers such as Jean-Jacques Rousseau. In his essay 'The social contract', for the first time in European history, he challenged the absolute right to parental authority, ushering in the 'enlightened' supposition that each individual is born free. The 'Romantic' ideals of this age aroused a new sentimentality about the family and the child. Rousseau advised people to love childhood, and to indulge its games and pleasures.[1] People began to suspect that it was alright for children to have fun, but this fresh tolerance took many decades to take hold and spread throughout the west.

Rousseau wrote a stinging denunciation of wet-nursing. He attacked the unscrupulous use of swaddling, comparing it to crucifixion. Rousseau pleaded with parents to nurture their babies at home, to throw out their swaddling bands and allow them freedom of movement.

A small but growing band of sympathetic authors voiced genuine concern for children. Such was Hanway's *A Sentimental History of Chimney Sweepers,* published in 1785, which contained some of the earliest suggestions in any literature that children should be cherished. Although strides were taken, the lives of most children were still full of woe. Not even Rousseau's civilising philosophy was matched by his actions. He abandoned every one of his five children at foundling homes, without bothering to record their birth-dates. While he recognised what children need better than any of his contemporaries, he was himself a product of 'ambivalent mode' parenting, and thus lacked the emotional capacity to meet these needs.

The idea of the stay-at-home, modest, loving and devoted mother was fabricated by Rousseau and the other Romantics. No doubt this newest trend would have improved the lives of many children. But as a fashion of the times, the new doting mother was largely driven by guilt and social expectation – she followed a formula not familiar through personal experience. Her sincerity as a mother may have been compromised by a doctrine that cautioned women to remain meek, powerless and subservient. Not surprisingly, mothers did enjoy closer bonds with their children, but perhaps with limited emotional authenticity and enthusiasm. How freely can anyone love if imprisoned by social pressure, rather than bonded by choice?

It can take generations for close and loving ties to become spontaneous rather than contrived, or merely in compliance with a chic recipe such as Rousseau's.

Certainly, the subjugation of children became increasingly methodical. Victorian England imposed impossible standards of manners, self denial and restraint. Philosopher John Locke spoke out against corporal punishment, but instead he advised that children's lives should be regulated by rigid schedules. Locke recommended strict toilet-training, and warned against indulging children's cries – supposedly in order to encourage the child's faculty of 'reason'. The idea was to raise dispassionate children – a formula not altogether unfamiliar in modern times. It was then – and in some families still remains – a universal tenet that children should ask for nothing, show no preferences, and eat what was in front of them without complaint. The assertion that 'children should be seen but not heard' was now at its zenith.

The treatment of babies was heavily influenced by 18th century doctor William Cadogan, who had persuaded parents to renounce the worst excesses of wet-nursing and swaddling. Like Rousseau, Cadogan testified to the superior health and robustness of unswaddled babies.

Having liberated babies in one way, Cadogan went on to entrap them in another: by promoting rigid schedule-based child-rearing methods. So, the quirky western caprice for schedule-feeding babies arose from ignorance; in a time when the art of breastfeeding had been completely lost. Cadogan's program for infant care appeared in his widely-read article, 'Essay upon nursing and the management of children from their birth to three years of age'. Based on the instruction of Cadogan and others, babies began to be fed and put to sleep according to the clock, rather than according to their obvious need. Faced with added intimacy with their children, and the discomfort this brings, parents seemed to resort to more intrusive and regimented methods of child-control. The parenting approach of the time was by-the-book; rather clinical and mechanical. Mothers were not encouraged or helped to tune in emotionally, and intuit their baby's changing needs and feelings. Nevertheless, in spite of its rigidity and invasiveness, 'intrusive' parenting was undeniably an improvement on past practice. This excessive preoccupation with routine remains an outdated but decreasingly common feature of baby-health practice to this day – although it is discredited by modern infant health know-how.

Child-rearing manuals of the 19th century may have urged closer bonds, but parenting was still expected to be cold and emotionally distant. The physicality of hugs and cuddles was shunned. Victorian parents were emotionally remote, and fathers were often referred to as 'Governor'. Those parents who had the means renounced any involvement with the day-to-day task of child rearing.

With the decline of wet-nursing came the rise of the nannies. While more parents began to allow their children to remain at home, they were still emotionally unready to engage directly with their children for more than a few moments each day. The daily task of upbringing was left in the care of nannies, as well-to-do parents devised new ways to distance themselves from their children. Historian Jonathan Gathorne-Hardy, who investigated hundreds of British biographical accounts from this era, described the nannies as "total strangers, nearly always uneducated, about whose characters [the parents] must usually have had no real idea at all".[2] Nannies were used by hundreds of thousands of British parents, and this practice peaked towards the end of the 19th century. The proliferating system of boarding schools further ensured that children would be kept at arm's length. Parents could monitor their children's progress from afar, through scheduled visits, often without the tedium – nor the pleasure – of emotional intimacy. 'Intrusive mode' parents tended to abandon their children emotionally rather than physically.

Trends in punishment

Victorian standards of manners and conduct were strict, and often backed up by severe corporal punishment. Though perhaps with less savagery and frequency than in earlier times, brutality continued at home, and at schools. The French abandoned school floggings by the 1840s, but it continued in British schools and homes for some time. Both in England and America, pictures of pedagogues typically showed them holding a birch – child battery was central to education.

Besides being incompetent, nannies tended to be domineering, strict, and cruel. Personal accounts and biographies abound which depict nannies as brutal, even sadistic disciplinarians.[3] Memoirs of the time are replete with stories of beatings, of children being locked up for hours in rooms or closets. Children were regularly put to bed tied up by the hands, wearing corsets, iron bodices or steel collars. They were forced to sit for hours tied to backboards in order to teach them 'self-restraint'. If punishment was a little less savage than in earlier times, the methods were more bizarre and elaborate. Some remarkable effort and inventiveness went into the creation of punishment and restraint devices.[4]

Chronicler Gathorne-Hardy also uncovered innumerable accounts of nannies who were alcoholic, many of whom would get children in their care drunk in order to subdue them. It was common for nannies to use ether to expedite their charges to sleep at night.[5]

Even potty training was punitive, beginning as early as one month. The enema, a painful invasion of the child's body, came into widespread use at this time. Ostensibly, enemas were meant for 'purification', though the grounds for this are dubious, especially as they were used so frequently. We can only marvel at the enthusiasm this fetish attracted at the time. The popular obsession with enemas was part of a collective compulsion to control children, and their most intimate bodily functions.[6]

Methods of psychological control were also quite popular, and parents had an assortment of bogeymen with which to threaten and terrify their children. Disobedient children were told that "the Werewolf" would eat them up, "Blue Beard" would chop them up, "Boney" (Bonaparte) would devour their flesh, or the "Chimney Sweep" would take them away at night.[7] In Germany, the infamous book of nursery rhymes *Struwwelpeter* was filled with stories of children suffering mutilation, starvation, incineration and other torments, all for failing to obey their parents.[8]

Late in the 19th century, there appeared in England and France the first child-rearing manuals urging gentleness. These new guidebooks encouraged fathers to be more directly involved with their children, and to spend time playing with them. They espoused a new view – inspired by Rousseau's earlier works, that children were born 'good'. Parenting should therefore be about bringing forth children's natural, 'good' impulses. This contrasted with the earlier idea that the goal of parenting was to punish the 'badness' inherent in all children. There was much opposition to this new perspective, however, and the goal of breaking the child's will continued to predominate.

The earliest accounts of children who suffered no beatings appear in the late 18th century, but according to de Mause these are precious few. In 19th century USA, where child beating was less popular, visitors from strict, disciplinarian Europe commented that the children were 'spoiled'.[9]

Child labour

Child labour proved difficult to eradicate, but was *officially* prohibited in England through the *Factory Act 1874*.[10] Meanwhile in the USA, child protection laws were unpoliced and ineffectual, and in 1880 there were still one million 10–15 year olds at work. Not until 1938 was American child labour legally abolished.[11]

This problem continues in many nations today, where millions of children are denied education and forced to work tedious, repetitive or dangerous jobs for long hours. The International Labour Organization estimated in 2002 that 110 million children under 15 were working in conditions hazardous to their health.[12] Almost 250 million children worldwide are forced to work.[13]

Sexual abuse

Striking at the heart of children's autonomy and their sense of their own bodily rhythms and pleasure, there arose in these times an obsession with prohibiting masturbation. Parents and doctors spared no effort nor inventiveness, in their determination to interfere with this natural activity. Victorian England saw an obsession with bondage to prevent children from masturbating.

The fear of child sexuality peaked to irrational extremes through the late 18th, 19th and early 20th centuries. The medical profession was fully behind this assault on infantile sexuality, making wild and unfounded claims through the most reputed medical journals and texts, such as the *Lancet* and the *Continental Handbook of Medicine*. Doctors in Europe and the USA maintained that masturbation could lead to a plethora of diseases such as epilepsy, spinal tuberculosis, impotence, sterility, psychosis, and early death was assured. For a 'cure', some doctors were advocating cauterisation of the prostate gland, others the cutting of nerves leading to the penis. Throughout Europe and North America, parents went as far as having their daughters' clitorises surgically removed (and we in the west thought this practice belonged only to Africans and Muslims!). Just as we tend to do today, the general public believed doctors unquestioningly. The reason circumcision of boys became so popular among non-Jews was due to the belief that this would inhibit masturbation. In 1905, several hundred inmates of the Indiana State Reformatory (a boys' home in the USA), were sterilised in order to prevent their 'sexual misbehaviour'.[14]

Doctors were also prescribing a range of gruesome genital restraint devices that would prevent self-touch, or pierce the genitals upon arousal. People went to astounding lengths to intrude upon this most private of bodily functions – one wonders at the ingenuity of the restraint devices manufactured for this purpose. Some nurseries were equipped in ways reminiscent of modern S&M dungeons. Many children were put to bed nightly with their hands tied. Boys' penises were fitted with corsets, padlocked chastity belts, penis-rings, metal cages with inward-pointing spikes, and plaster casts in order to prevent nocturnal erections. Some of these devices would make erections extremely painful, and many were sold with handcuffs to prevent the child from attempting to dismantle them. It's a wonder children could get to sleep at all. These devices, of a myriad shapes and forms, were abundantly available at any pharmacy, and were widely used. More elaborate machines sounded alarms or administered electric shocks to the wearer who got an erection. In the USA between 1856 and 1932, the Government Patent Office awarded 33 patents to new inventors of anti-masturbation devices.[15] Such restraint devices would have made night time for children, and especially pubescent children, an agony, a violation, and a sexual trauma. The lack of release of sexual charge through masturbation would have compounded the psychological anguish suffered by countless boys, night after night. The cumulative impact on adult social and sexual behaviour would have been disastrous.

By the 1920s, after two centuries of this barbaric assault on children's genitals, these methods began to die out in Europe. The USA was tardy in following suit, where the prohibition of children's masturbation began to abate by the 1950s.

While adults obsessively policed their children's behaviour, their own urges seemed to remain unchecked, and child molestation was running amok throughout Europe. The repressive and often violent attitudes toward child sexuality were a rather transparent cover for adult sexual perversions – born of the infantile traumas they themselves had once endured. As during the witch-hunts, children were being punished for the adults' sexual guilt and shame. For adults in Victorian England still harboured paedophile urges in huge numbers. There was, during this period, an explosion of erotic and pornographic literature around Europe. In Victorian England much of this literature depicted sex with minors.[16]

The child–as–sex–object was evident in the suffocating, metal-braced corsets that girls as young as three were squeezed into.[17] These corsets were at times so restrictive as to cause damage to internal organs and permanent back injury. The corset was an attempt to impose an adult, feminine figure on a child, and had more than a little in common with Chinese foot-binding and other culturally sanctioned disfiguring practices around the world.

Except in brothels, the sexual exploitation of children was well hidden under a cloak of collective denial. The growth of psychoanalysis uncovered an epidemic of sexual molestation by nannies. Sigmund Freud reported countless cases of clients who had been molested by their nannies and governesses in childhood. Historian Gathorne-Hardy also exposed the tendency for nannies of this era to be sexually exploitative. It was common for nannies to masturbate little boys in their care.[18]

Incest was still so widespread, that doctors who visited men suffering from venereal disease, frequently remarked that their children were also infected. Doctors concluded that the sexual abuse of children by their fathers was very common. European adults tended to believe that children could not remember anything before the age of five, and this meant they could be molested without harm. Ordinarily, sex with children was not considered destructive to the child. If pederasty was suppressed, this was because it was considered sinful or dirty, not because it was seen to be damaging to children. The concern was for a pure moral record, rather than for how children felt.

Child prostitutes were cheaply available in every European city. In London, about one house in every 60 was a brothel, and child prostitutes made up a large part of the trade. In Vienna, over 50 per cent of non-registered prostitutes were minors. All over Europe, North and South America a flourishing trade in child prostitutes meant that children were abducted or enticed into the business by the thousands. By the end of 19th century, the age of consent in England was still only 13.

Child prostitutes received no protection from government or non-government organisations, until the late 19th century, when Benjamin Scott formed the Committee for the Exposure and Suppression of Traffic in English Girls for Purposes of Continental

Prostitution. His organisation found abducted English girls aged five to 11 enslaved and working all over Paris.[19]

It is no wonder that Freud and his colleagues were treating patients with dissociative symptoms, such as hysteria, in such vast numbers. Previously, the same individuals would have been burnt as witches.

Today, the 'hysterical' patients that were so common in Freud's day, are increasingly rare. This indicates that the circumstances that led to 'hysteria', that is severe child sexual abuse coupled with suffocating emotional repression, are on the wane. From the 'intrusive' mode to today's 'socialising' mode, the evolution of parenting has altered the psychological profile of western societies.

Some improvements

Some of the earliest medical interest in children's health came from Scottish doctor William Buchan, who suggested in his book *Domestic Medicine* (1775) that doctors should see to children. Until this point, doctors had paid scant attention to kids. The separate field of paediatrics was not developed as a special branch of medicine until 1872. William Cadogan has been given the epithet 'Father of Paediatrics', but it was long after Cadogan that the practice of paediatrics was widely known. The first American and British hospitals just for children appeared in the 1850s.

The Society for the Protection of Children was formed in France between 1865 and 1870. At the time, the Society for the Protection of Animals had more members.[20] In England, the Society for the Prevention of Cruelty to Children received its royal charter in 1895.

The 19th century hosted the growth of literature especially devoted to children, such as Peter Pan, and novels such as those of Charles Dickens, that championed children's causes. Toys, and games especially designed for children proliferated. The first urban playgrounds in the world made their appearance in Boston in 1885. These social innovations indicated that children were finally starting to be recognised for their special and unique needs. This was the dawn of an acceptance of children's right to have fun.[21]

Around the same time, free schooling became available to all in North America and Europe (although in the USA it was racially segregated, and severely under-funded for African–Americans). Finally, children were at school and away from the workplace, set apart from the world of adults, and hence considered to be different, with their own needs and rights. The concept of childhood cannot be fully realised in any society, until all children are guaranteed education and freedom from exploitation. Throughout most of the western world, children weren't given this status until late in the 19th century, and around the turn of the 20th century. Until a society has designated provisions for their special care, children have not been recognised as a vulnerable and valued group, fundamentally distinct from adults – and this places them in grave danger.

New insights about the nature of child development came once people began to be genuinely interested in children's wellbeing. The concept of 'adolescence', for instance, was coined by G Stanley Hall in 1904, and had not been understood as a distinct developmental stage until then.[22]

The next parenting mode –'socialising mode'– is characterised by a growing social recognition of children's needs, as they are gradually released from being seen as objects, existing to serve adults' needs. The progress made in child rearing over the next period is based on a growing public awareness of developmental norms, thanks to the rapid dissemination of the social sciences.

Endnotes
[1] Rousseau in Greenleaf (1978).
[2] Gathorne-Hardy (1972) p 19.
[3] Gathorne-Hardy (1972) p 19.
[4] De Mause (1982) pp 43–44.
[5] Gathorne-Hardy (1972).
[6] De Mause (1982) p 45, (2000) p 419.
[7] De Mause (1998) p 232.
[8] *Struwwelpeter* was first published by Dr Heinrich Hoffman in the 19th century. An English version was reprinted in 1990 by Forum Books, Surrey.
[9] Greenleaf (1978).
[10] Child labour did not end with the *Factory Act 1874*. This was neither the first, nor the last, *Factory Act*. See for example, http://www.spartacus.schoolnet.co.uk/IRchild.main.htm (last accessed 1 December 2004).
[11] Greenleaf (1978). Just because child labour was legally abolished this does not mean it was abolished altogether. For example, you can read about child labour in the USA in the 1973 publication of a book called *Sweatshops in the Sun: Child Labour on the Farm*

http://www.questia.com/PM.qst?a=o&d=96273903 (last accessed 1 December 2004), and this is only one example. You can find many other examples http://www.questia.com/popularSearches/child_labor.jsp (last accessed 1 December 2004); http://www.georgemeany.org/archives/child.html (last accessed 1 December 2004).

[12] See the International Health Organization (2002).

[13] See United Nations Children's Fund (UNICEF) 'Child labour' http://www.unicef.org/protection/index_childlabour.html (last accessed 1 December 2004).

[14] Piers (1978).

[15] Schwarz (1973).

[16] Rush (1980).

[17] Edgerton (1992).

[18] Gathorne-Hardy (1972).

[19] Rush (1980).

[20] Badinter (1981).

[21] Greenleaf (1978).

[22] Greenleaf (1978).

7

THE SOCIALISING MODE

As we enter the modern age, the evolution of child rearing seems to progress at a faster pace, aided by a prodigious growth in communication technologies, availability of public education, and rapid advances in the social sciences. From the late 19th century, through the 20th century, and into the new millennium, there have been many significant changes in the way we bring up our children. Most of these changes have been positive, though there have been a few setbacks. Children from most cultures have benefited, but modernisation of parenting has eluded those societies that are mired in fundamentalist religious dogma, autocratic and repressive government, or extreme poverty.

The aim of socialising parenting practices is to train the child to conform to cultural norms, to adopt the manners and behaviours that will enable his or her seamless acceptance into the surrounding social milieu. The socialising parent, while not lacking in affection, tends to view the child through a moral lens that dichotomises behaviour into 'good' and 'bad'. The end goal of parenting is to produce a 'good' child; one that is courteous and well mannered, a productive and law-abiding member of society. Though most children are now cherished more than at any other time in history, and they are given more freedoms than ever before, fulfilling social expectations still takes precedence over individual creativity and self-actualisation.

One formidable change wrought by the socialising mode has been the entry of the father, and his hands-on involvement with child rearing. As early as 1866, French author Gustave Droz, produced the first parenting manual that encouraged dads to participate in play and affection. His book *Monsieur, Madame et Bebe* had huge print runs and multiple revised editions, attesting to its popular appeal throughout Europe. Until this point, fathers had, on the whole, been remote and disinterested at best, or violent and exploitative at worst.

Another improvement of this era was a significant drop in women's fertility rates. Whereas on average, women were bearing seven to eight children previously, now they were only having three or four. Since this drop in birthrates took place before modern contraceptive methods were available, it may have reflected parents' desire to give more care to each child. Socialising mode parents offered more and better quality attention to children than their predecessors.

Before socialising mode parenting had taken hold in the western world, the stages of childhood development were not at all understood. This allowed enormous confusion and misconceptions about how children should behave. As a result, they were constantly being punished for failing to perform as the adults wished. Until child development is adequately understood, the doors are left open to the dangers of the unrealistic expectation. Modern advances in parenting have been possible owing, in part, to the revolutionary discoveries made by pioneers such as Sigmund Freud and Jean Piaget.

The late 19th century was the dawn of genuine, scientific inquiry into the mind of the child. Austrian doctor, Sigmund Freud, was the first to thoroughly study the effect that childhood experiences have on adult functioning, and in this way he fathered the modern field of psychology. Over the 20th century, psychologists continued to unlock the secrets of adult behaviour, based on the formative early years of life. The portentous value of childhood has now been confirmed by a formidable body of clinical and research evidence. As the new field of psychology flourished internationally, the world was forced to accept that childhood experiences have a considerable impact on adult behaviour. This idea still receives mixed reviews. However, as this idea continues to gain cultural acceptance, the way we think about parenting is profoundly and irrevocably altered.

Freud initiated the discourse about the devastating, long-term psychological effects of child sexual abuse. He and his followers fostered the understanding that sexual exploitation of children is wrong because it is profoundly hurtful to children, rather than because it breaks some code of ethics. The focus of attention shifted onto the child's need for protection and empathy, rather than the narcissistic pre-occupation with adult sin. Freud lived and worked at a time when the sexual abuse of children was more prevalent than today, but its ubiquitous actuality was still largely denied.

Freud himself struggled with the truth of his patients' abuse memories. Unable to sustain his belief alone, he eventually repudiated his patients' reports of childhood sexual abuse, labelling their abuse memories as 'infantile fantasy'. Nevertheless, he somehow managed to expose the rampant incest that, under cover of civility, was a hallmark of his time. Freud certainly led the charge for the beginning of genuine concern for children, and the depth of their suffering at the hands of abusers. Owing to his personal difficulties in accepting his patients' abuse memories at face value, Freud is accused of whitewashing the issue of sexual abuse of children. Yet he was merely subject to the same denial that the rest of the world insisted on. It must be remembered that he lived in a world that either denied or tolerated child abuse, or ignored its harmful effects. In fact, he went much further than anyone in his era in so far as he insisted that this taboo subject be brought to public awareness. Over the decades that followed, it has become progressively harder for society to avert its gaze from this disturbing but frightfully common phenomenon.

As a result of the psychoanalytic movement, and subsequent growth of many forms of psychotherapy, the sexual abuse of children at last became the subject of widespread clinical concern, and psycho-therapeutic treatment became available for the victims. Children are better protected since all but those on the fringe of western society conceive of paedophilia as a perversion. Nevertheless, it took until the close of the 20th century for child abuse to become openly acknowledged in the general media, and for the reporting and prosecution of perpetrators to become commonplace. It is now an Interpol priority to track down and dismantle the international child pornography trade, and secret paedophile societies. Clergy or other professionals who misuse their contact with children are exposed and shamed by the media, and more frequently prosecuted. Survivors of sexual abuse are finally being given a voice in court. However, though progress has been made, the world has not yet come to terms with the extent of sexual interference that goes on behind closed doors.

Freud was also the first to strongly advocate that children should be allowed freedom of self-expression. His efforts to liberate the spirit of the child were endorsed by many subsequent luminaries, such as Jean Piaget, Erik Erikson, John Bowlby, and Wilhelm Reich. But even Freud did not identify beating as harmful to children, and this idea was not suggested by psychologists and social-learning theorists until much later. Though it is generally less frequent and less severe, child beating is still a regular feature of child rearing in most homes around the world. Traditional instruments of punishment have disappeared from most homes and schools, and today's children tend to be beaten with an open hand.

Social scientists have led the growth of public awareness about the need to protect and care for children as a society, rather than just leaving childcare entirely up to parents. There has been a flurry of legislation enacted around the world to protect the interests of children. Late 19th century laws in France enabled governments to remove abused or neglected children. In 1909, the first White House Conference on Children was convened in the USA. In 1912, the US Children's Bureau was established.[1]

It would take many more years for children to be accorded full personhood and legal rights, for history's parents preferred to consider them possessions, to do with as they pleased. In 1957, The United Nations produced the Declaration of the Rights of the Child, nine years after the Universal Declaration of Human Rights. In 1969, the United States Supreme Court declared children to be 'persons' under the United States Constitution. Up until then, American children had been legally the property of their parents.

In 1989, the Convention on the Rights of the Child was passed by the United Nations General Assembly and has now been ratified by every country except the USA and Somalia. This convention recognises the child as an independent being with freedom of thought and speech. Signatory states are obliged to take steps to protect children from economic or sexual exploitation, and traditional practices prejudicial to their health (such as genital mutilation).[2]

The Convention on the Rights of the Child also stipulates that children must not be executed, jailed for life or imprisoned with adult offenders. This might be a contributing factor behind the USA's refusal to sign, since this country was until 2005 one of only five that executed offenders who are minors.[3]

The Convention is the first explicit, near-universal agreement about the supreme importance of protecting and cherishing children, but it is a document that has yet to acquire legal teeth. Though it certainly signifies a growth in human consciousness, the spirit of the Convention has yet to permeate the depths of our collective conviction. Hatred toward children is still alive and well. Among many countries that have ratified this Convention, implementation of its tenets remains inconsistent, if not downright shoddy. Nevertheless, the uneven but almost global recognition of children's rights represents a formidable leap forward in our evolution. The socialising mode parenting style is the precursor of these social advancements.

Since the 20th century, the toys and games industry has boomed beyond what anyone could have imagined (although this is not always necessarily for the benefit of children).[4] This has been accompanied by boundless production of children's movies, songs, theatre and pantomimes. Not only are children receiving superior care, parents have also become much more supportive of their children's essential right to have fun.

Limiting self-expression

Though parents have become more accepting, and children are allowed a fuller range of self-expression, generally their full gamut of emotional expression has not yet been embraced. Socialising mode parenting places little value on the realm of feeling and emotion. Children are not encouraged to voice their feelings, and their opinions don't count. Their emotional inner-world is seen as trivial and irrational, and is therefore of little worth. In fact, emotionality is largely seen as a nuisance, so strong displays of feeling are either ignored or castigated. There is still little understanding about children's emotional needs and emotional development. It is still widely believed – though science has shown this to be false – that children less than two years old remember nothing, and therefore their early childhood experiences are of no lasting consequence. Parents of this mode are only partially coming to terms with the idea that psychological make-up is mediated through childhood emotional experience.

Socialising mode parents decry showing children 'too much' empathy. They believe that to meet a child's emotional needs might encourage him or her to be eternally dependent. Certainly, babies are kept safe and warm, cuddled and fed, and their physical health is fastidiously monitored. But socialising dogma warns against regularly picking up a crying infant, as this might 'spoil' the child, or reward his cries and thus teach him 'bad habits'. A favourite warning of the socialising mode is 'you mustn't let your baby get control over you!' This is a categorical denial of babies' abject helplessness. Crying babies are frequently left unattended, lest they 'become too dependent'. The expression of feeling is expected to be restrained in children of all ages. Unlike the 19th century belief, children are to be seen *and* heard – just not taken very seriously.

Rather than trusting, allowing and encouraging natural development, the socialising parent believes in actively shaping and moulding the child's character. Children are pressured to absorb and reflect parental values and goals, rather than becoming self-directed and free-thinking individuals. When parents view – and treat – their children as psychological extensions of themselves, they retard their children's individuation.

Gender roles
Boys are especially discouraged from feeling and expressing emotion, while girls are trained to be passive, so as to comply with unwritten social gender-roles. The family, though generally more democratic than in 'intrusive mode' times, tends to be – at least outwardly – patriarchal. Though it is held to be sacred, the role of mother is regarded to be of inferior social status.

Authoritarian parenting and the 'good child'
The focus of this mode is on pedagogy (child training). A strong emphasis is placed on 'taming' toddlers or 'disciplining' adolescents. The child is to be trained, as early as possible, to conform to social norms, to venerate authority, to be a well-behaved or 'good' child. The good child is the measure of successful socialising mode parenting: he or she is obedient, does not question or negotiate, and restricts passion and emotion. The authoritarian quest for the good child sets the stage for a battle of wills, where the parent must at all costs be the victor. The parent must remain dominant, let the child know who's 'boss', and never let the child 'get her own way'. Even babies are expected to be good. One of the most frequently asked questions regarding infants seems to be 'Is he/she a good baby?'

The belief persists in 'respect for elders' – no matter what – and absolute parental authority. In other words, authority is based on age, not on merit. Democracy plays a limited role in the socialising mode home. Socialising mode parenting is therefore authoritarian in style, based on domination rather than partnership. The socialising parent is a benign authority, usually kind. But in order to create 'well socialised' children, the parent's chief role is that of disciplinarian.

Discipline and control

Only a few generations ago, whenever our forebears felt overwhelmed by the demands of parenting, they would perceive their children as evil or demonic. They were convinced that severe punishment or even exorcism were the answers. These days, whenever their needs are too great for our limited or exhausted patience, we are more likely to see our children as small tyrants or manipulators. The delusions about children's malicious intentions are certainly less dramatic. Not surprisingly, the relentless brutality of earlier modes has all but disappeared from the mainstream of socialising cultures. All-out child battery has been replaced by spanking, or smacking. Socialising parents feel horrified by the brutality of earlier 'discipline' methods, but they remain insensitive to the effects of less severe physical assault.

A concept now widely familiar, the expression 'battered child syndrome' was not conceived until late in the socialising mode era. This term was coined in a landmark study published by C Henry Kempe[5] and his associates in 1962. This study has been enormously influential in raising public awareness about the dire consequences of attacks upon children. Kempe explicitly placed responsibility on doctors to investigate signs of child battery, and be bold enough to report it, thus making the victim a priority. The article offered guidelines for evaluation of battered children, acknowledging that there are usually great pains taken by the parents to cover-up the abuse, and to present an aura of civility. Kempe was perhaps the first to shake the world into awareness of this issue, and how frequently it goes unnoticed, unrecognised and misdiagnosed.

While most people in modern societies take it for granted that child battery is a ghastly crime, few realise that only decades ago, this problem scarcely attracted any attention. Up until very recently, the issue of child abuse and battery lay dormant, the adult world refused to acknowledge its existence. Child battery was universally buried under a cloak of denial. As American social worker and author Mary Katherine Armstrong says of child abuse at this time: "It was everywhere, yet nobody saw it".[6] The world was not emotionally ready to accept that parents could be so vicious toward their children, so frequently. The collective need to fantasise a 'just world' required the idealisation of the parent–child relationship. Today's increasing public acceptance of the existence of child battery and abuse speaks of a greater, collective emotional maturity. Our awakening to this unpalatable truth is painful, but an essential step toward further reducing – and finally, eliminating – child abuse. Nevertheless, denial thrives in lesser forms. Our threshold of what constitutes abuse remains high, such that many people still don't consider a 'good spanking' to be abusive.

When a child's behaviour is challenging, the automatic socialising mode response is to control the child's behaviour; rather than to understand it, or to educate the child about the impact their behaviour has on others. Behaviour control methods fall into three categories. Corporal punishment is the first. Though generally less barbaric than in days gone by, corporal punishment of children is still accepted throughout most of the world. There is a global trend, however, towards banning this practice from schools, and even from homes, which indicates a continuing evolution away from physical violence.

The second approach to behaviour control involves shaming – a kind of verbal punishment aimed at making children more docile. Shaming works like a psychological spanking, and thus the long-lasting injuries wrought are invisible to the naked eye.

The third category is the most covert and sophisticated, and it involves psychological manipulation. Control over the child is gained by rewarding their efforts to please, and by withdrawal of approval or affection when they fail to do so. Manipulation can be so subtle, that often neither the parent nor the child are consciously aware that it is going on. Children are easily seduced into compliance and obedience, when promised prizes, and conditionally made to feel special. When shrewdly combined and dispensed, praise and disapproval can lure any child away from their authentic selves, and condition them to become pleasers. No doubt this makes the adults around them more comfortable, but at a cost to honesty in relationships. The manipulated grow up to become manipulators. In Part IV, we will more closely examine these three approaches, and assess their impact on the development of emotional intelligence.

In the new millennium, we have certainly become progressively less extreme in our efforts to dominate children.

Instead, we resort to more sophisticated and subtly manipulative behaviour modification methods. These methods gain enormous popularity because they successfully do away with behaviours that make parents uncomfortable. Scant regard is given, however, to the possible emotional consequences for the child. Fortunately, we are at the same time allowing our children a far greater range of self-expression and liberty than ever before.

Bottle feeding

For centuries, European mothers have sought to escape the burden and the intimacy of breastfeeding, by feeding their infants artificially. When wet-nurses were unavailable, babies were fed mixtures of animal milk, water, or wheat flour (pap or gruel) through teats fashioned from clay, metal, leather, animal horns, or cow udders. The rubber teat was eventually developed in 1850.

When increased production resulted in a surplus of dairy produce in Europe, the industry was faced with the dilemma of what to do with the excess. The invention of baby-formula did more than solve the problem of surplus. Driven by marketing campaigns in which formula was presented as 'similar to human milk', an enormously profitable commercial juggernaut was created.[7] Though it is a welcome development in cases where there are medical, psychological or circumstantial impediments to breastfeeding, the spread of artificial feeding has been indiscriminate. Women were somehow persuaded en masse that breastfeeding was inferior or unseemly. Throughout the developing world, even where there was no medical reason for mothers to abandon breastfeeding, they were encouraged to do so. Babies ingested formula mixed with contaminated water and this created catastrophic health consequences.[8] In industrialised nations also, research suggested that the increased use of artificial feeding was associated with deterioration in infant health and increased infant mortality.[9] Whether it was attributable to the success of 'marketing' campaigns or to cultural forces, across the world, women in their millions lost touch with the skills of breastfeeding.

Many of the problems with breastfeeding experienced by women today – such as sore nipples or insufficient milk supply – are the result of a lack of role models, knowledge and experience. In societies where breastfeeding mothers are always in view, problems such as those encountered by western women are a rare occurrence. Professional lactation consultants are fulfilling a vital role that was once the province of the elder women of families and societies.

The global retreat from breastfeeding is one instance in which evolution in parenting has gone backwards. In the USA, after World War II very few women were left who knew how to breastfeed.[10] Nursing one's own, a practice considered unseemly, antiquated and unhygienic, was emphatically discouraged by many health professionals. Similar campaigns to discourage women from breastfeeding were common throughout much of South America. It has been argued that the gains achieved through the abolition of wet-nursing were reversed by the profit motive of corporate entities.[11] At least, the bottle-feeding mother maintains regular and close contact with her baby, unlike her ancestors whose wet-nursed babies were ejected from the home.

The socialising approach to feeding of babies is dominated by the peculiar belief – dating back to Dr William Cadogan and educationist John Locke – that feeding and sleeping must be regimented. Babies are to be fed prescribed amounts at fastidious intervals. To some extent this exigency is imposed by hospital staff, as it works more conveniently for them.[12] Intervention by health-care professionals grew enormously in the 20th century. Even when mothers wish to follow their maternal instincts, keep their babies close to them and feed them 'on demand', they are discouraged from trusting their natural impulses. A pleasing baby is, supposedly, a well-controlled baby. The idea of routine does not necessarily reflect the baby's needs, but those of the busy or otherwise overwhelmed parents and health practitioners.

The baby of socialising mode parents must at all costs sleep when the parents want them to, and feed when it is convenient for the parents. The baby who cries for a feed before 'time', or refuses to sleep alone in a separate room when expected to, is likely to be branded a 'difficult' baby. As in the past, babies are still blamed, though the vitriol against them is not as extreme as that of former child rearing modes. The socialising mode shuns 'demand' feeding, irrespective of what babies might feel about this decision made on their behalf. It is still demand feeding though: when the parents or nurses demand it.

Sexual abuse continues
In the socialising age there is near universal abhorrence for paedophilia, and outrage toward perpetrators when molestation

is uncovered. However, there is still great public confusion about how sexual molestation harms under-aged victims. Not everyone recognises the uniformly devastating effects. There remains a disturbing number of health professionals who fail to recognise the sadistic element in paedophilia, and many paedophiles are themselves convinced that they love and care for children. Since the long-term emotional damage to children often escapes their conscious awareness, the less perspicacious health professionals fail to see the harm done. Consequently, they doubt the existence of any psychological injury caused by incest or other sexual molestation of children.

There is still much denial about the prevalence of sexual abuse. Sexual seduction of children is still alarmingly common even in societies where the socialising mode of parenting predominates. But it is forced deeper underground as paedophiles are increasingly hunted by the law. As recently as the 1930s, movie theatres in New York had special seating designated for unaccompanied children. These separate areas were supervised by a matron and cordoned off, since the incidence of molestation in theatres was so high. Today, the most conservative estimates are that at least one in four children in modern societies have undergone some form of sexual molestation. In the USA since 1950, 4450 Catholic priests have been accused of child sexual abuse – a number representing four per cent of all priests serving in that period.[13]

It is estimated that there are still millions of child prostitutes throughout the world. Since abuse tends to be passed down from generation to generation, it may be a long time before it becomes a rarity.

Innovations of late socialising mode
A key turning point in child-rearing attitudes came as a result of the immensely popular Dr Benjamin Spock's parenting manual, *The Common Sense Book of Baby and Child Care*.[14] Through his book, Dr Spock became a household name worldwide, and he is still cited to this day. Dr Spock was a focal point for an era that was starting to reject the common penchant for authoritarian and punitive parenting, and his manuals were immensely influential in the USA, at least. He was a powerful force for eliminating morbid social hang-ups about masturbation, and he led an emphatic campaign to end its prohibition, and all the shaming associated with it. Spock and others like him presented

a powerful challenge to the child-punishing customs that predated him. He favoured gentle and non-punitive approaches to 'discipline', strongly advocated the developmental importance of free play, and helped fathers loosen up and become more closely, playfully and lovingly involved with their children. Spock articulately rejected antiquated notions of unquestionable parental authority and obedience, and instructed parents not to punish what is normal toddler developmental behaviour, such as selfishness, aggressiveness, or lying. In all these ways, Spock and many like him played a significant role in liberating children, and may have thus contributed to the irrevocable social-liberating changes of the 1960s. Although he was clearly innovative for his era, many of Dr Spock's influential ideas have already been superseded in the wake of newer understandings about early childhood development.

Conclusion

The dawn of the socialising mode era heralded the beginning of the end to the child-as-sex-object, as servant, and as insurance against old-age destitution. Child-protection legislation began to be both policed by designated government officials and enforced through strict penalties. This was the beginning of the child-as-a-person, with his or her own needs and rights. It began to be expected that each parent's role is to serve the child's need, and not the other way around. The vulnerability inherent in childhood is more universally recognised now than at any other time in history.

The socialising mode continues to guide and inform most parent–child relationships today.

The next mode of parenting, the 'helping mode', is the result of significant advancements in the way we understand what helps children to grow *emotionally* healthy.

Endnotes

1. Greenleaf (1978).
2. See UNICEF, 'Convention on the Rights of the Child' http://www.unicef.org/crc/faq.htm (last accessed 1 December 2004); Office of the High Commissioner for Human Rights http://www.unhchr.ch/html/menu3/b/k2crc.htm (last accessed 1 December 2004); see National Children's and Youth Law Council, 'What's up CROC?' http://www.ncylc.org.au/croc/home.html (last accessed 1 December 2004).

[3] The US Supreme Court only re-evaluated the constitutionality of the death penalty against 16 and 17-year-old offenders as recently as 2005. See the American Bar Association, 'Juvenile death penalty' at http://www.abanet.org/crimjust/juvjus/juvdp.html (last accessed 1 December 2004).

[4] Increasingly, excessive consumerism is exploitative of children rather than beneficial. Whereas originally, toys were designed to bring pleasure and learning to children, these days children are increasingly seen as a 'market'. Children are milked for their parents' wealth by corporate over-production of trendy toys and gadgets, and aggressive advertising campaigns.

[5] Kempe (1962).

[6] Armstrong (2001) p 48.

[7] Palmer (1988); Smibert (1988).

[8] See Palmer (1988); Minchin (1985). "The World Health Organization estimates that 1.5 million deaths per year could be prevented by effective breastfeeding protection": Costello and Sachdev (1998) pp 104–105.

[9] Smibert (1988) pp 15–16; Chen and Rogan (2004) pp 435–439; Stein (2004) p A03; Oddy (2002) pp 5–-18; Smith, Thompson and Ellwood (2002) pp 543–551.

[10] In 1946, only 38 per cent of American mothers were exclusively breastfeeding their newborns at hospital discharge. This dropped to 18 per cent by 1966: Riordan and Auerbach (1999).

[11] Palmer (1988).

[12] Smibert (1988) p 16.

[13] *The Australian* 8 February 2004 p 8.

[14] Spock (1946).

8

THE HELPING MODE

We find ourselves at the cusp of an emergent mode of child rearing, which Lloyd de Mause dubbed the 'helping mode'. With each step forward in child-rearing evolution, we learn to see and understand children more clearly. We become better at seeing each child for whom he or she is, instead of what we imagine or 'project' onto the child. As we release children from our customary judgements (little devil, little brat, 'difficult' child, etc) the way becomes open for a deeper quality of empathy. When our vision is less clouded by projection, we can more accurately recognise and appropriately respond to children's changing emotional and physical needs.

The most progressive modern parenting practices arose from significant improvements in our understanding of *emotional* development. Originating in the 1970s and 1980s, helping mode parenting places a great deal of attention on children's emotional needs, at each stage of their growth. Since the end of World War II there have been a number of revolutionary insights in the field of psychology. A veritable explosion of interest in psychology has fuelled a boom in psychological research. The rapid growth in this field has given rise to new bodies of thought such as attachment theory, object–relations theory, self-psychology, social learning theory and somatic psychotherapy. Family therapy systems have also advanced in leaps and bounds. We have learned volumes about how family dynamics drive the way children feel, behave, and grow. We know so much more about how children's unique personalities, relationship style and emotional make-up develop in infancy. Most parenting and educational practices have been at least tinged by this growing emphasis on emotional intelligence and relationship skills. A clearer understanding of healthy emotional development is slowly filtering into households, transforming the way we parent without our realising it.

Helping mode parents attend to their children's emotional development by listening with empathy to their children's expressions of need. Children's unrefined and spontaneous expressions of feeling and need are validated as never before, and this process begins at birth. Increasingly, we are coming to believe that babies know when they are hungry, how much they need to consume, when they are tired, when they need to be held, and when they need engagement or attention. A baby's cry, no longer thought to be capricious or meaningless, is warmly attended to without delay. It is the baby's natural biological and emotional cycles, not the clock on the wall, that govern the ebb and flow of nurturance – and the carer is led by the baby's cues. For this reason, the newest mode is often referred to as 'natural parenting'.

Toddlers and older children are benefiting from a greater tolerance for their expressions of feeling, opinions, wants and needs. In contrast to the censure of earlier modes, they are more likely to encounter empathy. What motivates helping mode parents is the desire to allow and support the natural unfolding of each child's unique individuality. This means less interference, less emphasis on adherence to convention and rigid social norms, and less pressure on the child to reflect adult ideals. New child-rearing ways show an added respect for children's liberty, and a growing sense of trust in their *natural* tendency to develop into socially functional and loving adults. Parents, teachers and other significant adults are increasingly helping each child to discover and pursue his or her own personal goals, rather than follow a pre-arranged path. We are spending less time admonishing our children to be quiet or still; and instead we are more likely to support their natural curiosity, their thirst to explore, discover and play.

Rather than imposing 'good' values through punishment and reward, and rather than enforcing blind obedience, the helping mode parent fosters the child's autonomy and self-regulation. As we learn to feel less threatened by the child's developing strength and will, we give the child more permission to self-assert. We are collectively beginning to learn how to set boundaries strongly and clearly without recourse to corporal punishment, shaming or manipulation. In contrast to the top-down, authoritarian power-dynamics of earlier modes, helping mode interactions are two-way and mutually respectful.

Perhaps the most significant departure from previous modes involves a better psychological differentiation between parent and child. In other words, helping mode parents have learned to distinguish more clearly between the child's need, and the adult's wishes. Many of the socialising mode practices were done ostensibly 'for the child's own good', when it was really the adult's need being served. We convinced ourselves, for instance, that it was for the child's own good that we spanked them, dispatched them to regimented, rote learning and competition-based education, or forced them into rigid feeding and sleeping routines.

An icon of the late socialising mode era, Dr Spock has been left behind by helping mode advances. It is now recognised that his weaknesses were many, and these included his feeble advocacy for breastfeeding, his ambivalence about 'demand feeding' and his support of scheduled feeding, his advice against co-sleeping, and his claim that it would not be damaging to leave a baby to cry alone for up to 20 minutes. Like most of his contemporaries, Dr Spock was subject to the widely held cultural fear of babies' dependency needs. He warned against yielding to babies' and toddlers' need to be held and comforted to sleep, lest they become habitually attached. (This was a bewildering self-contradiction, since his own advice was that security is what creates independence. Obviously, he did not realise that becoming attached is *precisely* what babies need in order to feel secure.) While he challenged the harshness of authoritarian parenting, Dr Spock offered very little modelling for asserting effective interpersonal boundaries with children. Many people blame Dr Spock for the social excesses and personal confusion arising from ungrounded, 'permissive' parenting.

These days, parenting manuals crowd our bookstores in unprecedented abundance. It is now possible, throughout the developed world, to attend a variety of parenting courses. There has never been such a level of public interest in learning how to give children our best. Nor have we ever seen such a widespread realisation that the skills and knowledge required for good parenting do not magically appear at childbirth – as they do for other species. Almost all contemporary parenting manuals advocate practices that reflect socialising mode and helping mode approaches, with an increasing tendency toward the latter.

Part VI of this book contains an in-depth exploration of

childhood emotional development. We will discuss the five stages of early childhood core emotional development, and look at how our experiences in each of these stages impact on our adult character, behaviour and relating style. The helping mode is the closest humankind has come toward nurturing emotional intelligence, by meeting the psychological needs of children at each of these five stages.

The main touchstones of helping mode parenting are emotional support for mother during pregnancy, gentler childbirth methods, home-birthing, 'rooming-in' at hospital, on-demand breastfeeding, co-sleeping, baby-wearing, and fathers who attend childbirth and share in the nurturance through all stages of childhood. Beyond infancy, the emphasis is on strong rather than violent boundary-setting, and empathic listening. Each of these aspects will be elaborated in detail in chapters to follow.

Helping mode in practice: the return to breastfeeding

An important example of the helping mode transition can be seen in society's changing perceptions of breastfeeding. If the art of breastfeeding was not totally lost to women of the industrialised world, this is due to the concerted effort of a number of sympathetic organisations. In 1956, the 'La Leche League' was formed in the USA to combat the misinformation propping up the artificial formula industry, and to support mothers to reclaim their ability to nurse. La Leche has expanded worldwide and now spearheads a global return to this natural maternal function.[1] In Australia, the Australian Breastfeeding Association serves the same function.[2] Organisations such as these have undertaken the enormous task of re-educating mothers, and convincing hospital staff to support mothers appropriately. Despite initial resistance from powerful commercial interests (we can't sell breastmilk!), there have been substantial gains. Scientific research into the immunological benefits of breastmilk, and the health and psychological benefits to both the baby and mother, have finally tipped the scales in favour of the breast connection. Non-profit organisations and medical researchers have convincingly re-established that, under normal circumstances, breastfeeding is superior.

A further challenge to the formula industry came from the World Health Organization (WHO), and the United Nations Children's Fund (UNICEF). Both organisations recommended that artificial feeding should not be promoted within the health care system, nor should there be any advertising of formulas (see International Code of Marketing of Breast Milk Substitutes). The code also demands that "All information on artificial infant feeding, including the labels should explain the benefits of breastfeeding and the costs and hazards associated with artificial feeding."[3] These days, lactation consultants are available in most hospitals to provide support for mothers to master, as well as to enjoy, nursing their infants. Gradually, artificial feeding is being relegated to its proper and truly helpful role as a substitute, when breastfeeding is impossible due to untreatable medical, psychological, or circumstantial reasons.

This is a welcome development, since it was estimated by the WHO, toward the end of the 20th century, that 1.5 million babies were dying worldwide because they were not adequately breastfed.[4] Though these deaths tend to occur in the developing world, even in the industrialised world bottle-fed babies can be more vulnerable to disease. Helping mode parenting is also animated by a new awareness that the *emotional* nourishment provided by breastfeeding is a centrepiece of optimal emotional development.

Impact of research into parent–child attachment

We have collectively come to understand that secure attachment early in life is essential for the development of mature and empathic humanity. This link was first elucidated by English psychiatrist John Bowlby, and developed into attachment theory in the 1960s. Since then, a massive body of international research has sealed the credibility of Bowlby's theory (see Chapter 26). Modern science has also detected benefits to the baby's immune system when they are held in constant closeness. Attachment theorists worldwide have helped to popularise the commitment to infants' emotional security through consistent and tender touch.

A more in-depth discussion of early attachment needs, and their relevance to adult relationships, will be presented in Chapter 25 and Chapter 26.

Healthy interpersonal boundaries: a new approach

The helping mode heralds an end to the ethic that sees parenting as a battle between good and evil. Instead, effective parenting is based on teaching children to be aware of others' boundaries, and to understand the impact of their behaviour on others. Whereas it was once thought that all children were born in a state of sin, Rousseau and the other 'Romantics' idealised children, and professed that they are all born 'good'. The Romantic movement was a reaction against the brutality of earlier modes, and thus they replaced one projection for another, more idealistic one. The helping mode rejects either pole of a moral verdict on children. Each child is seen to evolve through many stages of development where both narcissism and altruism play a natural and vital role. We are learning to avoid judging children against a moral matrix, since selfishness, aggression, and generosity are all recognised as normal impulses, which children are learning to master.

Whereas socialising parents are *authoritarian* – meaning that they insist on unquestioning obedience – helping parents have learned to be *authoritative*, based on their interpersonal skill and having gained the child's trust. Authoritative parenting embraces the parent's leadership role, while recognising the essential liberty and dignity of the child. Helping parents set boundaries by fostering respect, rather than fear – while the socialising parent does not properly distinguish between these two.

Part IV explores in greater depth the changes from socialising disciplinarian approaches, to a new paradigm for boundary-setting.

New approaches to education

Helping mode schools focus beyond academic intelligence. They embrace a wholistic emphasis on development, especially concerning emotional intelligence and social skills. It is not unusual to see a school that includes classes in appropriate assertiveness and conflict resolution, people management and leadership skills, recognising and articulating emotions, and critical reasoning skills. The goals of discipline and knowledge are no longer sufficient, we strive also for our children to be skilled in human relations.

Although the more wholistic and child-centred teaching methods are appearing in mainstream schools, these values are particularly evident in the steady growth of alternative schools, such as those aligned with the Democratic Education movement. The option of home schooling, a favourite among helping mode parents, is also rapidly gaining in popularity.

Who does the upbringing?

Helping mode parents recognise that this mode requires more input in the earliest years. Since we are now wanting to devote more energy and resources to each child, it comes as no surprise that in many modern societies, fertility rates have dropped yet further, even below replacement levels. To some degree, the increased commitment to childcare is offset by having fewer children. However, even parents with one child can experience strain unless help is at hand.

As tired parents, when our baby's cries meet with our despair and exhaustion, do we look to silencing the baby – do we decide that there is something wrong with the baby who cries at night? Or, instead, do we seek more support from people around us, replenishing ourselves so that we can meet our baby's needs? It makes more sense for us as parents to be surrounded by supportive friends, family and community, helping us to fulfil the enormous task of child rearing, than it does to behaviour-modify infants to fit more neatly into our harried lifestyles. Rarely do helping mode parents choose to do it alone. They choose additional carers scrupulously, who love and know the child and can be consistently available.

The old adage 'it takes a village to raise a child' is particularly true when we commit to meeting the child's emotional needs. Raising children under any circumstance is in fact not easily done by two parents. To a large extent, it is the responsibility of every society to support parents and their children. The quality of parenting that any family can offer depends, to a large extent, on the community support available. Conversely, the health of any community depends on the way it supports its families. Government sponsored parent support centres have been springing up around the world, and they have been instrumental in reducing child abuse, and a host of other social problems.

It is difficult for families to pursue more evolved parenting styles on their own, unless they feel some level of social and cultural support for their added commitment. The evolution of parenting modes therefore tends to occur on a large-scale social level, as the society in question devotes more resources to the support of families and their children.

In Chapter 31, we will take a detailed look at the multiple dividends that can be gained by any society that invests in the emotional intelligence of its children.

Social results

Children of helping mode parents tend to be self-possessed rather than imitative, they tend to be outspoken and less intimidated by 'authority'. Emotionally secure individuals are more difficult to seduce or intimidate, they tend to be assertive and self-motivated. Although this parenting style may initially consume more time and energy in children's early years, the children develop a greater degree of independence and self-responsibility later. Having encountered sufficient empathy, these children are less likely to act out frustrations destructively as they grow up. They are also likely to be more empathic towards others. Clearly, not just children but all of society benefits from non-violent and emotionally connected parenting.

The Quarry Hill Community in Vermont, USA, is one of many examples of the social benefits of helping mode parenting. This community was explicitly formed by parents who were seeking communal support for raising their children non-violently. For decades, they have been witnessing their children growing up along the lines described above.[5]

Though emotional intelligence can be cultivated throughout life, it is given the most powerful foundation in childhood, through this newest mode of parenting. Good interpersonal skills, and the ability to create and maintain healthy relationships, are hard-won attributes for many. For the children of helping mode parents, these abilities are more likely to be second nature and spontaneous responses.

Endnotes

[1] See La Leche League International http://www.lalecheleague.org/ (last accessed 1 December 2004).

[2] See the Australian Breastfeeding Association website at http://www.breastfeeding.asn.au/ (last accessed 1 December 2004).

[3] In Exibit E of the World Health Organization Summary of International Code of Marketing of Breast Milk Substitutes see http://www.i-case.com/newdemo/inffeed/docs/052if.pdf (last accessed 1 December 2004).

[4] See Baby Milk Action and go to 'Your questions answered' http://www.babymilkaction.org (last accessed 1 December 2004).

[5] Fiske-McFarlin, Nelson and Sherman (1993).

9

WHAT THE HISTORY
OF CHILDHOOD TELLS US
ABOUT OURSELVES

Our societies are only just beginning to be confronted by the haunting truth of the widespread maltreatment of children throughout history. The awakening from the slumber of denial is as painful as it is necessary. Faced with this new view of ourselves, with this unsettling new information that has been smoked out from its hiding places, we are forced to make new conclusions about ourselves and our humanity. I propose the following lessons.

Lessons from the history of childhood:
1. Humans are as likely to be dreadful parents as devoted, kind and attentive parents. Although we have historically exceeded all other animals in cruelty and destructiveness, we have also exceeded them in nurturance and love.
2. Mistreatment of children, even to the point of sadism, is so universal and intrinsic to human social behaviour that it has been stamped into culture and folklore, written into religious scripture and civic law, and even rationalised as 'necessary' by medical theory or healing arts. The urge to hurt and exploit children is almost as central a human trait as the urge to protect, nurture and liberate them.
3. Considering the wholesale torture of children (the witch-hunts of the 14th to 16th centuries, the near-universal practices of child mutilation), the mass slaughter of children through sacrifice or infanticide, the abandonment of millions, if not billions, the widespread sexual abuse of children (acceptable in many cultures until recently), we

should view much of human history as a holocaust against children.

4. Throughout most of our history, and across much of the world today, childhood was – and in many places continues to be – a hellish experience.

5. Child abuse and neglect has only recently become a minority occurrence, and only in some of the world's societies. Until relatively recently in our history, abuse and neglect was what happened to most children.

6. Although more of us in modern societies can claim to have not been battered or neglected as children, most of us are the children of, or descendants of, battered and neglected children.

7. In the western world at least, the idea of a loving family is a recent development.

8. The parenting instinct is not what we thought it was. It cannot be taken for granted. It is eminently open to environmental influence. Two conditions are essential: unless there are minimally favourable material circumstances and social support, and unless parents have themselves been shown some genuine nurturance in their lives, the 'parenting instinct' might not manifest, and parents can be indifferent, hostile, even brutal toward their children. 'Good' parenting does not emerge spontaneously. It has to be learned by example; it has to be role-modelled, and it depends on the extensive support of a loving family and community.

9. Alongside the 'parenting instinct', there is also a strong tendency for parents to safeguard their own equilibrium; to lighten the parental load by ignoring or downplaying children's needs. Sometimes this impulse takes the shape of violent rejection, or outright neglect. At other times, it might just be a distortion or denial of what children need.

10. Emotionally immature parents will attempt to satisfy their un-met emotional, physical and even sexual needs through their children.

11. Since parenting capabilities are influenced by the parents' childhood experiences as well as their current social circumstances, parenting skills can and should be taught to all. It behoves every government and community to be pro-active in ensuring that every parent is both educated and supported.

12. It would be myopic to blame the suffering of children on their parents. All parents are limited in their capacity to give. Parenting behaviour is a direct reflection of the quality and quantity of support available for the parent throughout their lives. All humans contain the potential for profound love and devotion, subject to their own state of emotional nourishment.

13. Parenting has been slowly evolving, and it is likely that improvements will continue. But in order to safeguard this positive evolutionary process, effort is required from individuals, communities and governments to ensure a general flow of social assistance for families in need, and parenting education.

14. Because parenting evolves, by definition, we have not arrived at some final evolutionary destination. At the current pace of social evolution, the way most of us parent now might be superseded in 50 years, if not sooner. We are all learning, collectively and individually, and parenting tends to improve from generation to generation.

15. If child rearing continues to evolve, we will be rewarded with extremely positive changes in areas of social justice, social harmony and ecological sustainability.

So much of our past needs to be re-evaluated in terms of collective adaptations to early trauma. Megalomania, sociopathy, and credulous adoration of charismatic leaders, are but some of the results of childhood neglect and abuse. Humanity has been split into delinquent leaders, and those who were mesmerised or submissive to their power. This perilous social combination has ensured that war, abuse of power, and environmental devastation followed humankind wherever we set foot. But this kind of society is inevitable when a significant portion of individuals are living out symptoms of untreated post-traumatic shock; the product of collective early life trauma. Violent and autocratic societies suffer a kind of social retardation, borne of tortured and loveless childhoods. When we contemplate the horrors of dysfunctional human relations, past and present, we should not say 'this is humanity', but instead 'this is traumatised humanity', or 'humanity in shock'. Human madness is the howl of a child with a shattered heart.

Children hurt in exactly the same way, and for exactly the same reasons, in any era, and in every culture. As members of the Homo Sapiens Sapiens species, we all share the same basic biological and psychological structures. The horrors suffered by history's children caused them to hurt in the same way as our own children would today, if they suffered a similar fate. The fact that most other children were in the same boat at the time, did not make their plight any easier. The long-term psychological effect of culturally normal abuse would be the same, if not worse, for they were told this was 'normal' life, and thus they never had recourse to protest their torment. To a large extent, our societies and our histories are founded on childhood pain.

We now know enough about human psychology to realise that an individual cannot kill or abandon his or her own child, and subsequently carry on as normal. A substantial emotional dissociation is inevitable, which would leave deep life-long psychological scars. More likely, severe emotional dissociation would predate the murderous act. Generally speaking, individuals belonging to earlier child-rearing modes are of poorer emotional development, irrespective of how well developed their intellects may be. Humanity is a long way from collectively achieving its full potential of emotional intelligence, but in earlier days we were emotionally retarded, distorted or deeply detached – en masse. How can it be otherwise, considering the constancy of war and brutality, the ubiquitousness of dictatorships, and the careless attitude to our natural environment? Can this be surprising, since before the 20th century, there may have been few who escaped some form of abuse or neglect?

Since abuse and neglect has occurred on such an all-encompassing scale, it still tinges our way of relating to each other – and to our natural environment. Much of what we take for granted as 'normal' social behaviours are in fact defensive vestiges, remnants from inter-generational mistreatment spanning thousands of years. Humanity has not completed its recovery from its traumatic past, and is still acting out this collective trauma in a thousand ways.

Even today, we cannot pretend to have escaped from the legacy of our historically horrible childhoods by convincing ourselves that it all took place in a distant past, somewhere far away. My own grandmother was, at 19 years of age, forced to marry a man for his status. He was a stranger to her, and she did not like him initially. Being in love with another man, she protested her fate vigorously. Her protests fell on deaf ears. Having given birth to her first child – my mother – and probably suffering post-natal depression, she escaped back to her home town in Romania. Her older brothers, incapable of empathy, 'disciplined' her by beating her. They dispatched her back to her husband, with whom she resigned herself to remain for life. The practice euphemistically referred to as 'arranged' marriage is prohibited today under the Universal Declaration of Human Rights,[1] and other human rights instruments.[2] Sexual relations within a forced marriage are now viewed as a form of rape. The beating suffered by my grandmother at the hands of her brothers is now recognised as domestic violence, punishable by law in modern societies. Yet her treatment was all perfectly sanctioned by her society. If world affairs are as they are, it is because everywhere human beings are recovering from childhood trauma that has been transmitted and restaged through countless generations.

Parenting modes have long been evolving and, as they do, the lot of children keeps improving. Some parents have somehow managed to provide for their children a better emotional climate in which to grow, than they were themselves given. Their numbers must be sufficient to cause entire societies to edge forward and make social advances. Societies have been known to stagnate or regress, but mostly they slowly advance, as parenting modes evolve. Lloyd De Mause sums up our social evolution in this way:

"The fundamental evolutionary direction of *Homo Sapiens Sapiens* is toward better interpersonal relationships, not just the satisfaction of instincts. While adaptation to the natural environment is the key to genetic evolution, relationship to the *human* environment is the key to psychological evolution, to the evolution of human nature."[3]

There are encouraging signs of improvement in human relations and positive social changes – driven by improvements in childcare practices – in many parts of the world. Thanks to the progress made in child rearing, the western world – and increasingly, much of the developing world – have accomplished unprecedented levels of democracy, welfare, gender equality, fairness in labour laws, and awareness of ecological issues. This bears exciting implications for future societies. What is even more exciting is that improvements in child rearing are accelerating, propelled by our current information revolution. So, although we remain a long way from a just, equitable and sustainable global society, the continuing evolution of child rearing may give us reason for hope.

Psychohistorians have managed to trace a large number of significant world events – whose repercussions profoundly affect all our lives to this day – to their origins in prevailing child-rearing customs. The link is clear, as we shall see in Part III, between major social changes – both calamitous and positive – and how societies treated their children. Once the extent to which childhood drives history has truly dawned on us, we cannot avoid making children's emotional wellbeing our top social priority. Our commitment to meeting each and every child's emotional needs, for his or her own sake, brings benefits for all of humanity – in ways we could not have imagined.

Endnotes

[1] Article 16(2) "Marriage shall be entered into only with the free and full consent of the intending spouses."

[2] See for example the Convention on Consent to Marriage, Minimum Age for Marriage and Registration of Marriages http://www.hri.ca/uninfo/treaties/64.shtml (last accessed 1 December 2004).

[3] De Mause (1999) p 649.

III

HOW CHILD-REARING FORGED THE DESTINY OF NATIONS

The ultimate source of all advances in human civilisation – political, social, individual – can be found in the day-to-day innovations in child rearing invented by each caretaker and child in their developing relationship.
Lloyd de Mause[1]

10

DEMOCRACY STARTS AT HOME

Every abandonment, every betrayal, every hateful act towards children returns tenfold a few decades later upon the historical stage, while every empathic act that helps a child become what he or she wants to become, every expression of love toward children heals society and moves it in unexpected, wondrous new directions

Lloyd de Mause[2]

How child rearing affects world affairs

We saw in the preceding chapters that until quite recently, childhood was a nightmare for most people, in most civilisations. What impact could this massive historical maltreatment of children have had on the functioning of societies? How many of the social and global problems we face today could be alleviated or eliminated if the way we raise our children continues to improve? Since childhood is a powerful governing force behind our thinking, feeling and behaviour, it follows that social policy bears the marks of each policy-maker's childhood experiences – for better or for worse. In fact, the collective childhood of a society is probably the single most important factor driving group decisions made at political, business and social levels.

Part III looks at child rearing as the driving force behind a number of major historical events. The following are the main messages I hope to convey in this part.

Messages of psychohistory

1. In every troubled part of the world, we should first and foremost be paying more attention to how the children there have been treated. Just as harsh or neglectful parenting

is an established risk factor for delinquency, the same conditions on a large scale have moved entire nations, as we are about to see, toward a greater acceptance of violent and oppressive means of social 'discipline' – such as war or dictatorship.

2. No ethnic group can be intrinsically war-like or peaceful (as we will see in Chapter 21, there is no real genetic basis for either trait). The role of child rearing is the same in any nation's destiny. The particular nations that we will be looking at here were chosen only because psychohistorians have closely examined how child-rearing customs have influenced historical events in these places.

3. While ethnicity cannot predispose people towards either violence or pacifism, culture can. Authoritarian or harshly patriarchal child rearing can incline any nation or ethnic group towards violence. This means that a tyrannical government cannot seize control over an otherwise peaceful people and fan the flames of war amongst them. People are not so malleable. Tyrants can drive a nation to war only when the prevailing culture has already prepared a large enough proportion of its people's minds for violence. Even in non-democratic nations, as we will see, leaders are products of their cultures – not the other way around.

4. Legislative and political measures cannot by themselves alter social forces that are largely shaped by cultural approaches to child rearing. The most powerful and reliable tools for positive social change are nurturing, respectful parenting practices, and compassionate education. Any effort to advance the way we bring up our children is vindicated by one of psychohistory's most consistent findings – that, throughout history, major positive social changes have always been preceded by improvements in the ways that societies bring up their children. In the pages to follow, we will see that the steady improvements in childcare we have witnessed in the last 200 years have produced some astonishing socio-political advances internationally.

Patriarchy and violence – are they linked?

What is the relevance of patriarchy to our discussion? Why is it that, as anthropologists have noted, strongly patriarchal societies seem to generate more brutality?

In any patriarchal system, a handful of men assert dominance through constant intimidation, brutality and manipulation. Over and above the trauma of punitive, repressive parenting, children suffer from being witness to the subjugation of their mothers and sisters, and the humiliation of any male relatives who display softer emotions. Since children in strongly patriarchal families are exposed to more physical and psychological violence, they tend to grow up with more violent attitudes. It is inevitable that the resulting society is more prone to autocratic rule, and more violent conflict. When enough children in a society grow up in violence, this makes the whole society more violent. Pronounced patriarchy is synonymous with misogyny, and it is associated with child abuse. In fact, family-types that emphasise obedience, rigid and authoritarian codes of religion, and male dominance are known risk factors for child abuse – and hence they raise levels of social violence.[3]

The link between patriarchy and social violence is demonstrable. When anthropologists John and Shirley McConahy conducted a comparative study of 17 different cultures, they found consistently that the more rigid the gender-roles set by the culture, the more violent and war-like the culture becomes.[4] Another cross-cultural study[5] confirmed an association between rigid sexual mores and social violence. A submissive wife, a domineering husband, and a family system that restricts its members' personal autonomy – these are the hallmarks of the patriarchal family. This family style is also an established risk factor for incest,[6] with all its attendant social consequences. As we saw in Chapter 3, anthropologists have found that infanticide is highest among the most patriarchal societies.

It is impossible for one group to dominate another without using violence, or some other potent form of manipulation. Rigid gender roles, and male dominance over women, cannot be maintained without resorting to physical or psychological violence. From the time of toddlerhood, healthy human beings of both sexes spontaneously resist oppressive domination. That is why it is not possible to make children unquestioningly obedient without using violence against them. It is also impossible to make men habitually war-like and violent unless a great deal of violence is used against them as children. Whatever material benefits might exist for men in patriarchal systems, these benefits are completely cancelled out by the psychological or emotional costs. In terms of emotional health and development, rigid and authoritarian patriarchy is equally

The Edinburgh Bookshop
219 Bruntsfield Place
Edinburgh, EH10 4DG
Telephone 0131 447 1917
E-mail mail@edinburghbookshop.com
VAT 150 5493 22

First Sticker Book Space   £5.99

Subtotal.   £5.99

Total.   £5.99

Payment

Card: £5.99

---- VAT SUMMARY ----

Vat @ 20%.   £0.00

Date   24-Jul-2018 16:07:22
Receipt 93,588

disastrous for men and women, and equally damaging for boys and girls.

A mother who is downtrodden cannot help being compromised in her ability to mother, and thus a 'vicious cycle' is created. The boy who feels maltreated, emotionally neglected or smothered by his mother is more likely to grow up harbouring resentment against women. Men are not born to be oppressive. Patriarchy is a systemic dysfunction that feeds upon itself. Neither gender bears sole responsibility for this social malaise, and neither gender benefits.

Archaeologists have recently unearthed a number of highly sophisticated ancient civilisations throughout Eastern Europe and Central Asia, which showed no signs of warfare; no evidence of weaponry or fortifications. These societies endured for centuries in peace, having developed complex administrative institutions, highly stylised arts and crafts, some even had running water and underground sewage. Such civilisations were excavated at sites including Vinca, Butmir, Petresti, Cucuteni, Catal Huyuk, and Vacilar around Eastern Europe,[7] and Harapi in Central Asia.[8] What was particularly remarkable about these societies was that their power structures were gender-balanced; neither male nor female were especially dominant in any institution of authority. This was the key factor under-lying their long and peaceful existence. Alas, relatively balanced cultures such as these have always been a tiny percentage of the world's population and eventually, they were destined to be over-run by their more violent, patriarchal neighbours. Nevertheless, they hail from our ancestry as evidence of what is possible through a gender-balanced society, where authority is not characterised by domination nor imposed by force.

Child rearing reform brings democracy

Democracy is still in its infancy. At its best it remains partial, crude, corrupted, tampered with, or merely symbolic. Nevertheless, democratic processes have been slowly spreading throughout the world since their inception in 18th century Europe and the USA. With the globalisation of democratic processes, we can take heart from the observation that 'democratic' nations are statistically far less likely to make war against each other. However, rarely does a country take to democracy immediately, like a duck to water, when it is given the chance. As we will see, comparative studies among European nations have found strong links between harsher child rearing modes and increased levels of civil or cross-border armed conflict, delays in democratic reforms, and greater public resistance to the responsibilities associated with democratic freedoms.

As democratisation gathers momentum, an unprecedented number of social and international disputes have been resolved through non-violent means (some examples will be discussed later). Egalitarian and democratic systems are an antidote to war. But democracy only tends to emerge, and firmly take hold, when the people are ready for it – a development that seems to follow quantum improvements in child-rearing practices.

In an effort to put to the test the premise that more democratic family types lead to more democratic nations, psychohistorian Lloyd de Mause[9] examined the order in which Eastern Block countries would transfer to democratic government. As a measure of child-rearing attitudes, de Mause chose to look at each Eastern Block country's infant mortality rate (IMR). This technique is commonly used by psychohistorians to gauge how nations treat their children.

Before the onset of recent Balkan conflicts, Yugoslavia's IMR (28.8 per thousand) was second only to Albania's (44.8) in Eastern Europe. Just as de Mause predicted, these two countries took the longest, among the Eastern Block countries, to produce successful democratic movements. Political reform was moderately speedier and accompanied by less violence in countries with medium-range IMR, namely Romania and the USSR (23.4 and 26.0 respectively). In contrast, transition to democracy has been earliest or smoothest in Eastern Block nations with the lowest IMR around the same time, that is, the German Democratic Republic (9.6), Czechoslovakia (15.3), Bulgaria (15.4), Hungary (17.0) and Poland (18.5).[10] These figures speak volumes for the idea that democracy starts in the home.

What follows is a look at some remarkable historical events, then an examination of the child-rearing modes and family styles that predominated one generation earlier – when the adults who wielded power, and those who gave them their power, were being reared. We will also see how a steady evolution towards more empathic child rearing has generated the unprecedented growth of democratic processes, the promulgation of human rights, and the modern environmental movement. I hope (and predict), that in the near future the study of child-rearing customs will become a standard way to deepen our understanding of the motivating forces of history.

Endnotes

[1] De Mause (1999) p 656.
[2] De Mause (1999) p 655.
[3] Breiner (1990).
[4] McConahy (1977).
[5] Prescott (1996).
[6] Thorman (1983).
[7] Eisler (1995).
[8] Pearce (2002).
[9] De Mause (1990).
[10] De Mause (1990).

11

YUGOSLAVIAN CHILDHOOD: FROM WAR TO DEMOCRACY

The relationship between parenting and a nation's destiny is clearly evident in the Balkan states, where psychohistorians have linked bygone child-rearing customs that were harsh and authoritarian with Balkan wars. On the other hand, modern child-rearing reforms in the former Yugoslavia produced a Ghandian, non-violent revolution that ushered a new, democratic era.

Once comprising the former Yugoslavia, the Balkans have been hosts to violent ethnic conflict and political oppression. Some of modern history's most shocking waves of genocide, and human rights atrocities such as systematic mass-rape, sexual enslavement and torture have swept through all parts of the former nation.[1] The level of barbarism we have witnessed there in recent years cannot be understood simply in terms of historical, economic or political forces. By some reports, for instance, soldiers were allegedly ordered to rape and impregnate an estimated 35,000 Bosnian women, whom they held captive and only released once abortion was impossible.[2] During the 1992–1995 Bosnian war, thousands of Muslims were rounded up and killed in fields near Srebrenica, and in the three-year siege of Sarajevo, snipers shot children, women and the elderly on the streets and in their homes.[3] These are just a few examples of violence carried out in this troubled land.

Social or economic adversity does not of its own accord drive people to such acts of carnage. The methodically brutal ethnic 'cleansing' policies of the former Yugoslavia demand a deeper level of explanation, a social-psychological one.

Drawing from the collected works of numerous historians and social researchers – mostly from the former Yugoslavia –

journalist Alenka Puhar[4] managed to trace the frenzy of ethnic 'cleansing' to its psychological origins in rigid and punitive child rearing. One of Puhar's principal sources is a comprehensive survey of rural family life in 300 Yugoslav villages, which was compiled during the 1930s by psychologist Vera Stein Erlich. The data was carefully collected by trained interviewers, mostly doctors and schoolteachers from every region of Yugoslavia including Serbia, Montenegro, Croatia, Bosnia-Herzegovina and Macedonia. The results were published in a book called *Family in Transition – A Study of 300 Yugoslav Villages*.[5]

The study found that the states that comprised Yugoslavia tended to lag far behind western European nations in child-rearing reform. The diverse ethnic groups in the former Yugoslavia once lived in large, extended family households known as *zadruga*. In the 1930s, at the time of Erlich's ambitious research project, most older Yugoslavians had grown up in a *zadruga*. "In the *zadruga* culture", writes Puhar, "people could be extravagantly generous and kind, sharing everything with a perfect stranger, but, on the other hand, extremely harsh, brutal and aggressive".[6] A *zadruga* provided security and a strong sense of solidarity, kinship and belonging. However, with the curtailment of personal freedoms and the harsh, authoritarian, and patriarchal dynamics, this environment did not foster individuals' autonomy nor personal development. Extremely rigid gender roles placed significant restrictions on psychological and emotional growth. Although these types of family structures began to disappear from Croatia about 100 years ago, and from the rest of Yugoslavia about 50 years ago, many contemporary policy-makers would have been reared in a *zadruga* or had parents who were reared in a *zadruga*.

Zadruga family dynamics were extremely lopsided in favour of male dominance: women held a particularly low status. The abode housed several men related by blood, their wives and their children. The household consisted of elderly parents, their married sons with their wives and children, and any unmarried children of the elderly couple. Male members seldom left their natal household. The homes were chronically overcrowded, with extended-family sizes ranging from 10–15 members, up to 100 in some areas. Between the two world wars, there was a gradual modernisation and dissolution of the traditional *zadruga*, leading to smaller family units. But some of the old patriarchal culture of obligation and obedience remained.

The head of the *zadruga* household was the elder or grand old man, (*staresina* or *domacin*), who usually remained the head of the household until his death. This position went automatically to the oldest male, except in a few places where the head of the household was elected by the elder males. In most places surveyed, he was unconditionally obeyed.

Marriages were arranged by the elders, and fear of the head patriarch prevented protest. Of all the couples surveyed by Erlich, 75 per cent listed property gains as a reason for their parents choosing their partner, and parents were expected to pay a bride price. At the time of the survey, the custom of bride abduction – known as *otmica* – was still common in Bosnia and Serbia, and was practiced in 75 per cent of villages. Though *otmica* was sometimes a charade staged by both lovers, it could also be brutal and clearly against the abductee's will.[7]

Newly married women held the lowest rank in the household, and were little more than servants.[8] Each woman was subordinated to all men of the household, and female disobedience was commonly punished with beatings.[9] In some areas, patriarchy was so pronounced that women were subservient to the smallest boys in the house. Erlich's research found that even in areas where the zadruga system had dissolved, there remained strong vestiges of traditional patriarchal authoritarianism. Erlich uncovered many stories of women's despair and heartbreak at being sold into a family of strangers, to become the lowest ranking member.[10]

In over 50 per cent of Bosnian and Serbian villages, women's subservience was ritually reinforced and cemented. They were obligated to submissively greet men by kissing their hands, by removing their footwear and washing their feet. It was a fading but still common custom for women to stand in silence behind their men, while they ate. The men were first to eat, taking the best parts of the meal for themselves. This custom was most common in Serbian villages, where women stood at meal times in 75 per cent of villages surveyed.[11] Women were lavishly generous with food, but were downtrodden, to be seen and not heard. Erlich states, "Many interviewers were revolted by the position of the wife".[12] In many areas of Yugoslavia, but more especially in Moslem parts of Bosnia, women were expected to behave with extreme modesty. Their movement was restricted, they were expected to wear head coverings, to talk little and to have their eyes downcast.

Men fared no better under the patriarchal system. In Macedonia, even adult sons were known to be forbidden to laugh, smoke, display any merriment or speak to their wives in the presence of their father or other senior.[13] In some households, men well into their middle age were not even allowed to look at their wives in the presence of their fathers.[14] For most Yugoslavian sons, the father was an object of deep respect and awe. The aura of paternal power permeated every space and activity. It was considered improper for women to show affection for husbands, cuddle or breastfeed their children in front of other male family members.[15] In some places it was considered too intimate for a married couple to refer to each other by name. Men who were demonstrative were said to "grovel under his wife's petticoats".[16]

Machismo in the *zadruga* world was such that verbal and physical abuse of one's wife was expected as proof of manliness. A man was not considered a true man if he refrained from violent behaviour, which generally meant that men could ill-afford to express affection or tenderness. Male violence toward women was easily forgiven if not condoned. In Croatian villages, it was common for gangs of young men to roam at night, seeking out unprotected young women to prey upon, even entering their homes.[17]

Wife beating was extremely common. Erlich's research revealed that it occurred "fairly often to very often" in over 80 per cent of Serbian villages surveyed, and over 50 per cent of Bosnian and Croatian villages.[18] In some areas, even the women thought there was something wrong with their husbands if they didn't beat them from time to time. Popular sayings such as these were commonplace: "Beat a woman and a horse every three days", and, "He's not a man if he has not boxed a woman's ears."[19]

Along with women, children were oppressed from the very beginning of their lives. The act of childbirth itself was shrouded in shame, and babies were often delivered in solitude and without assistance, in cellars, barns, stables, even outdoors and in hiding.[20] Many villages did not even have midwives. Childbirth and the room it was conducted in were thought to be 'impure'. Women were expected to continue to work hard during and immediately following pregnancy, and were given little or no care for the agonies of childbirth – in some cases they even risked being ridiculed or ignored. The resulting high maternity death rate (in some parts of Bosnia and Macedonia over half of the women who died did so in childbirth) and the preferential treatment of boys, were clearly reflected in population statistics. Before World War II, south Slav patriarchal regions showed a surplus of men, whereas in the rest of Europe (with the exception of Bulgaria and Ireland) women outnumbered men.[21] Erlich explains that since boys were preferred, they were "nursed more carefully".[22] One wonders what kind of 'less careful' nursing would lead to elevated death rates for infant girls.

Each stage of childhood in traditional families brought its own torment. Purification rites to protect babies from 'evil spirits' – such as holding the baby upside down by one foot over a flame – persisted into the early 20th century in some parts of the former Yugoslavia.[23] The prolonged and total immobilisation of babies[24] in tight swaddling bandages, a practice long abandoned throughout western civilisation, has persisted into modern times in the Balkans, with the predictable deleterious affects of withdrawal, passivity, and late walking. As we saw in Part II, this extreme kind of swaddling can upset neuro-chemical balance, and thus contribute to long-term anxiety and hostility.

Older children were severely punished throughout their lives, with absolute deference to their elders expected and violently extracted. Erlich's survey found no place in Yugoslavia where the beating of children with sticks was not favoured. Child beating was frequent and severe in at least a quarter of the homes surveyed. Additionally, children were confronted by the trauma of witnessing their mothers and sisters being dominated, disempowered and beaten. Not surprisingly, the areas exhibiting more vigorous child beating coincided with districts where fighting traditions were more firmly rooted.[25]

Fortunately, some of the worst excesses of the *zadruga* had disappeared by the second half of the 20th century, with a resultant growth of families that were more compassionate and egalitarian. Erlich's far-reaching survey revealed how rapidly the South Slav family was being modernised. Signs were plentiful that the harsh discipline of patriarchy was starting to be relaxed. The advent of smaller family groups and the dissolution of the patriarch's absolute authority allowed for a significant decline in family violence. New laws institutionalised such changes (for instance, it is now against the law in Croatia for parents to corporally punish children). These changes eventually bore fruit in the form of powerful, non-violent pro-democracy activism.

In Serbia, increasingly liberal child-rearing modes produced a younger generation that led a successful, non-violent resistance to Slobodan Milosevic, and toppled his autocratic regime. In 1996, when Milosevic annulled the election that made an opposition party the winner, marchers filled the streets of Belgrade for three months, in peaceful protest. This is unprecedented in Yugoslavian history, which is marred by bloodshed. There had already been numerous anti-war and pro-democracy demonstrations in 1991, 1992, and 1993. In 1998, young students formed 'Otpor', a pro-democracy organisation committed to non-violent confrontation.[26] Their sole weapons: anti-Milosevic slogans on stickers and t-shirts using humour and ridicule to undermine the dictatorship, programs of coordinated civil-disobedience, workers' strikes, mass protests involving hundreds of thousands of civilians, and long convoys of buses and trucks that paralysed the streets. Without leaders or hierarchy, Otpor grew to have 70,000 members. Through all these protests, not a single shot was fired. On 5 October 2000, a democratic government was installed, and Milosevic was eventually arrested by Serb police.[27]

What finally dislodged the Serbian dictator Milosevic from office was not NATO aggression, but the Serbian people's resolve, led by young students, to refuse to bow to paternalistic authority. In fact, while earlier NATO negotiations with Milosevic and bombings of Serbia may have been intended to remove him from power, they had the opposite result. NATO bombings gave Milosevic a pretext to suppress opposition, they helped to increase his support base and legitimise his hold on power.[28] NATO bombing was far more destructive than it was preventive, causing widespread civilian casualties and damage to civilian infrastructure.[29] The most powerful and effective challenge to Milosevic came from the unwavering commitment of the youth leaders to refuse to take up arms, or use any kind of violence.[30] This level of maturity may not have been possible in earlier, more traditional patriarchal Serbia, when principles of non-violence were seen to lack honour, when the rage born of harsh childhood would have demanded the spilling of blood. Back then, in the age of the *zadruga*, violence was seen as one of the only legitimate means of conflict. What will give Serbian democracy a chance to endure and grow is the fact that its democratic government was not installed by outside forces. The culture of non-violence and democracy that has begun to flourish in Serbia came from within – it was a grassroots movement that resulted from an evolution in family relations and child rearing.

Endnotes

[1] The violence has been long and bitter, extending far further than the Balkan crises we saw during the 1990s. For example see the hotly debated accounts of deaths on all sides throughout World War II: McAdams (1998). The accounts and numbers of deaths vary depending on sources, one thing remains certain: many people died, more than we can ever accurately estimate, in more battles than this book has scope to discuss.

[2] Coleman (1993) p 162.

[3] 'Charges faced by Milosevic' CNN 24 April 2002 http://www.cnn.com/2002/WORLD/europe/02/12/milosevic.charges/index.html (last accessed 1 December 2004); 'Timeline: the Milosevic years' CNN 31 August 2004 http://www.cnn.com/2004/WORLD/europe/08/31/milosevic.timeline/index.html (last accessed 1 December 2004).

[4] Puhar (1994).

[5] Erlich (1966).

[6] Puhar (1994) p 133.

[7] Erlich (1966) pp 199–206.

[8] Erlich (1966) p 228.

[9] Erlich (1966) pp 258–271.

[10] Erlich (1966) see especially Chapter VIII 'Husband and wife' pp 227–286.

[11] Erlich (1966) p 234.

[12] Erlich (1966) p 227.

[13] Erlich (1966) pp 61–68.

[14] Erlich (1966) pp 61–68.

[15] Erlich (1966) p 237.

[16] Erlich (1966) p 239.

[17] Erlich (1966) p 167.

[18] Erlich (1966) p 258.

[19] Erlich (1966) p 263.

[20] Puhar (1993b) p 183.

[21] Puhar (1993b) p 188.

[22] Erlich (1966) pp 180–181.

[23] Puhar (1993a) p 374.

[24] Old style swaddling was in another category to the type of swaddling people do today. Babies were left swaddled most of the day, and they were infrequently changed. Today in Australia

parents practice what is euphemistically called 'wrapping', which is less tight than the old style, uses less cloth, and it is done to induce sleep, not all day long.

[25] Erlich (1966) p 77.

[26] For a history of this peaceful organisation see Melicharova (2001–2002); Chiclet (2001).

[27] Ackerman and Du Vall (2000) pp 478–489.

[28] Ackerman and Du Vall (2000) pp 484–485.

[29] A report by Human Rights Watch lists NATO attacks on non-military targets such as bridges and television stations, and a high number of civilian deaths caused by the use of cluster bombs near densely populated areas http://hrw.org/reports/2000/nato/Natbm200.htm#P39_994 (last accessed 1 December 2004).

[30] Ackerman and Du Vall (2000) pp 485–489.

12

TRADITIONAL RUSSIAN CHILDHOOD AND THE STALINIST HOLOCAUST

The moves toward democracy already in place all across Eastern Europe are the by-product of the considerable progress made in child rearing over the past 50 or so years; from Mediaeval-style swaddling, beating and sexual abuse of children, to more gentle and respectful modes. But in some places, the transition to democracy appears to be tenuous and subject to challenges and resistance. Since the days of *perestroika* and *glasnost* in Russia for instance, there have been signs of nostalgia for the certainty of iron-fisted centralised rule. New freedoms have been abused by opportunists, profiteers and racketeers, and this has caused social chaos in Russia. Since the liberating days of Gorbachev, popular sentiment has swung back towards hardline, nationalistic and militaristic leaders. The unabashedly xenophobic and sabre-rattling Zhirinovsky attracted enormous popular support. The government headed by Vladimir Putin, the newest president, is suspected of extensive human rights abuses in its military suppression of Chechnya. Moreover, this government is methodically dismembering freedom of the press.

If the birth of a new regime that embraces individual freedoms is a halting and complicated one, this is because Russian family structures have historically been based on rigid patriarchal authority, just as with traditional Balkan families. Democratic processes and the responsibilities that accompany them had, in the past, scarcely been modelled in Russian homes or schools, and thus increased freedom, with its uncertainties, at first seem alien and threatening. Russian voters chose a return to the familiar comfort of 'strong', authoritarian leadership.

Democracy struggles to take hold wherever it contravenes

the family atmosphere to which people have grown accustomed. Democratic reforms in Russia can only spread in pace with the steadily growing liberalisation of family dynamics and with increasingly gentler attitudes to babies and children. One of the key founding fathers of Russian communism, Leon Trotsky, asserted that communism became totalitarian because it failed to bring about a change in patriarchal relations within Soviet families.[1]

The suffocation of children's freedoms was an enduring theme that spanned both the imperial (Tsarist) and Soviet eras. Patrick P Dunn's thorough review of literature describing Russian childhood reveals a pattern of parenting that relied upon fear and corporal punishment.[2] If heavily patriarchal societies are extremely tough on children, imperial through to early Soviet Russia was no exception.

Effective opposition to abusive child-rearing practices did not begin in Russia until well into the 20th century, which explains the two-century delay in political reform here as compared to the west. Infanticide and child marriage in Russia were widespread well into the 19th century. Nowhere is Russian antipathy to freedom more poignantly evident than in the tardy relinquishment of the outdated practice of baby-swaddling. Folk beliefs that unrestrained babies would hurt themselves, even tear out their own eyes, prevailed throughout Russia far longer than in western Europe.[3] Infant ice-bathing, with its sometimes fatal effects, was a practice that had long fallen out of favour throughout Europe – it persisted longest in Russia.

Russian parenting in the 19th century has been described as detached and hostile, restrictive toward children, and violent. A predominantly 'traditional' society until at least 1890, Russia's peasant life was full of flogging, beating and neglect of children. The whip was so often used on children and wives that it was presented to the husband as part of the wedding ceremony. Beyond the whip, it was common for children to be beaten with ropes, fists, sticks, switches, dragged by the ears or hair, or kicked. Popular culture reflected this attitude towards children with sayings such as "Love your child with your heart, but crush him with your hands".[4] In this way, parental – usually paternal – authority was ruthlessly enforced. Individuals' aspirations were suppressed, and rigid roles were ascribed to each family member by virtue of their position in the family. If that sounds exactly like the Russian politics of much of the 20th century, that's precisely because political systems have always been a facsimile of the predominant family dynamics. Just like in any ordinary, traditional Russian family, the 'good authority' was a duplicate of the 'good father': stern, protective, punishing and controlling. How can this approach to parenting produce anything but tyrannical hierarchies?

Violence toward children was backed by religious dogma. The *Domostroi,* a traditional guide to household management compiled by churchmen in the 16th century, continued to be an influential guide to parents well into the 19th century, around the time when the future Soviet power-mongers were being reared.[5] It counselled fathers, in their interactions with their sons: "do not smile at him, do not play with him, for having been weak in little things, you will suffer in great ones". It also said, "Punish your son in his early years and he will comfort you in your old age and be the ornament of your soul. Do not spare your child any beating, for the stick will not kill him, but will do him good; when you strike the body you save the soul from hell" and, "Raise your child in fear and you will find peace and blessing in him" and, "inflict more wounds on him and you will rejoice afterward…crush his ribs while he is not yet grown, or else he will harden and cease to obey you".[6]

The *Domostroi* of the Russian Orthodox Church advocated violence against women. Typical of doctrines contrived to serve patriarchal rule, the *Domostroi* stated that wives should be beaten by the husband 'carefully' and 'politely' – with a whip. The concept of 'careful' or 'polite' whipping would be a challenge for the most agile imagination. Traditional Russian proverbs taught: 'Beat the child from infancy, beat the wife from the beginning', 'A wife is always guilty before her husband', 'The wife who got away from under her husband's control is worse than Satan'. As in Yugoslavia, and elsewhere in the world, misogyny is always accompanied by child abuse. In an authoritarian society, no one escapes violence. Though the 1917 Revolution ostensibly gave women legal equality, this did not immediately translate to equality at home. It took a long time for the concept of gender equality to start filtering into Russian family dynamics. In his psychohistorical analysis of Russian culture, Juhani Ihanus concluded: "Authoritarian child rearing, subordination of the young to elders, and women to men has reproduced authoritarian political, religious, and social structures".[7]

Russian schools were a continuation of the rigid, authoritarian, harsh and punitive theme that characterised the traditional family.[8]

In these institutions children were moulded, subordinated and strictly socialised into subjugated and acquiescent followers, or unbending and despotic leaders. The political environment of Tsarist Russia, and later the Soviet Union, was consistent with the prevailing climate of familial and educational repression, and blocking of personal autonomy.

Biographical accounts of the childhoods of the world's most brutal leaders teach us much about the making of tyranny in the family home. What was behind the viciousness that drove Georgian-born Joseph Stalin to massacre millions of men, women and children during his reign of terror in the Soviet Union? Stalin was the son of a violent alcoholic father, who would randomly and capriciously subject him to severe beatings and whippings.[9] As a child, Joseph Stalin regularly witnessed his mother being verbally humiliated and physically assaulted by his father. There is an account of little Joseph running, with blood pouring from a wound in his head, to the neighbour's house, screaming for help as his father attempted to strangle his mother.[10] What must be understood is that, if Stalin the dictator was not short of followers, this was because his family history was not too unusual or extraordinary. The Georgia of Stalin's boyhood was an honour and shame based society, honour being largely a man's concern. 'It is better to lose your head than your honour' goes an old Georgian saying. In this hyper-masculine world where honour was everything, a man was expected to be fearless, aggressive, and more significantly, to emphatically scorn emotional vulnerability.[11] Drunkenness was integral to the traditional culture and carried no social stigma. At the time, in parts of Russia and Georgia, acceptable behaviour for 'true men' included brawling and heavy drinking.[12]

The oppressive atmosphere of Stalin's home life was carried on in his schooling, where a strict religious tutelage continued to thrash the individuality out of him and his contemporaries. It should not be surprising, given the atmosphere that many children grew up in, that the political movement which dominated Soviet life was hostile to open personal expression, demanded uniformity, and denied the importance of the individual. Neither should it be of any surprise that Stalin was destined to become one of the leaders of this regime. One of the most depraved of all European despots, he was supported by a sophisticated political power structure (made up of other adult survivors of child abuse), and a prevailing culture of 'might-is-right'.

117

Vladimir Lenin, one of Stalin's most ruthless predecessors, was emotionally cold, violent and brutal toward his enemies. As with all other tyrants, his political life was a re-staging of his childhood and family history. Lenin's mother had suffered traditional 'hardening' practices such as being put to bed wrapped in cold, wet towels, and she consequently brought up Vladimir in the traditional, spartan manner. This included extreme swaddling and being sent out to wet-nurse – so that Lenin could scarcely walk until three years of age.[13]

Although there were some efforts to change traditional child-rearing practices after the 1917 Revolution, it wasn't until the 1930s that childhood in Russia began to resemble that of the rest of the modern world. It was around this time that the prolonged swaddling of babies was phased out, and whipping started to become unacceptable. Education was extended to all, boys and girls alike. This growing spirit of empowerment of children of both sexes began to soften the patriarchal constitution of traditional Russian society. It was in this new child-rearing era that Mikhail Gorbachev was born. By comparison to Stalin and Lenin, Gorbachev had received considerably more respect from his parents, and was said to be rather joyous as a child.[14] By the time Gorbachev came to power, the nightmare of traditional Russian childhood had slowly been dissolving for five decades. Increasing numbers of Russians were prepared to commit their support to a more liberal society. As a result, Gorbachev was able to spearhead the momentous democratic reforms of *glasnost* and *perestroika,* which altered the course of Russian history.

Certainly there has been democratic progress in Russia, but there remains considerable inertia, and nostalgia for the old ways. If hardline leaders still magnetise substantial public support in Russia, then perhaps this indicates that child-rearing reforms continue to lag behind those of western Europe. How can an adult embrace the responsibilities that freedom brings: the burden of choosing, questioning, and challenging one's leaders, the yoke of participation in group decision making, the boldness of expressing dissenting opinion, the accountability for one's own mistakes – when these urges have been crushed, or at least discouraged, from the earliest days of life? The temperament and maturity required to be one's own authority, to feel the equal of all others, to be a responsible and active participator in public life and decisions – the inner strength to refuse tyranny or autocracy; all these qualities are second nature to those in whom they have been fostered from the very dawn of youth. They are qualities that are hard-won through years of maturation and acceptance of responsibility for one's destiny. Individuals who have never been exposed to democratic notions of personal responsibility and egalitarianism in their upbringing cannot be expected to automatically absorb themselves in democratic living as soon as democracy is foisted upon them.

The continuing democratisation of Russian childhood is likely to further the process of political liberalisation. The emergence of Russian schools that follow the 'democratic edcuation' model and a 'natural parenting' movement are signs that this process is firmly underway. As prominent Russian educator, Olga Leontieva, explains: 'If they [the children] are to live in a free world, they must be educated as free persons'[15]

Time and again history teaches us that the first lessons in democracy must be delivered, through example, at school and in the family home. It makes no sense to fixate on particular totalitarian nations or their dictators and think of them as 'bad'. War and dictatorship are no more than mass delinquency, perpetrated by abuse survivors acting out their pain. This can and does happen *anywhere* in the world where a significant proportion of children are oppressed.

Endnotes

[1] Trotsky in Eisler (1995) p 164.
[2] Dunn (1988).
[3] In western Europe extreme forms of swaddling were phased out during the 18th and 19th centuries, Russians completely immobilised their babies, and released them infrequently for cleaning, until just a few decades ago: Ihanus (1994) p 193.
[4] Ihanus (1998).
[5] Ihanus (1998).
[6] Dunn (1988) pp 392–393.
[7] Ihanus (1998) p 248.
[8] Ihanus (1996).
[9] Miller (1998) p 583.
[10] Rhodes (1997) p 378.
[11] Rhodes (1997) p 379.
[12] Ihanus (1999).
[13] De Mause (1990) pp 341–352.
[14] De Mause (1990) pp 341–352.
[15] 'Education Revolution' newsletter, Summer 2002.

13

NAZIS AND THEIR OPPONENTS: HOW DID THEIR CHILDHOODS DIFFER?

Consider the words 'every child is a battle'. What kind of attitude to children do these words convey? These were the portentous words shouted in an address to the National Socialist Women's Organisation of Germany, by Adolf Hitler in 1934.[1] Far from being alone in this attitude to children, a look at parenting manuals of pre-World War II Germany exposes a prevalent hostility to children. Swiss psychologist and author Alice Miller states that around the turn of the 20th century – roughly the time when Nazis, their collaborators and their sympathisers were children – German upbringing manuals generally deplored physical demonstrations of affection toward children, and were filled with warnings against 'spoiling' children by indulging their emotional needs.[2] Of course, many German families bucked this trend, but as far as the manuals were concerned, rigorous obedience training from the earliest time of infancy was the dominant ideal. This is the kind of childhood atmosphere that, when taken to extremes, gave rise to the hatred, the lack of compassion and the blind obedience that comprised the engine of the Nazi phenomenon.

We will never know exactly how many German families upheld the austere standards espoused in the parenting manuals, and I have no doubt that many German parents were highly empathic. What researchers have made clear, as we shall see in this chapter, is that there was a marked difference between the childhoods of Nazis, their supporters and apathetic bystanders, and the childhoods of German humanitarians who were committed to resistance. Only a critical mass of harsh, authoritarian upbringing is needed to skew a nation towards dictatorship and war. I believe the evidence shows that this critical proportion existed when Nazis were babes.

The parenting mode of this era has left a clear footprint in the numerous German autobiographies from around the turn of the 20th century. One study that compares 90 French and German autobiographies from this time found that German childhoods were "far more brutal and unloving".[3] Another study of 154 autobiographies reveals a formidable degree of cruelty against children at this time – an extremely grim picture found nowhere else in Western Europe.[4] Foreign visitors to German homes reported a lack of glee or exuberance in children. It was not uncommon, at that time, for German childhood to be joyless and full of fear. A distinct preference for boys abounded, as did greater neglect and maltreatment towards girls. Hence, Germany lagged behind the rest of western Europe in the advancement of women's rights, and in the education of girls. Beatings in schools were routine and plentiful, with an arsenal of whips, canes and birches.

As a rough indicator of cultural attitudes to children, infant mortality rates (IMR) at the end of the 19th century were breathtakingly high; much higher in Germany and Austria than in the rest of western and northern Europe. IMR was 21 per cent in Prussia and 58 per cent in rural Bavaria (German provinces). Overall for Germany it was 20 per cent at the turn of the century.[5] Just as in France one century earlier, babies were kept unwashed and tightly swaddled up to nine months, and more women sent their babies to wet-nurses rather than breastfeed. There were variations from province to province, but in some parts of Germany, it was considered 'swinish' to breastfeed. For convenience, it was common to stuff the mouths of babies with a linen cloth drenched in meal-pap or gruel, called *zulp*. This method gagged the babies' cries while supplying automatic – though woefully inadequate and unsanitary – nourishment.[6] No parent would go to such lengths to avoid intimacy with their child, unless the infant was seen as little more than an irritant or a burden. Given the high IMR, these practices bespeak a level of neglect such as had not been seen around the rest of western Europe for a century. Even Martin Luther, the father of German religious 'Reformation', considered small children to be "obnoxious with their crapping, eating, and screaming".[7] Luther is credited for having once said, "I would rather have a dead son than a disobedient one."[8]

Perhaps the most widely read parenting writer of the times was Dr Daniel Gottlieb Moritz Schreber.[9] Historian Maria Piers sums up Schreber as a "consummate sadist, whose methods epitomize totalitarian behaviour modification worthy of the Gestapo".[10] According to this popular parenting guru, even four-month-old babies should be denied empathy – in his view, they should be discouraged from crying through the use of "physically perceptible admonitions".[11] One loathes to imagine what his method of admonishment might have consisted of, when "such a procedure is only necessary once, or at the most twice and then one is master of the child for all time".[12] Schreber professed a kind of grip over the child's mind such that "one look, one single threatening gesture will suffice to subjugate the child".[13]

Schreber advocated the use of metal jackets, which children would wear all day in order to enforce a straight-backed posture. Piers (1978) recalls that these devices were still in use in Vienna when she was a child. Schreber suggested recipes for teaching self-denial to children, which consisted of eating or drinking the child's favourite foods in his or her presence, and then: "However urgent the infant's oral needs may become in this situation, they must not be gratified."[14] Far from being a marginal trend, Schreber's books were a major influence on German parents: some of his tracts ran into 40 editions, its sales only exceeded by the Bible.[15] With little to advocate the promotion of children's individuality or creativity, life under the 'Schreber' regime must surely have been barren, fearful and tormented for German children.

The quintessential pedagogical handbook of the Third Reich was *The German Mother and Her First Child*, by physician Johanna Haarer. Hardly a break from tradition, this manual maintained the heavily authoritarian obsession with obedience, with statements such as "Babies and young children won't obey, don't want to do what grown-ups want them to do but instead test them, and tyrannise them. By nature they are impure, unclean, messy, and soil every thing they can get their hands on."[16] German mothers, according to Haarer, needed to arm themselves with "strictness", "persistency" and "will power", for "the child's training must begin directly following birth".[17] Haarer emphatically discouraged tenderness or responsiveness in mothers, for fear of "spoiling" babies or making them "too soft".[18] She advised that babies should be separated from their mothers immediately after birth, and kept separate for 24 hours. Daily meals were to be ruled by punctuality, and Haarer insisted on "breaking off the meal early and relentlessly letting the child go hungry if it resists".[19] A crying child, according to Haarer, should be "removed to a quiet place, where it will stay alone… until the next meal".[20] When babies' attachment needs are so rigorously denied, there are dire psychological and neurological consequences that can last a lifetime (see Chapter 25 and Chapter 26). To compound this early deprivation, parents were admonished to be "tough with the child that has hurt itself", to demand absolute obedience, and not to shy away from giving their children "an immediate slap".[21]

One of the most popular of all German children's story books, and a staple of the family bed-time reading scene, was *Struwwelpeter*. Written and compiled by Dr Heinrich Hoffman (1809–1894), this compendium of moralistic sing-song rhymes presented typical, rule-setting parent–child interactions. Each time, the hapless child suffers a gruesome fate for his or her disobedience. There is the little boy whose thumbs are hacked off by a mad, scissor-wielding tailor – just as his mother had warned – for the crime of persisting to suck his thumbs in her absence. Another boy gradually withers to an emaciated shadow of his former, sturdy self, and eventually falls down dead; all for refusing to submit to his parents' force-feeding soup-regime. A young girl who accidentally sets fire to herself after not heeding her 'good' mother's warnings about playing with matches, is watched by her cats as she agonisingly dances, all aflame, ending up on the floor as a pile of ashes. What is most disturbing is that each anecdote is illustrated cartoon-style with the most graphic of pictures, such as 'Johnny Suck-a-Thumb' succumbing to the amputation of both thumbs, complete with blood squirting from the remaining stumps.

These days, more people would find it unthinkable to expose a child's susceptible and vulnerable mind to images as atrocious as those that German children were routinely treated to at bedtime readings. If *Struwwelpeter* were a cartoon-movie, it would never make it past the 'G' rating censors. We take care to shield young viewers, via censorship laws, from images of violence and horror less monstrous than those that German children were subjected to daily. The 'G' rated viewing category exists in recognition of the fact that small children cannot properly distinguish between fact and fantasy, and do not have the psychological resources (or twisted sense of humour) to safely process images of shocking violence or catastrophe.

Around the turn of the 20th century, German child–suicide rates were *three to five times higher* than in other western European countries. Investigations revealed that the most common cause of suicide was the children's terror of their parents' severe corporal punishment. German psychiatrists who commented on this trend almost unanimously recommended stricter obedience training for children, concluding that the victims suicided due to their psychological "weakness". The prevailing professional advice was that children suicided because they were "too soft" and "spineless", and so they needed "toughening up".[22] The 'cure' for the victims of child abuse was more abuse. Perhaps those who were 'tough' enough, rather than jump out of their windows in despair as so many others, would grow up to volunteer for service in the ultra-violent paramilitary SA troops.

The morbid Dr Hoffman's tutorial to children was clear: a horrible fate awaits those who displease authority. To a certain degree, this threat was grounded in reality – the all-too-real pall of the Haarer and Schreber methods; a pedagogical style that said, 'Obey, or else.' Adherents to this style of parenting were unwittingly preparing their children psychologically for the acceptance of national fascism. This is precisely what took place one generation later, when rather than repel German voters – or at least arouse their suspicion – Hitler's unrelenting belligerence made him all the more attractive and popular. German fascism, like every other fascism of history, was born in the family home – the offspring of a pervasive antagonism toward children's individuality. After World War II, psychiatric studies of SS officers found that most of them had been beaten frequently by authoritarian fathers.[23] Nazism was no more than a parenting mode – the insistence on defeating children's wills through terror, was projected onto a big, national screen.

The terrorised child will, in many cases, grow up to terrorise, tacitly approve of, or overlook the persecution of the vulnerable. It's not only the perpetrators and oppressors that we should focus on, when sufficient public disgust with Hitler's call to violence simply failed to materialise. There have been many Hitlers who faded into obscurity in free-thinking societies where, thanks to more advanced parenting styles, iron-fisted toughness is simply not tolerated, and is nipped in the bud. In early 20th century Germany, a large portion of the population, mollified by an early crushing of the spirit, failed to respond with the spontaneous and unanimous outrage and revulsion that would have nullified the young Hitler and his supporters from the moment they made their first public appearance. Those individuals who were psychologically mature enough to recognise the danger and protest against it from the beginning, were tragically (but not surprisingly) insufficient.

In a modern, democratic society such as Germany is today, most parents would find the child-rearing mode that predominated when Hitler was a child, to be unthinkable and repugnant. The only way to come to grips with the social effects of such child rearing, is to realise the extent of the public participation, tacit approval, indifference or denial regarding the calamities of the 1930s and 1940s. The anti-child climate that existed before World War II accounts for why Hitler was able to count on more than just a handful of followers in order to execute his master plan. Hitler was aided and abetted by so many ordinary citizens. At the very least, Hitler benefited from an appalling public toleration or non-reaction to his many explicit promises of violence. He was tacitly approved of or altogether ignored by large sectors of the public who were too accustomed to seeing brutal 'fathers' as nothing out of the ordinary.[24]

The Nazi party enjoyed massive compliance – both enforced and voluntary. At its peak, it had eight million members. Hitler had clearly and publicly advocated a bloody elimination of the Jewish race; as a centrepiece of Nazi party policy. This did not prevent him from receiving 37.4 per cent of popular votes in the free elections of July 1932, which made the Nazis the largest and most powerful party in the German Parliament. This success gave the Nazis further confidence to intimidate their political opponents. Such undemocratic tactics should have deterred voters. In fact, in the March 1933 elections, 43.9 per cent cast their ballots for Hitler. Immediately following these tainted elections, Hitler dismantled what was left of the tattered democracy that had helped him into power. Even Hitler's public declaration of his desire to kill off hundreds of thousands of disabled, deformed or mentally ill people did not dissuade voters. A sizeable proportion of voters were either excited by, or absolutely indifferent to, the Nazi promises of horror and violence. The increasing waves of Nazi-sponsored violence against Jews and political opponents failed to repel voters.

In Hitler's many public speeches, as well as his widely read book *Mein Kampf* (over 280,000 copies sold *before* he was elected to power) he laid out his plans for violence clearly for all to see. Here he spoke of *Lebensraum* – the need for Germany to acquire more land by force, and even mentioned 'poison gas' as an appropriate treatment for the Jewish peoples. Anyone with a passing interest in social policy might have deduced that something horrible was afoot. Hitler had already served a jail sentence for attempting to take political power by force. It could not have been more plain that he was a tyrant with tyrannical plans. Notwithstanding, Hitler enjoyed considerable popularity before he sealed his final grip on power by force.

When Germany exploded into violence, atrocities were committed with substantial nation-wide support. The SA (*Sturmabteilung*) were zealous and merciless instruments of state-sponsored brutality, whose ranks were filled by volunteers. In every district of the country, they battered, tortured and humiliated old people, men, women and children. No efforts were made to hide the brutality of the SA, which often took place in the street, in full view of the public.

The SA gained their grisly notoriety one fateful night in 1938, which was henceforth to be named *Kristallnacht* – the 'night of the broken glass'. *Kristallnacht* was an orchestrated detonation of savagery led by SA troops throughout the country. Hundreds of German Jews were killed, 7500 Jewish-owned businesses were destroyed, hundreds of synagogues were burnt, and 30,000 Jews were hauled off to concentration camps. Far from causing an outcry of revulsion at sites of slaughter and vandalism, the SA were cheered on by onlookers, many spontaneously joining the violence.[25] It was a titanic achievement to execute this much damage in just one night, from one end of the country to the other. This necessitated the co-ordinated efforts of a nation-wide mass of survivors of child abuse. The following day, Nazi sympathisers somehow managed to orchestrate a 100,000-strong gathering in Nuremberg in support for the atrocities.

Historians who specialise in World War II and the Holocaust agree that among the executioners of the Nazi genocide were many willing participants. A particularly chilling account of this enthusiasm for killing is reported by historian Daniel Goldhagen (1996). According to Goldhagen, approximately 15,000 members of German police battalions were directly involved in the massacre of unarmed civilians, including children and babies. The staff of the police battalions were rarely content with mere murder; they toyed with their victims in the most bizarre and macabre ways. The legacy of child abuse is evident not only in the vast numbers of obedient killers, but in the blatant pleasure some of them took in their savagery.

Historians may forever debate the proportions of the German popular support for Nazi violence – how much of it was enforced, and how much was voluntary.[26] What prevails is the sense that co-operation or tacit approval was discomfortingly widespread. Says Clendinnen, "The speed and efficiency of the implementation of the Furher's decision were the contributions of a bureaucracy ready and eager to execute its leader's will".[27] Breitman[28] also saw that Hitler's eliminationist dream could not have thrived unless it germinated in a population that already contained a large number of virulently racist people. Breitman[29] suggests there was stunning public indifference to the considerable leaks of information about the genocide taking place all around them. Even some surreptitious bureaucratic foot-dragging would have slowed the progress of Hitler's macabre ambitions. But this foot-dragging did not materialise. Co-operation with the eliminationist scheme was more than efficient; it was sometimes unwavering and enthusiastic. The astonishing efficacy with which over six million were identified, collected, transported, tortured and murdered, in such a short space of time, was nothing short of a logistical marvel. Support for Hitler's genocidal designs was abundant.

We may never know exactly how much the general public knew about the full extent of the horrors, but the campaign to eliminate Romany and Jews was, effectively, not a very well-kept State secret. State-sponsored atrocities were often unconcealed.

Deportations to extermination camps were brutally conducted in full view of the general public. Neither children nor the old and frail were spared from being savagely beaten, spat upon and humiliated as they were herded and crammed into trains and trucks – while spectators stood and watched. Thousands of soldiers returning from the Russian front brought home stories of mass extermination of Jews. The organisation of Hitler's master plan relied on an immense number of co-operative and efficient staff, which included the police battalions, administrative bureaucrats, railway workers, concentration and labour-camp staff, and communications officers. There were scores of concentration camps and ghettos all over Europe, relying on a monumental rotation of dutiful crew. Overall, the personnel of the massacre was legion, it would be naïve to imagine that there were no leaks of information about some of the goings-on inside extermination camps and in the killing fields. Hundreds of thousands of emaciated and dying Jews were marched back and forth, from one end of the country to the other, in open and public display. Of course, many Germans may have simply not known the full extent of the horrors going on around them, and the internment in concentration camps of thousands of German opponents did much to silence and intimidate potential resistance. It cannot be denied, however, that a large proportion of the population aided the Nazi program with their full co-operation, their tacit approval, their extreme fear or their indifference.[30]

The mood of hatred was broadly fomented by anti-Semitic church authorities, in whom congregations placed their trust. The church was another 'absolute authority' whose anti-Semitic propaganda was often accepted. Both Protestant and Catholic officials gave considerable support to Hitler's annihilationist policies. Anti-Semitism was the official church line, as regularly reflected in anti-Semitic religious publications. While condemnation of the Jewish 'race' issued from almost every church authority, there was only a trickle of church protest against racist violence. Religious leaders did however demonstrate some disapproval of Nazi policy. It was united church protest that forced the Nazis to repeal their euthanasia programmes for the disabled. Regarding the exterminationist policy, however, Lutheran and Catholic authorities were, on the whole, either supportive or silent – and by their inaction complicit. The bloodbath of *Kristallnacht*, for example, did not draw protests from the church.[31] Despite such an abrogation of humanity from a supposedly 'Godly' institution, the people did not abandon their churches. If church authorities said that Jews are evil, that was not to be questioned. Undemocratic child rearing makes for an easily seduced congregation. Had there been concerted civic outrage at the vilification coming from both the Catholic and the Lutheran churches, long before there was any threat of retribution, Nazi eliminationism may not have ensued. The general public either endorsed the prevailing church view, or were willing to let it go unchallenged. The church, after all, was an authority that must never be questioned, and always obeyed.

What could have caused such public approval and co-operation with the horrors, how did such a chillingly large percentage of the population become absorbed in irrational racist hatred? Hitler's 'willing executioners' were acting from a powerful and unconscious rage, accumulated from years of austere childhood 'discipline' in the style of Schreber and Haarer. The racism behind the Holocaust was collectively justified by the most absurd and ludicrous beliefs, to which many gave irrational and uncritical credence. Can you imagine a sizeable portion of a population succumbing to the belief that an entire ethnic group, including its children and babies, were morally tainted from birth by virtue of their race? Hatred annuls common sense in even the most intelligent minds. This is an unforgettable example of the dire results of cold and punitive upbringing; it stamps in our collective consciousness that violence towards children, and neglect of their emotional needs, creates a violent society. The gratuitous violence displayed by so many ordinary Germans was a misplaced explosion of revenge for acute childhood suffering.

In their struggle to comprehend what could have caused outrages of such magnitude, many historians have tended to rationalise the public support enjoyed by Hitler in terms of the economic despair that plagued the population following World War I. They emphasise causes that are economical, historical, political or religious. These causes are real enough, but only partial to our understanding of what occurred.[32]

When contemplating the terrible events of the Holocaust, this should also conjure in our minds images of those German babies who were left tightly and painfully swaddled for hours at a time in the hands of wet-nurses, their mouths stuffed with *zulp* so their cries were drowned out. It should also conjure up images of children who were denied empathy and open displays of warmth and affection lest they be 'spoiled', and who were trained to be mechanically obedient through systematic and vigorous beatings. The multitudes who joined in the racist violence and hatred, and the many more who failed to deplore it, suffered from arrested emotional development – they were crippled in their ability to feel human compassion, to be outraged by the suffering of fellow humans. Their sense of self, their personal autonomy and confidence was damaged such that they were overly compliant, susceptible to propaganda and intimidated by 'authority'.

Germany was only the prime instigator, however. There were various levels of contribution to the Holocaust across Europe, and even amongst the Allied powers. Large-scale atrocities were committed by Romanians, Poles, Ukrainians, and many others.

The Allies knew of Hitler's plans and of their execution long before they acted decisively. For a long time, the Allies behaved little better than apathetic or appeasing bystanders. Then again, child abuse went unchecked throughout the west, and was simply not considered a problem until the 1960s, when for the first time it began to receive sustained attention. World War II has been a turning point in our understanding of how human monstrosity is created in childhood.

Resisters, rescuers and their childhoods

While many who did not approve of the Nazis were understandably afraid, and were convinced that resistance would have been futile, there were many pockets of successful resistance to the policies of ethnic cleansing. Many who stood up to the Nazis and refused to do their grisly work managed to force the Nazis to back down. In Denmark there was a groundswell of people who quickly understood Hitler's intentions and would not abide by his atrocious intent. At grave risk to themselves, the Danish simply refused to co-operate when required to yield Jewish citizens. In this instance, a unified humanistic response rendered the Nazi tough-guy stance completely ineffectual.[33]

Similarly, the Italian army flatly disobeyed Mussolini's orders to round up Italian Jews and hand them to the Nazis. The unified resistance was too great for any retribution to take place, and Mussolini was unable to impose his will. In Berlin, around 600 implacable German women staged a protest against their Jewish husbands' detention. Even when the fearsome SS fired bullets to disperse them, the women re-grouped, and simply would not go away. Their determination to stare down an 'authority' whom they did not respect, finally paid off, and none of these protestors were injured. Their refusal to submit forced the embarrassed SS to release their husbands from custody. As mentioned previously, the Nazi campaign of euthanasing tens of thousands of children with congenital disabilities was brought to a halt by a passionate, church-led public protest – without retribution from the Nazis. This demonstrates that resistance to the massacres and deportations was possible, for those who were united and committed to humane values. If an overwhelming number of committed Germans had so wanted, they might have blocked the genocide before it gathered pace. Many of those who had the inner strength and emotional maturity to be committed to refusing the horrors, prevailed – even against the seemingly indestructible might of the Nazi machine of oppression.[34]

Naturally, a lot of Germans felt sickened by what they saw happening all around them, but were simply paralysed with fear, and their protests were swallowed back. They felt horror and pain for the victims of persecution, but these feelings failed to translate into action. Yet even in the midst of this calamitous chapter in human history, many people risked their lives to protect Jews, both friends and strangers, from persecution. Ordinary Germans – who fully understood what the Nazis were up to – saved the lives of around 10,000 Jews by hiding them, at great personal risk, for the duration of the deportations. What was it that distinguished those people whose integrity actually pressed them into action, just like the Danes, or like the women of Berlin? What made those people whose conscience translated into committed action so different from the rest? What is it that enables an individual that abhors injustice, to renounce passivity and take action?

Interestingly, it has been found that there were discernible differences in the childhoods of the rescuers that distinguished them from the war criminals, collaborators or passive bystanders. In a detailed and comprehensive study titled *The Altruistic Personality: Rescuers of Jews in Nazi Europe,* sociologists Samuel and Perl Oliner[35] interviewed over 400 individuals who had placed their own and their family's lives at risk in order to hide and rescue Jews. These rescuers were compared to a group of non-rescuers, who disagreed with the persecution of Jews but took no action to protect them. Both groups were asked an exhaustive battery of questions about a wide range of personal attributes, their personal and family backgrounds. The results of this survey are eye-opening, and they carry profound implications.

Following a thorough and painstaking interview process, the Oliners found that there were no significant differences between rescuers and non-rescuers in almost any of the categories of attributes. The two groups were not dissimilar in economic status, in exposure to opportunities for rescuing, in religious faith, or in risks involved. Rescuers and non-rescuers were equally likely to live among Jews and know them as friends or acquaintances. Members of both groups were asked for help by Jews with the same frequency. So why if both groups were equal in their circumstances, was one group's caring and conviction strong enough to motivate life-risking action? The only distinguishing feature that set apart the rescuers from the non-rescuers, was the way they were reared as children. No other personal or circumstantial attributes could adequately explain the difference between the two groups. Over half the rescuers acted alone and spontaneously, and did not belong to any kind of resistance group that aided them or supported them. Over half of them rescued complete strangers on principle, not just friends or relatives. The researchers discovered that the only real difference between the two groups was the difference in how they had been parented.

Rescuers reported that their parents had placed much less emphasis on 'obedience'. They tended to describe their relationship with their parents as closer and warmer. Both groups reported being 'disciplined' by their parents with equal frequency, but the parents of rescuers had used non-violent methods of 'discipline'. Rescuers reported having been beaten a lot less as children, and certainly not with objects such as rods, wooden spoons or birches.

There probably is no clearer evidence that childhood shapes society. There is no more compelling and convincing imperative to abandon violent and punitive child-rearing methods. The willingness to take altruistic action, even when this poses a risk, and the willingness to defy dishonourable authority, these are signs of emotional maturity – the product of non-violent and respectful child rearing. If more Europeans had been raised in this way around the turn of the 20th century, there would not have been a Holocaust.

Holocausts – a worldwide phenomenon

The holocaust is certainly not a German phenomenon. There have been countless holocausts involving sometimes more, sometimes less victims, but the same level of horror. There have been holocausts in China, the Soviet Republics, Turkey, Cambodia, Chile and Argentina, the former Yugoslavia, Rwanda, Burundi, and even in Australia. As historian Inga Clendinnen clarifies, the only thing that makes the German-led Holocaust stand apart is the method: the modern capacity, the advanced logistical and technological endowments that enabled the prosecution of such massive atrocities, across so many nations, in so little time.[36] The enormous scope and speed of the Jewish Holocaust was made possible through computer-age communications technology, advanced transport infrastructures, and a highly methodical and efficient bureaucratic organisation. The popular proclivity toward hatred or indifference, and the acute cruelty and heartlessness, are no different to similar explosions of human savagery all across the globe, and throughout history.

The suffering of children ends up producing human rights abuses anywhere in the world. Every war and every genocide has been a direct consequence of society's war against children. Similar patterns of abuse toward children would be discovered if we examined Rwandan childhoods, or the childhoods of the supporters of the apartheid regime in South Africa. The same would have been true of the childhoods of that sector of Australian society which perpetrated atrocities (or remains unmoved by these atrocities) against indigenous people – including the removal of Aboriginal children from their families, which was finally officially acknowledged with an apology from the government, in February 2008. A reprehensible 'White Australia Policy' defined Australian immigration laws until 1973.

Today, Australia has a particularly high indigenous death rate, and on general measures of indigenous health it has been rated amongst the worst in the world.[37] The current policy of mandatory detention of asylum seekers, political refugees and their children is extremely contentious and out of step with other modern democracies.[38] (The topic of children in detention will be discussed in a postscript at the end of this chapter.) The fact that Australia has a comparatively high rate of youth depression and youth suicide,[39] speaks of a collective failure to safeguard children's emotional health – a fact that may well have contributed to this tragic record of race relations.

No ethnic group or nation is naturally more violent than another. The actions and inactions that made holocausts possible are simply the all-too familiar human result of abusive child rearing, and arrested emotional development. Violence is a cultural *trend,* not an ethnic *trait* (in fact, as we will see in Chapter 21, when it comes to personality there is no such thing as an ethnic trait). Violent leaders and their willing followers emerge wherever there has been violence against children.

A new Germany

Fortunately, it is possible for cultural shifts to take place quite swiftly. German child rearing changed rapidly in the decades following World War II. Harsh and authoritarian parenting manuals such as those of Haarer and Schreber have long been out of circulation, and with them the vogue for disciplinarian upbringing. As a result, there has been a dramatic social evolution. Following a recent wave of Neo-Nazi attacks against immigrants, 200,000 Germans – including political *and* religious leaders – rallied in Berlin in protest.[40] Organisers were surprised by the strength of the turn-out, which was twice what they had anticipated. This tide of passion for human tolerance and brotherhood stands in stark contrast to the state of affairs just over one generation ago, when merely a fraction of the population showed any such commitment; when almost half of all voters knowingly elected the very party that now attracts legal sanctions and massive, nation-wide condemnation.

In today's Germany, it's highly unlikely that someone like Hitler would attain any meaningful position of power. On average, there is a much higher level of emotional development. This evolutionary progress is the result of gentler child-rearing modes that foster the development of emotional intelligence. In fact, today's Germany is inching to the forefront of the world in child-rearing attitudes. In July 2000, the German Parliament passed an absolute prohibition on any kind of corporal punishment against children, and this ban explicitly included the use of psychological injury and any other humiliating measures. Germany is one of only 13 nations to have done this, and this puts her ahead of other west European nations for the first time. The national ban is backed by a large-scale government-sponsored education of parents regarding alternative, non-injurious means of boundary-setting with children. Changes such as these are likely to transform Germany into one of the world's leading forces for peace, democracy and human rights advocacy, less than a century after World War II. In fact, the connection between child-rearing evolution and peace advocacy is already evident in a heart-felt repentance for the Holocaust that was recently proffered by German churches,[41] and in the unflinching German stance against the war on Iraq in 2003.

Origins of hatred

So, how do repressive childhoods produce adult persecutors? The mechanism is quite simply explained. As Miller says, "An animal will respond to attack with 'fight-or-flight'. Neither response is open to an infant exposed to aggression from immediate family members. Thus the natural reaction remains pent up, sometimes for decades, until it can be taken out on a weaker object. Then the repressed emotions are unleashed against minorities. The targets vary from country to country, but the reasons for that hatred are probably identical the world over."[42] Whether it be the Jews, the Romany, homosexuals, Croats, Serbs, Bosnian Muslims, Kosovo Albanians, Cambodians, Tibetans, Chinese democrats, or Australian Aborigines, all holocausts have this in common: they are perpetrated by survivors of tyrannised childhoods. A glut of evidence links punitive or authoritarian upbringing to violent attitudes and behaviour in adults (as we will see in Chapter 21, violence in childhood can have permanent neurological and neuro-chemical effects on the developing brain, thus predisposing individuals towards violence). On a larger scale, the relationship between child abuse and war is therefore only logical, and to be expected.

Not surprisingly, just like Stalin's, Hitler's childhood was a torment of unrelenting and methodical violence perpetrated by his sadistic father, who would daily take out his rage with impunity on the young Adolf. Hitler learned to ignore human pain and tragedy as he impassively counted out loud the blows raining down upon him. Hitler was whipped or caned up to 200 times in a day, which sometimes put him into a coma.[43] Mao Tse-Tung, another victim of regular fatherly whippings in the name of 'discipline', was later to send 30 million Chinese people to their deaths.[44]

A glimpse at Saddam Hussein's childhood sheds light on what predisposed him to become one of the world's most barbaric dictators. Hussein was fatherless, and his mother viciously rejected him. Both his father and elder brother died while he was still growing in his mother's womb. His mother subsequently attempted suicide, and when this failed, she tried to abort Saddam by beating her belly against a door. Rejected at birth, Saddam was reared by an uncle. When he returned to his mother's home at three years of age, Saddam was physically and psychologically abused by his new step-father. As an older child, he returned to the care of his uncle, who was a brutal ultra-nationalist. Saddam Hussein has never experienced the love of a mother or father, but he is intimately familiar with brutality from his earliest moments of life. Such bleak circumstances would have made it impossible for him to develop any semblance of a capacity for remorse, empathy or compassion.[45]

Recent world events have aroused much discussion and debate about the influence of religious extremism upon social, political and international affairs. But it is rare for commentators to pose the questions: What is childhood like among radical or fundamentalist religious families? Can the study of fundamentalists' childhoods promote more understanding of the way they function within – and impact upon – the larger world? The next chapter looks at what many studies have revealed about the child-rearing styles of religious extremists.

Postscript

A case study of child abuse[46] in Australia – *Jessica Perini*[47]

> *The arrest, detention or imprisonment of a child shall be in conformity with the law and shall be used only as a measure of last resort and for the shortest appropriate period of time.*
> Convention on the Rights of the Child, Article 37(b)

In Australia, children are imprisoned in immigration detention centres for months and sometimes years. These centres have been found, time and again, to be wanting by any number of human rights standards.

During 2001 representatives from the Human Rights and Equal Opportunity Commission (HREOC) made many visits to immigration detention centres around Australia. By the end of that year it had received numerous reports of abuse and harm to children and adults held in such centres. In November 2001 HREOC announced that there would be an inquiry into the treatment of children held in immigration detention.[48]

In May 2004 HREOC published its report, 'A last resort?', the result of two years of investigation which included interviews with detainee children and their families from all immigration detention centres including those on remote islands off the coast of Australia. It had also received reports from organisations representing detainees, human rights and legal bodies, members of the public, religious bodies, state government agencies and a range of non-government policy and service-providing organisations. Inquiry staff also interviewed medical care professionals, teachers and guards who had been involved with children in the centres.[49]

The resulting 900-page report contained overwhelming evidence that holding children in detention centres was cruel, inhumane, damaging and absolutely contrary to Australia's international obligations under the United Nations Convention on the Rights of the Child (CROC).

An overwhelming majority of the children (over 90 per cent) were found to be refugees and now live in Australia. But what damage was done during their average 20 months[50] in immigration detention can only be gauged over the years as they grow.

As of January 2005, eight months after the release of the report, there were still at least 90 children in immigration detention.[54] This is despite the fact that human rights abuses continue to be reported, by visitors to the facilities,[55] medical health professionals,[56] the press and politicians.[57]

The Australian government has fought cases against the human rights of children all the way to the High Court and won. Former prime minister John Howard authored a so-called 'Pacific Solution' in 2001, which established camps on two small, remote Pacific islands in an attempt to deter illegal immigrants entering Australia. Immigrants and asylum seekers were summarily detained in these camps awaiting processing. The Howard government was widely criticised nationally and internationally for the conditions of the camps and the poor treatment meted out to the camp-dwellers.[58] In 2007, the incoming government led by new prime minister Kevin Rudd began dismantling the camps, terminating the 'solution'.

In the UK, there have been a number of reports of children held for long periods in the Yarls Wood immigration removal centre in Bedfordshire, awaiting assessment and possible removal from the UK.[59] Parents have protested at the living conditions, and the enforced detention and confinement of their children.[60]

Endnotes

1. Gruen (1999) p 141.
2. Miller (1998).
3. De Mause (2000) p 407.
4. De Mause (2000) p 408.
5. De Mause (2000).
6. De Mause (2000).
7. De Mause (2000) p 414.
8. De Mause (2000) p 416.
9. Miller (1998).
10. Piers (1978) p 85.

11   Miller (1998) p 575.
12   Miller (1998) p 575.
13   Miller (1998) p 575.
14   Miller (1998) p 575.
15   Miller (1998) p 574.
16   Quoted in Gruen (1999) p 142.
17   Chamberlain (2004).
18   Chamberlain (2004) p 379.
19   Chamberlain (2004) p 382.
20   Chamberlain (2004) p 385.
21   Chamberlain (2004) p 392.
22   Baartman (1994).
23   Milburn and Conrad (1996) p 185.
24   Goldhagen (1997); Breitman (1998); Clendinnen (1999).
25   Goldhagen (1996).
26   Burleigh and Wippermann (1991); Burleigh (2001) see Chapter 2 and Chapter 4; see Hoffmann (1988); Gellately (2001) Chapter 6; Newton (1990).
27   Clendinnen (1999) p 97.
28   Breitman (1998).
29   Breitman (1998).
30   Goldhagen (1996); Clendinnen (1999).
31   Goldhagen (1996).
32   The 'economic hardship' rationale for understanding the Nazis' support base is important but limited in scope. Hitler wore his bloodlust on his sleeve for all to see. To any who looked upon him with open eyes, he must have radiated the promise of eventual chaos and ruin – the exact opposite of what impoverished people needed. We should never presume that the choice of tyrannical leaders is based on rational thought. There are further questions that remain unanswered by this 'economic' theory. If economics was behind the violence, then why were Jews attacked, and not rich gentiles? Why was anti-Semitism the official stance of the church long before the German economy collapsed? What was the economics behind slaughtering Romany and homosexuals? Why did some countries suffering deep economic pain through the Great Depression not produce fascist dictatorships? Why did most German workers, those who were worst affected by the Depression, not vote for the Nazi Party? Some of the insufficiencies of the economic theory are discussed by de Mause (2000) p 406. Traditional historians often overlook psychological factors. Fascism is, at its core, a

psychological phenomenon – this makes more sense when we consider what childhood was like for many Germans of that era. The Holocaust was largely the product of child abuse and neglect. Every holocaust in history has been the product of a holocaust against children.

[33] Ackerman and Du Vall (2000).

[34] Ackerman and Du Vall (2000) pp 207–240.

[35] Oliner (1988).

[36] Clendinnen (1999).

[37] See Henry, Houston and Mooney (2004).

[38] Human Rights and Equal Opportunity Commission (2004).

[39] Cantor, Neulinger and de Leo (2004).

[40] See 'Celebrities join Berlin anti-racism rally' (2000) CNN 9 November 2000 in http://www.cnn.com (last accessed 1 December 2004) and 'Germans unite against racism' (2000) BBC 9 November 2000 http://news.bbc.co.uk (last accessed 1 December 2004).

[41] 'Changing the future by confronting the past' is a full report of the 'Talks and testimonies' given at a convention held in Jerusalem on 17–20 April 2001, convened by the Evangelical Sisterhood of Mary of Darmstadt-Eberstadt, Germany. See also http://www.kanaan.org/main_frames.htm (last accessed 1 December 2004).

[42] Miller (1998) p 581.

[43] Miller (1998).

[44] Miller (1998).

[45] Bone (2003).

Postscript

[46] The Australian Democrats commonly refer to the imprisonment of children in immigration detention as "institutionalised child abuse": see http://www.democrats.org.au (last accessed 1 December 2004).

[47] Media officer for ChilOut (Children Out of Detention).

[48] Human Rights and Equal Opportunity Commission (2001) Media releases 28 November 2001. The inquiry considered whether Australia's immigration detention laws and its treatment of children in immigration detention complied with the United Nations Convention on the Rights of the Child (CROC): see the Human Rights and Equal Opportunity Commission (2004) introduction. See also Lateline (2001).

[49] The Department of Immigration and Multicultural and

Indigenous Affairs (DIMIA) and ACM were also consulted during the process and given several opportunities to make submissions and amendments to the report: Human Rights and Equal Opportunity Commission (2004).

[50] See Human Rights and Equal Opportunity Commission (2004) Chapter 3.

[51] Human Rights and Equal Opportunity Commission (2004) Chapter 9. National Council of Churches in Australia (NCCA) (2004). The NCCA consists of 15 major churches and has consistently called for the release of all children from immigration detention.

[52] Human Rights and Equal Opportunity Commission (2004) 17.3 The Inquiry's recommendations, Recommendation 1.

[53] 'HREOC inquiry into children in immigration report tabled' Joint media release VPS 68/2004.

[54] ChilOut http://www.chilout.org/ (last accessed 17 January 2004). On 6 July 2004, the Minister for Immigration stated that there was only one child left in immigration detention. The minister did not count the boat arrival children imprisoned in Nauru, Christmas Island or the Port Augusta Residential Housing Project, nor did she count children who arrived by plane imprisoned in Villawood, Maribyrnong and Baxter detention centres: Human Rights and Equal Opportunity Commission (2004) Press release 6 July 2004 http://www. humanrights.gov.au/media_releases/2004/40_04.htm   (last accessed 17 January 2004); Minister for Immigration and Multicultural and Indigenous Affairs (2004) Press release 6 July 2004 http://www.minister.immi.gov.au/media_releases/ media04/v04096.htm (last accessed 17 January 2004). Human Rights and Equal Opportunity Commission (2004) Press release 6 July 2004.

[55] ChilOut http://www.chilout.org/ (last accessed 17 January 2004).

[56] Lateline 12 May 2003 reported on a study compiled by 12 authors, including psychiatrists (with the backing of the Royal Australian and New Zealand College of Psychiatry), the New South Wales University and the New South Wales Institute of Psychiatry. In this report 95 per cent of the children reported seeing a physical assault; nearly 40 per cent claim to have been assaulted by camp officers; 25 per cent claim to have been kept in solitary confinement and around 10 per cent allege sexual harassment: see Royal Australian and New Zealand College of

Psychiatry http://www.ranzcp.org/ (last accessed 17 January 2004). See Steel and Silove (2001) pp 596–599; Norden (2004).

57 Reynolds (2004). The Australian Democrats constantly raise the issue of child welfare in detention: see http://www.democrats.org.au (last accessed 1 December 2004).

58 http://news.bbc.co.uk/1/hi/world/asia-pacific/1802364.stm

59 http://news.bbc.co.uk/1/hi/england/beds/bucks/herts/6710105.s

60 Independent, April 11, 2008. http://www.independent.co.uk/news/uk/home-news/mothers-detained-in-immigration-centre-hold-naked-protest-807802.html

14

RELIGIOUS EXTREMISM: A PARENTING STYLE

Religious organisations generally address our common need for spiritual sustenance, and for community. They uphold the concept of 'family' in an era when economic rationalism is tearing families apart. Historically, religions have spawned and championed countless humanitarian causes, such as the anti-slavery and (American) civil rights movements, Ghandist non-violence and the Islamic *zakat* (alms tax for the needy), to mention but a few. In modern times religious institutions have often been at the forefront of human rights and social justice movements. For instance, church authorities have stood up against repressive regimes in Latin America, and in Australia they are an essential part of the fight to protect the rights of asylum seekers (see Chapter 13 postscript).

This chapter, however, is not about religion *per se*. It is about the use of religious extremism, radicalism or fundamentalism as a rationalisation for repressive or punitive child-rearing styles. In contrast to mainstream religion, religious extremism has historically been associated with increased social and international violence. I simply wish to pose the question 'Might this have anything to do with the way religious extremist communities relate to children?'

Scriptures cannot be blamed for their believers' attitudes. We all interpret according to our personal predispositions, and therefore we each should be held responsible for our interpretations. Those who favour violence will find justifications for violence in any text. The rage of the battered and maltreated child lives on in an adult body, hiding itself behind scriptural justifications, insatiably seeking others to punish. Even if we give our hatred a religious rationale, what underlies it is always childhood pain.

Thus we persecute the infidel, or in the name of God and 'good discipline', we punish the next generation.

Religious extremism can therefore not be particularly associated with a specific denomination or sect. It is people, not texts, who perpetrate violence. In fact, extremism is not intrinsically problematic, unless it involves punitive approaches to child rearing.

What follows is a look at what social researchers have identified as the child rearing practices of extremists from four of the world's main religions.

Child rearing and Islamic extremism

Fundamentalist religious societies in general are patriarchal, and Islamic fundamentalism is no exception. In July 2002, the United Nations Development Program and the Arab Fund for Economic and Social Development jointly issued the 'Arab Human Development Report' (AHDR 2003) in order to assess blocks to development in the Arab world, where Islamic extremism has been enjoying an extensive revival. The report was compiled by a team of specialists from across the Arab region headed by Nader Fergany, director of the Cairo-based Almishkat Center for Research and Training. This report concluded that Arab women's economic and political participation is the lowest in the world.[1] It also underscored cultural blocks to development such as "authoritarian and over-protective child rearing ... curricula in schools that encourage submission, obedience, subordination and compliance rather than free critical thinking".[2]

The suppression of children increases in direct proportion to the degree of patriarchy and misogyny. In fact, punitive attitudes towards children seem to be a salient feature of fundamentalist communities. In Egypt, where fundamentalism is prominent, a report by the Department of Public Health in Alexandria,[3] stated that one in four Egyptian children had suffered injuries such as fractures, concussion or permanent disability as a result of parental 'discipline'. Radical Islam has embraced and propagated the African custom of female genital mutilation. Around the world, 130 million women have suffered this fate, dooming them to a life of sex without pleasure, or worse: making sex with their future husbands an excruciating ordeal.[4]

Throughout the Islamic world modernisation, liberalisation and moderate forces are at work. Fundamentalist politicians were soundly rejected by Malaysian voters in 2004. Reformists such as Iranian Jamaluddin Afghani and Egyptian Muhammad Abduh were agitating for a liberalisation of Islam as far back as the late 19th century.[5] Perhaps the advent of Islamic feminism constitutes one of the strongest contemporary bulwarks against archaic traditions. A growing number of voices from within the Muslim world are speaking out against oppression of women and children.

One such voice is that of Moroccan scholar, Fatna A Sabbah,[6] who says that fundamentalists expect women to be silent and immobile, to act meek and remain with eyes downcast, and to lead a life of near-total seclusion. Women in fundamentalist families, as depicted by Sabbah, are possessed as property, shunned as temptresses, and blamed as the inspirers of lust — an evil and destructive emotion. When a mother is crushed underfoot, and when she lives under threat of violence, how can she be the kind of mother she wants to be, the mother her children need her to be? Children are the ultimate victims when their mothers live in bondage.

Palestinian researchers Haj-Yahia and Tamish[7] echo Sabbah's assertion that women are given a low status because traditionally, they are seen as the source of evil and anarchy. They demonstrate how this attitude to women has had disastrous ramifications in traditional communities. Female victims of sexual abuse are often accused of bringing the abuse upon themselves. A family's honour is based on the sexual purity of its girls and women. Since a girl's 'loss of honour' reflects on her whole family, even if she has been raped, she risks severe punishment for being found out. This makes girls easy targets for sexual abuse. Meanwhile boys, from a very young age, are pressured to be overly aggressive and dominant. The genders thus become polarised to extremes of hyper-masculinity and ultra-submission.

Much of what researchers Haj-Yahia and Tamish have to say about Arab families would be enviable by western standards. For instance, traditional Arab families are known for their generosity and hospitality. Children certainly benefit from the kind of security that the Arab extended family, with its shared or communal parenting practices, can provide. However, wherever traditional patriarchy has not been tempered by modernisation, gender roles and relations are still rigidly — even violently — delineated.

The imprint of Islamic fundamentalism on parenting and family dynamics has been closely studied in Saudi Arabia. Two extensive and independent surveys of Saudi Arabian families were conducted by Arab academics Soraya Altorki[8] and Mona AlMunajjed.[9] Both reported a kind of sexual apartheid, where women were segregated from men at home, in most public buildings and in public transport. Even at university, male teachers were viewed by female students through closed circuit TV. At the time of conducting her survey in the 1970s, Altorki was not even able to move around on her own, unchaperoned. As an anthropologist, she considered Saudi Arabia one of the most closed cultures in the world.

As in other fundamentalist havens, a Saudi family's honour is tied to its women's sexual conduct, and to the males' capacity to control their women. Strict codes of honour are the prime responsibility of women, and the slightest infractions – which include talking or flirting with unrelated males – bring shame upon their family. Women are severely punished by their own male relatives, and the penalty for adultery is death. Male infidelity, on the other hand, is tolerated, though it is preferred that philandering is done with non-Saudi women. If sex occurs outside the rigidly prescribed boundaries, the woman is invariably blamed for leading the man astray. In marriage, her duty is to be sexually available to her husband – whether or not she chose, through love, to be his betrothed.

The suspicion and disgust with which feminine sexuality is viewed by fundamentalists is unfathomable. Only recently, religious police in Saudi Arabia forced 15 girls back into a burning building. Their crime? Trying to escape with their lives, uncovered by traditional dress. For this infraction they were burnt to death.[10]

In Saudi homes, obedience to the father or husband is usually the overriding principle. Most children and women do not leave their homes without permission – a privilege that is infrequently granted by the male heads of the household. From both women and children, total obedience is expected, and children are obligated to their parents for life. They are told that they are doomed to hell, after judgement day, if they displease their parents. At the time of Altorki's survey in the 1970s, children were still expected to stand when adults entered the room, and to kiss their hands in the morning, and not to laugh 'excessively'. The Saudi father loomed as a distant and aloof disciplinarian. His children always stood in his presence, and they were never observed by the researcher to defy him.

Interestingly, AlMunajjed found that as modernisation chips away at patriarchal oppression, children are gradually treated with more kindness and patience. It is precisely this kind of reform, as we will see later, that will allow democratisation to evolve naturally throughout Arab societies.

Though there are signs of change toward liberalisation, until recently Saudi marriages were arranged, based on commercial or status-related considerations. A 'dowry' was paid for the bride by the groom's father, and partners did not see each other until their wedding day. Obedience, instead of love, was the glue that kept the family together.

Al Munajjed insists that patriarchal tribalism has distorted the true message of Islam, which originally was infinitely more liberal toward women. Middle Eastern writer and journalist Ziauddin Sardar argues that nowadays, the puritan imposition of Shari'a Law – which entraps countries like Sudan and Saudi Arabia – is not based on the teachings of the Koran.[11] In Sardar's opinion it was constructed by jurists in the Abassid period, between the 8th and 13th centuries. Shari'a Law erases many of the egalitarian teachings of the Koran, says AlMunajjed, which explicitly recommends the empowerment of women in the spheres of politics, religion, commerce, and education. According to Amina Wadud, Islamic Studies Professor, contrary to the practice found in many Islamic regimes, the Koran guarantees women rights to inheritance, independent property, divorce, and the right to testify in a court of law, and it forbids violence against women and girls.[12] Edicts such as these go unheeded in conservative Islamic regimes.

Elsewhere, in Afghanistan, a survey of women recently conducted by Physicians for Human Rights found that under the yoke of the extremist Taliban regime, 78 per cent suffered symptoms of a major depression. More than one in every three women admitted having suffered at least one incident of serious physical abuse, such as beating, rape or detention. Even in parts of Afghanistan not controlled by the Taliban, over half of all women suffered from symptoms of major depression.[13]

In recognition that violence in the family home is endemic in many Islamic nations, a manual for combating this problem was recently developed.[14] This manual was compiled by a largely Muslim group of women campaigning against the high incidence of violence in radical Muslim families. It highlights the existence of stoning for adulterous women, polygamy, child marriage, and grossly unequal grounds for divorce; across a range of countries where fundamentalist Islam is powerful. The manual also exposes the loathsome custom of 'honour killing',[15] which, it states, is common in Jordan, Turkey, Iraq, Syria, Egypt, Lebanon, the Gulf countries and in Palestinian territories. ('Honour killing' of women and girls is rare in the non-Islamic world, but exists to a lesser degree in Ecuador, Brazil and Uganda.) As an example of honour killing in Jordan a father stabbed his daughter in the groin because she had gone unaccompanied to talk to a boy. She was left to bleed to death.[16] This kind of incident is not unusual, according to this manual, and honour killings are actually on the increase in the Middle East.

A girl's own father, brother or uncle can kill her if she is perceived to have brought shame upon her family. The dishonourable acts which merit her murder range from chatting to a neighbour, holding hands with a man other than her husband, flirting, indulging in illicit or pre-marital affairs, committing adultery, and in some places being the victim of rape. In the community's eyes, the family's name and reputation will not be cleansed until the offending girl is brutally killed. The more brutal the killing, the more complete the restoration of the family's honour, and so victims tend to be strangled, knifed or hacked to death. Only those whose hearts are already brutalised through years of abuse could possibly accept this kind of atrocity in their community, let alone perpetrate it. In some Islamic countries, women who report being raped face adultery charges and the possibility of jail or even death by stoning.[17]

Honour killings are most common in Pakistan, and the government's response to this custom has left a lot to be desired. Most cases go unpunished, and even those who are prosecuted receive lenient sentences. Several hundred honour killings are reported each year in Pakistan, and it is estimated that many more go unreported.[18] Honour killing is also found in Palestinian territories. In 1997, Khaled Al-Qudra, Attorney General of the Palestinian National Authority, said that he suspected 70 per cent of all murders in Gaza and the West Bank were honour killings.[19] In Jordan, where a forensic medical examiner estimated that 25 per cent of all murders are honour killings, the Criminal Code is explicitly and selectively lenient towards the perpetrator.[20] 'Honour' in this twisted form, seems to be valued above love and life.

A recent Pakistani conference on child abuse reported

a huge incidence of infanticide, abandonment, and violent physical abuse throughout the nation. Islamic schools in Pakistan are found to practice severe forms of corporal punishment. According to *The State of Pakistan's Children – 1998*, Pakistan tolerates a very large number of child workers: 3.3 million aged between five and 14, or one in 12 of all in this age bracket. The female literacy rate is 24 per cent – half of the male rate. The state of Balochistan has the lowest level of female education in the world: two per cent. Though Pakistan is a signatory to the United Nations Convention on the Rights of the Child, it does not enact its obligations under this charter. Governmental foot-dragging ensures the dereliction of its duty to establish and protect children's rights. From 1990–1997, central government expenditure was 31 per cent for defence, two per cent for education, and one per cent for health.[21] A conservative estimate of Pakistan's Infant Mortality Rate (as at 1998) was 9.5 per cent – the highest in the world.[22] How might this level of attention to children's wellbeing impact on this nation's quality of democracy, its state of social harmony and cohesion, and its foreign policy? Could this explain the preponderance of militant groups who find haven in parts of this country?

This report on Pakistan's children has been updated and a 2004 edition has been released (at http://www.sparcpk.org). This version finds that the Pakistani government has made some effort to improve children's educational opportunities, but their efforts have been rather slow and insufficient. The section on violence against children reports that it is rising, and it is carried out with impunity. There is a tacit acceptance of abuse and violence in many areas of Pakistani society, and unchecked cultural practices that aid and abet violence against children. The practice of child marriage continues unchallenged, particularly in the rural areas of Pakistan. The child labour situation is 'dismal' and getting worse. If the lack of educational opportunities exposes children to violent influences, so does an education system that has been annexed by radical religion. The recently imprisoned Abu Bakar Bashir, accused of masterminding numerous terrorist strikes around the world including the Bali bombings of 2002, was also head of a boarding school in Java which is notorious for militant religious indoctrination.[23] Too often when a government fails to provide well for education, the slack is taken up by well-funded religious–extremist groups eager to indoctrinate children's minds.

148

The long-standing troubles in the Middle East have had disastrous worldwide ramifications. Israelis have been relentlessly attacked, and the Palestinian people have suffered considerable injustice and human rights violations (the latter has been acknowledged by rabbinical sources).[24] A significant element of the Palestinian 'Intifada' – literal translation is 'shrugging off' – was originally based on a movement committed to non-violent resistance led by Palestinian–American psychologist, Mubarak Awad.[25] So far, militarism has done nothing but scuttle Awad's work and undermine the Palestinian cause. Violent extremists have reversed the gains made by the non-violent elements of the Palestinian struggle, and contributed to a bloody stalemate in the Middle East. Could it be that the choice of brutal means has more to do with people's own childhood trauma, than with the historical injustices they are trying to redress?

A clarion call for peaceful reform comes in Irshad Manji's: 'The Trouble with Islam' (Random House, Sydney, 2003). Manji gives testimony through her own life experience and Islamic education to the misogyny endemic to many sections of Islam, and calls for feminist reform throughout the Islamic world. Manji focuses on cultural reform as essential to addressing the root causes of violence and of terrorism. Reforms to gender relations and family dynamics – by implication child-rearing reforms – have historically been effective where a 'War on Terror' cannot hope to be. It is these kinds of reforms that the relatively democratic nations should be sponsoring in authoritarian states.

Some of the recent developments in the Arab world offer signs of a growing rejection of authoritarianism. Multi-party elections have taken place in Egypt and Kuwait, and municipal elections were allowed in Saudi Arabia along with promises to give women the vote in four years.. Millions of Iraqis braved dangers to cast their votes. At the time of writing, a massive wave of peaceful demonstrations in Lebanon – pertinently, one of the most modern and gender-egalitarian of Arab nations – ousted a repressive, Syrian-backed government. No doubt some analysis will credit western interventions (such as the American-led military invasion of Iraq) for igniting this liberating chain of events throughout the Middle East. I contend that this sustained, popular insistence on liberalisation could not have taken root had it not been already manifesting itself in recent decades in modern Arab family dynamics.

Child rearing and Hindu extremism

Much of India is progressive, modern and tolerant, as evidenced by the recent election results in which for the first time a non-Hindu was chosen as prime minister. But religious extremism thrives in a number of Indian provinces, where, in accordance with ancient tradition, each year hundreds of women are burned alive, where female infanticide continues, and where, to a much lesser degree, even child sacrifice is not unheard of – among some radical sects.[26]

As elsewhere around the world, the suffering of children bears sour socio-political fruit. In 2002, more than 1000 people, mostly Muslims, died in inter-religious violence in the Indian state of Gujarat. Bellicose Hindu-extremist leaders earned the censure of Amnesty International, who even accused the ruling party, BJP, of sponsoring violent vigilante attacks against Muslims.[27] Reportedly, some prominent Hindu leaders publicly warned Muslims that a certain "Hindu deity wears a garland of human heads", that a third of Indian Muslims – amounting to 50 million people – should be executed, and that what happened in Gujarat would happen throughout India.[28] The extremists who made those public statements would surely have earned the most stringent condemnation from Mahatma Gandhi, if he was still alive.

Child rearing and Christian extremism

In the Christian world, religious fundamentalism is characterised by the insistence upon a literal, non-interpretive reading of the Bible. Christian fundamentalism is often associated with the belief that human history will come to an end in the near future in an apocalyptic battle between forces of good and evil.[29]

Christian fundamentalism emerged in the USA around the time of Charles Darwin, as a reaction against the growing influence of scientific thought. The World Christian Fundamentals Association was formed in 1919.[30]

As the boundaries between mainstream faith and fundamentalism are open to debate, it is impossible to decide how many of the world's estimated two billion Christians[31] can be categorised as fundamentalists. One source[32] estimated in 1996 that there are 60 million in the USA, with a growing worldwide following. In the same year, another survey[33] stated that only nine per cent of Americans considered themselves as fundamentalists, although – seemingly in contradiction – 54 per cent insisted upon a word-for-word literal interpretation of the Bible.

Are there distinguishing features in the way Christian fundamentalists relate to children? It does appear so, according to a number of studies showing that Biblical literalists practice more authoritarian child-rearing methods than mainstream Christian families. A recent American survey compared hundreds of parents belonging to Christian denominations espousing literal, versus non-literal interpretations of the Bible.[34] The survey was intended to measure the social impact of Biblical passages that seemingly encourage parents to corporally punish their children.[35] The most well-known of these being Proverbs 13:24, which says, "He who spares his rod hates his son". The Book of Deuteronomy contains a recommendation that rebellious sons should be stoned to death.[36]

The researchers found that members of literalist denominations were significantly more inclined to hit their children. What's more, literalist parents had more inappropriate expectations from their children, and showed less empathy toward their needs.[37] Several surveys conducted since[38] have consistently replicated these findings. In the USA, the corporal punishment of children is most favoured in the southern and mid-western states known colloquially as the 'Bible Belt'. Two fundamentalist parenting manuals in the USA have offered this advice: "The spanking ... should be painful and it should last until the child's will is broken" and "Even though Mom spanks him, he wins the battle by defying her once again. The solution to this situation is obvious: outlast him; win".[39]

The corporal punishment of children is anything but synonymous with Christianity, and some Christian groups are salient for their stance against it. In the USA for example, a General Conference of the United Methodist Church has passed a resolution calling for the complete abolition of corporal punishment.[40] Citing the teachings of Jesus, the group 'Christians for Non-Violent Parenting' aims to persuade Americans to reject corporal punishment at home, school and at childcare facilities.[41] Some of the most authoritative, empathic and scientifically sound parenting manuals have been written by Christian authors.[42]

Fundamentalist groups, on the other hand, are notorious for their accent on obedience. One Missouri reform school for troubled teenagers purporting to use Biblical methods has been the subject of many allegations of physical abuse.[43] In a Texan home for girls run by a Christian group, girls were subjected to whippings, paddlings, hours of kneeling on hard floors and solitary confinement.[44] A nun from a Canadian religious commune faced charges of assaulting children in her care, to some of whom she had administered over 30 blows at a time. In court, she was cool and unrepentant as she recounted how God had instructed her to paddle the children, and she maintained that her punitive practices were in accordance with scripture. The judge ruled that her discipline methods constituted abuse, and police were called in to remove children from the commune for their safety.[45] Also in Canada, a judge ordered the removal of seven children from parents belonging to a fundamentalist denomination, as their parents had been assaulting them with implements such as belts and clothes-hangers. In court, the parents and their pastor defended their brand of 'discipline' as prescribed by scripture.[46] Their solution? Twenty-eight of the mothers belonging to this denomination fled across the border, where they found a legal haven for their spanking habits.[47] In Georgia, USA, authorities acted to protect 60 children who had been severely beaten by parents and church leaders, under supervision from their church elder. When the church leaders were charged with cruelty to children, the parents refused court rulings to tone down their abusive practices, protesting that they were raising kids according to the Bible.[48] Some of the harshest detention centres in America for 'reforming' unruly or substance-addicted youths are run by church groups. They have attracted considerable media attention for their commitment to corporal punishment – often severe.[49]

Twenty-two American states still allow corporal punishment in schools, where teachers favour the use a long-handled wooden paddle to redden their pupils' buttocks. The states that hold on to this approach to 'discipline' are strongholds of conservative Protestantism. How successful is this approach to 'discipline'? The 10 states that paddle students most frequently (in order: Arkansas, Mississippi, Alabama, Tennessee, Georgia, Texas, Louisiana, Oklahoma, South Carolina, Missouri) have higher murder rates, and higher incarceration rates.[50]

The conservative Christian approach to pedagogy, with its tolerance for corporal punishment, is by no means limited to the USA. When the caning of school children was recently abolished in the Australian state of New South Wales, religious schools were conspicuous for voicing strong objections.[51] In the state of Victoria corporal punishment is banned from public and Catholic schools, but remains legal for independent schools. In 2001, a Victorian Christian Community Schools group issued a statement saying "the hand or flat instrument on the buttocks is appropriate in some circumstances".[52] Meanwhile, an Australian man was awarded an enormous sum of money in damages for the strapping he received as a boy in a religious school.[53] In South Africa, where the corporal punishment of children is banned from schools, a Christian organisation representing 196 schools lobbied to have this ban lifted, on grounds of 'religious freedom'.[54] Near to the time of writing, the principals of four Christian schools in the UK attempted to overturn a ban on corporal punishment on the basis that this ban infringed on their human rights. This move was rejected by the House of Lords.[55]

Child rearing and Jewish religious extremism

Despite Israel's strong democracy and a majority population of liberal, mainstream orthodox and secular individuals, Jewish religious extremism is still a powerful force. According to the ex-chairman of the Israeli League of Human Rights, Israel Shahak, only 20 per cent of Israelis are considered religious, and perhaps only five or six per cent[56] belong to radical extremes of religion. (Jewish religious extremism must be distinguished from the highly developed tradition of reformist and liberal Judaism – they are poles apart on many key issues. It should also not be confused with moderate orthodox communities.) Since the racism and sexism of Jewish religious extremists are virtually unknown outside Israel, says Shahak,[57] the degree of their oppressiveness would surprise and shock most of the world's Jewry. On the other hand, secular and moderate religious Jews dwelling in Israel, are painfully aware of this small but politically powerful extremist minority.

In his two books *Jewish History, Jewish Religion* (1994), and *Jewish Fundamentalism in Israel* (1999), Shahak describes the family dynamics of the Jewish religious extremists as patriarchal domains, where the education of children is dominated by the grandfather and women 'know their place'. According to Shahak, rigidity in sexual mores is manifest through strict regulation of male and female roles, as well as draconian attitudes on sexual preference. This is what prompted liberal Rabbi Donna Berman to write in protest about the "many centuries of Jewish misogyny", calling for Jews to "honestly confront the sexism inherent in our tradition".[58]

Some Israeli religious extremists repeatedly refer to women engaged in politics as witches, bitches or demons.[59] The same extremists forbid women from driving taxis or buses, or from taking up any employment where they might lead or oversee men. Just as in Saudi Arabia, the most extreme sects advocate the separation of men and women in public places. In some neighbourhoods, women who go about 'immodestly' dressed have been insulted or beaten. Men are forbidden to listen to the voices of women singing, for this is a sin as grave as adultery.[60] This stands in contrast to the relatively gender-egalitarian attitude of the Jewish mainstream.

It should be emphasised that religious attitudes such as these are not representative of mainstream Jewish faith. What's more, Jewish religious practice is traditionally characterised by open debate rather than by dogma. Harsh and authoritarian upbringing is not a salient feature of mainstream Jewish culture. A survey conducted in the USA in 1965 found that Jewish ethnicity was proportionally under-represented in national statistics of child abuse, domestic violence, alcohol and drug abuse.[61]

Shahak introduces readers to communities in Israel whose children are trapped in religious schools where 'secular' subjects such as mathematics, science and literature are eclipsed, and where they are forced daily to cram religious scriptures for hours on end. The head of the more extreme *yeshiva* (scriptural schools) has absolute authority. In Shahak's view, he even arranges marriages for the students – an act that violates international human rights conventions. Students are excluded from the outside world and are forbidden contact with 'unbelievers'. Once they reach the age of 16, they are indoctrinated with scriptural texts for 12–14 hours a day. Each day contains tedious study of God's punishments, which threaten to befall those who have the temerity to break religious rules. God is believed to punish all Jews for communal lapses in Talmudic adherence – even children! Incredibly, there have been rabbis who professed that the Holocaust was one such punishment.[62] What kind of attitude towards children, and towards justice generally, would have to precede the acceptance of the idea that children should be horribly and fatally punished for their parents' lapses in piousness? What happens to the hearts and minds of children who are shut off from the rich and diverse world that surrounds them, and shackled daily to the study of such a vengeful God?

When, in the year 2000, Israel became the tenth country to abolish all corporal punishment against children, strong opposition came from religious circles invoking Biblical and Talmudic sources.[63] In keeping with world trends, a survey conducted by a major Israeli newspaper found a broader acceptance of corporal punishment among religious communities.[64] The acceptability of corporal punishment among conservative religious schools was cited in an Israeli court, in defence of a rabbi and teacher who was recently jailed for child abuse.[65]

Besides Shahak, a number of analysts (Marc Ellis, (1999) Jewish theologian and professor of American and Jewish studies, Yehoshafat Harkabi, (1988) professor of International Relations and Middle East Studies and ex-intelligence advisor to the Israeli Prime Minister, and Uriel Tal, (1985) professor of Jewish History at Tel Aviv University) have commented that the influence of religious extremism on Israeli politics has been deleterious, having contributed to a hardening of Israeli domestic and foreign policy. Opinion surveys have shown that secular Israelis see Jewish religious extremists as a greater threat to Israel than that posed by Arabs.[66] Liberal Jewish religious groups, on the other hand, are vigorous activists for justice and peace in Israel and the Middle East.[67]

Despite all the violence that plagues our world, humanity is witnessing a remarkable growth of democracy and respect for human rights, beyond what has ever been known. The following chapter looks at how the evolution in child rearing has fuelled this welcome trend.

Endnotes

[1]   Hewitt (2003).
[2]   Raphaeli (2003).
[3]   Youssef, Attia and Kamel (1998).
[4]   De Mause (2002b) p 341, (2001) p 384.
[5]   Sardar (2002).
[6]   Sabbah (1984).
[7]   Haj-Yahia and Tamish (2001).
[8]   Altorki (1986).
[9]   AlMunajjed (1997).
[10] 'Saudi Arabia – improperly dressed' (2002) *Time* (1 April 2002) p 12.

[11]   Sardar (2002).

[12]   Wadud (2003).

[13]   See Physicians for Human Rights http://www.phrusa.org/ (last accessed 1 December 2004).

[14]   Afkhami (1998).

[15]   Honour killing is when a male member of the family kills a female relative for tarnishing the family image.

[16]   Afkhami (1998) p 47.

[17]   Terzieff (2004); Mydans (2002).

[18]   United Nations Foundation (2003); Amnesty International USA (2004) 'Violence against women continues: Pakistan' http://www.amnestyusa.org/women/interact/women_pakistan.html (last accessed 1 December 2004), 'Pakistan: human rights concerns, women and religious minorities at risk' http://www.amnestyusa.org/countries/pakistan/summary.do (last accessed 1 December 2004).

[19]   Ruggi (2004). To find 'Women and the United Nations – Directory' (Autumn 2002) p 5 search http://www.findarticles.com (last accessed 1 December 2004).

[20]   Hewitt (2003) p 65.

[21]   Ahmad (1999) p 119.

[22]   Ahmad (1999) p 124.

[23]   Powell (2002).

[24]   Ellis (1999); Cohn-Sherbok and el-Alami (2002); Rabbis for Human Rights http://www.rhr.israel.net/ (last accessed 1 December 2004).

[25]   Ackerman and Du Vall (2000) pp 397–420.

[26]   Atapur (2002).

[27]   See the September 2002 issue of Amnesty International's monthly magazine *The Wire* available at http://web.amnesty.org/web/wire.nsf/september2002/Gujarat (last accessed 1 December 2004).

[28]   'Hindu right threatens to strike Islam' (2002) *The Australian* 23 October 2002 p 9; Perry (2003). For a summary of events in 2003 relating to religious extremism and India see Amnesty International Report 2003 http://web.amnesty.org/report2003/ind-summary-eng (last accessed 1 December 2004).

[29]   Milburn and Conrad (1996) p 75.

[30]   Family Encyclopedia of World History 1996, Reader's Digest.

[31]   'Alive and kicking – the facts' (2004) *New Internationalist* August 2004 Vol 370 p 18.

32   *Family Encyclopedia of World History 1996* Reader's Digest.

33   Milburn and Conrad (1996) p 76.

34   Wiehe (1990).

35   Proverbs 13:24, 19:18, 22:15, 23:13–14, 29:15.

36   Deuteronomy 21:21.

37   Wiehe (1990).

38   Grasmick, Bursik and Kimpel (1991); Grasmick, Morgan, Kennedy (1992); Ellison and Sherkat (1993); Ellison, Bartkowski and Segal (1996); Gershoff, Miller and Holden (1999).

39   Quoted in Milburn and Conrad (1996) p 76.

40   'Getting your state to ban corporal punishment: a youth campaign to end school corporal punishment' http://www.stophitting.com/disatschool/YouthCampaign.php (last accessed 1 December 2004).

41   See Christians for Non-Violent Parenting in Project No Spank http://www.nospank.net/cnpindex.htm (last accessed 1 December 2004).

42   For example, Sears (2001); Hendrix and Hunt (1997).

43   'Acting on faith: desperate parents; unregulated reform schools in Missouri' *St Louis Post–Dispatch* 19 November 2002 see Project No Spank http://www.nospank.net/n-j70.htm (last accessed 1 December 2004).

44   Colloff (2001).

45   Cox (2002); CBC news 26 October 2002: see Project No Spank http://www.nospank.net/n-j68.htm (last accessed 1 December 2004).

46   Blatchford (2002).

47   Clairbourne (2001).

48   Firestone (2001).

49   Kilzer (1998). A sizeable compilation of media reports on the pedagogical methods used by many fundamentalist Christian institutions can be found at http://www.nospank.net/ (click on these links, 'Flogging for God' and 'Boot camp for kids') (last accessed 1 December 2004).

50   Guthrow (1998).

51   Baird and Verghis (2000); Noonan (2000).

52   Tomazin (2004).

53   'Man awarded $2.5 million for strapping' *National Nine News* 14 February 2001; Connolly (2001).

54   Maurel (2001).

55   Howard S (2005); See 'UK: Christian Schools Lose Smacking Legal Battle', News.scottsman.com, 24 February 2005 at http://

nospank.net/n-o17r.htm (last accessed 13 April 2005)

[56] Shahak (1994); Shahak and Mezvinsky (1999).

[57] Shahak and Mezvinsky (1999).

[58] Berman (1995).

[59] Shahak and Mezvinsky (1999).

[60] Shahak and Mezvinsky (1999).

[61] Breiner (1990) p 215.

[62] Harkabi (1988).

[63] Ezer (2003).

[64] 'Not with brawn but with brains' *Yedi'ot Aharonot* 2 January 2000 p 7.

[65] See Itim (2004).

[66] Ben Cramer (2004).

[67] See the website of Rabbis for Human Rights http://www.rhr. israel.net/ (last accessed 1 December 2004).

15

CHILD-REARING REFORMS:
THE SEEDS OF DEMOCRACY
AND HUMAN RIGHTS

If abusive and authoritarian upbringing leads to war and political tyranny, what kinds of social change are brought about when a large enough proportion of any population shifts to more supportive and empathic parenting? In this chapter we will look at the growth of democracy and social justice in nations such as France, the USA and Sweden, and how these developments have closely followed child rearing reforms.

Further on, we will look at some of the remarkable social changes brought about by the advent of modern child rearing (socialising mode) in the 20th century. Even more exciting improvements in social harmony and sustainability will be possible as 'helping mode' or natural parenting styles begin to germinate. Whenever I look at this historical and sociological data I'm reassured that prioritising support for families and child rearing will produce inestimable social rewards. I have found this discovery extremely encouraging – a sense I wish to share through this chapter.

Early French flirtations with democracy
One of the most significant turning points in history, a cataclysmic moment which marked the birth of modern nation-state democracy, was the French Revolution of 1789. Though French democracy was to falter and stumble many times, with governments often reverting to tyranny or military rule, the remarkable events of 1789 and the years that followed shunted the world toward democracy beyond the point of no return. Some of the more momentous products of the French Revolution

included the Declaration of the Rights of Man and of the Citizen, the abolition of feudal power, of church power, and aristocratic privilege. For the first time a nation upheld that its citizens (though at first only males) – rather than individuals claiming the fatuous doctrine of 'Divine right' – are the only legitimate source of civic power. Certainly, the ideals of liberty, fraternity, and equality remain incompletely manifest in modern democracies, but it is clear that they germinated in the collective imagination of the French middle class toward the end of the 18th century. For the first time, masses of ordinary people stood up to oppressive authority, and demanded more freedom, equality and respect for human rights than had ever been available in any nation.

Undoubtedly, there are many factors which helped to precipitate the birth of French democracy. But what was it that enabled the psychological shift in the minds of the many who came to be convinced that a freer society was possible? What made the emergence of democratic thinking, and the progressive ideas that were expounded in the French Revolution, possible in the minds of so many French citizens? It is no accident that this maturation in French society followed a transformation in parent–child relations that had begun one generation earlier.

The ideas of 'family love' and 'mother love' first appeared in French literature in the middle of the 18th century. For the first time publications dealing with parenting issues began to emphasise parents' obligations to their children, rather than the reverse. If the concept of 'mother love' as depicted in Jean-Jacques Rousseau's highly influential *Emile* seems unremarkable now it was a revolutionary idea in 1762, the year of publication. The French Revolution, a fulcrum in the history of democracy, came 27 years later.

During the 1760s in France, a flurry of publications urging mothers to keep their own babies at home and to breastfeed them appeared. Although still rife in 1780, the practice of wet-nursing had begun its decline in 1770. The horrendous statistics relating to its incidence in 1780 indicated that authorities had begun to take an interest in measuring, then curbing this disastrous practice. Though it took decades for wet-nursing to disappear, increasing numbers of French babies were remaining near their mothers through the 1760s. These developments in child rearing, affecting firstly the French middle class, were sufficient to sow the seeds of a more liberal society. The French middle class was the main intellectual driving force behind the Revolution.

The emergence of this new appreciation of children was sufficient to ignite a spark of democratic thinking – alas, it was not to be too much more than an ideal for some time to come. Rousseau himself proved unable to live up to his own ideals of a loving parent – he abandoned all his children in foundling homes. Soon after this initial burst of democratic reform, revolutionaries in power seemed unready to sustain democratic responsibilities, and the nation slid into mob rule and terror. Child-rearing innovations were slow to spread to a majority, and a limited French democracy and dictatorship interchanged for a century. Nevertheless, the core democratic values were never to be entirely rubbed out, and France became an example for other nations to follow. Once the virus of democracy was caught, it remained entrenched in the social organism, and France continued its march toward democracy, thanks to the process begun in 1789. Further hallmarks of social justice, such as universal suffrage and fair labour laws, were to develop just as in other democracies, in step with additional improvements in child rearing.

American reforms set the pace

At around the same time, in 1790, the USA was to become the most democratic nation at that time. What was it that released the fierce individualism that fashioned, through the American Revolution, the world's first enduring nation-state democracy, producing also the most liberal society of the times? What was it that enabled democracy to gain its tentative toehold in the New World while it faltered in Europe? American achievements included: gradual abolition of slavery (in northern states to begin with), banning of hereditary titles, and the breaking down of the political powers of the church. Enshrined in the 1791 Bill of Rights were freedom of speech, press, worship and assembly. These were all quantum leaps toward a fairer and freer society at the time. However, America's fledgling democracy was deficient, as it excluded women and non-whites and even today, American democracy is quite flawed.[1] Nevertheless, despite these failings, this embryonic 'democracy' created in 1790 was a significant discontinuity in history, a social 'great leap forward' in which the USA was – at the time – the undisputed leader. American prosperity has been the reward for a culture whose support for the individual, and for freedom of self-expression, has set a benchmark for the world to aspire to. Pioneering Americans dabbling with democratic processes provided a powerful example that helped other nations follow suit. Why did these liberal forces gain such momentum in the North American colonies, in particular, and not in other resource-rich colonies or countries?

Lloyd de Mause's research has unearthed a clear pattern of child-rearing reforms that produced individuals who, relative to their times, were more emotionally mature.[2] It was these individuals who blazed a trail for modern egalitarianism, respect for basic human rights and freedom of thought.

What de Mause's research uncovered is that the bulk of the people who fought (with quite a bit of fervour and subsequent success) for the values of liberty, equality and fairness, were drawn from waves of middle class English migrant families and their descendants. These families came from a time and strategy of English society that, around the 17th century, produced a turning point in the evolution of childhood. To begin with, there is evidence that the practice of infanticide – mostly of daughters – then commonplace throughout Europe, had abated and all but ended in England by this time. Census figures showed that whereas boys had previously outnumbered girls by about one third, the ratio had evened up by the 17th century. England was at the time about a century ahead of France and 200 years ahead of the rest of Europe in such key indices as the decline of infanticide, the rejection of baby swaddling, and the cessation of farming out babies to wet-nurses. Mainland Europeans were still practicing abusive 'purification' rites on babies and children. England was ahead of other European nations in child rearing, but it was particularly middle class parents among whom close and nurturant parent–child bonding appeared for the first time.[3]

From the start then, parents in the American colonies, particularly in the north-east, were measurably closer to and more nurturant toward their children. It was the first time in western history that mothers were beginning to spend significant time empathically caring for their infants. Colonial America had the most even boy:girl ratio and the least child abandonment and infanticide in the world. At a time when abandoned infants could still be found in European streets, 'foundlings' were comparatively low in numbers in American cities, as noted by European travellers. In 1685 it was remarkable, and worthy of note, for English traveller Samuel Sewall to record the "first child that ever was…exposed in Boston".[4] The rates of infanticide and abandonment were much lower than anywhere in Europe, and thus the need for foundling homes was drastically reduced. Except among some of the stricter, more authoritarian religious communities, the wet-nursing, swaddling, and cold disciplinarianism that prevailed in Europe was largely absent from the American colonies. Before becoming the doyens of the world's first democratic nation, the Americans were also the first to end wet-nursing and swaddling.[5]

Children of early American colonists tended to be breastfed on demand, a significant advantage over their European counterparts.[6] European visitors to these colonies during the 17th century frequently commented on the greater liberty, precociousness and self-assurance of American-born children. Europeans were often shocked by American children's tendency to be outspoken and go about unchaperoned. Many of these children did not exhibit the unquestioning obedience instilled in their European counterparts. (Notable exceptions existed among Puritans, who preached minimal affection, strict obedience, and who frequently sent their children away to work for friends or relatives.)[7] In addition, the USA was to become the earliest country to set up mass public schooling, and one of the earliest to campaign —with limited success – against the beating of children both at home and at school. The state of New Hampshire abolished corporal punishment in schools toward the end of the 19th century. It was this unusual concentration of comparatively advanced parenting that caused American social structures to evolve beyond the rest of the contemporary world.

In contrast to the migration of colonists into New England, which generally contained more 'advanced' parents, the demographic profile of migrants to the south was quite different. Many of those who migrated to the south did not do so as intact families: these waves of migration comprised a high proportion of indentured (abandoned) children. Migrant families who came to the southern colonies were on average less educated, and they practiced more old-fashioned forms of parenting. As a result, the south lagged significantly behind the north in their average style of child rearing.[8] The cultural lag of the south was most evident in their defence of slavery during the American Civil War.

In the north-east, it was those Americans who had been allowed to be closer to their parents than anyone before in history, who formed the driving force behind American liberalism and the formulation of the Bill of Rights.

In recent years, however, the USA has fallen from its historic position of leadership in terms of human social advancement. There are probably many factors contributing to this, but it's worth taking into account the failure to progress on children's wellbeing.

On most key indicators, the care of children in USA lags badly behind the rest of the industrialized world. Corporal punishment is still legal in schools in 22 states (for a fuller discussion on this, see chapter 17), and there is a plethora of American parenting literature, much of it religious in nature, which instructs parents on how to use corporal punishment on their children.

The impact of TV viewing – its amount, and its content – means that by age 18, the average young American will have viewed 200,000 acts of violence on television alone; there are now many well-conducted studies that link this to increases in aggressive behaviour and attitude [9].

The USA has one of the lowest maternity leave provisions in the world [10]. It has the second worst newborn death rate in the developed world (www.thebusinessofbeingborn.com) and a very low percentage of babies born in Baby Friendly Hospital (BFHI) (see page 00). In 2007, the USA earned second last place in UNICEF's list rating children's wellbeing among 21 of the world's affluent and developed nations (the UK was at the bottom) [11]. In addition, the USA remains one of only two nations, along with Somalia, not to have signed the UN Convention on the Rights of the Child.

Sweden reaps benefits of better nurturance of children

One of the world's leading examples of peace and social justice achieved through child-rearing reform exists in Sweden. How did the Swedes manage, despite their relative scarcity of natural resources, and their Arctic climate, to prosper so much and advance so far socially? For instance, Sweden was one of the first countries to enshrine in law equal pay for men and women, in the *Act on Equality Between Men and Women at Work*. Sweden has for a long time led the world in the care of children. Swedish churches instigated a universal literacy program over 200 years ago. Universal elementary education began in Sweden in 1842. Sweden lowered its infant mortality rate before any other country in the world and continues to lead the world in this area.

In 1979, the new Swedish 'Children's Code' stated that

children "shall be treated with respect for their person and their distinctive character and may not be subjected to corporal punishment or any other humiliating treatment". Sweden was effectively the first country on earth to make hitting children, in any shape, form or intensity, explicitly illegal. Hitters are not criminalised, but counselled and educated. Since this law was passed, there has been a cultural shift, with measurable benefits for children. Firstly, there has been a sharp and near total reduction in public acceptance of corporal punishment, which demonstrates that legislation can alter public attitudes. Secondly, there has been a marked reduction in assaults on children. The death of children caused by their parents' abuse has been almost totally eliminated: the child homicide rate was zero for 15 years running.[12] In the decades since the legislation, children's own reports of being hit have plummeted dramatically, below that of other industrialised nations.

Any fears that an end to corporal punishment would lead to 'undisciplined' children are groundless, and invalidated by the results. Since 1979, there has been a steady decline in youth crime, youth alcohol and drug abuse, rape and youth suicide. There has also been an increase in the reporting of youth violence, caused by a country-wide zero-tolerance policy toward bullying in schools. Clearly, this legislation giving children the same protection as adults, has been remarkably successful for Swedish children, as well as for Swedish society as a whole.

As at 1998, Swedish mothers were entitled to 450 days of paid maternity leave.[13] The rest of the world would reap immeasurable benefits from adopting similar initiatives. Far from being a costly exercise, this will save masses of money in the long term, by helping to create happier, healthier, and better-adjusted children. Consider this: it is no co-incidence that, as the world leader in the care of children, Sweden has managed to stay out of war for almost 200 years, and its homicide rate is amongst the lowest in the world.[14] This is an enviable state of affairs, but one that is demonstrably within the reach of any country that chooses to put its resources and political will firmly behind improved nurturance, protection and education of parents and children. UNICEF's 2007 report on children's wellbeing placed Sweden second from the top of the list.

It may also be no accident that a nation that leads the world in its treatment of children should also be such a courageous leader in environmental policy – the Swedish government has committed itself to a 100% reduction in their fossil fuel dependency by 2020 [15]. The progressive aspects of Swedish society and politics go hand in hand with its attitudes towards children.

Because it has been such a successful measure, the Swedish legislation banning the corporal punishment of children both at home and at school has now been imitated in over twenty countries, and proposals for controls on hitting are under discussion in yet more countries.

Social rewards of reforms in Uruguay

Another inspiring example comes from the South American nation of Uruguay. Corporal punishment was banned from Uruguayan schools in 1876. At the same time, free, compulsory and secular education was made available to all children.

In November 2007, End All Corporal Punishment of Children (http://www.endcorporalpunishment.org) reported that Uruguay became the 20th nation in the world to legally ban all corporal punishment of children. Uruguay has for a long time held fast to a tradition of freedom of religion, coupled with a requirement that all public institutions, including schools, universities and hospitals, remain strictly secular. This has made it impossible for fundamentalist religion, with its rigid, authoritarian family structures, to gain a foothold in this country. Uruguay's early commitment to protecting its children from violence or indoctrination brought inestimable social rewards.

Uruguay's children benefited from perhaps the most liberal developmental environment in Latin America, from well over a hundred years ago. These liberal and progressive reforms to education, based on a fundamental respect for individual children's rights, brought about outstanding social reforms one generation later. Predictably, Uruguay was to become the first welfare state in South America in the early 20th century. Described as a 'model country', it was also the first to introduce universal suffrage in 1932, unemployment benefits, old-age pensions, the eight-hour work day in 1916, paid holidays, and subsidised medical care. Today, the capital city municipality of Montevideo boasts one of the world's most democratic community decision-making processes. Their 'participatory budgeting' system engages members of all echelons of society in every major decision regarding development. This style of 'open-door government' is reputed to provide an enviable record of administrative accountability and transparency. [16]

Time and again we see remarkable social dividends such as these manifest in countries that take progressive steps toward child-rearing reform. (Sadly, the abject poverty of this small and under-resourced nation may stall further progress there, at least until neighbouring powers move forward.)

Social dividends of socialising mode parenting

'Socialising mode' parenting emerged toward the close of the 19th century. As these child-rearing innovations were embraced by people in growing numbers, this gave rise to what we know as our modern societies, with their increasingly egalitarian and democratic character. There is no modern democracy that cannot boast a greater degree of social justice, than what was available 100 years ago.

The advent of this new parenting mode, being more benign than the previous modes, facilitated some momentous social changes wherever it took hold. Compared to our forebears, we enjoy a marked reduction in gender-based inequities, laws that protect minorities from vilification, discrimination or attack, a liberation from rigid or repressive social mores, some social welfare safety nets for the old, the sick and the unemployed, and significantly fairer labour laws. These are advancements we take for granted today, but such ideas were considered 'pie-in-the-sky', utopian flights of fancy in our grandparents' time. Just as these realities seemed no more than idealistic dreams not long ago, how many of our present day hopes, dismissed by many as 'unrealistic', might come to fruition in the future? Is the hope for world peace, for instance, merely a fool's fantasy? Or would it be the readily attainable outcome of continued child-rearing improvements?

The more we examine historical childhood, the clearer it becomes that family relationships are the blueprint for the way public and political life unfolds in any nation. If child rearing continues to evolve and improve throughout the world; if we continue our steady trend away from authoritarian, punitive, shaming and manipulative child-rearing methods, we should expect a collateral improvement in key aspects of social, national and international affairs.

Movement away from 'might-is-right'

There is reason to be excited about future probabilities. According to the Conflict Data Project of the University of Uppsala, Sweden, the number of worldwide armed conflicts dropped from 55 in 1992, to 24 in 1997. The Worldwatch Institute found that global military expenditure in 1996 was 2.6 per cent of global economic output, down considerably from 5.7 per cent in the mid-1980s. More and more, albeit imperfectly, the world acts in concert through the United Nations to bring swifter ends to conflict or famine. Between 1946 and 1988, 13 international peacekeeping operations were established. This has grown to 21 such missions that were carried out between 1988 and 1995. It was a world-first when United Nations' peacekeeping troops were deployed, on human rights grounds, to put a stop to the Balkan atrocities of the 1990s. These are the early signs of a small but growing multinational movement that denies the legitimacy of warfare, and acts against it.

The World Trade Centre attacks, the subsequent American-led war on Afghanistan and Iraq, and the deterioration in the Middle East situation seem to negate recent gains toward an era of peace. On the other hand, the recent war on Iraq was protested by the largest anti-war marches the world has ever seen.[17] Humanity has never before displayed so comprehensive and passionate a rejection of the call to arms, with up to ten million marchers in 60 countries.[18] Nevertheless, recent escalations in war and terrorism highlight the urgency of further reforms in the child-rearing practices of the USA, Britain and Australia, throughout the Middle East and the Muslim world. In 2000, Israel passed a law that fully prohibits the use of corporal punishment against children, both at home and at school. It is more than feasible that such cultural changes – that honour children and their vulnerability – will eventually turn Israel into a major force for peace and development in her area.

The idea of inalienable universal human rights only began to gain global credibility in the 20th century. The Universal Declaration of Human Rights was signed by 48 nations in 1948.[19] The human rights watchdog, Amnesty International, was created in 1961. It now has over a million members worldwide, and its goals and work are shared by 900 other non-government organisations (NGOs) worldwide.[20] The term 'crimes against humanity' was coined at the post-World War II trials of Nazi war criminals at Nuremberg. The Nuremberg trials signified the very first act of international intolerance toward war criminals, which at the time was a revolutionary concept, since war objectives were once reason enough to justify any atrocity. It was the first time in human history that butchery was formally put on trial at an international court of justice, rather than passively accepted as an unavoidable fact of politics, or a necessary evil.[21] These modern developments represent a sensational forward shift in human consciousness. No act committed under the rubric of 'warfare' was ever given a second thought, let alone considered a crime, up until recently. In this new era of universal human rights, launched in Nuremberg in 1948, we have come closer than ever to rejecting once and for all the belief that 'might-is-right'.

The momentum toward a new world, where universal human rights form the basis of every society, has not been lost. New and remarkable precedents were set when Augusto Pinochet (Chilean dictator), and later Slobodan Milosevic (Yugoslavian dictator), were captured, detained and brought to trial. These were the first former national leaders who were denied diplomatic immunity, and forcibly deported to answer for crimes against humanity. For the first time, even presidents are no longer above the international rule of law. The extradition of Ricardo Cavallo to Spain to face charges for his part in Argentina's 'dirty war', also broke new ground in international prosecution, prompting a lawyer for Human Rights Watch to say that this "sends a message to soldiers and police officers around the world that if they commit torture today, they could be prosecuted somewhere tomorrow".[22] As the world community continues to gain confidence in bringing war criminals to heel, we are edging closer toward the set-up of an International Criminal Court (ICC) with a permanent residence at The Hague.[23] The establishment of a permanent ICC has been supported by 120 nations, and only opposed by a handful of recalcitrants including Iraq, Iran, and the USA. The ICC at The Hague has already successfully prosecuted a number of Yugoslavian and Rwandan war criminals, who are now serving time for crimes against humanity. It was not unwarranted for Mary Robinson, Human Rights Commissioner to the United Nations, to dub this the Age of Prevention, or for eminent human rights lawyer Geoffrey Robertson to talk of a new "Age of Enforcement". It is not inconceivable that we might be approaching an era when war and dictatorship will be considered illegal, and will be nipped in the bud by immediate, decisive and united international prevention. In his book *Crimes Against Humanity*, Geoffrey Robertson suggests that if this trend continues – especially if the USA finally gets behind it – all war and dictatorship will be classified as a crime against humanity, and perpetrators will be held accountable before an international court.[24]

All around there are encouraging signs that humanity is finding powerful alternatives to violence. Certainly, the most casual glimpse at any newspaper reveals that we are a long, long way from abandoning war and terror. But it cannot be denied that new, violence-free methods of conflict resolution are burgeoning, with increasing frequency, in ways that are utterly unfamiliar from our collective past. The 20th century welcomed many instances of non-violent struggle as a means of defying undemocratic authority and combating injustice. Peaceful resistance has frequently been far more successful than violence, in achieving its aims of justice or freedom. Some of the most notable examples, key transformative moments in our bloodstained history, include: Mahatma Ghandi's success against British colonial hegemony, Nelson Mandela's peaceful transition to post-apartheid power, the dogged non-compliance with Nazi directives by Danish citizens, the women of Berlin who stood up to the Gestapo, Otpor's defiance of Serbian dictatorship, and Burmese democrats' valiant face-off against the military junta – to name but a few.[25]

For the first time, human rights concerns are translating into international pressure, in protest against brutal regimes. Though it does not materialise often enough, this new phenomenon has had a powerful impact in South Africa, and in East Timor.

Many times over, peaceful citizen action has brought brutal and oppressive government to a standstill, forced concessions from powerful and irresponsible multinational corporations, even deposed autocratic leaders. Naomi Klein's *No Logo*[26] examines the growing, worldwide phenomenon of well-organised, peaceful demonstrations and boycotts, which attract tens of thousands of individuals from all walks of life and political persuasions, to protest against damaging corporate activities. Consumer boycotts forced a major food manufacturer to stop aggressively marketing baby-formula in the developing world. In 1997, there were co-ordinated protests in 85 cities across 13 countries against the exploitative use of sweat-shop labour by a leading sports-shoe maker. This popular protest precipitated a massive drop in this company's share price. A series of student boycotts of a popular soft-drink forced the manufacturer to sever all ties with the repressive Burmese military regime, and to withdraw its business there. An oil company intent on dumping a decrepit oil platform into the North Sea was stopped by a citizens' boycott that spanned the European continent. In many places around the world, people are increasingly convinced that peaceful means resolve conflicts more effectively, that violence is inexcusable and that it never achieves its goals. Bloodless strategies are increasingly the norm in the human striving for justice.

Wherever family dynamics become more democratic, and children cease to be regarded as property, relatively democratic governments come into being. Democracy, with its freedoms, continues its global expansion, slowly chipping away at hallmarks of tyranny such as gender inequality, child labour, military or religious power, and the curtailment of free speech. As the influence of human rights advocates like Amnesty International increases, domestic injustices are increasingly exposed to international criticism. National governments are becoming more transparent to the watchful eyes of the United Nations. These exciting social advances are the predictable result of the continuing evolution of child-rearing practices.

Shortfalls of socialising mode

It would be simplistic to suggest that socialising mode parenting has created a completely fair and egalitarian society. Certainly, it can be said that this mode of parenting has furthered our psychological and emotional development, and this has enabled us to make considerable progress in areas of social justice. However, celebration of our social progress needs to be tempered. While socialising mode child rearing has moved us away from strong-arm styles of dictatorship, it has not eliminated strategies for attaining power that involve cunning. In modern societies, illicit and improper advantage is more often won through sleight-of-hand, rather than through overt intimidation. Sophisticated techniques of psychological manipulation are used to win votes, and to garner market domination irrespective of the quality or integrity of a product or service. Highly paid 'public relations' professionals – recruited by corporations or by industry-funded 'think tanks' – are able to whitewash the most unscrupulous activities, thanks to a blindly trusting, and largely undiscerning public.[27] Politicians win over a credulous public thanks to charisma, and the wiles and tricks of their professional spin-doctors, rather than the merit of their policies or their personal integrity. Some of the worst and most toxic products and ideas can be widely sold thanks to our modern methods of psychological manipulation – 'image building' and advertising. Not with invading colonial armies, but under the guise of 'free trade' and 'economic reform', all-powerful western corporations are bleeding developing nations, causing an explosion of poverty and civil unrest. Crippling loan packages carrying conditions of austerity and excessive privatisation are seductively imposed on poor nations 'for their own good'.[28]

When it comes to corrupt attitudes to power, the iron fist has been superseded by the con. A cavernous inner emptiness makes us insatiable consumers, bewitched by the latest trend, easily suckered by handsome or smooth-talking politicians, and slick advertising campaigns. It is all too easy to manipulate public opinion for personal gain, when a wounded or ill-formed self-esteem makes us so open to manipulation (we will see in Chapters 19, 26 and 27, that the conditions that render individuals more vulnerable to psychological manipulation arise from specific, painful childhood experiences). On average, our collective level of emotional maturity has yet to make us immune to psychological manipulation.

Socialising mode child rearing has not eliminated social ills such as substance addiction or depression, but once it has taken hold for at least one generation, it has the potential to end extremes of human suffering such as the brutality of war and dictatorship. If these are the social dividends brought by socialising mode child rearing, imagine what could happen as 'helping mode' child rearing takes hold, what additional social problems can begin to dissolve.

Conclusion

Once we fully comprehend the far-reaching implications of our collective parenting choices, the idea that a mother or father in the home are of lesser status than an executive in the boardroom, will be dumped in the deepest corner of the trash-bin of history. Parenting or school teaching are no less momentous and influential career choices than joining the diplomatic corps or registering for a Masters of Business Administration. Parents and teachers can be the most powerful and effective social-change agents – as long as they are given the resources and social support they need to fulfil their potential.

Peaceful and prosperous communities, societies and nations are wholly possible when children's wellbeing is made a top priority. If we continue to actively pursue the path of child-rearing reform and evolution throughout the world, then

172

utopian ideals such as world peace and ecologically sustainable development are entirely within our grasp.

Many modern nations have succeeded in safeguarding the physical development and education of the majority of their children. However, this is not enough. The next task before us is to pay closer attention to children's emotional development. We need to continue to explore how to best help our children to develop a rich and balanced emotionality, for this underscores their ability to form and maintain harmonious relationships. With the help of modern advancements in psychology, we are gaining a much deeper understanding of human emotions. We have come to realise that 'emotional intelligence', a faculty that is nurtured in childhood, is the most vital ingredient of psychological health, it is also the key to good relations with others, and with the world around us. A harmonious society arises when children are nurtured at all levels.

So far we have looked at how, for better or for worse, the way children are cared for can literally change the course of history. Before we look at natural parenting (de Mause's 'helping mode'), the newest development in the evolution of parenting, we need a clear picture of socialising mode parenting – the most common in modern societies – to help us distinguish one stage in the evolution of parenting from the next. The following section looks at the behaviour control methods that characterise the socialising mode approach to children, followed by a discussion of non-authoritarian ways to set interpersonal boundaries with children.

Endnotes

[1] Though it can boast some enviable freedoms, today's American democracy is no longer the most advanced in the world. It has fallen behind other, relatively more progressive, dynamic, open and responsible democracies, such as Switzerland, where citizens have a direct say on most major governmental decisions. See http://www.wikipedia.org/ and search for 'Direct democracy'. By contrast in USA, the First Amendment gives constitutional protection to corporate financing of elections, a measure that gives corporations extensive control over the electoral process. For a rather chilling account of this subsuming of democracy to corporate interests see Bakan (2004) pp 85–110. See also American Civil Liberties Union under 'National security' http://www.aclu.org/ (last accessed 1 December 2004).

2   De Mause (1982).

3   De Mause (1982) pp 109–110.

4   Cited in de Mause (1982) p 110.

5   De Mause (1982) p 110.

6   It is interesting to note that this exceeds what many American infants are offered today.

7   Greeenleaf (1978).

8   De Mause (2002a).

9   Sigman, A (2005).

10 http://www.apesma.asn.au/women/maternity_leave_around_the_world.asp

11 http://news.bbc.co.uk/1/hi/uk/6359849.stm

12 Durrant (1999a).

13 See Human Rights and Equal Opportunity Commission (2002).

14 Keeley (1996) p 32·

15 http://en.wikipedia.org/wiki/Oil_phase-out_in_Sweden

16 McFarland (1999)

17 See 'Global protests against war on Iraq' Wikipedia (last accessed 1 December 2004).

18 See 'Millions join global anti-war protests' BBC News 17 February 2003 http://news.bbc.co.uk/ (last accessed 1 December 2004).

19 It celebrated its 50th anniversary in 1998. See United Nations http://www.un.org/Overview/rights.html (last accessed 1 December 2004).

20 See Amnesty International http://www.amnesty.orgl (last accessed 1 December 2004).

21 The proceedings of the Nuremberg Trials have been preserved for the world to see by Yale University, see The Avalon Project at http://www.yale.edu/lawweb/avalon/imt/proc/v1menu.htm (last accessed 1 December 2004).

22 'Argentinian extradited to Spain' The Sydney Morning Herald 30 June 2003 p 7.

23 See International Criminal Court http://www.icc-cpi.int/ (last accessed 1 December 2004).

24 Robertson (2000).

25 Ackerman and Du Vall (2000).

26 Klein (2000).

27 Rampton S. and Stauber J (2001)

28 Stiglitz (2002); Pilger (2002); Klein (2002).

IV

TO SOCIALISE OR HELP?
FROM AUTHORITARIAN TO
AUTHORITATIVE PARENTING

*There is a time to admire the grace and persuasive power
of an influential idea, and there is a time to fear its hold
over us. The time to worry is when the idea is so widely
shared that we no longer even notice it, when it is so
deeply rooted that it feels to us like plain common sense.
At the point when objections are not even answered any
more because they are no longer even raised, we are not in
control: we do not have the idea; it has us.*

Alfie Kohn[1]

16

THE CARROT AND THE STICK

The majority of parents in so-called 'developed' nations are now parenting in the style which Lloyd de Mause calls the 'socialising mode'. Although increasing numbers of child-rearing manuals are now advocating aspects of 'helping mode' parenting, many still contain ideas about discipline and behaviour control that hark back to the earlier socialising mode.

The passing of socialising mode parenting

Most readers would have been brought up along socialising mode principles. To the degree that we are immersed in this mode, we take its doctrines for granted, passively accepting them as 'the way it is done'. Thus it can be difficult to view this parenting mode objectively. We think of it as 'common sense' parenting, rather than as a choice; even less as a stage in the continuing evolution of parenting. Although our parenting customs are a product of our particular era, many of us imagine them to be universal and timeless, and so we don't question our methods, nor do we wonder if any better practice is possible.

This chapter defines and describes socialising mode parenting. Since this mode is primarily concerned with controlling and adjusting children's behaviour to make them fit in with social and cultural norms, we will closely examine the three behaviour control methods that define socialising mode. Beyond authoritarian discipline methods, there exists a more effective and more emotionally sustaining paradigm for relating to children, based on 'contact' rather than 'control'. In Chapter 20, we will be discussing this new paradigm, which is more conducive to the development of emotional intelligence in children. As we will see, setting boundaries effectively with children entails being assertive, rather than authoritarian.

In a nutshell, socialising parents are more affectionate

and more tolerant of their children's playfulness than parents of earlier modes. They listen to their children's feelings, offer comfort for their pain, and support their personal aspirations to a greater degree than was previously done. Consequently, their children have tended to develop further, in terms of emotional intelligence, than those of earlier modes.

But punishment and the desire to control have not been altogether abandoned. Instead, control methods have become more subtle, less extreme or less overt. Certainly, we can say that we have moved away from the excessive brutality, neglect, abuse and exploitation of earlier modes. In fact, today we penalise people who practice earlier modes of parenting, which are now considered abusive. But parent–child conflict is often still blamed on the child's 'misbehaviour', and this is responded to with 'discipline'. The gist of socialising parenting is to punish 'bad' behaviour corporally or verbally, and to manipulatively reward 'good' behaviour with a show of approval, or other secondary goodies. This stands in contrast to the helping mode, which aims to engender pro-social behaviour by promoting healthy emotional development. Socialising mode parenting places more emphasis on the child's 'good' behaviour, than on his or her emotional wellbeing – without realising that the former springs naturally from the latter. Essentially, socialising parenting is still authoritarian; though it is the last – and therefore the mildest – version of authoritarianism.

Most children of socialising parents grow up relatively 'normal', that is, free of the dysfunction, psycho-pathology, deviation, coldness, violence or dissociative disorders commonly found among survivors of earlier parenting modes. But this does not mean that the authoritarian flavour of socialising mode parenting has no negative effects. Part IV will look at how socialising mode methods of 'discipline' affect the development of emotional intelligence, and therefore social behaviour.

Differences between authoritarian and authoritative parenting

The terms 'authoritarian' and 'authoritative' bear some explanation. As we begin to leave socialising behind, we enter what de Mause calls the helping mode, which is authoritative rather than authoritarian parenting.

The fully authoritarian parent insists that his or her parental authority, however benign, is not to be questioned. Parental power and domination is automatically legitimised by their position in the family, and by their age. Thus, the parent relates through a *role*, or a rank, and can seldom afford to be seen by the child as a *real* person. This is the 'do as you're told' approach, that denies or at least downplays children's right to an explanation – let alone negotiation – regarding decisions that affect them personally.

Punishment, threats and rewards are the centrepieces of authoritarianism, which views parenting primarily as a process of training the child. This pedagogical orientation exists to serve the parents' need for order, discipline and predictability, and so authoritarian parenting can be said to be principally parent-centred.

The idea that children need coercive discipline has always seemed so cardinal, that no one thought to genuinely put it to the test – at least until recently. In the last few decades, there have been numerous efforts to investigate how children fare in authoritarian family environments, and the results belie some long-held assumptions. Research psychologists have found that parents who employed absolute moral imperatives, and who were more punitive, tended to have children who were more discontent, withdrawn and mistrustful.[2] A study of mothers and their two-year-olds found that mothers who used more criticism and physical coercion, had more defiant, rather than more obedient children.[3] Another study examined 11–14-year-old school children who reported being bullies and/or victims. Both types of children were found to come from homes where authoritarian styles of parenting were employed.[4] Not only does authoritarian parenting appear to be less effective, it can also be associated with a number of undesirable social problems.

In the western world, we have barely begun our transition from an authoritarian to an authoritative model of parenting. Many modern parents seem to straddle both, as we continue to evolve by degrees toward progressively more authoritative interactions with our children. The shift from 'socialising' to 'helping' mode actually spells the end of authoritarian child rearing; the helping mode being the first truly authoritative style (see Figure 1).

Aspirants to authoritative parenting seem more transparent; their children can more directly experience them as real persons. In relation to their children, they take charge assertively rather than through domination or manipulation. A growing number of parenting manuals already teach assertive ways to set strong boundaries with our children, while rejecting physical and verbal aggression or manipulation. Examples of such manuals include those of Thomas Gordon,[5] Steve Biddulph[6] and Louise Porter.[7] Though I cannot say that I agree to the letter with everything these authors say (nor would they necessarily agree with me!) they certainly represent a positive and clear departure from outdated authoritarian methods of boundary setting.

Figure 1: *Socialising mode parenting is the last and the mildest form of* **authoritarian** *parenting, whereas helping mode is* **authoritative**.

Socialising mode	Helping mode
Parental power is authoritarian	Parental power is authoritative
Parents' power exists by virtue of their rank and age. It is not negotiable	Parents' power is *earned* through trust
'Disciplines' the child	Models healthy boundaries.
Tries to control the child	Establishes 'contact', authentic emotional connection with the child
Manipulates the child's behaviour through rewards and/or punishment	Invites mutual expression of needs and feelings
Goal: obedient, socialised, 'well-behaved' or 'good' children	**Goal:** autonomous, self-actualised, considerate, empathic, emotionally mature children

Socialising mode	Helping mode
Teaches *rules* of behaviour, morality	Role-models caring, empathy, responsibility and openness

The authoritative parent uses power *with* the child, not *over* the child. Their authority is based on respect rather than fear – a distinction that the socialising parent has not quite learned to make. True authority is earned, through a trusting connection with the child, and it relies on inspiration rather than coercion. Whereas authoritarian parents teach children to obey abstract rules about 'right and wrong' (external frame of reference), authoritative parents teach them to follow their hearts and listen to their feelings (internal frame of reference), and thus to be guided by natural compassion and empathy.

Authoritative parenting is neither parent-centred nor child-centred, but relationship-centred. Thus it also guarantees the child an age-appropriate amount of power and responsibility, while also recognising the rights that parents have in relation to their children. It should not be confused with the short-lived trend of permissive parenting: which has been a polarised overcompensation to the excesses of authoritarian parenting. Authoritative parents do give their children responsibilities, and they demand considerate behaviour from them, at levels that are appropriate to each child's stage of development. In Part VI, we will take a detailed look at authoritative (or helping mode) parenting as it applies to the critical early years of core emotional development.

The border separating authoritative from authoritarian parenting will become clearer once we have closely examined the three authoritarian control methods pertaining to the socialising mode.

Social implications of authoritarian parenting

Because authoritarian approaches to child rearing are more controlling and punitive, this has a measurable social and political effect. Studies conducted by social psychologists have found that authoritarian individuals are more supportive of punitive national policies, such as the death penalty (in the USA) and the use of military force.[8] Authoritarian individuals have been found to be more hostile towards the environmental movement, while tending to express more leniency towards polluters.[9] Our collective evolution beyond authoritarian control methods is a necessary step towards a peaceful and sustainable world.

Three 'authoritarian' control methods

The three behaviour control methods commonly used to 'discipline' children are: corporal punishment, shaming, and manipulation. Most people see nothing wrong with any of these strategies; they are viewed by the majority of parents as 'common sense'. Most people are either surprised or annoyed to hear that so much of what is considered 'good parenting' might have some negative psychological and social consequences. But there is mounting evidence, as we shall discuss, that rather than create 'good behaviour', these formulas for 'discipline' limit the development of emotional intelligence, and therefore bring about a host of relationship and social problems.

What follows is an evaluation of each of these three behaviour control methods, examining how each can harm children's emotional development.

Endnotes

[1] Kohn (1996) p 3.
[2] Baumrind (1967).
[3] Crockenberg and Litman (1990).
[4] Baldry and Farrington (1998).
[5] Gordon (1975).
[6] Biddulph (1993).
[7] Porter (2001).
[8] Milburn and Conrad (1996) pp 58, 69.
[9] Milburn and Conrad (1996) pp 204–205.

17

AUTHORITARIAN CONTROL
METHOD 1:
CORPORAL PUNISHMENT

Corporal punishment is still widely used. While some forms of physical punishment are considered abusive and illegal, smacking or spanking remains culturally sanctioned throughout most of the world. Recent studies have shown that between 57 and 90 per cent of American parents use corporal punishment.[1] Around the world, over 80 per cent of French parents, 92 per cent of Irish parents, and 69 per cent of parents in Ontario, Canada have admitted to hitting their children. With the exception of a handful of countries such as Kenya and South Africa, corporal punishment tends to be quite severe in schools throughout Africa.[2] Twenty-two American states permit corporal punishment in schools. Though it has finally been banned from most Australian schools, many Australian parents would feel put-upon if legislators interfered with what they perceive as their 'right' to smack their children. But this kind of attitude is on the retreat, as it becomes increasingly harder to defend it against the tide of evidence as to the damage it causes.

In modern societies, the flogging or whipping practiced by our forebears has been replaced by spanking or smacking. Socialising mode parents maintain that hitting children in this way causes them no harm. In fact, many are convinced that a 'good smack' is necessary for teaching children 'discipline' and 'respect', and that without an occasional spanking, children would run amok. As we saw in the last section, this negative view of children is particularly clung to by some religious groups. So, what happens to kids who are hit? Do they actually become more self-disciplined? What happens when we take the trouble to measure the effectiveness of corporal punishment? It will come as a great surprise to many that it actually does not work.

Over decades it has come to be agreed upon by psychologists and learning theorists that punishment is generally an ineffectual and problematic learning tool. American psychologist and social researcher Elizabeth Gershoff[3] recently examined 88 pieces of research designed to measure the effects of corporal punishment on children. Overwhelmingly, according to Gershoff's extensive analysis, researchers have found that the most spanking or smacking can hope to accomplish is immediate, short-term compliance. You can hit a kid, in other words, and you're likely to force them to do what you want. But this only works for the short term, and the behaviour enforced soon wears off. This means that spanking does not cause children to internalise any moral message. Punishment does not deliver a lesson on ethics, even if it ensures the child's compliance while the discipliner is around. To put it in another way: a smack can induce children to learn ethical rules with their heads, but not with their hearts. So far, no one has managed to demonstrate that spanking works. As psychologist George W Holden said after a review of Gershoff's analysis, "corporal punishment does not accomplish the goal for which it is used".[4]

Perhaps it would be OK for us to keep spanking our children if the results were no worse than irregular, superficial and temporary compliance. However, there is much worse to be said about corporal punishment. There are scores of studies demonstrating that it is actually harmful, in a number of ways. And the indications regarding harmful effects are 'remarkably consistent' throughout all studies.[5] Moreover, unlike the rare and dubious 'positive' effects of corporal punishment, the harmful effects last well into the long term.

Why is corporal punishment harmful? And exactly how is it harmful?

Family violence breeds social violence

A prodigious number of studies, replicated worldwide, have shown that violence is trans-generational.[6] In other words, violence in the home (both physical and verbal) is what produces violent children. Few notions are so well supported by the research literature, and so well agreed upon by psychologists across the board. One researcher[7] was able to accurately predict boys' criminal behaviour, based on which boys had a history of violence in their upbringing. People who were severely corporally punished as children are more commonly found amongst jail inmates and juvenile delinquents.[8]

Even ordinary spanking or smacking is harmful

There is a growing acceptance that children's violence and delinquency springs from the kind of family violence that is culturally recognised as 'abusive'. But surely, an occasional smack on the bottom or on the wrist isn't an act of violence! Or is it? With some incredible leap of fuzzy logic, socialising parents emphatically deny that spanking is violence, when the very same spank, applied to a nursing home resident, or a psychiatric patient, would be unequivocally treated as assault.

When we deny the violence of a smack, this simply means that we have become personally de-sensitised to violence at that threshold. Since a smack does not feel violent to the smacker, this seems sufficient justification to carry on smacking. There appears to be an endlessly shifting imaginary line separating 'normative' smacking – a completely arbitrary and subjective definition – from definitive violence. Simply put, we think of something as 'normative' because that's what we grew up with. The hitting we experienced as children has made us insensitive to the pain and humiliation suffered by our own children as we swat them in the name of 'discipline'. So we don't see our blows as 'violent', but our children – who are much more vulnerable and sensitive than ourselves – certainly experience them as violent. In 1998 in the United Kingdom, the National Children's Bureau asked a large group of five to seven year old children how they felt when they got smacked. All of them spoke of wounded feelings, hurt, embarrassment, and shock. The children's responses, reproduced in their own words, are a moving testimony to the violation they experience at the receiving end of parental 'discipline'.[9] It would take a very thick skin for anyone to read these children's messages, and continue to deny that smacking or spanking constitute violence.

It is easy, for those who want to, to overlook the harm caused to children by corporal punishment. Mostly this is because the evidence of the child's emotional wound does not appear until later. Furthermore, because not all children who are hit by their parents become violent or depressed, many of the negative effects are less obvious.

Nevertheless, the effects of even ordinary corporal punishment are real, and the evidence to support this is massive. One study of elementary school boys found that their 'behaviour problems' were consistently traceable to two things: lack of parental affection, and parental use of spanking for discipline.[10] Another study of over 270 boys and girls from diverse backgrounds showed that those who had been spanked were more likely to be aggressive towards their peers.[11] A German study that looked at 570 families found a direct path between harsh punishment and anti-social behaviour in children.[12] In a two-year study of 900 American children, it was discovered that those who were spanked more often acquired more problem behaviours, such as lying and bullying. The same children showed less remorse for hurtful behaviour, were more destructive and more disobedient, regardless of how warm their parents were.[13] These results have been replicated in a similar follow-up study.[14] The link between corporal punishment and aggressiveness in children is so strong, that the best predictor of violent behaviour is the frequency with which children have been spanked.

So, even culturally accepted corporal punishment tends to make children more aggressive, if not in behaviour, at least in attitude. Gershoff's review of studies revealed that children who are hit more often are more likely, later in life, to hit their romantic partners, their spouses and their own children.[15]

The popular myth that hitting children in 'moderation' can make them 'better behaved' is rapidly being debunked. In fact, toddlers of mothers who rely most on physical punishment are less likely to listen to them, they tend to be less compliant, and they show lower levels of physical skill development.[16] A new international study assessing the impact of mothers' use of corporal punishment in China, India, Italy, Kenya, the Philippines and Thailand found that in all these countries, it was associated with more aggression and anxiety in the children.[17] Not all the spanked become more aggressive in thought or deed. Corporal punishment has been linked to a host of psychological problems. A history of harsh punishment has been found to underlie 'conduct disorder', and anxiety disorders in children.[18] Adults who were physically punished as adolescents are more likely to suffer from depressive symptoms, suicidal thoughts and alcohol abuse.[19] Finally, Gershoff's study found a strong association between corporal punishment and adolescent depression, decreased confidence and assertiveness, low self-esteem, and alcoholism.[20]

A group of psychologists conducted a longitudinal study of about 400 people spanning over 22 years. They began by interviewing each person at eight years of age, as well as interviewing their parents in order to assess their parenting styles. They interviewed everyone again at 19, and finally at 30, in order to assess their developing personalities. These researchers found that those individuals whose parents had favored authoritarian, harsh and punitive child-rearing methods lagged behind in the development of empathy, social skills and personal autonomy.[21] Even if authoritarian parenting does not necessarily create 'damaged' individuals, authoritative parenting helps individuals to mature further in terms of their emotional intelligence and relationship skills.

How corporal punishment engenders violent attitudes and behaviour

The main reason why children learn to be violent is that they are natural imitators.[22] They continually reproduce the things they see their role models do. This means that parents who rely on corporal punishment or verbal abuse to 'control' their kids are unwittingly acting as models for bullying behaviour.[23] In a series of groundbreaking experiments, psychologist Albert Bandura demonstrated how faithfully children would imitate adults who acted aggressively toward toy dummies.[24] The same principle applies when it is the child himself who is being hit.

For role-modelled behaviour to be efficiently transmitted, three main conditions must be met. Firstly, children are more likely to imitate role models that they look up to or love. That's why parents can be such powerful role models. Secondly, the role model's actions are more likely to be imitated if they are seen to meet with success. In other words, the attitude that 'might-is-right' is passed on when a spanking disciplinarian actually succeeds in changing a child's behaviour, and remains unchallenged. The third condition is that violence must be legitimised and sanctioned in order to be imitated. In other words, children more readily adopt violent attitudes if they have been made to believe that harsh punishment is 'deserved'.

It's been shown that violent children come from violent or neglectful homes. This matter has been put to rest. But only about half of abused children grow up to be abusive. Why? Individuals who remain convinced that verbal or physical assaults against them were 'deserved' are significantly more likely to act out violently. This is also true for those who are not victims, but witnesses to violence against others. Children are more likely to imitate violent behaviours when the violence has been approved by an adult.[25] For this reason, children who are told they deserve to be hit go on to be more accepting of violence. They are potential candidates for the ranks of bullies, victims, or both.

A side-effect of harsh punishment is that it de-sensitises children to their own pain, which in turn makes them insensitive to the pain of others. De-sensitisation facilitates the acting out of violence. The process of de-sensitisation to violence begins when a child who, branded as 'bad' or 'naughty', accepts the blame and the assault that comes with it. A 'tough skin' grows over the wound, which obscures or masks the depth of the pain that throbs beneath. The feelings of pain and betrayal are sealed off, minimised, trivialised, or denied. Deafness to one's own pain entails indifference to the pain of others. Those whose anger boils over become bullies, those who are paralysed with fear, the victims. While some children of violent parents become de-sensitised, others become hypersensitive. They grow up to be timid, unsure of themselves, they are easily intimidated, downtrodden and manipulated. The fact that they are not threatening and willing to please makes them easier to like than bullies, but they are socially handicapped nonetheless. Others who have been brought up by 'the rod' hover in between the two poles of insensitivity and hypersensitivity. They harbour a predilection to retributional and 'might-is-right' attitudes, such as seen among the religious extremists discussed in earlier chapters.

Everywhere we find the punished and the beaten; who grow up to make light of it, or to stoically profess that 'It never did me any harm!' By contrast, those who are in touch with their pain, humiliation and anger, are better able to heal their emotional wounds and thus avoid passing on the violence.

The power of denial should never be underestimated. Many adults tend to grossly dilute or whitewash any violence they suffered as children. In two studies, researchers spoke to people who remembered having been punished so brutally as to require hospitalisation. Only 43 per cent in one study and 60 per cent in the other considered themselves abused![26] If it is hard to imagine being hospitalised by a violent parent, and not recognising this as abuse, it is even harder to conceive how widespread this level of denial is. Yet all of us in one way or another minimise, deny, even entirely forget our own childhood pain.

The cycle of violence can be broken by those willing to express the hurt inflicted by punishment. People who are openly angry about any abuse they suffered as children, are statistically less likely to transmit this abuse onto others.[27] If we are to reduce the levels of violence in the world, it is absolutely essential that we openly decry all physical chastisement of children, and correctly name it as violent. Beaten children who are at risk of becoming bullies, offenders or habitual victims can be helped once somebody can make it abundantly clear to them that spankings or thrashings are not just, nor deserved.

Social consequences of corporal violence

Violence is an adaptive behaviour learned within a family system. The school bully or juvenile delinquent is an emotionally injured individual trying to compensate for an inner feeling of powerlessness. The same is true for those who grow up to become autocrats, dictators and bullies in business. To consider bullies as offenders is superficial, when in fact, they are first and foremost victims.

As long as any kind of violence – and smacking is definitely a kind of violence – is sanctioned in the home, there will be bullies in schools, in business and in politics. Bullies are not a fact of life, but an artifact of history. Child rearing has historically been so violent, as we saw in earlier chapters, that almost all of us are either battered children or descendants of battered children. It is no wonder that violence persists in so many forms, across all age groups, and that most of us are capable of slipping and treating our children violently on occasions, even if we strive against it.

So, this is how violence against children – at home or at school – creates social violence, and when it is severe enough crime and war. Clearly, hitting children does not bring about 'discipline'. What it does bring about is a broad range of social problems.

Can punitive child rearing create a punitive society? Certainly, there is an abundance of social research suggesting this link. In their book *The Politics of Denial* (1996), social psychologists Michael Milburn and Sheree Conrad review a collection of studies showing that individuals who were brought up in punitive, authoritarian families tend to favour harsher aspects of law and order policy – such as the death penalty – they are more likely to support war and less likely to support the environmental movement. Evidently, the political opinions of the punished seem to reflect their childhood environments. The evidence we looked at in this chapter – showing that childhood punishment tends to make us more aggressive in attitude – would seem to explain Milburn and Conrad's findings. Authoritarian child rearing – in religious *and* secular environments – can radicalise individuals' worldviews, and collectively it can leave its mark on a nation's political landscape.

We cannot claim absolute certainty about the broader social impact of punitive childrearing and education, and more research is warranted to explore this link. The USA, for instance, is quite unusual among modern democracies in its retention of corporal punishment in schools. It would therefore seem important to investigate to what extent this style of child rearing may have influenced some of the harsher aspects of American social and foreign policies. For example, the USA has the second highest rate of gun ownership and the highest homicide rate among affluent democracies.[28] It also has the highest documented incarceration rate in the world,[29] and it is the only western democracy to have retained the death penalty – despite there being no evidence that it deters crime.[30] The USA remains one of only a few nations that sentence juveniles to Life Without Parole (LWOP), and one of only two countries, alongside Somalia, that has not signed the Convention of the Rights of the Child. There are at least 2,225 child offenders serving life without parole (LWOP) sentences in US prisons for crimes committed before they were aged 18 (http://www.hrw.org/english/docs/2005/10/12/usdom11835.htm).

As yet, the USA has not signed the United Nations Convention on Discrimination Against Women, or the Kyoto Protocol on Greenhouse Gas Emission Control. It refuses to support the International Criminal Court at The Hague (along with countries such as Iran, Iraq and China), and the international ban on the use of land mines. A vast body of psychological research has explained the mechanics of how the child-rearing modes of our forebears created the war and tyranny that has plagued humanity through the centuries. By the same token, wherever violence against children becomes less severe, the first signs of democracy and rationality begin to appear. This evolutionary process seems to be gathering pace across many nations.

Is corporal punishment here to stay?

The good news is that the beating, spanking and verbal abuse of children is on its way out, as an overall world trend. An American survey conducted in 1987 found that although there is still an extremely high incidence of serious violence against children in the USA, it had decreased from 1975–1985 by a factor of 47 per cent.[31] Another study confirmed a decrease in the American rates of violence against children: in 1968 it showed that 94 per cent of parents approved of corporal punishment. By 1994 the approval rate had dropped to 68 per cent (note however, the 'approval rate' is probably less than the actual hitting rate. Many parents hit their kids regularly though they regret it). The highest rate of approval of corporal punishment was in the southern states.[32] Another American researcher found that whereas in 1992 over 90 per cent of parents admitted to hitting their kids, by 1999 this rate had dropped to 57 per cent.[33] The proportion of Americans who disagree with the statement that 'spanking is necessary' grew from 16.5 per cent in 1986 to 26.6 per cent in 1994.[34]

Since the 1970s, when we first began to talk in earnest about 'the battered child syndrome', the fruits of psychological research have begun to filter out to the world community. We have come a long way in changing attitudes to corporal punishment en masse. In 1979, Sweden became the first country to officially recognise that smacking children is a form of domestic violence, and they banned this practice accordingly. As we saw in Part III, this prohibition has yielded measurable social benefits.

Countries that had banned hitting children before the year 2004, when the first edition of this book was being written, are Sweden, Finland, Norway, Austria, Cyprus, Denmark, Latvia, Croatia, Germany, Israel, Iceland, Romania, Ukraine. Since 2004, several more countries have joined them. These countries are: New Zealand, Holland, Portugal, Greece, Uruguay, Spain, Chile and Venezuela. [35] New Zealand is the first English speaking country to have enacted this law, and also the first in the southern hemisphere. The UK banned corporal punishment (by birching) of juvenile offenders in the 1940s, and corporal punishment ended in state schools in 1987 and 1998 the few independent schools that still used it were finally subjected to a ban. It remains legal for UK parents to carry out corporal punishment on their children, defined as 'reasonable chastisement', though there have been amendments to the law proposed and enacted by the Welsh assembly and the Scottish Parliament.

Nevertheless, the UK government has fallen foul of the Council of Europe for being one of the few recalcitrants still eschewing reform. The European Court of Human Rights has found unanimously that the "reasonable chastisement" defence fails to give children adequate protection. Among the British people however, the call for abolition is gathering momentum. This movement is spearheaded by umbrella organizations such as: 'Children are unbeatable!' - an alliance of more than 300 groups including the NSPCC, Save the Children, Bernardo's and the National Children's Bureau.[36] Insofar as corporal punishment in schools goes, every industrialized country in the world now comprehensively prohibits school corporal punishment, the U.S. and Australia are the only exceptions. (http://www.stophitting.com/disatschool/worldwide.php).

At the current rate of change, we may be only years away from an era when hitting children will be considered unthinkable throughout the entire Western world and beyond.

A global initiative to end all corporal punishment of children was launched at the United Nations in April 2001,[37] and it is likely that most readers will see this practice altogether terminated throughout the western world, and further, in our lifetime.

It would be unfortunate if the global debate about the merits of corporal punishment were treated solely as a scientific issue, when ultimately it is a question of justice. In the USA, all forms of corporal punishment are forbidden against soldiers, felons and murderers, "but it remains legal and acceptable for children who are innocent of any crime".[38] If a welt shows up on the body of a US soldier, it can be used as evidence of excessive disciplinarian force. Australian psychologist Louise Porter points out that when elderly persons in nursing homes are rude to the staff, we don't hit them to "teach them a lesson".[39] So why do we need research and health professionals to tell us that hitting children is not OK? It is a pity that we need social scientists to 'prove' to us what should be manifestly obvious. We have passed laws against hitting men, and more recently we prohibited men from hitting their wives – without waiting around for someone in a lab coat to 'prove' to us that this was harmful.

As parents' self-awarded 'right' to hit their children retreats around the world, some forms of social, inter-ethnic and international violence will go with it. But by itself, the elimination of corporal punishment will not be sufficient. There are other causes of violence, including shaming, neglect, emotional manipulation and exploitation. Shaming is a kind of verbal violence that for most people appears normal and unremarkable, because we are barely beginning to understand the damage it causes. In Chapter 18 we take a closer look at this method of control.

Endnotes

[1] Straus and Kaufman (1994).
[2] Maurel (2001).
[3] Gershoff (2002a), (2002b).
[4] Holden (2002).
[5] Holden (2002).
[6] Spatz Widom (1989).
[7] McCord (1979) pp 1477–1486.
[8] Maurer and Wallerstein (1987).
[9] See End All Corporal Punishment of Children http://www.endcorporalpunishment.org/
[10] Sheline, Skipper and Broadhead (1994).
[11] Strassberg, Dodge, Pettit and Bates (1994).
[12] Muller, Hunter and Stollak (1995).
[13] Straus and Paschall (1997).
[14] Straus and Mouradian (1998).
[15] Gershoff (2002a), (2002b).
[16] Power and Chapieski (1986).
[17] Lansford et al (2005)
[18] Engfer and Schneewind (1982).
[19] Straus and Kaufman (1994).
[20] Gershoff (2002a), (2002b).
[21] Dubow, Huesmann and Eron (1987).
[22] Walters and Grusec (1977).
[23] Bandura (1973); Baron (1977).
[24] Bandura (1973).
[25] Bandura (1973).
[26] Berger, Knutson, Mehm and Perkins (1988); Knutson and Selner (1994).
[27] Hunter and Kilstrom (1979).
[28] See Handgun-free America at http://www.handgunfree.org/HFAMain/research/abroad (last accessed 1 December 2004).
[29] Milburn and Conrad (1996) p 110; see Human Rights Watch report on the USA http://www.hrw.org/backgrounder/usa/

incarceration/
30 Milburn and Conrad (1996).
31 Gelles and Straus (1987).
32 Straus and Mathur (1996).
33 Dietz (2000).
34 The study was cited in Milburn and Conrad (1996) pp 21–22.
35 See End All Corporal Punishment of Children 'States which have prohibited' http://www.endcorporalpunishment.org/; the Center for Effective Discipline http://www.stophitting.com.
36 http://www.childrenareunbeatable.org.uk/
37 See End All Corporal Punishment of Children http://www.endcorporalpunishment.org.
38 Maurer and Wallerstein (1987).
39 Porter (2001).

18

AUTHORITARIAN CONTROL
METHOD 2:
SHAMING

Shaming is the second authoritarian control method used by socialising mode parents. Shaming has received little attention and little condemnation in comparison to hitting, which is increasingly meeting with legal prohibitions around the world. Shaming is harder to define; its wounds are impossible to photograph, they are harder to detect or measure. In many ways, this makes shaming more insidious than hitting. What does shaming look like? Here are a few examples – all real-life observations.

A five-month-old baby is lying in his mother's arms. He is close to sleep, then wakes and begins to grizzle. His mother tells him that he should stop being a naughty boy, and that she will be cross with him if he doesn't sleep.

An 18-month-old child is taken to a restaurant with her father and uncle. Her father goes to the bar, leaving the child with the uncle at the table. The child gets down from her chair to follow her father. She is grabbed by her uncle and told that she is a bad child, and to stay in her chair. She looks around worriedly for her father.

At an adult's birthday party a six-year-old is awake long past his bedtime. He is running around the hall with helium-filled balloons. His father yells at him to leave the balloons alone, and tells him to stop being a trouble-maker.

What did these children learn from these experiences? Many would say that the adults' responses were necessary to teach the child 'self-discipline', and the difference between 'right' and 'wrong' – between 'good' and 'bad' behaviour. Verbal punishment is common in almost every home and school. It relies on shame as the deterrent, in the same way that corporal punishment relies on pain. Shaming is one of the most common methods used to regulate children's behaviour. But what if shaming our children is harming our children? Could it be that repeated verbal punishment leaves children with an enduring sense of themselves as inherently 'bad'? If so, what can we do differently?

What is 'shame'?

Shaming is designed to cause children to curtail behaviour through negative thoughts and feelings about themselves. It involves a comment – direct or indirect – about what the child *is*. Shaming operates by giving children a negative image about their *selves* – rather than about the impact of their behaviour.

Feelings of shame make us want to hide, to conceal ourselves. Typically, we avert our eyes, we look down, we hunch over, make ourselves appear smaller, withdraw and become quiet. It is shame that makes us say things like: 'I could have died on the spot', or 'I wanted to sink through the floor' or 'I wished the earth would swallow me up'.

What does shaming look and sound like?

Shaming can take many forms – here are some everyday examples.

Shaming type	Examples
The put-down	You naughty boy! You're acting like a spoilt child! You selfish brat! You cry-baby!
Moralising	Good little boys don't act that way! You've been a bad little girl

Shaming type	Examples
Age-based expectation	Grow up! Stop acting like a baby! Big boys don't cry
Gender-based expectation	Toughen-up! Don't be a sissy! That's not very lady-like! Girls don't do that sort of thing
Competency-based expectation	You're hopeless!
Comparison	Why can't you be more like your brother? None of the other kids are acting like you

How common is shaming?

Shaming is central to socialising mode parenting, and all earlier modes. As a hallmark of authoritarian parenting, shaming is everywhere. It's as common and ordinary as a cup of tea, only not quite so innocuous. The habit of shaming children is a good example of what psychologist Alfie Kohn calls an idea "so widely shared that we no longer even notice it … so deeply rooted that it feels to us like plain common sense".[1] Shaming is even more common than corporal punishment. It is not restricted to 'abusive' families, in fact it occurs in the 'nicest' of family and school environments. A recent study of Canadian school children found only four per cent had *not* been the targets of their parents' shaming, which included "rejecting, demeaning, terrorising, criticising (destructively), or insulting statements".[2]

Shame: a new frontier of psychological study

The issue of shaming as punishment has been largely overlooked. Only recently have psychologists begun to discover that shaming has serious repercussions.

Daniel Goleman, author of *Emotional Intelligence*, says that we are now discovering the role that shame plays in relationship difficulties and violent behaviour.[3] New efforts by psychologists to study shame look at how it is acquired, and how it affects a person's relationships and functioning in society. The study of this previously 'ignored emotion' is such a new frontier because it is the most difficult emotion to detect in others. Shame is the most private of emotions, mainly expressed through hiding, and humans have yet to evolve a distinct facial expression that clearly communicates it. Perhaps this is why we might easily overlook it when our children are suffering from this secret emotion.

How shame is acquired

No one is born ashamed. It is a learned, self-conscious emotion, which starts at roughly two years of age with the advent of language and self-image. Although humans are born with a *capacity* for shame, the propensity to become ashamed in specific situations is *learned*. We learn exactly what we are expected to be ashamed of based on the things that others shame us for.

In other words, this means that wherever there is shame, there has been a shamer. We become ashamed of ourselves because someone of significance in our lives put us to shame. Shaming messages are more powerful when they come from those we are closest to, from people we love, admire or look up to. That is why parents' use of shaming can have the deepest effects on children. Our parents socialise our shame, and to a lesser extent so do our teachers, older siblings and peers. Since children are more vulnerable and impressionable than adults, shaming messages received in childhood are significantly more difficult to erase.

Messages of shame are mostly verbal, but there can be great shaming power in a look of disdain, contempt, or disgust. Sometimes, a parent's look of disgust is enough to lead a child to self-loathing.

Why is shaming so common?

Shaming acts as a pressure valve to relieve parental frustration. Shaming is anger-release for the parent, it makes the shamer feel better – if only momentarily.

When made to feel unworthy, children often work extra hard to please their parents. This makes the parent think that the shaming has 'worked'. But has it?

How shame hurts children

To understand the damage wrought by shame, we need to look deeper than the goal of 'good' behaviour. If we think that verbal punishment has 'worked' because it changed what the child is doing, then we have dangerously limited our view of the child to the *behaviours* that we can *see*. It is too easy to overlook the inner world of children; the emotions that underlie their behaviour, and the suffering caused by shame. It is also easy to miss what the child does once out of range of the shamer!

Even well-meaning adults can sometimes underestimate children's sensitivity to shaming language. There is mounting evidence that some of the words used to scold children – household words previously thought 'harmless' – have the power to puncture children's self-esteem for years to come. Children's self-identity is shaped around the things they hear about themselves. A ten-year-old girl, for example, was overcome with anxiety after spilling a drink. She exclaimed over and over 'I'm so stupid! I'm so stupid!' These were the exact words her mother had used against her. She lived in fear of her parents' judgement, and learned to shame herself in the same way that she had been shamed.

If children's emotional needs are dismissed, if their experiences are trivialised, they grow up feeling unimportant. If they are told that they are 'bad and naughty', they absorb this message and take this belief into adulthood.

Like crying for sadness, and shouting for anger, most emotions have a physical expression which allows them to dissipate. Shame doesn't. This is why the effects of shame last well into the long term.

Shame makes us feel diminished. It causes us to be inhibited and held back. When we are ashamed, we are powerlessness to act, and to express ourselves: we want to dance, but we're stopped by memories of being told not to be 'so childish'. We seek pleasure, but we're hindered by inner voices telling us we are 'self-indulgent' or 'lazy'. We strive to excel, or to speak out, but we're held back by a suspicion that we are not good enough. Shame takes the shape of the inner voices and images that mimic those who told us 'don't be stupid', or 'don't be silly!'

Shame-based suppression begins in childhood. Having felt the sting of an adult's negative judgement, the shamed child censors herself in order to escape being branded as 'naughty' or 'bad'. Shame restrains children's self-expression, it crushes their natural exuberance, their curiosity, and their desire to do things by and for themselves.

How shame hurts relationships

This shame-based self-consciousness carries well into adulthood, and it profoundly affects the way we relate to others. The shame we acquired in childhood makes us chronically afraid that our true nature might be exposed to the world's gaze. This can lead us to withdraw from others, to retire into our own private world, to become isolated. Even individuals who seem outgoing can be hiding; presenting a sociable, carefully crafted façade that protects an agonising sense of shame underneath. Shame is at the root of falseness.

Finally, the shamed tend to anticipate feeling humiliated and disapproved of by others, and this can lead to hostility, even fury. Quite often, shame makes us want to punish others. When angry, shame-prone individuals are more likely to be malevolent, indirectly aggressive or self-destructive – their anger finds no appropriate expression. A study revealed that children who had experienced higher levels of verbal aggression at home (being sworn at or insulted) exhibited higher rates of delinquency and interpersonal aggression.[4] The explosive anger that can result from accumulated feelings of shame has been variously identified by psychologists as 'shame-rage' or 'humiliated fury'.[5] Shame-rage is often what underlies bullying, delinquency and vandalism in young people. This rage is not always acted out on other people or property. Those who harbour a deep sense of shame about themselves can end up sabotaging, even destroying themselves.

Thomas Scheff, a sociologist at the University of California, has said that shame inhibits the expression of all emotions – with the occasional exception of anger. People who feel shamed tend toward two polarities of expression: emotional muteness and paralysis, or bouts of hostility and rage. Some swing from one to the other. In close relationships, unconscious and unresolved feelings of shame keep partners stuck in discordant shame-rage cycles. That's what Scheff refers to as a shame-rage spiral.[6]

Many studies have indicated that shame causes a host of

relationship difficulties. This is not surprising, since relationship skills depend on emotional intelligence. The shaming we receive as children wounds us emotionally, and thus slows the development of emotional intelligence. Shaming blocks the healthy development of empathy and self-responsibility. The legacy; a lack of empathy and a tendency to blame, can certainly place a strain on relationships.[7]

In one way or another, almost all of us suffer from deep-seated shame. Almost all of us were unnecessarily shamed as children, by our parents, our siblings, our teachers and our peers. We have become experts at disguising the emotional pain of shame wounds – and the disguises are many. While some people tend to compensate for deep feelings of shame with attitudes of contempt, superiority, domineering or bullying, others become compulsively obedient, easily intimidated, self-deprecating, and obsessively perfectionistic – they choose to be overly self-critical in order to 'beat others to the punch'.[8] So many of our most problematic social behaviours are compulsive covers for inner feelings of shame. To conceal our shame, we sneer at others, we criticise, we moralise, we judge, we patronise and we condescend. We compulsively strive for positions of social dominance, or we use our humour compulsively to hide our discomfort.[9] That is, if we are not overcome with shyness. The worst of these defensive behaviours would disappear as quickly as parents and teachers give up the habit of shaming children.

And that's why shame has, until recently, had so little attention; it often shows its face through mannerisms which we take for granted as natural and unchangeable 'personality' traits. So many of the behaviours which we brush off as 'that's just the way I am' or 'that's just the way he is', are actually symptoms of shame – and they are problematic for our relationships. We all carry something that we are ashamed of, perhaps to do with our looks, our performance, our accomplishments, or our sexuality. Sadly, it is often quite wonderful and unique aspects of ourselves that have been put to shame.

Severe shame and mental illness
When shaming has been severe or extreme, it can contribute to the development of mental illness. This link has been underestimated until now. Researchers are increasingly finding connections between early childhood shaming and clinical conditions such as depression, anxiety, personality disorders,

and obsessive-compulsive disorder. In his book, *The Psychology of Shame*, Kaufman goes further to say there is a strong link between shaming and addictive disorders, eating disorders, compulsive disorders, phobias – especially social phobias – and sexual dysfunction.[10]

Although shame has been linked to a number of mental illnesses, the idea that shaming leads to depression is the most thoroughly supported association made by psychological research.[11]

As we saw earlier, some people react to shame by becoming self-deprecating, self-loathing, even self-destructive. When the shame is severe and depression sets in, there is a risk of suicide.

Why shaming doesn't work

The main reason shaming does not work, is that it teaches nothing about relationships. While shaming has the power to control behaviour, it does not have the power to teach empathy. When we repeatedly label a child 'naughty' or otherwise, we condition them to focus inward negatively; they become pre-occupied with themselves and their failure to please. Thus children learn to label themselves, but learn nothing about relating, considering, or comprehending the feelings of others. For empathy to develop, children need to be shown how others feel. In calling children 'naughty', for example, we have told the child nothing about how we feel in response to their behaviour. Children cannot learn about caring for others' feelings, nor about how their behaviour impacts on others, while they are thinking 'there is something wrong with me'. Not surprisingly, psychotherapists and researchers are finding that individuals who are more prone to shame, are less capable of empathy toward others, and more self-preoccupied.

The only true basis for morality is a deeply felt empathy toward the feelings of others. Empathy is not necessarily what drives the 'well-behaved' 'good boy' or 'good girl'.

The myth of morality

We are naïve to confuse shame-based compliance with morally motivated behaviour. At best, repeated shaming leads to a shallow conformism, based on escaping disapproval and seeking rewards. The child learns to avoid punishment by becoming submissive and compliant. Children that have been shamed may do what they're told, but not from any desire to help you. They are just trying to avoid your reprisal. They are ashamed of themselves, and afraid of you. The charade of 'good manners' is not necessarily grounded in real interpersonal respect.

Deconstructing shame: What should we consider shameful?

Shame varies among cultures and families: what is considered shameful in one place may be permissible, un-remarkable, even desirable in another. What is called 'naughty behaviour' is usually arbitrary and subjective: it varies significantly from family to family.

In one family, nudity is acceptable, in another unthinkable. Being noisy and boisterous is welcome in one family, frowned upon in another. While one family might enjoy speaking all at once around the dinner table, another family might find this rude. Such examples help us to realise that our way is not the only way: that our own way of deciding what is shameful behaviour can be arbitrary and variable. It behoves us to be thoughtful about setting boundaries with our children, as strongly as we need to, but in a way that doesn't blame them or make them wrong for their behaviour.

In the next chapter we look at the third authoritarian control method: manipulation.

Endnotes

1. Kohn (1996).
2. Solomon and Serres (1999).
3. Goleman (1995).
4. Vissing, Strauss, Gelles and Harrop (1991).
5. Lewis (1992).
6. Scheff (1987).
7. Tangney, Wagner and Gramzov (1992); Tangney and Fischer (1995).
8. Loader (1998).
9. Kaufman (1989).
10. Kaufman (1989).
11. Andrews and Hunter (1997); Tangney, Wagner and Gramzov (1992); Lewis (1992).

19

AUTHORITARIAN CONTROL
METHOD 3:
MANIPULATION

As the 20th century unfolded, there was a gradual decline in the reliance on corporal punishment and shaming. But this evolution away from violence has not meant a rejection of authoritarian control. While moving away from being overtly punitive, we have become more adept at being manipulative. Punishment is out, and rewards are in. Why use the stick, when we can better 'teach' a child by using a carrot? Instead of using force over children, we win control seductively, we use cunning, psychological manipulation. When material or emotional rewards are conditionally tied to our children's compliance, or their pleasing us, this is authoritarianism with a kinder face.

Our modern trend to be manipulative brings with it new kinds of problems. In a different way to corporal punishment and shaming, manipulation hinders the development of emotional intelligence in children, and impairs their relationship skills. Nevertheless, the manipulative use of praise and rewards is so common, ordinary and accepted these days, that most parents would be shocked to hear that it may not be such a good method after all.

It would be hard for many of us to detect the manipulative use of rewards with sufficient objectivity, since this kind of interaction is so deeply entrenched in western cultures. The use of rewards to manipulate others' behaviour pervades 'new age' thinking in personnel management, business, education and parenting, and its image is tinged with the rosy glow of success.

Rewards and praise
We give our children ice-cream if they're 'good', chocolate if they're quiet, little gold stars if they eat their greens, maybe

even money if they get good marks at school. We praise them with a 'good boy!' or 'good girl!' if they do something that pleases us.

The modern hype about praising and rewarding children for what we call 'good' behaviour has gained massive popularity. 'Find something good your child has done, and praise them for it!' say the nouveau 'how–to' books and seminars. Psychologists all over recommend the 'star-chart' treatment to modify your child's behaviour. This trend is the offspring of a particular school of psychology – the 'behaviourists' – whose thinking currently dominates much of mainstream psychological and educational theory.

In fact, these days praising or rewarding your kids' 'good' behaviour is so customary that almost nobody – until recently – has thought to question its validity. Praising or rewarding kids is just plain common sense, *and* good parenting – isn't it? Who would doubt that it's good to give children praise, or prizes when they perform to our liking?

The praise–and–reward method has a scientific seal of approval, since it is backed by a ton of evidence from the most methodical and ingenious research that money can buy. Actually, it springs from the work of psychologists who painstakingly discovered that they could train rats to run mazes, pigeons to peck at coloured buttons, and dogs to salivate at the sound of the dinner bell – by giving them a controlled schedule of rewards. Psychologists soon became titillated about the idea of controlling human beings, by applying to us the same principles that worked on animals. Imagine their excitement when they realised that rewards work exactly the same on humans as on rats, pigeons and dogs. Modern psychological know-how has enabled us to manipulate children's behaviour, thoughts and emotions in the same way as we can teach a seal, with a few sardines and a little flattery, to balance a ball on its nose.

One problem, though. We don't particularly care about the quality of relationship we develop with a lab-rat. We are not concerned with rodents' developing self-esteem, their sense of autonomy or independence, nor do we give a hoot whether the rat will get interested in trying bigger and better mazes of its own accord, long after we stop rewarding it with little food pellets. And that, as most of our experts have failed to tell us, is where the whole fancy technology of 'reward, praise and reinforce' falls to pieces.

Over and over we have been taught that we should praise and reward our children a lot more. What could be wrong with that? On the surface, praise looks marvellous – *the* key to successful children! Scratch this surface, however, and the results look very different.

But, rewards improve children's behaviour and performance, don't they?

For a long time, that's what we thought. When the little gold stars or jelly-beans stop coming, the behaviour we were trying to reinforce tends to peter out. Children who have grown used to expecting praise, can feel crushed when it doesn't come. This dampens their perseverance. There is plenty of evidence that in the long term, reward systems are ineffective.[1]

Contrary to popular myth, there are many studies showing that when children expect or anticipate rewards, *they perform more poorly*. One study found that students' performance was undermined when offered money for better marks. A number of American and Israeli studies show that reward systems suppress students' creativity, and generally impoverish the quality of their work. Rewards can kill creativity, because they discourage risk-taking. When children are hooked on getting a reward, they tend to avoid challenges, to 'play it safe'. They prefer to do the minimum required to get that prize.[2]

Here is a good illustration of why we made the mistake of believing in rewards, based on benefits that appear *on the surface*. When an American fast-food company offered food prizes to children for every book they read, reading rates soared. This certainly looked encouraging – at first glance. On closer inspection, however, it was demonstrated that the children were selecting shorter books, and that their comprehension test-scores plummeted. They were reading for junk food, rather than for the intrinsic enjoyment of reading. Meanwhile, reading outside school (the unrewarded situation) dropped off.[3] There are many more studies showing that, while rewards may well increase activity, they smother enthusiasm and kill passion. Individuals anticipating rewards lose interest in activities that were otherwise attractive. It seems that the more we want the reward, the more we come to dislike what we have to do to get it. The activity required of us stands in the way of our coveted prize. It would have been smarter to just give the kids more interesting books, as there is plenty of evidence that intrinsically enjoyable activity is the best motivator and performance enhancer.

Can rewards and praise harm our relationship with our children?

You wouldn't think that the positive things you say to your child can be as destructive as negative labels. But there are times when this is true.

Thanks to modern advances in behavioural science, our ability to seduce or manipulate children (and animals! and grown-ups!) to do what we want them to has become increasingly sophisticated. But the cost of manipulating through rewards has been great.

Below are 10 ways praise and rewards can damage our relationship with our children.

1. Rewards and praise condition children to seek approval; they end up doing things to impress, instead of doing things for themselves. This can hold back the development of self-motivation and makes them dependent on outside opinion. When children get used to getting goodies for 'performing', they become pleasers, over-reliant on positive strokes. Rewards and praise can create a kind of addictive behaviour: children can get addicted to recognition, and thus lose touch with the simple joy of doing what they love. So many of us are addicted to prestige: we get depressed when admiration fails to come. Instead of doing what we do for its own sake, we fish for flattery or reassurance, and when the applause dies away, we sink into despair. Giving rewards or praise can be habit-forming. This is because the more rewards we use, the more we have to use them to keep children motivated. Praise cannot create a personal commitment to 'good' behaviour or performance. It only creates a commitment to seeking praise.

2. One of the worst things we can do is to praise a child's *potential*. Acclamations like 'I just know you can do it', 'You're getting better!', 'I know you've got it in you!', 'You'll get there!' sound supportive on the surface. But these compliments are loaded with our expectation that the child must improve in some way. It tells the child there is a target to keep reaching for in order to get the full 'bravo!' Praising children's potential does not help them

206

to like themselves for who they already are, and can make them feel disappointed with themselves. Underneath the praise is the silent implication: 'you're not good enough yet'. This seduces children to work harder to impress us, at the expense of their own self-esteem. As Australian psychologist Louise Porter says, "If you want children to develop a healthy self-esteem, stop praising them."[4]

3. Rewarding children's compliance is the flip side of punishing their disobedience. It is seduction in the place of tyranny. Many studies show that parents who use more rewards also use more punishment, they are more likely to be autocratic. Praise is the sweet side of authoritarian parenting. It reduces the relationship to one of controller and controlled. That is why the more astute – or less gullible! – children feel something 'icky' in praise; it makes them feel like they are being condescended. Praise is a reminder that the praiser has power over them. It diminishes the child's sense of autonomy, and, like a little pat on the head, it keeps them small.

4. Meanwhile, the rewarder is like an assessor, judging what merits praise and what doesn't. This makes them somewhat scary to the child. Praise or rewards do not make children feel supported. It makes them feel evaluated and judged. Although 'Good boy!' or 'Good girl!' is a positive judgement, it is still a judgement from on high, and ultimately it alienates the child.

5. Perceptive children can see through manipulation. They are onto us, they think our praise is slimy, and they are not easily outwitted by seductive tactics. In particular, when praise is a technique we have learned from a book or a seminar, it is likely to come across as false and contrived. Praise and rewards, like flattery, can reek of our efforts to control, and lose our child's respect.

6. Children, just like adults, naturally recoil from being controlled. We all want to grow toward self-determination. Praise can therefore create resistance, since it impinges on a child's developing sense of autonomy.

7. Rewards punish, because the child is denied the reward, praise or approval unless he or she 'comes up with the goods'. Moreover, the child who is used to being praised begins to feel inadequate if the praise doesn't come. Nothing feels more defeating to a child than to miss out

on a reward that he or she had been conditioned to expect. Inside every carrot, there is a stick.

8. When children are bribed with rewards for 'good' behaviour, they soon learn how to manipulate us by acting the part that is expected of them. They wise up to what it takes to get the goodies from us: the approval, the ice-cream, whatever. They become superficially compliant, doing what it takes to flatter or impress us, and honesty suffers. After all, who wants to be honest or real with a person who is evaluating them? Once relating is reduced to mutual manipulation rather than authenticity, this sets the stage for manipulative and dishonest relationships later in life. Manipulation erodes the functions of mutual trust, vulnerability and transparency, which are vital to healthy intimate relationships.

   As a result of early manipulation, we grow up trying hard to please, or we learn to use our wiles to impress, in order to get the goodies – at the expense of being our natural selves. We develop a phoney or false self that distorts our relationships with others.

9. Among siblings, or in the classroom, reward systems create competition, jealousy, envy, and mistrust. Rewards or prizes for 'good' performance are a threat to co-operation or collaboration.

10. Praise can make children feel robbed. If we are hungry for admiration ourselves, we can sometimes err by deriving it through our children's triumphs. We use them to make up for our own wounded self-esteem or pride. If we are praising them because they have made us feel good about ourselves, they sense this. This takes away from their good feelings about themselves; our praise can act as rain on their picnic. Some children refuse to produce what they are naturally good at, because they are repulsed by their parents' gloating.

Why are praising and rewarding strategies so popular?

Rewards are an easy way out, easier than trying to understand why a child is, as many like to glibly call it, 'misbehaving'. For example, why bother to find out why a child refuses to go to sleep at our convenience (Is he afraid? Is she feeling lonely? Is he still hungry?) if we can simply reward him or her with a trinket for going to bed on time? It feels easier to fudge over the underlying problem by using a bribe. This gives the child the clear message that we are not interested in how he or she feels. Worse still, we risk overlooking a serious emotional problem. Rewards and praise can be a gimmicky quick-fix that ignores the child as a whole person.

Rewards work well for getting children to do something that they don't naturally want to do, for the short term only. This immediate behaviour change rewards us, and keeps us addicted to rewarding. The negative consequences of rewards and praise don't materialise until later, so we fail to recognise rewards and praise as the culprit.

What can we do instead of praising them?

Often we want to express our delight and appreciation for our children; who they are as individuals, and the amazing things they do. Appreciation is different to praise because it is not manipulative. Manipulative praise, as opposed to spontaneous expressions of appreciation or acknowledgment, is loaded with the covert expectation that the child do the praiseworthy act again. Most children can sense this; they can feel the difference between genuine acknowledgment, and a deliberate strategy to reinforce their behaviour. So, how do we give our children positive feedback?

Avoiding praise or rewards does not mean holding back the love and delight we feel for our children, nor our instinctual desire to encourage them – far from it! It is perfectly possible to join in with our children and celebrate every step of their unfolding, without being manipulative. Here's a few suggestions for how to acknowledge and encourage your children to your heart's content – and theirs – while avoiding the use of praise.

Focus the child on his/her own pleasure at achieving

Instead of lavishing children with congratulations, it's better if they focus internally on the pleasure they derive from accomplishment. Children are naturally thirsty to achieve, learn and conquer. They are born with an insatiable zest for mastery, and each new attainment fills them with delight. It is this self-enjoyment that provides the greatest fuel for perseverance and further learning. When you see your child do something new, it can be wonderfully encouraging and supportive to say, 'you look like you enjoyed that!' or, 'How did it feel to do that?' 'I'm glad you did that, you look happy with yourself!'

Help your child to self-evaluate

Whenever possible, it is a good idea to ask your child about their own self-evaluation. For instance, 'How do *you* like your drawing?', 'Are *you* happy with how that piece fits into the puzzle?'

Ask them about their inner experiences

Say, for instance, your child reads you a story he just composed. After sharing how the story made you feel, you could ask, 'How do you feel about the story you wrote?', 'How did it feel to write it?', 'Did you enjoy telling it?', 'How did you come up with those ideas for your story?'

There are few things so nourishing to your child's self-esteem, and so enriching to your relationship with him, than your interest in his inner world of feeling and imagina-tion.

Use 'I' statements, instead of labelling the child

Your appreciation touches your child more deeply when it is expressed in terms of your feelings. For instance, 'I like the colours you chose!', or 'I love how you sang that song!' – instead of 'what a good drawer you are!', or 'gee you're a good singer'. Avoid labelling statements like, 'Good boy for sharing your toys!' – say instead, 'thanks for sharing with your friend, that felt good to him – and to me'. Focus on your feelings, not on a moral or quality-oriented label. An 'I' statement keeps you from holding a position of power over your child. It creates an honest and fulfilling connection between you while not interfering with the child's experience of himself.

Comment on the behaviour, not on the person

Feedback and acknowledgment are definitely important. Imagine your child has just played you a new piece she has learned on the piano. Instead of saying, 'What a good player you are!', you could tell her how much you enjoyed the piece. Better still, be specific. Tell her what in particular you liked about her playing (the passion or emotion, the beautiful melody, how carefully she played, her sense of rhythm).

When are 'positive comments' manipulative?

Ultimately, the problem is not about the perfect choice of words, or how much or when to make positive comments. When you do the right thing for the wrong reasons, it ends up being the wrong thing. Since the problem is one of intent, there is no other way but to become good examiners of our own motives. This takes practice, and the courage and humility to look within. When giving a positive comment, are you trying to seduce the child into pleasing you again, into making Mama or Papa proud? Or are you genuinely glad to see the child accomplish something that pleases *him,* or genuinely delighting in *her* being? Therein lies a paradox: that which is not intended to reinforce, but merely to 'connect', is the most reinforcing.

Is praise *ever* OK?
There is no need to muzzle ourselves, praise is wonderful when it is not used manipulatively. For instance, rewards should not be promised in advance, nor guaranteed every time the child does something you like. Positive feedback is best for your relationship with your child when it is offered spontaneously, when it springs from your heart, and not as a deliberate ploy to get more of what you want from the child.

Social results of manipulation
The adverse effects of shame and hitting are instantly recognisable. When hit or shamed, a child can identify the source of his pain. Children have a better shot at recovering from hurt when they are conscious of the fact that they have been hurt. The same cannot be said of manipulation. Manipulation through conditionally offered rewards – whether material or emotional – is superficially pleasing to the child who, more often than not, fails to react against this control tactic. The blow to emotional development comes when a child submissively accepts adults' manipulation. It is because so many of us have grown up accustomed to being manipulated, that we have collectively become so susceptible to further manipulation. Advertising, marketing and PR industries owe their billion-dollar success to a high level of public vulnerability to seduction. When the general public is susceptible enough, clever spin-doctors are able to sell us the most appalling products, policies and ideas by simply beguiling us with an appealing 'image'.

A final word about rewards and praise
Praising and rewarding are deeply ingrained habits, particularly as that's how most of us were raised and educated. It may take practise to replace them with appreciation and

acknowledgment, but the latter feels more fulfilling, and can bring you and your child closer.

Children can certainly be made to do what they don't want or love, by offering them approval, praise or other rewards. But this does not make them happy. Happiness can only be derived from doing what is intrinsically rewarding to us, and this does not require others' applause. Do we want kids to become reward-addicts, crowd-pleasers, and recognition-seekers, or do we want them to be self-motivated, faithful to themselves, following their own interests? If the latter is true, then the way is not to praise them but to appreciate them. At school, when the work is made intrinsically interesting, enjoyable, meaningful and relevant, this works better than reward systems to improve both the quality and the commitment to the work.

Children are born with an enormous desire to learn. They also have an innate capacity for honesty, empathy and considerateness. These qualities come forward as a result of our guidance, our role-modelling, and our appreciation. Rewards and praise for 'good behaviour' or 'good performance' simply get in the way.

Endnotes

[1]   Kohn (1996).
[2]   Kohn (1996).
[3]   Kohn (1996).
[4]   Porter (2001).

20

THE AUTHORITATIVE PARENT:
FROM CONTROL TO CONTACT

The goal of authoritarian parenting is to produce an obedient child who pleases the parent, and conforms to the prevailing culture. What most authoritarian parents and teachers fail to realise however, is that obedience is the opposite of autonomy. Obedience-trained children tend to lag behind in the development of creativity, self-responsibility, independence and empathy towards others. The 'good' child is good in order to gain approval and escape punishment; his 'good morals' and 'good manners' are acted out but not deeply felt. Remember: obedience is extracted through punishment and reward, and thus obedient behaviour is based on fear.

The emotionally maturing child, on the other hand, is sometimes selfish, sometimes defiant, but often deeply empathic and caring. Her consideration of others comes spontaneously and from deep within; it is not motivated by fear of punishment or need for approval. She is assertive instead of aggressive. She naturally loves to help out and to contribute to household activities.

The goal of creating compliant children is a shallow and self-serving goal. History has shown us over and over that the pre-occupation with obedience can be dangerous. In Part III we saw dire results in countries whose parents placed a high emphasis on unquestioning obedience. Psychologist Louise Porter agrees that the goal of obedient children is "a dangerous aim". She argues, rightly, that children who are trained to do as they're told are at risk of succumbing to abuse or exploitation, or of following ringleaders at school.[1] Porter has joined a chorus of voices clamouring that societies would be safer if people did not automatically follow the orders of questionable leaders. History bears out the prime importance of raising individuals who think for themselves and stand up to authority when it deserves to be challenged. Porter concludes that "[o]bedience is a fine aim for household pets, but we do not usually expect our pets to grow up and leave home".[2] Instead of obeying the powerful or the charismatic, children need to learn to obey their own instincts for considerate and caring behaviour, and for self-preservation. These kinds of impulses are innate and emerge as a result of empathic and authentic parenting.

What we need from our children is not their obedience. We need their *trust,* so that when we say 'No, don't run out onto the six-lane highway', or, 'No, don't play with that electric plug', they believe that we have their interests at heart, and they follow our lead with no bruising to their self-esteem. We also need our children to learn to show appropriate consideration towards the feelings and needs of others. Neither punishment nor manipulation can ever hope to achieve these goals.

In this time of transition, we are learning to replace a controlling attitude towards children that is as old as human civilisation. This makes a lot of us feel sceptical, even frightened, and thus we cling to the security of the old and familiar. We doubt that children could ever learn to behave pro-socially without being punished or manipulated. This reflects a pessimistic view of children, and of humanity. We fear that in order to quit our traditional demands for obedience, we have to become overly permissive with our children. Many authoritarian parents and teachers, when asked to give up smacking or shaming, react as if someone is trying to disempower them and burden them with guilt. This is not the case. Authoritative parenting is more effective, since it is assertive rather than aggressive or manipulative.

Assertion instead of aggression – contact instead of control

For any parent, the dilemma of when and how to use one's authority arises most strongly around the need to set boundaries with children. Boundary setting is pivotal to child rearing: on average, some kind of conflict or disagreement occurs between parents and their children from 3 to 15 times an hour. Boundaries are, of course, essential for any child's safety. But they also play a vital role in the development of healthy emotionality and relationship skills. It is through clear and realistic interpersonal boundaries that children learn how to balance their own needs with the needs of others. Healthy interpersonal boundaries are necessary for the development of empathy, and close relationships.

When we have some difficulty with our children's behaviour, it is our responsibility as parents to let them know this clearly. But why do most of us find it difficult to do this without blaming or shaming them? Why do we find it difficult to know how to be assertive – even appropriately angry – when our children do something inconsiderate, without resorting to punishment? Mostly, the way we relate to children is a reflection of the way we were once related to ourselves. To the degree that we were raised with punishment at school and at home, we associate anger with hurt. When our parents, teachers or peers were angry with us, this was usually followed by some kind of punishment, humiliation or attack. As a consequence, we confuse anger with hostility, not realising that the two are quite different. Few of us had good role models who showed us how to express anger responsibly and free of blame. Yet it is eminently possible to be angry without being hostile, to command a child's attention without threat or accusation. Usually, it is also possible to communicate strongly with children without the need for anger in the first place!

As we will see in detail in later chapters, most of what we call 'difficult' behaviour in children is a result of some emotional wound; a sense that they do not feel securely connected to their carers. When children's emotional needs are met from their earliest days, they tend to respond far more favourably to what their parents ask of them.

When setting boundaries with our children, we are in fact stronger and more effective when we avoid being punitive or manipulative. Real strength stands apart from toughness, harshness, or seductiveness.

The 'I' statement
A new paradigm for parent–child relationships emphasises 'contact' instead of 'control'. Effective 'contact' with our children requires our authentic and responsible self-expression. The idea of authentic 'contact' exists outside the paradigm of 'control', which forces parents to choose between coercive/aggressive or permissive styles. In fact, it rejects this polarity altogether. Setting boundaries assertively through authentic 'contact', is accomplished mainly by making 'I' statements to the child. Respectful boundary setting implies a strong

statement about *you,* and about how *you feel,* as opposed to a negative statement about *the child.* In this way, it's OK to occasionally be angry with children, because 'I' statements express anger in a responsible and non-hostile manner. An assertive 'I' statement gets the child's attention, it compels them to momentarily look beyond themselves (it is stage-appropriate for little children to be egocentric!), and at least momentarily, see you as a person. The focus is not on hurting, putting down, guilt-tripping nor shocking the child. Instead, the goal is to command the child's attention, to show yourself in a way that compels him to see you as an 'other', with your own separate needs and feelings.

Selfishness and being inconsiderate are merely the result of children's immature ability to see others as truly separate individuals. Small children tend to view others as extensions of themselves, and their behaviour reflects this. Fundamentally, emotional maturation involves awakening to the reality that others are separate individuals, with rights equal to our own, and with needs and feelings and perspectives distinct from our own. The more your child can see you *as a person,* rather than as an 'authority', the more this awakening process is facilitated.

It is through showing yourself, your willingness to be emotionally transparent, that your children gradually come to comprehend the feelings of others. Children benefit from open expression of emotions; from seeing when their parents are angry or vulnerable, as well as when they are happy and loving. There is much value in letting your children see you are annoyed, disappointed even hurt at something they have done. Children learn best when they can see the kind of impact that their behaviour has on the feelings of others. A study conducted at the Barnard College Toddler Centre in New York confirmed that mothers who openly – but appropriately – expressed anger had children who were more emotionally secure.[3]

Any book about conflict resolution will tell you that making others responsible for your feelings is destructive to relationships.[4] If you study these books you will learn a simple formula for the responsible expression of displeasure, along the lines of 'When you (do such and such), I feel (describe feeling), and what I'd like is (specify the desired change of behaviour)'. Exactly the same principles apply to our relationships with children, although the language needs to be simplified.

Example 1 For the third time in a row, your teenage daughter has made herself a snack in the kitchen, and left behind a pile of unwashed dishes.
You say, *'I'm really angry about this mess! I want it cleaned up!'*

Example 2 At the beach while you are trying to relax on the sand, your toddler keeps carelessly treading on your feet as he runs back and forth.
You say, *'Ouch! That hurts when you step on me!'*

Example 3 Your seven-year-old son starts shooting you with a water pistol just as you settle down to read a newspaper in the backyard.
You yell out, *'Hey! I'm not enjoying this game! Cut that out!'*

Example 4 You have been playing an intense game of cards with your six-year-old daughter, and you begin to feel worn out.
You say gently, *'OK...I think I'm getting tired of playing now, I'm going to need some space, and some time to myself.'*

Example 5 Your toddler insists on playing piano on your computer keyboard.
You say, *'This is my toy and it's really special to me. I'm afraid it might break, and that would make me sad. I don't want to share it.'*

Example 6 Your little boy wriggles around so much it is almost impossible to dress him to go out. You have already asked many times for his co-operation – to no avail.
You say, *'I feel really frustrated! It's too hard to dress you when you jump around like that! Please stay still!'*

Authentic self-expression

You can make contact more effectively with your children if your tone of voice and facial expression really show the emotion you are trying to convey. Children are more likely to take notice of you if your self-expression is congruent and authentic.

If you listen, your child might hear you

They are also more likely to listen to you when they are accustomed to being listened to themselves. What makes it OK to strongly voice your feelings is the fact that you also respect your children's right to voice theirs, whether positive or negative. They too have a right to be angry or disappointed with you sometimes, and they deserve to have those feelings heard. Kids learn to listen to you through the way you listen carefully and patiently to them, and the way you validate their feelings without trying to change them.

Own your feelings

Authentic contact with your children means *owning* your feelings. This means an honest expression of feelings, without blame. While we want our children to learn responsibility for their actions, we ourselves are responsible for our feelings – that is, our reactions. Showing your children how you feel only goes wrong when this is used to intimidate or manipulate. If your children are afraid of you, then you have been too overpowering. I make the distinction between being real and transparent, versus being emotionally annihilating or overwhelming. The goal of showing our feelings is to make contact, not to manipulate or frighten. It can be important to check back with your children after resolving a conflict: 'Were you startled when I raised my voice earlier?' or, 'How did you feel when I was grumpy with you?' Their feedback is essential in order to keep your interactions within emotionally safe bounds.

I would also caution that showing anger – or other 'difficult' emotions – to babies is inappropriate, and likely to be too overwhelming for them.

In sharing our feelings, we must also guard against using children to lean on as our counsellors or confidants, burdening them with our troubles, drowning them in our feelings, or worse still, making them feel guilty. Responsible self-expression must be sensitive to our child's age and level of understanding. While it is important to be emotionally visible with your children, the intensity of feeling needs to be measured and contained to a level where they demonstrably feel safe.

Many of us in western cultures seem to recoil from authentic expression of feeling – it frightens us. But when this is done authentically and responsibly, it is the very thing that builds intimacy and trust, not just with our children, but with all our loved ones. Being emotionally open is essential to a healthy relationship with our children, and this helps their own emotional development. They need to get to know us as *persons*, not as arbiters of power. We are their role models for how to share feelings appropriately.

'Contact' – instead of 'control' – takes time and practice, especially as good role models for this kind of relating have been scarce. Historically, the western way of relating has been dismissive of emotion, we have over-emphasised the 'rational'. This has made us too controlling, uncomfortable with spontaneity, at times even cold. Reading and commitment to practice are warranted, but the rewards are plentiful. An emotionally open relationship with your children is mutually satisfying and nourishing, and it provides for them a strong foundation for their developing sense of identity.

Demonstrating empathy – instead of preaching morality

Children do not become more moral by having morality drummed into them. Rules of morality are an abstraction, which can be adhered to by rote without any emotional conviction. I stress empathy instead of morality. Empathy is an internal and natural morality, it emerges spontaneously because it is fuelled by the heart. Children behave 'morally' as a result of having been loved and respected, and related to with authenticity. A better goal is therefore to promote and foster the natural development of empathy. Children are born with a natural drive to develop a social conscience. When treated with the same respect as adults, and exposed to adults who respect each other; children will naturally develop a capacity for empathic, considerate and respectful behaviour. This is the foundation of moral behaviour.

How can children learn to be empathic unless they are faced with a parent who is transparently real? When you play the role of authority, you are not being real, but distant and false. Here is what a real person is: sometimes sad, sometimes vulnerable, sometimes irritated, frustrated, elated, loving, angry, tender, confused, mistaken and uncertain. In other words, not so in-control. And it is your essential humanness that your children want (and need) to get to know. Your humanness is knowable to your children through your openness about your emotions. In this rich soil, their natural latency for empathy and caring can grow solid as a tree. When children are treated empathically, and when they can know their parents as real persons – that is, with their own needs, limits, and vulnerabilities – they mature emotionally. Ultimately, this is what best helps them to become naturally considerate, responsible and empathic individuals, with a strong self-worth and a keen social awareness.

Re-directing the child's impulses

From time to time we are compelled to intervene in our child's activity, when we fear that either a person or a treasured object might get hurt. Instead of just chastising or stopping the child, we can also provide a safer, alternative activity. For instance, occasional aggression is part of normal, balanced and healthy development. Children are often shamed and punished for this, when instead they could be shown ways to channel their natural aggression safely. For example, a friendly, humour-filled wrestle can help to release the child's aggression while taking the heat out of a potential conflict.

When a child wants to be strongly physical in his or her play, it is better to give them something unbreakable (or inexpensive!) to play with. This can allow their natural, aggressive charge to dissipate harmlessly.

Sometimes it is important to re-evaluate whether we need to chastise at all. A guideline comes from considering whether the behaviour in question is actually causing harm to anyone, or creating a concrete risk.

The role model

Role-modelling is the most powerful teaching tool. Children don't do what you say, they do as you *do*. The kind of respect they show others and themselves is a reflection of the kind of respect they have themselves been shown – and the respect they have witnessed displayed between the important people in their lives. Are we role-modelling the kind of behaviour that we want our children to display?

Changing the bottom line: our attitudes to children

Sometimes it is not enough to learn new parenting formulas or techniques. New ideas about 'what to do when my child does this or that' often fail to improve our relationship with our children. Sometimes what is needed is an attitudinal change on our part. The most lasting and powerful improvements come from fundamental overhauls of our most deeply held attitudes toward children.

We can do this by:
- avoiding projections;
- reassessing the label 'misbehaviour' in terms of the child's stage of development;
- reassessing the label 'misbehaviour' by truly trying to understand what is going on for the child;
- cultivating empathy by remembering what it felt like to be a child; and
- finally, taking care of our own emotional wellbeing.

Avoiding projections

The first fundamental attitude shift should involve a re-evaluation of what we think is motivating our children's behaviour. There is no question that parenting can be frustrating sometimes – even exasperating. But it is groundless to automatically assume that the child is out to upset us, or to attribute some kind of nasty intention to the child. This imagined malevolence is usually what underlies the impulse to shame and punish children. I wish I had a dollar for each time I heard somebody say that their children are deliberately trying to antagonise them – simply because they are crying, or asking for something that the parent cannot give. A surprising number of professional parenting advisors still maintain, for instance, that toddlers' temper tantrums are deliberate ploys to outwit their parents. This blaming idea persists despite modern scientific understandings about the toddler's immature brain, and its inability to regulate strong emotion.

When we automatically assume a deliberate intent on the part of our children, simply because we feel irritated by them, this is called 'projection'. A projection is an erroneous attribution about another person's motivation. In truth, what we project onto our children says a lot more about us than about them.

I do not believe that children are incapable of malice or cunning. As much as I deplore the odious, ancient idea that children are born sinful, I am also sceptical about the romantic, Rousseau–like fancy that all children are born 'good'. We should never judge children according to moralistic criteria of 'good' or 'bad'. All children are capable of a broad range of selfish, and as they mature, altruistic behaviours. Either way, they are loveable.

The more we learn to respond to our children without assessing or judging them – and the less we project onto them – the more effective we become as parents. Far too many of our children's awkward or problematic attempts to learn about human relations get punitively dismissed as 'misbehaviour'.

'Misbehaviour' – or developmental stage?

Sometimes what we condemn as 'misbehaviour' is simply the child's attempt to have some need met in the best way they know, or to master a new skill. The more parents can accept this, the less they are tempted to shame children into growing up faster. For instance, it is normal for toddlers to be selfish, possessive, exuberant and curious. It is not unusual for two-year-olds to be unable to wait for something they want, as they don't understand time the way adults do. It is quite ordinary for three-year-olds to be sometimes defiant or hostile. If we shame instead of educate, we interrupt a valuable and stage-appropriate learning process, and our own opportunity to learn about the child's needs is lost.

When three-year-old Alice defies her mother by refusing to pack up her toys – after being told to do so repeatedly – she may be attempting to forge a separate and distinct self-identity. This includes learning to exercise her assertiveness, and learning to navigate open conflict. Toddlers can be galling sometimes. But this does not mean they're 'misbehaving'. In fact, I would go further to say that in children, there is no such thing as 'misbehaviour', only attempts to learn the complex and difficult lessons of human relations.

Strong limits are essential, but if children are shamed for their fledgling and awkward attempts at autonomy, they are prevented from taking a vital step to maturity and confidence. In the period glibly called the 'terrible twos', and for the next couple of years, toddlers are discovering how to set their own boundaries. They are learning to assert their distinct individuality, their sense of will. This is critical if they are to learn how to stand up for themselves, to feel strong enough to assert themselves, and to resist powerful peer pressures later in life. If we persist in crushing their defiance, and shaming children into submission, we teach them that setting boundaries for themselves is not okay.

Consider the example of eight-month-old Jayden who crawls over to something that has flashing lights and interesting sounds. He pulls himself up to it and begins to explore. He does not know that it is his father's prized stereo. Jayden finds himself being tapped on his hand by his mother, who tells him to stop being naughty. He cries. At eight months', Jayden is unable to tell the difference between a toy and another's valuable property, and is incapable of self-restraint, even if he could make that distinction. Children's ceaseless curiosity – a frequent target for shaming – is what drives them to learn about the world. When children's exploration is encouraged in a safe way, rather than castigated, their self-confidence grows. Unfortunately, we frequently call a behaviour which may be entirely stage-appropriate 'naughty', simply because it threatens our need for order, or creates a burden for us.

A flustered mother and her distraught four-year-old daughter emerge from a local store. The girl is sobbing as she is forcefully strapped into her stroller. 'Stop it, you whinger!' screams the mother, as she shakes her finger in the little girl's face. Children are often berated for simply crying. Many people believe that a crying baby or child is 'misbehaving'. Strong expressions of emotion – such as anger and sadness – are children's natural way of regulating their nervous system, while communicating their needs. Children cry when they are hurting, and they have a right to express this hurt! Even though it is often hard to listen to, it must be remembered that it is a healthy, normal reaction that deserves attention. It is tragic to see how often children are shamed for crying.

Here's a further example of what happens when we are unaware of developmental norms. Until recently, toddlers were started on potty-training far too early, before they were organically capable of voluntary bowel control. Many found this transition to be a battle, and toddlers were commonly shamed and punished for what was a normal inability. What was once a struggle both for parents as for children has been greatly alleviated through more accurate information about childhood development. Shaming, punishment or manipulation often take place when we try to encourage or force a behaviour that is developmentally too early for the child's age.

We have come a long way in our understanding about child development in recent decades, and made many advances in childcare as a result. Children and parents are both happier when parents have 'reasonable' expectations of the children. An in-depth discussion of developmental norms pertaining to emotional development will follow in Part VI.

Understanding instead of control

Is it possible to *understand* what motivates children when they are 'behaving badly', instead of shaming, punishing or manipulating them? What might 'bad' behaviour be a *reaction* to?

When we don't seek to understand children's 'bad' behaviours, we risk neglecting their needs. For instance, sometimes children repeatedly behave aggressively – over and above what can normally be expected of children their age. This could be due to conflict in the home, bullying at school, or competition with a sibling. Often what we expediently label as 'bad' behaviour, is a vital signal that the child in question might actually be hurting. As we saw earlier, there is much research showing that a consistent pattern of antisocial behaviours, for example hostility and bullying, are children's reactions to having felt victimised in some way. Children often 'act out' their hurts aggressively, when they have not found a safe way to show that they have been hurt.

Ironically, authoritarian control methods can themselves be the underlying cause of difficult behaviour, as they tend to make children feel small and powerless. Sometimes, children turn the tables: they reclaim this lost power by finding another person to push around – usually someone smaller or more vulnerable than themselves.

There are many other common causes for difficult behaviour. Children are usually highly sensitive to the 'vibes' in their environment, they pick up tensions between their parents, or other family members. At times 'naughty' behaviour may be the child's way of reacting to this tension.

Kids are less given to acting out when they are receiving enough attention, when their hunger for play, discovery and pleasurable human contact is satisfied. Provocative behaviour can indicate boredom, or perhaps the need for another 'dose' of engagement with someone who is not feeling irritable or worn out, someone who has the time and energy to spare.

Finally, children can be grumpy or 'difficult' simply from over-tiredness. In this case, what is dismissed as 'bad' behaviour might be a child's way of saying 'I'm over the edge, and I can't handle it'. Ironically, when we as parents react with verbal assaults, we are communicating the same thing. Isn't yelling at children that they are 'naughty' or 'terrible' (or worse) a kind of adult tantrum, a dysfunctional adult way of coping with frustration?

It is worth remembering that some causes of 'misbehaviour'

are a lot less obvious. For instance, children need to feel our strength, they are uncomfortable with weakness in our personal boundaries. They need exposure to our true feelings, and they sense when we are hiding or pretending. They need their feelings and opinions validated, and are highly sensitive to poor empathy. Frequently, they react to any of these conditions by becoming provocative. They provoke us for a strong and authentic response that lets them feel our presence and attention. This tends to happen especially when we have been emotionally distant or remote. Sometimes we blame and shame children for their vexing behaviour, simply because the causes are initially hard to see.

Cultivating empathy: through remembering

As parents, we often do to our children as was done to us. It is known that violence can be passed down across generations. Those that have forgotten the sting and humiliation of being punished, risk being insensitive to the pain they inflict on their own children. Change requires deepening one's empathy toward the child, and this comes from remembering how it felt to *be* a child. There is probably no more important parenting skill than the ability to recall our own childhood feelings. The understanding that comes from seeing the world through a child's eyes can help adults to influence children without shaming or punishing them.

Parents need to manage their own emotions first!

As parents, it is not unusual to find ourselves struggling, frazzled, or nearing an emotional boiling-point. When we don't find healthy ways to discharge this frustration, we risk taking it out on our children. We might respond to our children in an authoritarian manner out of a need to vent frustration.

Although irritation is a normal part of parenting this is not because children are 'too demanding'. Of course, parenting is a demanding job, but children are children, and the fact that child rearing can be difficult is not their fault. There are many ways to re-route our excess anger, such as screaming into a pillow, chopping some wood, going for a walk, or talking our frustration through with friends. There are times when one or more sessions with a counsellor, psychologist or family therapist might be warranted, if a difficulty in relation to a child does not resolve.

Everyone's capacity for loving patience is finite; that's human. When parents experience excessive strain this is largely due to our adherence to this myth: that it takes just two parents to raise a child. Our society has grossly underestimated the energy required to truly meet children's needs. We can avoid shaming simply by sharing the load – by asking for, and accepting, practical help from trusted friends, family and community. When we hear ourselves shaming our children, we might take this as a sign that we need more assistance.

Early childhood experiences – both loving and painful – have a lasting impact because they powerfully determine the course of brain development. Part V will examine how personality is formed in the early years, through the neurological and biochemical effects that important relationships have on children's central nervous systems.

Endnotes

[1] Porter (2001).
[2] Porter (2001) p 4.
[3] Karen (1994) p 242.
[4] Cornelius and Faire (1999); Crum (1998).

EMOTIONS, PERSONALITY AND YOUR CHILD'S GROWING BRAIN

If we are to reach real peace in this world and if we are to carry on a real war against war, we shall have to begin with children; and if they grow up in their natural innocence, we won't have to struggle; we won't have to pass fruitless idle resolutions, but we shall go from love to love and peace to peace, until at last all the corners of the world are covered with that peace and love for which consciously or unconsciously the whole world is hungering.

Mahatma Gandhi[1]

21

THE SHAPING OF PERSONALITY AND HUMAN RELATIONS

I n this chapter we will be looking at how child rearing shapes society by conditioning each individual's style of relating to other people. Recent discoveries in the neuro-sciences have shed light on how the components of personality are etched into the child's developing brain, through his or her early interactions with care givers. The neuro-biology of emotional development is only a recently developed field of study, but discoveries made have not only explained, but confirmed, what psychologists have long been saying about children's emotional development and personality formation. Bruce Perry, a neuro-scientist, sums it up by saying that "early life experience determines neuro-biology".[2] Perry is referring to the hard-wiring in our nervous systems that animates personality.

To a significant extent, we develop emotionally according to how we are related to, from the earliest moments of life. Our emotional development underlies our predispositions to relate to others and to the world around us in characteristic ways. In a nutshell, this is how child rearing shapes society.

It's not that our genes have no influence on our behaviour, they do – though indirectly. A useful (if imperfect) analogy might be to say that genes are somewhat like raw ingredients, and childhood is the method of cooking. Alternatively, genes might be thought of as the seed of a tree, while childhood represents the complex set of conditions that support and direct the seed's growth: the soil profile, the nutrients, micro-organisms and toxins in the soil, the climate, and the precipitation. These environmental conditions sculpt the shape, size, colour, health and vigour of the tree, so that if two cloned seeds were germinated under different conditions – one on the side of a dry cliff, the other in an alluvial plain, one in dry, mild weather, the other exposed to violent storms – these trees would look very different from each other. Certainly, genes play an indirect role in some aspects of our emotional strengths and vulnerabilities, but this role is more modest than previously thought.

Thus, much of what underlies our most compassionate, loving, creative and 'moral' behaviours is the loving nurturance we received in childhood, and our more destructive urges are similarly the expression of childhood hurts. The same holds true for group behaviours including those that are embedded in traditional, cultural and religious practices. Anthropologist Robert Edgerton makes a powerful case for the idea that cultural behaviour is not necessarily healthy nor adaptive.[3] The stories told in Parts II and III corroborate Edgerton's idea. Much of what is customary around the world is a reflection of collective, early childhood emotional wounds. Lloyd de Mause sums it up in this way, "Societies are not constructed in the most logical or even most adaptive forms possible. Given the hominid brain we started with, even the most bizarre forms of society revealed by the historical record can be understood as the flawed products of evolving psyches and evolving brains."[4] Early childhood is the foundry of personality, and therefore society, because the earliest experiences of human relationships are encoded into the growing brain.

Not in our genes

We now know a lot more about the way genes interact with the environment. The genes are not the dictators we once thought they were. Our individual genetic blueprints have a significant say in such things as our physical attributes, or the diseases we might be prone to. What our environment affects is our emotional development, our attitudinal orientation to the world, the way we ordinarily and habitually relate to one another. Most people know these enduring traits as 'personality'.

When it comes to personality, genes do not seal our fate. New research has demonstrated that environments can actually change genetic expression. Genetic messages can be re-written, creating new behaviours, because some "genetic structure is wide open to environmental changes".[5] Gene mutations are not as random as we once thought, they can also be selectively made to accommodate environmental pressures. This means, for instance, that in an environment that is unpredictable or unfriendly, it is possible for an organism to make changes at the genetic level in order to adjust to this reality.[6] The role of genes in human relations is further diminished by recent studies stating that the same gene can be expressed in numerous ways depending on the social environment in which it exists.[7]

If the idea of genetically based personality traits is now receding into obsolescence, it is also because "there simply are no adequate studies of the heritability of human personality traits".[8] For a long time, scientists speculated a one-to-one relationship between genes and personality attributes. It was once suspected that every human trait was the direct and inescapable result of a single gene, or a group of genes. In particular, scientists preoccupied themselves with trying to find a gene that can be blamed for delinquency or criminality. In every case, they have come up empty-handed. With regard to what is perhaps the most problematic of all human characteristics, the link between violence and genes is the most tenuous of all. There is also mounting evidence that violence is one of the least heritable of all human traits.[9] It is now widely thought that there are no specific genes for any behavioural traits.[10]

While some personality dimensions are influenced by the genes, these hereditary factors are neutral; that is, they only become troublesome as a result of some emotional injury. Even severe psychotic illnesses such as schizophrenia are explained by a combination of genetic and environmental factors.[11] A child's complex genetic profile may have *some* influence – alongside age and a host of other circumstances – on whether she tends to favour 'fight', 'flight' or 'freezing' responses when met with harshness. In other words, under intense stress some children might naturally favour more aggressive responses, others might favour escape, and others might tend to become detached or 'play dead'. It is only if these responses become habituated and exaggerated, that they begin to interfere with relationships. So, although there are some genetic differences in the nature of emotional vulnerability, all children are profoundly vulnerable in relation to adults. All are injured by harshness or emotional neglect, and these injuries are compensated for in their developing personalities.

Not the genes, but early experiences with care givers "sculpt the enduring temperamental features of the child's emerging personality".[12] "Experience, not genetics, results in the critical neurobiological factors associated with violence."[13] With these words, foremost neuro-biologists Allan Schore and Bruce Perry (respectively) confirm that the violence of history, the violence we face today, is *learned*. The passing down of violence – and every other emotional dysfunction – from one generation to another, is a function of the developing human brain. These advances in the neuro-sciences are indeed reassuring for our ability to reduce social and global violence. It is well within our grasp to abate social dysfunction with each passing generation.

Neuro-biology and neuro-chemistry of violence

Much of what we have learned about how experience affects emotional development comes from studies of the neurological impact wrought by neglect and abuse on the child's brain. The experience of violence in the first three years of life profoundly alters the course of brain development. Once certain neurones (brain-cells) become over-sensitised as a result of persistent or intense emotional trauma, they can more easily be re-activated by similar but less threatening provocations. The result is that an emotionally wounded or traumatised child too readily interprets situations as threatening, and inappropriately reacts defensively. The brain of the maltreated child has been conditioned to be hyper-vigilant. It is because of this over-sensitisation of areas of the brain concerned with self-protection that children who are maltreated can become developmentally retarded, depressed, aloof, disruptive or hostile.[14]

Stressful parent–child relations impact children's behaviour by altering their brain chemistry. This holds true for animals as well as for humans. When some female macaque monkeys were placed under stress, their offspring developed altered brain chemistry. As a result of this imbalance, the young macaques behaved more timidly.[15] In human children, overwhelming and persistent emotional stress causes an imbalance in noradrenaline[16] and serotonin[17] levels, as well as a disruption in cortisol[18] levels.[19]

When an infant receives too little direct loving contact, this causes the areas of his brain that regulate emotion, self-image and beliefs about relationship to become atrophied, with serious and long-lasting – often permanent – consequences for behaviour.[20] Touch deprivation releases steroids that damage the hippocampus,[21] leading to cognitive and behavioural problems later in life. That is why the practice of baby swaddling, for instance, can be so damaging for the long term (see Chapter 5). Swaddling enforces immobility, and deprives the baby of the essential experience of tender touch.[22]

There are many other ways in which trauma alters the course of a child's brain development. The hippocampus is a part of the brain concerned with inhibiting impulses; it allows us to delay responses, to think before we act, as it were. When trauma happens before the hippocampus is fully operational (at roughly three years of age), or if the trauma is emotionally too overwhelming for the hippocampus to process, the memory of the trauma is stored and coupled with acute emotions such as terror or rage. These emotions are subsequently triggered by situations that barely resemble the original traumatic incident. For instance, a child who is bitten by a dog may later be terrified of all dogs – even small and friendly ones. Another child who has been abused might become enraged and uncontrollably hostile when triggered by relatively inoffensive provocations or frustrations.

When an infant is most helpless and unable to escape a traumatic situation, this causes severe damage to the hippocampus – neurones and connective neural pathways are destroyed. The earlier the trauma therefore, the deeper the effects on the developing personality. An atrophied hippocampus is one of the main factors underlying the poor impulse control shared by survivors of childhood abuse. The hyper-reactivity that ensues can account for many social problems, including excess docility, bullying or compulsively dominant behaviour.

An area of the brain called the 'orbitofrontal cortex' is most responsible for 'emotional intelligence'.[23] Like the hippocampus, it is also involved in the regulation of our impulses, and it is responsible for our ability to feel empathy for others.[24] Emotionally traumatic experiences precipitate the secretion of a host of stress-related hormones and neuro-transmitters, such as cortisol. In excess quantities, these brain chemicals can damage brain cells – in the orbitofrontal cortex in particular – and can cause permanent disruptions to the balance of brain chemistry.[25] This can be truly costly for an individual's 'emotional intelligence'. The greatest damage is done when emotional stress is chronic and persistent. The damage to neurons and to brain chemistry in maltreated children contributes to many kinds of pathology later, including depression.[26]

The stress of emotional injury also decreases the production of thyroid hormone, which is associated with the healthy regulation of fear and anxiety. This process can contribute to anxiety disorders later in life. Hormonal depletions such as these can also compromise a child's capacity to moderate aggression and impulsivity – making violent behaviour more likely. In fact, new brain-scan technology allows us to see that the brains of violent individuals are damaged in the prefrontal area, responsible for the capacity for empathy, the regulation of emotion and behavioural self-control.[27]

If it's hard to envisage a purpose for the violent child-rearing practices of history - like infant cranial deformation, swaddling and body mutilation – then consider what advantages these might have brought to the perpetrating cultures. By subjecting children to chronic and extreme stress, brain cortisol levels would have remained at peak levels. The resulting damage to the hippocampus and areas of the prefrontal lobes concerned with impulse control and empathy would be likely to produce, in increased numbers, the kind of nervous systems that characterise remorseless fighters; individuals desensitized to the pain of others and hard-wired for hair-trigger violence. It is doubtful that the decision to traumatize children so severely in order to produce a warrior society is a consciously made decision. Nevertheless, societies the world over have acted intuitively to deprive children of tenderness and the battle-ready warriors that resulted have rewarded many of these harsh practices – well into modern times.

As with most problems of human relations, there is a distinct neuro-chemical basis for interpersonal violence. But biochemistry is not the cause of our troubled relationships. It is no more than the molecular mediator for learned patterns of behaviour – patterns which are more readily acquired when the brain is still immature. Since the child's brain is equally open to being imbued with predominantly compassionate and assertive (non-violent) responses, those are the traits any child will reflect if she is treated in kind, from the first moments of awareness.

Beyond the behavioural distortions mentioned so far, abuse and neglect also cause deficient integration between left and right hemispheres of the brain; so that abuse survivors are more likely to have epileptic seizures, they are twice as likely to have abnormal electrical activity in the brain (EEG), and they suffer more impairments to memory.[28] Abused children have a cortex that is 20 per cent smaller, on average, than children who have not been abused.[29] In fact, children who have suffered early trauma have been shown to have generally smaller brains as a result.[30]

Single-event traumatic experiences tend to be easier for children to recover from, if they are able to cry, scream if necessary, and be soothed. What is more likely to leave permanent imprints on the developing personality are the repeated or ongoing dynamics that characterise the relationships on which the child depends for his emotional wellbeing. In other words, frequent abandonment or non-responsiveness to a baby's cry, or frequent hostility or coldness directed at an infant, have a more profound and indelible impact on his brain than a single traumatic event. Early emotional stressors such as these leave children with a chronically over-activated biological stress response; as if permanently on high-alert, ready to respond to an unfriendly environment.[31] The over-responsive hyper-arousal apparatus that has been built into a traumatised child's nervous system makes him more anxious, gives him more muscle tone, a higher body temperature and higher blood pressure.[32] Unfortunately, his hyper-vigilant behaviours – such as suspicion, aggressiveness or evasiveness – ensure that many people he interacts with will find him unpleasant, and become unfriendly towards him. In this way, his defences create a social environment that confirms his negative worldview, locking him into a vicious cycle of conflict.

Unless early emotional needs are met adequately, children grow up more vulnerable to drug addiction, depression, dissociative disorders and personality disorders.[33] Emotional health is highly dependent on the quality of infants' relationship to their caregivers, and the quality of attention given to their changing emotional needs.

The excesses of violence that blight our world are a manifestation of emotional retardation. Early emotional injuries retard growth in the parts of the brain that enable us to feel empathy, remorse, and our essential connection to other humans.[34] A true commitment to 'moral' behaviour and the capacity for loving relationships cannot easily be taught; these abilities are built into children's brains when caregivers are empathically attuned to the children's emotional needs.

How shame affects the growing brain

It was mentioned in Chapter 18 that childhood shame can be psychologically damaging. Children commonly feel some shame, from around 18 months of age, as a result of the increasing imposition of limits on their behaviour. Some measure of parent–child conflict is unavoidable, and in fact necessary, to healthy emotional development. Humility – as distinct from shame – is important to the development of healthy social awareness, and a sense of self that is not grandiose but grounded in reality. Recent developments in brain research have helped us to understand the exact neurological basis for the life-long effects of humility and shame.

When a child is reprimanded, an image of the scolder's look of disapproval becomes stored in the lateral tegmental limbic circuit – a part of the brain concerned with emotion. Later in life, the growing child and adult judge their own behavioural impulses through the lens of these stored inner representations, which are imprinted as images charged with feelings of shame. These inner visual and auditory records of the shamer usually – but not always – operate beneath conscious awareness. The experience of parents setting healthy boundaries causes the orbitofrontal brain to grow, its purpose being to contain and regulate raw emotion (impulses from the limbic cortex). But when the parent sets a boundary or limit, for some time following the symbiotic time of infancy, the toddler feels a degree of hurt and betrayal. There is emotional stress associated with the change in the dynamics of the parent–child relationship heralded by the shift from babyhood to toddlerhood. A look of disapproval triggers cortisol secretion (a stress hormone) and inhibits the flow of wellbeing hormones such as endorphins and dopamine.[35] It is important that the parent soothe the toddler after imposing restrictions on him, to help him cope with what Schore refers to as "shame-stress".[36] Some reassurance of the parent's love repairs the child's wounded 'self' and restores his self-confidence. If parents diligently assist with their child's shame–repair, he soon learns to take over, and based on his parents' role modelling, repair his own shame when needed. Inner representations – stored as emotional and narrative memory in the brain – of a soothing and reassuring parent are used later in life for shame-repair. This internal portrait of a reassuring adult is essential so that as an adult the individual won't be disabled or overly inhibited by experiences of shame. Though this process is usually unconscious, it secures our ability to self-soothe, and to recover from shame when needed.

If we lack these positive images, stored in our emotional

memory centres, we are at risk of becoming hostile, or overly submissive – and possibly slipping into depression. Psychological and social problems arise when a child grows up with images of a disapproving face stored in the brain centres that constitute the unconscious mind, without the subsequent images of a soothing and reassuring adult. This child is likely to become either hyper-sensitive and defensive, or overly inhibited.

Further developments in neuroscience offer additional explanations why shaming children is, in the long run, such an ineffective way to set boundaries. When an adult shames a child, this triggers a chain reaction in the child's brain that kills the ability for empathy or attention to others. The emotionally-charged amygdala in the child's brain overwhelms the prefrontal cortex, so the child's ability to attend to others is drowned out by a self-focussed anxiety. The result is that any 'good' behaviour that follows is based on fear and a shamed preoccupation with self, not on any genuine concern for, or awareness of, the needs of others [37]. So shame, in fact, stifles the development of empathy.

The violent leaders and obedient followers that mar human history are a catastrophic combination of nervous systems excessively hard-wired for 'fight' responses (the violent leaders)— and shame-based or fear-based submission (the obedient followers).

Nurturance and optimal brain development
At birth, the brain is one of the most immature of the body's organs, and it is only a quarter of its full-grown size. The most consuming business of infancy is to develop the brain; a task that uses up over 50 per cent of the total basal metabolic rate. The brain attains nearly 70 per cent of its final mass by the first birthday, having gained in weight from 400 grams at birth to 1000 grams. This remarkably speedy brain growth begins to slow down in the second year. By the age of three, the brain has accumulated 90 per cent of its final adult mass.[38] This massive expansion of brain tissue involves the growth of a myriad connective pathways between neurones; the nature and direction of which is not pre-set. Brain growth is experience-dependent; it is guided by the child's experience of relationships.[39] If the child's environment is consistently empathic, loving and tender, the brain grows far differently than if he or she is met with coldness, inconsistency, or harshness. The brain's astounding capacity for transformation

decreases with age, so the tendencies established in these early, formative years are resistant to change later. The first few years are far more critical to emotional development – and so, personality – than any other time of life.[40]

The parts of the brain concerned with regulation of emotion and deeply held attitudes to human relations are particularly dependent on human contact in order to develop. A mother's joyful interactions with her baby actually provide an essential building block to these areas of the brain. Such interactions, including tender touch, sustained loving gaze and smile, and rhythmic soothing and rocking, are essential for healthy emotional development.[41] A secure attachment between a baby and her caregivers prepares the emotional and neurological foundation for harmonious and dynamic relationships in adulthood. Exactly what babies need in order to feel securely attached will be discussed in more detail in Part VI.

Let's take a closer look at how nurturance shapes the child's emotional make up by altering the course of brain-growth. One of the key elements of secure attachment is affectionate eye contact. A look of love cannot be faked, for only when it is genuinely felt in the caregiver's heart, it dilates his or her pupils. Experiments show that babies smile more when they are looking at eyes that have dilated pupils – they sense the difference between a dispassionate look, and a genuinely affectionate look.[42] A caregiver's sustained, loving gaze and smile suffuses infants with indescribable joy. What ensues is a cascade of dopamine, endogenous opioids, enkephalins and endorphins in the baby's brain – all feel-good chemicals associated with loving relations. This joy-precipitated surge of brain chemicals promotes the maturation of precise regions of the cortex, such as the orbitofrontal cortex (OFC), which are concerned with the healthy regulation of emotion later in life. Nerve projections travel directly from the eyes to the OFC and by meeting each other's gaze, parent and child are interlinking their OFCs and thus forming an empathy loop. The OFC contains neurons that specialize in detecting emotion in others' eyes and faces, as well as in their tone of voice. Eye contact provides a stream of rapport that builds intimacy between parent and child [43]. Each parental smile and affectionate look "actually helps the brain to grow".[44]

Every baby requires this kind of nourishing experience regularly and frequently, for healthy brain development. When a child is consistently treated gently and empathically, this produces in her brain a biochemistry that is incompatible with violence.[45] By implication, when most children will be raised in consistently loving and empathic environments, war will be neurologically impossible.

By the end of the first year, the infant has stored an internal representation of her mother's loving face in the area connecting the anterior temporal and the orbitofrontal cortices. It is as if the child has filed a video-clip of her mother in her brain's 'hard-disk'. Henceforth, these inner images, though rarely consciously remembered, will animate her core emotional responses, forming the basis of her fundamental relating style. When she feels her emotional needs are consistently attended to, this engenders in the child an enduring expectation of a supportive world. This attitude is pervasive and unconscious, and it inclines the child toward friendly and considerate behaviour.

Depending on severity, significant gaps in the fulfilment of stage-specific emotional needs can be a major contributing factor to serious psychopathology and developmental disorders. But much more commonly, the breaks in the emotional connection between child and parent are less severe: they don't interfere with basic social functioning, but they create deeply held unconscious attitudes about human relationships that are potentially problematic later in life. Within the realm of 'normalcy', there exists a huge range of persistent difficulties with human relations, particularly with intimate relations. These 'normal' but enigmatic blocks to intimacy are painful, and they are equally the product of breaks in emotional development that occur in childhood. A detailed account of common, problematic unconscious attitudes that arise from specific developmental arrests will be discussed in Part VI.

How the infant brain adapts to emotionally painful experiences

Each child gathers vital information about the nature of the world through the way she is related to. Since her parents are her universe, the way they respond to her reveal the kind of world she must prepare herself for. The nature of the parenting relationship is integrated into the infant brain as a template of human relations, a working model of the world. Accordingly, the child makes the best possible adaptation to that template, with whatever resources she has available. Her unique adaptations will be recognised as her 'personality'.

It is the brain's job to develop responses and abilities suitable to the environment it finds itself in, and to make those self-protective responses operate unconsciously, automatically and spontaneously for optimal survival. The human brain has amazing adaptive malleability. But once a part of the brain is organised, it is resistant to change. The part of the brain that deals with emotion is particularly resistant to change once it is organised. So, while areas of the brain concerned with cognition tend to remain more pliant, our individual psychological defences tend to remain fixed as distinctive features throughout our lives, becoming part of what we call 'personality'. The personality traits that we find problematic began as healthy and necessary adaptations to a range of difficult early childhood circumstances.

Most of us have been told many times over not to be concerned about our children's emotional hurts, because children are supposedly resilient. This is a misconception. *Children are not resilient; they are adaptive.* In other words, they don't simply 'bounce-back'; they re-shape themselves. The repeated disappointments, shocks, discomforts, pleasures and fulfilment they encounter are constantly used as feedback, from which they piece together a precise map of their human environment. It is around this unique topography that they will erect the framework of their personality. In order to adapt to the emotional ambience they perceive around them, infants unconsciously make conclusions about human nature: can others be expected to be reliable or untrustworthy, friendly or dangerous, honest or manipulative? Also as a result of feelings that arise from relationships, they compose a personal script about themselves, a complex self-image, silently reminding them that they are unconditionally lovable as individuals, or conversely that there are unwelcome aspects of themselves that must be compromised or repressed. These stored images of self and others are neurologically etched into emotional memory, acting as the unconscious guides for all relationship-oriented behaviour.

The basic themes of our individual strategies for relating are developed early, as are our deepest, most reflexive ways of meeting adversity. We each have a set of preferred responses to the stresses, the hurts and disappointments, the challenges of love, friendship and loss that we must inevitably face. Under stress, fear or discomfort, do we tend to avoid, withdraw, cling to others in hope, do we manipulate, seduce and trick, do we attack and dominate, do we bear up and endure, do we complain or do we armour ourselves and become insensitive? These are but some of the lasting adaptations that are created by each individual very early in life. They are encoded into the brain, to become some of the centrepieces of what we tend to take for granted as 'personality'. Our unique and individual adaptations to the combination of love and hurt that we experience in our formative years collectively create the kind of society that we live in.

Conclusion

Neuro-scientist Martin Teicher has come to the conclusion that "adequate nurturing and absence of intense early stress permits our brains to develop in a manner that is less aggressive and more emotionally stable, social, empathic" so that society "reaps what it sows in the way it nurtures its children".[46] The newest developments in brain science have repeatedly endorsed what psychotherapists and psycho-historians have been claiming for decades.

Since relationships in early childhood so strongly affect the way our brains develop, they deeply influence *emotional* development, and ultimately, the way we relate to one another. The next chapter looks at 'emotional intelligence': the foundation of personal fulfilment, healthy relationships, and harmonious societies.

Endnotes

[1] See the website of the Bombay Sarvodaya Mandal Gandhi Book Centre http://www.mkgandhi.org/momgandhi/chap58. htm (last accessed 1 December 2004); see also Attachment Parenting International http://www.attachmentparenting.org/ (last accessed 1 December 2004).

[2] Perry (1997) p 126.

[3] Edgerton (1992).

[4] De Mause (1997) p 125.

[5] De Mause (1999).

[6] Lipton (1997).

[7] Hrdy (2000) p 56.

[8] Lewontin, Rose and Kamin (1984) p 256.

[9] Gerhardt (2004) p 170; Belsky, Steinberg and Draper (1991).

[10] Dover (2000); Gerhardt (2004) p 170.

[11] Ellingsen (2002).

[12] Schore (1994) p 282.

[13] Perry (1997) p 125.

[14] Zeanagh and Scheeringa (1997).

[15] Rosenblum, Coplan, Friedman, Bassoff, Gorman and Andrews (1994).

[16] Noradrenaline assists in the regulation of the body's fight-or-flight responses.

[17] Serotonin is involved in the regulation of mood.

[18] Cortisol plays a key role in stress responses and has been colloquially dubbed the 'stress hormone'.

[19] Gerhardt (2004) pp 56–86.

[20] Miller (1998).

[21] The hippocampus plays an important role in the formation and storage of memory.

[22] Lamprecht, Eichelman, Thoa, Williams and Kopin (1990); Lipton, Steinschneider and Richmond (1965).

[23] See Chapter 22.

[24] Gerhardt (2004).

[25] Van der Kolk (1994); de Mause (1997); de Bellis, Keshavan, Clark, Casey, Giedd, Boring, Frustaci and Ryan (1999).

[26] Hart, Gunnar and Cicchetti (1996).

[27] Pearce (2002); Gerhardt (2004) pp 180–181.

[28] Patten-Hitt (2000).

[29] Brownlee (1996); Perry (1997).

[30] De Bellis, Keshavan, Clark, Casey, Giedd, Boring, Frustaci and Ryan (1999).

[31] Van der Kolk (1994).

[32] Perry (1997).

[33] Schore (1994).

[34] Perry (1997); Fonagy, Target, Steele and Steele (1997).

[35] Gerhardt (2004) p 47.

[36] Schore (1994).

[37] Goleman (2006) pp 53-4.

[38] Perry (1999); Miller (2001).

[39] Karmiloff-Smith (2000).

[40] Schore (1994).

[41] Greenspan (1999).

[42] Schore (1994).

[43] Schore (1994).

[44] Gerhardt (2004) p 41.

[45] Morrock (1999).

[46] Teicher (2002) p 75.

22

WHAT IS EMOTIONAL INTELLIGENCE?

Emotional intelligence, a term coined by Howard Gardner in *Frames of Mind*,[1] describes a domain of human consciousness that has, until recently, been seriously neglected. It is currently enjoying an explosion of academic attention.

There have been many efforts by psychologists and educationists to:

- define the concept of emotional intelligence;
- devise instruments for measuring it in individuals (commonly referred to as EQ); and
- teach its properties to both children and adults.

It has finally been acknowledged that EQ is more important than IQ when it comes to 'people skills' – success in career, in personal and business relationships, and in raising fulfilled children.

Emotional intelligence is a broad term that loosely defines a collection of skills necessary to navigate the realm of feeling and emotion. It includes a range of faculties, such as sensing the presence of emotions in your body, and the conscious ability to use language or otherwise express the emotion. It also includes the ability to contain (instead of repress) emotion, or to communicate emotion in a way that is appropriate to the relationship context, and the ability to choose when to do one or the other. It means the ability to process and let go of emotion in a healthy way, and the ability to give ourselves time to feel, and to enjoy the depths of our 'selves' through feeling.

A maturely developed emotional intelligence includes, among a host of other things, the ability to lead wisely or follow with grace, to honour our limits as well as celebrate and fulfil our talents, and to give and receive love and support.

Last, but by no means least, emotional intelligence involves the ability to listen and sense empathically the emotions of others. Our alertness to our own constantly changing emotions informs our acuity in detecting the many different textures of emotion in others. Most healthy individuals are surprisingly skilled at inferring others' intentions and emotional states merely from looking at their eyes. This is a function of emotional intelligence, and has nothing to do with IQ.[2]

Relationships cannot be truly intimate, nor can they grow, without a deep sharing of our emotional inner worlds. Many of us have learned early in our lives to hide or ignore our feelings, and that is why relationships can become stunted and dull.

More pertinently, our ability to inspire and impart emotional intelligence to our children rests on our own mastery of the realm of feeling, and our willingness to learn and grow in this area.

In one way or another, we are all struggling to refine, develop, and expand our emotional intelligence and relationship skills. Life, with its pain and joys, could be considered a 'big school' for the emotions. In many ways the development of emotional intelligence parallels the learning of a language. Just as a new language can be painstakingly learned by most adults, emotional intelligence can be cultivated through adulthood. However, learning a new language is an infinitely faster and smoother process for small children than it is for adults. When I was three years old, I learned to speak French as my second language in a matter weeks, through being in an environment where I spoke it for several hours each day. Similarly, the basis for emotional intelligence and healthy emotional communication is much easier to learn while the parts of the brain concerned with emotion are still growing – that is, in early childhood.

Although most of us can claim to be 'fine' or 'OK' most of the time, many of us have some trouble accessing our feelings, and appropriately communicating our feelings with others. Our relationships suffer as a result. Any committed relationship, whether business or personal, requires a great deal of emotional intelligence – not just to stay 'together', but to remain vital and dynamic.

Gauging emotional intelligence

Following are some questions you might ponder to gain insight into your own emotional terrain and to understand more about what is meant by 'emotional intelligence'. Please note that this is not a quiz; emotional intelligence is not quantifiable, and it is not my purpose here to provide a framework for interpersonal comparisons. When it comes to emotional intelligence, every last one of us is learning, evolving and developing, well into adulthood. These questions are designed to provoke reflection about areas of your emotionality, which you might like to expand or develop. They may also help you identify areas that are already well developed. It would be both unkind and unrealistic to expect perfect answers to all items – I doubt anyone exists who would not recognise some areas of personal difficulty in the questionnaire. Furthermore, as we collectively keep learning about the nature of emotionality and the human capacity for wellbeing and joy, I imagine that definitions of emotional health will periodically be revised.

Some of the questions below may seem a little banal at first glance, nevertheless, do take the time to weigh up how each item applies to you personally, as honestly as possible. The questions are arranged in a number of categories, and they do not represent an exhaustive scope of emotional faculties.

After you have answered 'yes' or 'no', ask significant people in your life how they see you in terms of these questions – their feedback could be both surprising and valuable. If your friend or partner answered 'no' when you answered 'yes' or vice versa, take the opportunity to re-consider the question. Much can be learned from another's perspective.

Communicating emotions

Question	Your answer		Your friend's answer	
	Yes	No	Yes	No
If you are sad, grieving or mourning, do you allow yourself to weep? Do you allow trusted others to see your tears?				
Can you express anger freely and non-destructively, then let it go?				
Do you quickly let go of grudges and resentment?				
When you are afraid, do you let trusted others see your fear?				
Do you let yourself know that you are afraid?				
Do you take notice of your emotional and interpersonal needs, and express these needs assertively? Respectfully?				
Are you able to recognise when you need help, then ask for help or support?				

Question	Your answer		Your friend's answer	
	Yes	No	Yes	No
Can you receive help, as well as give it?				
Can you say 'no' without feeling guilty?				
Can you strongly protest against mistreatment?				
Do you easily express, as well as receive, tenderness, love, passion?				
Can you enjoy your own company yet gladly and comfortably accept intimacy?				
Do you listen clearly to yourself, and to others?				
Can you empathise with the needs and feelings of others, without judgement or criticism?				
Can you accurately perceive what others are feeling, and feel compassion for them?				
Can you motivate others without resorting to fear tactics or manipulation?				

Emotional fluency

Question	Your answer		Your friend's answer	
	Yes	No	Yes	No
Do you allow yourself to frequently experience and enjoy pleasure?				
Do you allow yourself to experience bliss, ecstasy, excitement, fascination and awe?				
Do you often laugh out loud – a deep belly laugh?				
Do you sometimes feel moved by the courage or the spirit of others?				
When necessary, can you contain (rather than repress), your impulses and delay your gratification, without resorting to guilt, shame, or suppression of your emotions?				

Flexibility and balance

Question	Your answer		Your friend's answer	
	Yes	No	Yes	No
Can you focus your energy on work, yet balance this with fun and rest?				
Can you accept and even enjoy others who have different needs and world-views?				
Do you let yourself be spontaneous, play like a child, be silly?				
Are your goals realistic, and does your patience allow you to work towards them steadily?				

Self-esteem

Question	Your answer		Your friend's answer	
	Yes	No	Yes	No
Can you forgive yourself your mistakes, and take yourself lightly?				

Question	Your answer		Your friend's answer	
	Yes	No	Yes	No
Can you accept your own shortcomings, without feeling ashamed, and remain excited about learning and growing?				
Do you respect your strengths *and* vulnerabilities, rather than inflate with pride, or fester with shame?				
Would you say you are generally true to yourself without blindly rebelling against, nor conforming to social expectations?				
Can you bear disappointment or frustration, without succumbing to criticism of self or others?				
Are you kind to yourself, or hard – even punishing towards yourself?				
Can you self-motivate?				
Can you gracefully accept defeat and failure and still feel OK about yourself?				

Have a look at the questions where you answered 'no'. Your areas for potential growth are signalled by those questions. Areas of difficulty may well represent emotional wounds – possibly sustained early in life – that call for healing and growth. Your answers may also point towards areas of personal vulnerability where you might find your greatest challenges in parenting. For example, parents who have difficulty expressing anger may have the most trouble allowing their children to be angry, parents who find it difficult to express their needs may have the most trouble listening to their children's needs, and so on.

If any of the questions above feel particularly problematic to you, you could consider seeking the assistance of a counsellor or psychotherapist, or any other modality of healing and personal growth that you feel comfortable with.

Language of emotions

Until recently, it was popularly understood that reason and feeling were mutually exclusive. The world of emotion was 'irrational', and there was no place for passion in the realm of reason. Those neat distinctions no longer exist. We have come to realise that it is not possible to think rationally without emotion. Human feeling is integral to the process of reasoning and decision: we cannot make rational decisions without sensing how the probable consequences of these decisions would *feel*. The repression of emotion is as detrimental to the rational mind as the chaos of too much, unrestrained emotion.[3]

At the most basic level of emotional fluency, most of us can differentiate between six, basic universal emotions: happiness, sadness, fear, anger, surprise and disgust.[4] Some authors suggest a maximum of 10 basic emotions, adding to the list: interest, contempt, shame and guilt.[5] A more advanced level of acuity lets us differentiate between intensities of these emotions, such as 'a little scared', or 'very angry'. Ultimately, there are many more shades and subtleties of emotion that enrich our humanity and our interpersonal relationships. A well-developed emotional intelligence is what helps us discern between manifold textures of feeling in ourselves as well as in others.

For instance, there are different kinds of laughter for silly humour, for small mishaps, for children's cuteness, for revenge, for malice, for mania or craziness. Anger also manifests in an array of different hues; such as rage, outrage, indignation, hostility, frustration, annoyance and irritation. There are various meanings carried by the many qualities of sadness; such as grief, mourning, hurt, pain, anguish and loss. There are vital differences between the various self-conscious emotions; such as guilt (a wholly narcissistic fear of punishment), shame (a feeling of self-diminishment), embarrassment (a more superficial and communicable cousin of shame), remorse (shame mixed with genuine care for another's pain), and regret (an empathic wish that one had acted with more compassion). Some complex emotions, like horror, hopelessness or despair, do not fit into the basic categories mentioned above; they are blends of two or more emotions. There are palpable differences between happiness, joy, bliss, ecstasy and elation, and these differences are not merely a question of degree or intensity. Finally, there are differences between care, concern, affection, warmth, compassion, tenderness, and the many, diverse qualities of love we feel for each person in our lives, for ourselves, for nature, for God.

This colourful tapestry of emotion gives meaning to our lives, and depth to our experiences. Even when we are not consciously aware of emotion, it motivates our behaviour, and drives our every gesture and choice.

Fathomless depths and qualities of feeling that escape our ordinary language can often only be expressed through poetry, the arts, music, dance or bodily gestures. Your face, mouth and eyes constantly communicate complex emotions through the finest muscular adjustments. Your body and voice speak volumes through posture, skin tone and movement, and vocal timbre. We are in perpetual and profound communication with each other, though most of the time we are not tuned in to this mutual 'conversation' – our awareness is focussed elsewhere. Our emotional fluency entails our ability to sense and identify the changing feeling states in our own bodies. To the extent that we are tuned in to our own feelings, we are able to perceive and understand the feelings of others.

Emotion is an essential aspect of interpersonal communication. The capacity to feel is what makes us human, what connects us to one another. Thus, the more we develop and refine emotional intelligence the more we can enjoy fulfilling relationships, and a harmonious society.

Our ability to discern, communicate and empathically listen to emotion plays a vital role in parenting, for it helps us to respond appropriately to our children's emotional needs. For instance, our emotional attunement brings us closer to deciphering our baby's cries: when is it a tired cry, when is it a hungry cry, a lonely cry or a scared cry, a hold-me cry, a cry of pain, a discomfort cry, an angry cry or a bored cry?

If we are willing, emotional development can continue through life. We can grow through our relationships, through our work, through life's peaks and disappointments. Counselling and psychotherapy offer multiple means of developing our emotional intelligence and relationship skills. To a significant extent, the emotional injuries of childhood that influence our relating can be healed with therapy. Cautiously and gradually, we can sometimes move beyond places where our emotional development has been arrested. Our own healing and our growing understanding about childhood development can also enable us to better address our children's emotional needs.

Core emotional development

Not until recently, through the work of scientists such as Jean Piaget, did we start to recognise the distinct stages of children's cognitive (mental) development. Our way of relating to children has been altered accordingly, much to their benefit. These advances have helped us to give children stage-appropriate stimulation and education, while avoiding unrealistic expectations.

It is through the pioneering psychological works of Sigmund Freud, Eric Erikson, Alexander Lowen, Heinz Kohut, John Bowlby, and many others that we have come to recognise that emotional faculties also develop, stage-by-stage, along predictable pathways. This insight has helped us to tune-in more and more empathically to children; to better answer their developmental needs as they unfold. The fundamentals of our individual orientation to the world, that is our relating style or personality, are laid down over the first five to seven years.[6] The emotional development that takes place during this time is divided over five distinct stages, or rites of passage. Chapters 25–29 will each examine one of the five stages of core emotional development, the emotional needs specific to each stage, and the relationship functions that develop at each stage.

Universal pathways of emotional development

Our 'core' emotional needs are biologically inherent, essential to both our physical and psychological survival. Since these developmental needs are intrinsic to our species, they are fixed, and they represent a developmental trajectory through which we all must pass.[7] Although there are many aspects of socio-emotional functioning that develop at different rates for many children, the core emotional needs unfold along a common course, determined by our shared human biology. All children need acceptance, love, warmth, affection, empathy, tenderness, respect, freedom of self-expression, healthy boundaries, and the right of autonomy over their own bodies, no matter where they are born. The basic psychological needs are absolutes that exist independently of culture or epoch.

Psychologically, we are truly 'one people', since we develop along identical rites of passage the world over, and geneticists have now established that there are no biological differences between the 'races' – in fact, there is no genetic basis for the concept of 'race'.[8] It is nonsensical to talk about 'Blacks', 'Whites' or 'Asians', other than as an expedient – but altogether shallow – label.

This is not to say that biological differences do not exist beyond matters of external appearance. There clearly are a few biological differences, beyond skin colour, that distinguish human groups. Some diseases have a higher incidence among certain ethnic groups, there are differing capacities for digesting dairy foods, and differing side-effect reactions to some pharmaceutical drugs. It still holds, however, that the concept of race is a blurry one at best, and there certainly do not appear to be 'race'-based differences in emotionality or in stages of emotional development in childhood.

Since the birth of *Homo Sapiens*, we have migrated around the globe far too quickly for genetic mutations – bar a few cosmetic changes – to split us into truly new 'races'. Researchers have recently calculated that everyone alive today may have descended from one common ancestor who lived just a few thousand years ago.[9] Aided by modern transportation and globalisation, the growing rate of 'intermarriage' between diverse peoples will ensure that humanity will remain genetically homogenous; a single species. In the USA, for example, the number of inter-'racial' marriages has more than doubled, to 1.46 million, in the last 20 years.[10] Any psychological differences between groups of people are not genetically determined but culturally-derived, based on the diverse customary ways of meeting – or failing to meet – children's developmental needs.

Based on his extensive travels, Charles Darwin was the first to declare that emotions and their expression through the face and body are identical for all peoples, even among the most isolated cultures.[11] Darwin's discovery has been repeatedly confirmed. The facial expressions related to the basic emotions share a universal neuro-musculature.[12] Even complex emotions, such as contempt, are facially expressed in the same way around the world.[13] Sustained smiling emerges for babies aged between 2–4 months, and separation anxiety between 7–15 months, irrespective of the culture to which they are born.[14] This reflects a universal pathway of emotional development. There is one truly universal language, and that is the language of emotion: the language of the body and the tone of voice. Cultural differences reflect only which areas of our emotionality are customarily suppressed, and what areas are expressed. This means that the stages of core emotional development that we will look at in Part VI apply to all children, irrespective of what era they are born in, and irrespective of their ethnic background.

The phenomenon of parenting evolution has taken us steadily toward a closer emotional attunement with our children. Though we are now biologically the same humans we were thousands of years ago – a little taller perhaps – our emotional intelligence has been given more nurturance, and more room to develop. This has been the driving force behind the positive, social and cultural changes that have unfolded over the centuries.

Over recent decades, scientists from diverse disciplines such as psychology, neurology and learning theorists have been piecing together the puzzle of how early experiences leave such lasting impressions on the human psyche. As we will see in the next chapter, an additional and important piece of this puzzle has been recently put in place as a result of new breakthroughs in our understanding of memory. If even the earliest experiences of life can be so formative, this is because we all remember far more than was previously thought.

Endnotes

1   Gardner (1993).
2   Baron-Cohen, Wheelwright, Hill, Raste and Plumb (2001).
3   Damasio (2000).
4   Damasio (2000).
5   Mascolo and Griffin (1998).
6   Belsky, Steinberg and Draper (1991).
7   Hrdy (2000).

[8] Since the completion of the Human Genome Project, it has been made clear that there is no genetic basis for the outdated and discredited notion of 'race'. Strictly speaking, there are no 'races'; just an interesting diversity of physical attributes that defy categorisation. Search 'Race and the human genome: researchers definitively trump the notion of race with DNA research' in About Race Relations http://www.racerelations.about.com (last accessed 1 December 2004) and search 'Our genetic identity' in the American Museum of Natural History http://www.amnh.org (last accessed 1 December 2004).

[9] See Rohde, Olson and Chang (2004); see also a commentary about these findings by Hopkin (2004).

[10] Moore (2003).

[11] Rothschild (2000).

[12] Lewis (1992).

[13] Schore (1994).

[14] Broude (1995).

23

WHAT CHILDREN REMEMBER: AND HOW THIS AFFECTS THEIR DEVELOPMENT

Most of us have been told at one time or another that children aren't supposed to remember anything that happens to them before roughly two years of age. What goes on before this age, even if emotionally traumatic, will therefore have no lasting impact. These words might be reassuring, if they didn't also mean by implication that our infants don't remember the love we have given them. This would mean that our love at this time has no lasting impact either. As science continues to throw open the mysteries of the brain, and the nature of memory, this kind of advice will vanish. We can now verify that everything that happens to an infant is stored in memory. Every emotionally meaningful experience, whether joyous or painful, has a lasting impact on a baby's developing nervous system, whether or not it is *consciously* recalled later. The way our world feels to us as babies influences our unfolding personality, emotionality and relating style for the long term, even without our visual or narrative recall.[1] There are different kinds of 'memory', beyond the stories we can recount. And we 'remember' a lot more than we realise.

Two different kinds of memory

Within the limbic system of the brain – an area concerned with processing emotions – are the amygdala and hippocampus. The amygdala processes highly charged emotional memories, such as terror and horror. The hippocampus processes narrative, chronological memory, which then gets stored in the cortex.

The amygdala is mature at birth, so babies are able to intensely feel the full range of emotion, even though they cannot process the content of the emotion and its relation to what is going on around them in the same way adults can. The hippocampus on the other hand, does not mature until sometime between the second and fourth years of life.[2] While the hippocampus is immature, we are relatively unable to organise our memory meaningfully in terms of sequences of events. Only rarely does anybody consciously recall the content or context of early life memory. However, the storage of the *emotional* content of memory is facilitated by the amygdala. We therefore remember every emotion and physical sensation from our earliest days, and even if we have no clarity about the events that took place, these memories imbue the way we relate to each other as adults.

Just as memory can be divided up into the dual categories of 'short term' and 'long term', there are also two qualities of memory, 'explicit' and 'implicit'. 'Explicit' memory is the kind of memory that is conscious and enables us to tell a story that makes sense of what happened. This kind of memory does not reach full maturity until around three years of age. That is why most people feel as if their earliest recollections date back to around this age. 'Implicit' memory, however, is available from birth – more than likely earlier – it tends to be unconscious, and is encoded in emotional, sensory and visceral recall. In other words, what we don't remember with our minds, we remember with our bodies, with our hearts and our 'guts', and this has profound implications for our thinking, feeling, and behaviour through life.[3]

Traditional medical orthodoxy once held that children under two years of age cannot record memory because their nerve tracts are not fully myelinised. We now know that the absence of myelin (a fatty sheath covering the nerve) slows down nerve impulses, but it does not prevent them from passing. Immature myelinisation does not interfere with memory.[4]

The process of 'forgetting' is more superficial than we once thought: it only erases conscious recall. Even as adults we are mercifully capable of deleting any recall of traumatic events. If we are unlucky enough to face a situation of panic or terror that we feel helpless to escape, the brain secretes endogenous opioids in order to numb us to overwhelming emotional or physical pain. These brain chemicals also interfere with the storage of explicit memory,[5] though implicit memory of the trauma remains available. Additionally, the excess adrenalin associated with the traumatic stress suppresses the functioning of the hippocampus,[6] so we forget the context of the trauma (though it is possible to retrieve the explicit memory later, under hypnosis for instance).

Experiences that are emotionally too overwhelming to deal with are stored somatically, as a body memory. Thereafter they are expressed as an unconscious response to stress,[7] and thus they modify personality. Henceforth, we over-react to situations that are even vaguely similar to the trauma, without the slightest idea why. Our seemingly 'irrational' over-reactions to mildly stressful or even innocuous situations are often due to traumatic experiences, usually dating back to childhood or infancy, which we cannot consciously recall.

The memory centres that govern narrative recall and emotional memory (body memory) can operate independently of each other.[8] Despite being in a coma, one man went into physiological anxiety states when exposed to a smell that was associated with a personal trauma. Clearly, it is possible to have strong emotional reactions without conscious recall, even without consciousness! Another man whose damaged brain had lost all capacity for short-term memory, still reacted aversively to doctors who had conducted unpleasant tests on him, without any recollection of having met them. A brain-damaged woman who had also totally lost her short-term memory refused to shake the hand of a doctor who had earlier hidden a sharp pin in his hand. She was bewildered by her own refusal, since as far as she was aware, each time she met him was the first.[9] So, much of what we think, feel and do is induced by implicit memories written into our bodies' tissues.

The body remembers

Our brain has an amazing capacity to make associations. Something or someone that 'reminds' our brains of a traumatic situation — a smell, a song, a person who looks like someone from our past — triggers our automatic, self-protective 'fight, flight or freeze' responses. This reflexive reaction occurs too quickly; before the information reaches the cortex where it can be evaluated rationally. That is why we sometimes over-react to things, people or situations reminiscent of a traumatic event, without any conscious recollection of the event in question.[10]

There are occasions when implicit memory can be made explicit. Since implicit memory is 'stored' in the body, repeating certain movements, gestures, breathing patterns, or assuming certain postures associated with emotionally charged memories can bounce these memories into explicit, conscious awareness. It is as if the body releases its secrets to the mind. Many individuals have been able to retrieve traumatic memories, both from adult and infant experiences, when induced by strong emotions associated with the original experience. In certain states of consciousness, in psychotherapy, hypnotherapy or meditation, people have spontaneously recalled things that happened to them as babies. Many have remembered how it felt to be a baby, howling for a mother who would not come. In reconstructing a particular body posture, or talking about a similar emotionally charged event, the contextual memories of unbearable longing, rage or terror come back into focus. It is equally possible for sweet, joyous memories of a parent's loving face to resurface. This phenomenon is called 'state-dependent memory retrieval'.[11] Detailed explicit memories can come back to our conscious recall when we are brought back to the emotional state that we were in at the time of the trauma. If treated appropriately, and within certain guidelines, these spontaneous regressions can be extremely healing.

In my own therapy, I have re-experienced some of the intense terror, followed by elation and relief that surrounded the event of my birth. I have also remembered the all-encompassing adoration I felt for my mother as a baby. Although I cannot easily re-capture such intense, early-life feelings in my relatively armoured adult body, the memories are not altogether irretrievable. Not one of our experiences is lost to us. Each experience, particularly those that are charged with emotion, adds to the complex mosaic of our personality.

Even if not consciously remembered, early memories show themselves through behaviour.[12] It is intrinsically human to re-enact defensive reactions to forgotten traumas, though our reactions are no longer relevant. Often early memories become evident through persistent feelings that don't seem to relate to a present situation, or through bodily sensations that don't seem to make any sense. More commonly, these early implicit memories of emotional pain or hurt are indirectly evident through persistent difficulties in relationships, particularly in intimate relations. These relationship difficulties include the many social problems of chronic loneliness, isolation, violence, greed, power-abuse and addictions that beset our world. These are behavioural and relational symptoms of painful disturbances in our emotional development that elude our narrative memory. Often the task of psychotherapy is to help people make their own connections, between their actions and early emotional memory. More recently, it has been the task of psychohistorians to unravel the state of nations and link these to customary and common childhood experiences that escape discussion since they are stored as implicit, emotional memory.

How implicit memory affects relationships

For most of us, relationships are sometimes a struggle, though we might be unsure why this is so. Even the most 'functional' and successful among us can be evasive, clingy, or perhaps insensitive in relationships. These are just some of the problems of relationship that have their roots in hurts we felt at the advent of life. To some extent, most of us suffer from some behavioural manifestations of painful implicit memories.

Unwittingly, we each act as triggers for each other's defensive emotional reactions based on early traumas. This process underlies the dovetailing, dysfunctional social relationships that drive the disharmonious and exploitative aspects of societies. War, dictatorship and environmental abuse are collective defensive reactions based on early traumas that are stored as implicit memory, triggered by reminiscent situations. Our societies and cultures are collective expressions of both love and unremembered fear.

Here are some examples of commonly experienced relationship difficulties that are animated by painful childhood memories. Implicit memory – or body memory – explains why, for instance, a woman who was molested as a child remains fearful of intimacy – at least with men that 'remind' her of the perpetrator – even without a trace of conscious memory of the traumatic episodes.

A man fears being alone because it triggers emotional memories of terror as he cried in the crib, and no one came to comfort him. He has no recollection of these repeated events, and people in his life find him likeable and congenial. He has no understanding about his compulsive avoidance of solitude.

Another man, who experienced his parents' care as inconsistent and unreliable, learned to protect himself from unbearable feelings of loss by becoming overly clingy and possessive. As an adult, he is easily provoked into a jealous rage, and he is prone to co-dependent or enmeshed relationships. He is otherwise normal and happy and none but those who are closest to him notice his vulnerability.

Habitually violent or dominant behaviours develop along similar lines, as do a host of other defensive or compensatory attributes.

How implicit memory affects parenting

Unbeknownst to our 'rational' minds, we sometimes respond mistakenly to current challenges as if they were the hurts we suffered originally. This dynamic holds true in our relationships with our children. There are many reasons why, for instance, we might find our children's expressions of need aversive and overwhelming. Here is a common scenario: when a baby screams, our bodies react the same way as when our parents screamed at us as children, we are neurologically conditioned to escape or push away, rather than to respond with spontaneous compassion. Alternatively, our baby's cry might trigger in our bodies an implicit memory of a time when our own cries, as infants, were not met with a loving response. Either way, our baby's cries evoke our own painful memory, and so we seek refuge. We are all biologically capable of a wellspring of spontaneously loving responses toward our children, and toward each other. Sometimes this love is blocked by automatic defensive reactions to unresolved, implicitly remembered hurts. We are neither insensitive nor neglectful; we are *wounded*.

For centuries, parents have acted-out the symptoms of forgotten emotional injuries onto their children, through no fault of their own. The cruelties suffered by history's children have been the neurologically-mediated symptoms of the parents' own emotional traumas. Alongside the love we have received, we have all been, at one time or another, victims of parents' and teachers' unhealed post-traumatic stress reactions. The continuity of human suffering is the product of this cycle of violence and neglect, that ensues when the wounded, who have no access to healing, in turn wound the next generation.

Memories create 'personalities' – how 'states' become 'traits'

In most cases, a single painful event is not formative for a child's developing personality, unless it is intensely traumatic. Even small babies are able to process a certain level of anguish by crying,

261

screaming, suckling and resting in their carers' arms. These are natural, expressive reflexes that help to return their nervous systems to a healthy balance. It is the persistent or repeated dynamics, such as leaving a baby to cry unattended, or regularly punishing a child, that throw their nervous systems off-balance, creating neurological and behavioural compensations that may turn out to be permanent.[13] When recurrent, emotionally overwhelming experiences exceed the brain's capacity to return to the original balanced state, this alters beliefs, attitudes, and personality for the long term. That is how the emotional 'states' of early childhood can become personality 'traits'.

Once a neural response such as dissociation (freezing) or hyper-arousal (fight-or-flight) becomes over-activated, it takes lesser stresses to re-activate it. We either dissociate or over-respond more readily, even minor stresses set us off. That is because, as neuro-scientists believe, some of these early changes to brain chemistry and neuronal connections are long lasting, if not permanent. When parents repeatedly fail to tune-in to their child's emotional needs, the child gets over-sensitised to a broad range of even vaguely similar situations. He or she thus becomes predisposed to pattern-like, defensive responses.[14]

Here is an example of how this might work. A child who is terrified of her punitive parents learns to protect herself by withdrawing; she becomes resigned or over-compliant, and thus less of a target. If this type of escape happens repeatedly, her nervous system adopts it as her characteristic, automatic defence. Henceforth, she isolates herself, or she tends to respond passively or meekly in social situations that augur even mild conflict. This way of relating would persist well into adulthood, so that others would recognise it as part of her 'personality'.

Infants tend not to respond with fight-or-flight, but with a 'freezing' or 'dissociative' response that involves surrender, resignation and detachment. The compliance and docility that many parents and teachers admire in children is often a defensive response to early trauma, emotional deprivation or harsh, authoritarian control. This adaptive passivity is erroneously seen by many adults as evidence that the child is OK, when in fact their terror and despair is masked, and unrecognised. Neuro-biologist Bruce Perry explodes the contemporary myth that states "children are resilient".[15] They are not resilient, they are adaptive; their distinct personalities are cast around key emotional and relational experiences. Certainly, most children quickly 'forget' their hurts, and they bounce back full of playfulness and vigour. However, this does not mean they bounce back unchanged.

Adaptive defences are not pathological, they are skilful self-protective devices that make absolute sense given the way an infant experiences his or her world. Our interpersonal defensive patterns are solidly wired into our unique neurological and endocrinological systems, emerging as unconscious, automatic, and spontaneous impulses. It is this 'hard-wiring' that makes our interpersonal defences so reliable and protective, but also resistant to change. These defensive response tendencies comprise much of what we commonly refer to as our 'personality traits'. Each personality tends to be a unique blend of defences and gifts that are partly innate, and partly developed in response to the prevailing emotional and relational climate that it is born into.

Is healing possible?

We don't know exactly how completely the emotional hurts of childhood can be healed. Though some remarkable progress has been made in the psychological healing arts, we do suspect that there are limits to how much healing can take place once a child's immature and fast-growing brain has been subjected to chronic and persistent emotional stress. Some neuro-scientists go so far as to claim that "emotional memory is forever".[16] While I agree that there are some aspects of our unique character structure that resist change, I also believe that many of our problematic relating patterns are amenable to healing and growth.

Psychiatrist Bruce Perry,[17] founder of the Child Trauma Academy in USA, explains that healing requires repeated experiences of restorative relationship (loving care, safety, respect), and lasting changes happen only when these enriching experiences happen consistently enough to rebuild neural networks that animate a new repertoire of relating styles. Healing is a journey, it requires changes in the nature and feel of relationships, and it does not take place in a moment.

Australian psychologist Vicky Flory[18] investigated the use of Emotionally Attuned Parenting strategies to treat children suffering from severe childhood depression and anxiety. Flory's researchers did not treat the ailing children but the parents; giving them sessions aimed at increasing the parents' empathy for their child, helping them be more aware of their child's distress, and challenging their negative judgments about their children's behaviour. Even though they were dealing with severe and chronic psychiatric disorders – which on average the children had been suffering for five years – there was significant symptom reduction.

Every personality is a dynamic and growing system. We keep developing and adding new layers of wisdom to ourselves throughout life. Our emotional intelligence is open to learning if we are willing, and our childhood environment need not be a life sentence. However, the earlier the experience, the deeper the neurological impact, and the more the resulting behavioural patterns are resistant to change.

My experience as a psychotherapist – and as a client of psychotherapists – has shown me that profound healing and continued emotional development are eminently possible in adulthood. Nevertheless, it is wiser for us to place more emphasis on supporting emotional wellbeing from the very dawn of life – that is, when the brain is most absorbent and adaptable.

By tracing the universal pathways of early childhood emotional development, Part VI will offer many suggestions for how to secure your children's emotional health. As societies increase their efforts to protect children's wellbeing, we can achieve more than an alleviation of gross forms of suffering such as addiction and crime. We can also do much to alleviate more ordinary forms of suffering, among those we consider as 'well adjusted individuals' – the most 'normal' and 'ordinary' difficulties with human relations can also spring from painful implicit memories. Even in relatively democratic and functioning communities there is much we can do to deepen the fulfilment that is possible for the human heart.

Myth of the 'well-adjusted individual'

A number of child-rearing practices that are common these days can still be emotionally wounding to babies and children (as we'll see in Part VI), though they seem such ordinary practices that most people take them for granted. As most of us were raised in a 'socialising mode' era, we would have experienced these painful yet widely accepted practices, though we might dismiss them as 'normal'. In fact, many of our deepest emotional wounds may have resulted from practices that were considered 'good parenting' at the time. Though we might be essentially happy individuals, our bodies and nervous systems have not forgotten these hurts.

In this socialising mode age, few of us can claim that our

parents and teachers did not hit us or shame us as little children, few of us can claim that our parents did not leave us to cry in our cribs until we panicked, or as babies made us sleep alone in a separate room. Though such occurrences are so routine these days that they hardly attract attention, early experiences such as these shape our distinct personality quite profoundly – without necessarily making us 'pathological' nor hopelessly 'neurotic'. On an emotional level, we remember these incidents quite distinctly, and they silently but powerfully shape our behaviour, our beliefs and attitudes.

The 'ordinary' emotional injuries that are not given the legal classification of 'abuse' and 'neglect', tend to manifest as problems of intimacy. These are lesser injuries arising from gaps in emotional sustenance that are ordinary results of socialising mode parenting and education. They affect us as individuals, and permeate our relationships on many levels.

When trying to understand human suffering, most of us tend to simplistically divide humanity into two groups, those who are 'crazy' or 'sick', and those who are 'normal'. Similarly, we conceive of childhood emotional development in two categories: those who experienced 'happy' childhoods, and those who are abused and/or neglected. The threshold of what constitutes abuse and neglect remains high, we only use these terms to describe extreme traumas.

This superficial view of human relations is based on a disease model, and it obscures from our view the multi-layered complexity of 'normal' psychological suffering. If a child grows up to exhibit socially 'normal' behaviour we say he or she, like a loaf in the oven, has 'turned out alright'. To attain this bland tag of normalcy or 'OK-ness', it seems sufficient for a child to grow up able to work, get married and raise more children, and avoid criminal behaviour. It is as if there are no more dimensions to the human experience than the trappings that are superficially visible.

Almost all individuals I have worked with in my practice have been successful and admired individuals. Their friends and colleagues would consider them to be contented and doing OK. As far as their peers are concerned, many of my clients are the epitome of the 'well adjusted individual'. Nevertheless, within the relative safety of my consulting room, they speak of great pain, often life-long pain – a hurt that becomes highlighted through the challenge of close relationships. I have become accustomed to seeing that, alongside a well of 'good' feelings, many of the most 'normal' people harbour long-held emotional wounds. Most of us have buried within a considerable depth of hurt, anger and fear, which remains hidden – even from ourselves. We conceal our private anguish and shame from each other; it even defies detection by professional diagnosticians and personality tests. It is manifestly possible, and in fact extremely common, for us to function capably, and keep smiling, while enduring long-held, secret pain – much of it dating back to early childhood. Though we may not realise it, our emotional wounds and defensive reactions are enacted in relationships with our loved ones, as 'ordinary' difficulties with closeness and intimacy.

The thin veneer of 'normalcy' is also apparent among our animal cousins. When rhesus monkeys were maternally deprived early in life, they were subsequently observed to adjust normally to their social group. The monkeys that had suffered early deprivation were indistinguishable from the rest, and observers would have declared them to be perfectly 'healthy' and 'happy'. However, under situations of stress, their responses were quite different, more exaggerated than those of their peers, "as if they were being traumatised all over again".[17] It is similar with humans. Many of our unhealed emotional injuries are invisible to people around us, even to ourselves; they only emerge when we are emotionally stressed – or when we face intimacy and love.

'Normal' problems in relationships

So many of the behaviours we accept as 'normal', among 'well-adjusted' individuals, are unrecognised reactions to implicit memories of pain and loss. The 'normal' can be extremely jealous and possessive, while engaging in loveless sexual relations that lack contact or tenderness. Innumerable partners remain married for years with barely an inkling of awareness of each others' inner emotional worlds, not knowing how to – let alone why – share these with each other. The 'normal' have enormous difficulty exposing emotional vulnerability, we fear trusting each other with those parts of ourselves. Instead, we lose ourselves in a dizzying acquisition of excess consumer goods and capital, we anxiously hoard our resources – yet we scarcely enjoy what we have. Though life's beauty and riches surround us we are unable to be nourished to the depths of our being, and so, the 'normal' among us seek solace in gambling, tobacco, alcohol, pharmaceutical or recreational drugs, or endless hours in front of the TV. We have so strayed from our hearts and distrusted our passion that work has come to be synonymous with suffering and drudgery. Though we love our children, too often they feel burdensome to us – and in our overwhelmed states we hit them, shame them, or ignore their crying. All these are conventional social behaviours; they pass off as unremarkable in our culture – yet they speak of entrenched emotional pain.

Many ordinary traits that we take for granted, or blame on our genes – such as compulsive attention-seeking, seductive charm, paralysing shyness, gullibility, chronic discomforts around intimacy, an uncontrollable temper, mental or moral rigidity, self-effacing behaviour – are probably the results of child-rearing practices that are culturally accepted and integral to the socialising mode. These are our ordinary impairments to human relations. In fact, most of us would have answered a number of items in the questionnaire on 'emotional intelligence' (Chapter 22) in the negative. We endure or hide our pain, and 'get on' with our lives. We tell ourselves and each other that we are 'alright', doing 'just fine', content with our lot. But we remain a step back from the depth of joy, fulfilment and love that is the fullness of our human potential. A wholeness of intimacy with ourselves and those we love eludes us, we fear it and long for it all at once. While Part VI is intended to assist your understanding of your children's core emotional developmental stages, it may also help you to gain valuable insights into personal areas of emotional difficulty, since we have all passed through these key formative stages.

In Part VI we will look at root causes of ordinary emotional wounds, as well as causes of the most problematic social ills. There has been such an explosion of knowledge about how to promote healthy brain development and emotional intelligence, that we may have to reconsider the limits of human potential. I believe that we have barely begun to tap into the collective human capacity for joy, loving relationships and harmonious community.

Endnotes
[1]   Rothschild (2000).
[2]   Van der Kolk (1994).
[3]   Rothschild (2000).
[4]   Verny (1981).

[5] Van der Kolk (1994).
[6] Rothschild (2003).
[7] Van der Kolk (1994).
[8] Perry and Pollard (1998).
[9] Damasio (2000); Rothschild (2000) p 33.
[10] Perry (1999).
[11] Van der Kolk (1994).
[12] Van der Kolk (1994).
[13] Perry and Pollard (1998).
[14] Perry, Pollard, Blakley, Baker and Vigilante (1995).
[15] Perry, Pollard, Blakley, Baker and Vigilante (1995).
[16] Perry, Pollard, Blakley, Baker and Vigilante (1995).
[17] Perry (2006).
[18] Flory (2004).
[19] Van der Kolk (1994).

VI

THE FIVE STAGES OF EARLY CHILDHOOD EMOTIONAL DEVELOPMENT

The ideas presented in Part VI are drawn from a combination of published research data, my own experience as a psychotherapist, and the collective experience of a large number of eminent psychotherapists taken from their writings, seminars and training workshops.[1] Some of the propositions I make in this section are speculative, and would be difficult to prove. They are however what I believe to be the most reasonable conclusions based on the confluence of:

- the findings of current neurological and endocrinological research on the impact of early emotional experiences;
- current child development research;
- what psychohistorians have observed globally; and
- the combined wisdom of several streams of psycho-therapy.

24

FIVE RITES OF PASSAGE
IN CORE EMOTIONAL
DEVELOPMENT

The newest point in the evolution of parenting can be best referred to as 'natural parenting',[2] because of its accent on trusting children's emotional needs as natural and appropriate to each stage of childhood development – and responding to those needs. Natural parenting aims to offer what the child's growing brain, heart and body ask for in order to grow in physical *and* emotional health. We are currently in the early days of an era in which aspects of natural parenting are increasingly filtering into mainstream childcare policy and practice.

In Part VI, we will be looking at 'natural parenting' approaches as they would apply to five stages of emotional development in early childhood.

Five rites of passage
The following chapters provide a map of early childhood emotional developmental needs. Although these core rites of passage follow each other along the same lines for all children, there is considerable overlap between the stages, and some variation across individuals regarding the exact duration of each stage. The account assumes normal physiological development, and thus may not necessarily apply in the same way to children who are very ill, handicapped or otherwise developmentally impaired.

Our core emotional development takes place roughly over the first seven years of life, while important neural pathways are still rapidly being established in the child's brain.[3] It is during these first seven or so years that the deepest – and therefore the most enduring – aspects of our character are formed. There are of course later, key developmental stages, but these are beyond the scope of this book.[4]

Further endorsement for the formative significance of the first seven years of life comes from British psychologist, Margot Sunderland.[5] Sunderland states that the massive forming, reforming and dismantling of brain connections slows down at around age seven, due to the increased myelination (a fatty sheath covering nerve tissue) of brain cells that takes place around this time. This strengthens neural pathways and fixes them in place, which contributes to a cementing of the character structures that have been developing. A critical formative window is closed around this time, and henceforth change is more hard won.

Chapters 25–29 are assigned to each of five key stages of core emotional development, tracing children's developmental needs as they change through each stage. Each rite of passage or developmental stage is organised into the following sections:

What happens at this time
This section will be an account of the developmental changes taking place in the infant's, baby's or toddler's emotional reality.

Child's emotional needs at this time
This will be an account of the most basic and universal core emotional needs that need to be met to ensure the child's emotional health.

What baby (or child) is learning at this time
Specific relationship skills that the child is trying to master and that will prepare the ground for self-image and later relationships, will be examined.

The most wounding experiences
This is a non-exhaustive list of some of the most common hurtful experiences that can cause stage-specific emotional wounds.

How experiences shape emotional make-up and beliefs
Here we look at the personal and relational strengths that grow as the core emotional needs are met, and the kinds of attitudes and unconsciously held beliefs that arise from injurious experiences. For each rite of passage, I list some of the stage-

specific personality traits or relating styles that children tend to develop as adaptations to adverse circumstances that they might meet along the way.

How emotional wounds affect behaviour
Here we look at the kinds of defences that children develop in response to their emotional needs not being met, and how this contributes to their unique character profile and their way of relating to others. There are positive attributes as well as problematic attributes that arise as compensations for emotional wounding.

Social impact of wounds
Our personal journeys through each of these five rites of passage have profound consequences for our relationships – and hence for society as a whole. The social repercussions will be discussed here.

Why learn about these five rites of passage?
The main object of the developmental map offered here is to help parents and professionals that work with children relate to and understand children's emotional needs. This map can help readers identify the kinds of experiences that can be emotionally wounding for children, as well as gaining insights into how to address their changing emotional needs at each stage.

The more we familiarise ourselves with these stage-specific emotional needs, the better we can understand our children's behaviour, their responses to emotional hurts, and what we can do to provide healing.

Since we all have gone through these rites of passage, the following chapters can also be used to deepen our understanding of personal emotional issues affecting our lives and relationships that might have origins in our individual childhoods. This will in turn help us as parents, teachers or carers. The more we tune in to how it felt for us to be children, the more we can tune in to our own children's needs. Nothing can contribute more to our effectiveness as parents than a clear and grounded sense of our selves, and a sense of our own emotional histories.

Myth of 'perfect parents'
A rather large reservoir of psychological energy is needed in order to consistently (and pleasurably) nurture our children.

I doubt that any parents exist who can constantly meet their children's needs, as outlined herein. At times, our children's needs seem too great for any of us, and you should not feel surprised if some passages in the following chapters feel a little daunting to you. We all fall short of being able to meet our children's needs from time to time, for all sorts of compelling reasons that are circumstantial, social, medical, psychological or material. The main reason is, however, that no pair of parents is meant to care for their children unaided; nature has designed us to rear our children in supportive groups (this will be discussed in depth in Part VII).

Scars come from repetitive hurts

In every home around the world, children feel hurt from time to time. I want to emphasise that the more serious social repercussions don't tend to come from one single bad experience, but from persistent or repetitive shocks that are reinforced through painful experiences across various stages. Children are often able to heal from life's unexpected wounds if they are supported to express their grief, and their anger, and if they receive comfort.

Different child: different outcome

It is impossible to predict exactly how each child will adapt to persistent wounding experiences, since there are many possible manifestations of emotional injury. While this section is a guide for how early childhood experiences affect our social behaviour, it is not meant to be deterministic. It speaks about *likelihoods* rather than certainties, about causative *factors* rather than absolute causes. We cannot always predict the outcome of emotional blows: the same kind of hurt may manifest in a number of ways across different individuals. Furthermore, some people have managed to turn their emotional wounds into gifts or talents, and many of history's humanitarians were wounded individuals who, once given opportunities to heal, used their wounds as impetus for great works.

Non-traditional families

Throughout the next five chapters you will note I mostly mention 'Mum and Dad' as the principal carers, for that happens to be the predominant model for family structure. I do not intend to leave out other types of families. Modernity has released us from rigid views of what a family ought to be, and we have become inclusive of single parent families, homosexual parents, and other models for family. Although Mum and Dad are the most important, I believe it is also crucial for children that their parents are not alone, and that they feel supported by a close-knit and loving community. We can afford to be more flexible in our beliefs about family structure once we realise that child rearing should be a communal enterprise. The human family, and loving bonds, are not limited to the 'nuclear' model.

Children: the ultimate experts

Finally, I believe that the ultimate experts on child rearing are children themselves, if we choose to trust their cues, and to take the lead from them. Sometimes, what our children ask from us confounds our expectations. As parents, carers and teachers, we are most tuned-in to them when we listen to them closely, and when we keep an open mind.

Endnotes

[1]   The material in the following five chapters is to a considerable extent inspired from the course notes of one of my most influential teachers, psychologist Chris Campbell. Other psychotherapist sources include: Brennan (1993); Campbell (1980), (1990); Conger (1994); Johnson (1994); Kurtz and Pestrera (1976); Kurtz (1990); Lowen (1969), (1975), (1980), (1997); Totton and Edmondson (1988).

[2]   You will also hear this parenting style referred to variously as 'attachment parenting', 'continuum parenting', or as Lloyd de Mause has tagged it, the 'helping mode'. The jargon can be confusing; but the central emphasis of learning to meet our children's emotional needs is the common denominator. This new mode of parenting emphasises *natural* responses to our children's biological and psychological needs; it is a commitment to following children's *natural rhythms*. That is why some authors, like psychologist Jan Hunt, author of *The Natural Child* (2001), like to call it 'natural parenting'. Since the bulk of research into early childhood emotional development has been conducted by 'attachment theorists', others like to call this new parenting mode 'attachment parenting'. Yet others call it 'continuum parenting' in homage to Jean Liedloff's ground-breaking book, *The Continuum Concept*. All these terms really refer to the same thing: a new, natural parenting approach, the first to be solidly based on scientifically derived conclusions

about child development.

3   Gerhardt (2004) p 195.

4   Developmental rites of passage continue throughout life, and except under dire circumstances, we certainly do not stop growing emotionally at seven years of age. For instance, the period of early adolescence – when there is another surge in brain development – is quite critical to our psycho-emotional and social development, and we keep on growing well into old age. As we get older, our peers begin to be a stronger influence on us, as our parents' influence slowly diminishes. The nature of our passage through the first five stages has a strong bearing on how we deal with the challenges we face through later stages, since it is during these first five stages that the foundation of the self is structured, and it is in early childhood that most brain development takes place.

5   Sunderland (2006).

25

FIRST RITE OF PASSAGE:
THE RIGHT TO EXIST

At the dawn of life the baby wants to feel safe and welcomed; what helps him[1] to feel loved is the utmost sensitivity to his bodily and emotional needs. The experiences that make him feel carefully listened to and held enable him to feel, at the core of his being, that he has the right to exist.

What happens at this time

The first developmental stage begins in the womb, possibly as early as the second trimester. It spans through the ordeal of birth, to around the sixth month of life.

No one is yet sure exactly when a foetus becomes conscious inside his mother's womb. However, we do know that his brain is mature enough to support consciousness at 28–32 weeks, and perhaps mature enough to process emotions at the sixth month of gestation. The neurological capacity for storing memory is present in the third trimester, and possibly even in the second.[2] Some scientists suggest an even earlier presence of consciousness, since brain waves can be detected in the foetus at the eighth or ninth week, and purposeful movements such as thumb sucking commence at the tenth week. Certainly, a foetus is able to feel pain by the twelfth week of gestation.

In recent years, a considerable amount of research has been done around the world in order to gain better understanding about the nature of foetal awareness. A foetus is able to sense and respond to a range of stimuli such as bright lights and loud noises. He is able to learn, and can, for instance, tell the difference between people's voices. Even in the womb, a baby can recognise his father's and mother's voices. He can remember pieces of music he heard while still in the womb, through the uterine wall. After he is born he can be especially soothed by music he enjoyed in utero.[3] Research suggests that newborns are more responsive to their mothers than to others,[4] which indicates that some preliminary bonding is able to take place even before birth (although the bulk of bonding takes place immediately after birth, and over the months that follow). This is not surprising, since we now know that a foetus is deeply attuned to and responsive to his mother's changing emotional states. He is emotionally alert, and capable of a broad array of facial expressions.

A mother's emotional states are passed to her foetus hormonally, through the placenta. Consequently, her more intense or persistent feelings have a powerful effect on the foetus's behaviour. This effect is so strong it can be detected in the baby's behaviour after birth.[5] The foetus responds to his mother's stress or anxiety with visible signs of agitation: his heart rate goes up, he becomes more active or jumpy, the blood flow to his brain is altered. He appears to feel her feelings as if they were his own. When a mother experiences a lot of unresolved anxiety during pregnancy, this can impinge upon his neurological development.[6] Since the foetus is so sensitive to the emotional climate that surrounds him; his mother's wellbeing, and her positive feelings towards him lull him into blissful tranquillity. How the parents feel about him and his coming birth sends ripples through the baby's primitive consciousness – he records and senses their joy, their ambivalence or even hostility to his presence.

A number of longitudinal studies have linked behavioural problems in later life stages to stressful experiences in the womb.[7] Although research in this area is in its early stages and remains inconclusive, there are indications that when babies are 'fussy', unusually clingy, difficult to settle, even hyperactive, this may be the result of high maternal stress during pregnancy.[8] Behavioural disturbances as serious as delinquency, schizophrenia, attention deficit and hyperactivity disorder (ADHD), depression and substance abuse have been associated with highly stressful experiences in the womb; such as severe marital discord, or maternal hostility or rejection towards the foetus.[9] Very stressful and traumatic experiences in the womb, through birth, and in the earliest months are recorded as emotional memory, and they have an enormous impact on the developing personality. The way a mother is supported throughout this process can critically influence the child's emotional health.

There is growing evidence that we are able to remember the events leading up to and surrounding our birth, at least as emotional memory, with remarkable accuracy. This should come as no surprise since, as we saw in Part V, the mechanisms for recording memory are well and truly present at this time. Undisclosed details of the birthing process that resurface as memories in clinical trials have been verified for accuracy by checking medical records, and further substantiated through interviews with mothers.[10] Many people have reported recalling their own birth, with varying degrees of lucidity, during psychotherapy, hypnosis or meditation sessions. That is why the highly-charged drama of birth, which is filled with the most intense emotions – uncertainty, fear, terror, pain, anger, joy, ecstasy and tenderness – leaves a deep and lasting imprint on the baby's unfolding emotionality. Psychotherapists have known for some time that, under carefully monitored circumstances, the release of deeply held emotions surrounding birth trauma can bring much psychological healing.

The first hours after birth are very important to the bonding between mother and child. These primal moments of release into the larger world, when the baby is exquisitely aware and suffused with strange and wondrous new sensations, act upon him like a love potion: he absorbs her presence and identifies her with all his senses; and he falls deeply in love. The newborn's senses are keenly attuned to his mother immediately after birth. As soon as he can breathe, his mother's unique and recognisable smell becomes imprinted in his brain. From the very first moments, a newborn's vision is preferentially attracted to human faces, eyes especially, and he is able to make limited eye contact.[11] His brain is hardwired to respond to facial features at exactly the distance at which he would be held during breastfeeding, and his eyes are able to focus and discern his mother's face at that distance. If he can be brought to her breast according to nature's plan, within the hour, his mouth immediately learns the unique contours of her nipple and areola, and adapts solely to her shape. In every sense, she is 'the one'. By the end of the first week he is already familiar with her face; and he reacts visibly to her changing expressions. He is moved by her emotional states and is sensitised to – and helplessly dependent on – her affection and warmth. Babies are able to detect a lack of expression in their parents' faces, and they become upset in response to emotional detachedness.[12] Even newborn babies can discriminate if their carers are emotionally cold, distant or hostile. Although these moments and days immediately after birth are a potent window of opportunity for mother–infant bonding, all is not necessarily lost if this window is missed. The bonding that determines a person's inner sense of security is the major recurring theme for the duration of the first two rites of passage. However, the special, highly-charged post-partum bonding period can certainly be particularly helpful in honing a mother's attunement to her baby, and stimulating her subsequent responsiveness to his needs.[13]

This first rite of passage is perhaps the most critical because the brain's response to stress adopts its 'set point' by the sixth month of life, thereafter shaping – for the long term – how we react under stress.[14] Our characteristic responses to life's stresses are strongly influenced by our experiences in the womb, during birth, and through the earliest months.

Neither the foetus nor the neonate have a capacity for boundary formation: as far as the child is concerned, he and his mother are one, with no differentiation. Consequently, the newborn baby is highly absorbent of parental emotions. In this innocent and permeable state the baby registers how his parents feel toward him as the very nature of his own being, and begins to form around this experience his deepest attitudes to himself, to humanity, and to life.

For over 35 million years, primate infants survived and stayed safe by clutching onto mothers day and night. To lose touch meant an almost certain death. The same holds true for human babies. It is central to our genetic inheritance to be born with the need to be held or carried directly on our mother's body throughout the day, and to be held close through the night – at least until we display obvious signs of wanting to move around independently. It can be said that to be worn on his parents' bodies for most of the day is the baby's evolutionary expectation – it is a core emotional need, and his sense of security is compromised to the extent that this is denied him. No infant is prepared for physical or emotional separation; this causes him to feel uneasy. If the separation is prolonged, the unease escalates to alarm, panic, rage, followed by despair, and finally an emotional switching-off – the baby's way of giving up. Our modern, socialising mode expectations that our babies should sleep in separate rooms, or that they should withstand crying without being touched or held for minutes at a time, are unnatural and emotionally wounding.

At birth, and for months afterwards, the baby is extremely vulnerable, and so aloneness, non-responsiveness to his needs, or lack of human warmth can bring about the deepest of terrors and despair. The imposition of regimented feeding and sleeping routines is experienced by the baby as a shattering break from his own natural inner rhythms, and an emotional abandonment from the ones he loves.

Baby's emotional needs at this time

The ideal situation is one in which both parents long for the child from a position of emotional and material preparedness. Both parents are sufficiently emotionally fulfilled and ready to give and love, and are able to pleasurably meet the enormous demands of the helpless infant. Ideally, help is at hand from a supportive family and community (it does take a village!) when the parents are otherwise occupied or feeling exhausted. It is essential that both parents feel loved and supported during pregnancy, by each other, their extended family and their community. The mother's emotional wellbeing, her sense of being safe, supported and fulfilled, and her enjoyment of life's pleasures, are all directly transmitted to the foetus.

To be talked to in the womb

Parents should talk lovingly to the baby in the womb, since he recognises both of their voices. It is also a good idea to let the foetus hear soothing and beautiful music. There is evidence that these kinds of communication directly benefit the psychological as well as physical health of the baby later.[15] Studies also show that when mother–infant bonding is well attended to in utero and at birth, this facilitates more maternal patience and affection later.[16] Increasingly, research is demonstrating that if infants' early security needs are satisfied, this helps to prevent behavioural problems later, such as fussyness, excessive clingyness, irritability, and difficulties with sleep.

To have a natural and gentle birth

There are medical reasons why a natural birth is not always possible. Nevertheless, non-traumatic birth is free of emergency or defensive obstetrics, which the acutely sensitive newborn can experience as violating. Unfortunately, many modern labour ward birthing methods focus on emergency measures while paying insufficient attention to the emotional and psychological needs and fragility of mother and child. The unnecessary physical separation of mother and baby soon after birth is an abrupt and shocking discontinuity from the intimate contact of the womb. The transition into the outside world is critical in giving the baby information about the nature of the environment he has entered. Therefore, his arrival needs to be extremely gentle and sensitive, into a warm, holding and non-violent world where the child will be joyously welcomed, and where his contact with his mother will not be broken.

Few people have so far witnessed the unspeakably moving phenomenon of a compassionately managed birth. We are so desensitised to the starkness of our labour wards, and the cold mechanics of modern-day obstetrics, that few give an alternative a second thought. In order to gain an appreciation for what is possible when parents' and babies' emotional needs are attended to at labour, it is extremely worthwhile to read French obstetrician Frederick Leboyer's *Birth Without Violence*. The sublime images shown in this book make the case for non-violent birth with heart-rending eloquence. It is through Leboyer's pioneering work and the work of others[17] that a healthier and more appropriate approach to birth has begun to spread. The growing use of cosy and home-like birthing centres, home birthing, water birthing, and the shift toward midwifery instead of obstetrics, are helping to soften the impact of birth trauma on the human psyche.[18] New, natural birthing methods such as Leboyer developed insist on soft lighting, avoiding loud or sudden noises, delaying the cutting of the umbilical cord, handling the newborn with great tenderness and bringing him immediately to the mother's breast, engaging the support of the father, and generally safeguarding the natural processes of labour as much as possible. The first hour or so after birth can be a life-changing and powerful experience of indescribable love and unshakeable bonding – and much has been learned about why this is the case.

At the moment of birth, mothers experience huge surges in levels of several key hormones: oxytocin, the hormone producing loving feelings, beta-endorphin, the hormone of pleasure, and prolactin, the hormone that induces tender and maternal behaviour. These hormones are enhanced again through direct, skin-to-skin contact with the baby, and through breastfeeding. In undisturbed birth, when this hormonal cocktail reaches its zenith, it brokers the deepest and most loving bond between mother and newborn. It results in a loving attachment that reverberates for a lifetime, informing all future intimate relationships.

This whole process can be severely disrupted by the drugs administered in modern obstetrics, which suppress the natural secretion of the hormone cocktail. The blissful feelings that can arise during birth and bonding can be diminished or numbed altogether under medicalised birth conditions.[19]

To be tenderly welcomed into the family
The parents' joy at receiving their baby is the essential ingredient of his emotional nourishment. Baby and mother need to remain physically together constantly in order to foster bonding and healthy attachment. Warm, tender and supportive holding bathes the baby in feelings of contentment and security, orienting him toward emotional balance and wellbeing. Skin-on-skin contact and stroking allows the infant to receive his mother's loving presence directly through his delicate nerve endings. Excessive clothing or swaddling can act as a barrier that deprives the baby of this essential sensory nourishment. This most intimate kind of contact (known as 'kangaroo care') is of vital importance in the early months, and has been shown to improve the development of physiological, emotional and cognitive faculties.[20]

To be in a gentle and peaceful home environment
Babies are extremely sensitive to others' emotional charge and volatility, they can be easily shocked when there is intense conflict going on around them. Infants require protection from excess conflict or disharmony during this fragile time.

To sleep close to Mum and Dad
When newborns are allowed to sleep close to their mothers ('rooming-in'), they spend more time quietly sleeping, and they retain healthy body temperature better than those who are removed from their mother's presence.[21] Babies strongly prefer to be near their parents at night; they are not ready to cope with the anxiety that physical separation provokes. They need to be at least close enough to hear their parents breathing, and to be within arm's reach so they can be rocked or touched if they need to be soothed back to sleep, and quickly picked up for night time feedings. The issue of co-sleeping will be dealt with in more detail in the next chapter.

To be held throughout the day

In terms of his emotional wellbeing, a baby thrives best when he is carried on his parents' bodies whenever possible, in a sling or similar device, throughout the day. There are many kinds of activities, both work and home-related, that can be comfortably carried out while wearing a baby. Babies love to be included and to observe our day-to-day lives. An American study found that when babies were routinely carried in a sling, directly on their mothers' bodies, mothers became more responsive to them, and the babies appeared to be more emotionally secure.[22]

In fact, to be carried on his mother's body might be the infant's most important developmental need, according to Dr James W Prescott, developmental neurophysiologist and former health-science administrator at the US National Institute of Child Health and Human Development. Prescott's studies demonstrated that the unique and irreplaceable stimulation provided by baby-wearing is essential to healthy brain growth, and the development of trust and intimacy. He considers baby-wearing a potent vaccine against depression, social alienation, violence and substance addiction later in life.[23]

Jean Liedloff, in her seminal book, The Continuum Concept,[24] aptly refers to this stage and the next as the 'in-arms phase'. The need for near-constant physical proximity is very high during this and the next developmental stage. Many parents have found that if they meet their infants' attachment needs in this way, their baby is significantly more serene, and he relaxes into sleep with Comparative ease. Emotionally secure children are not necessarily the ones that are held the most, but the ones who are held on their own terms, in other words, the ones who are hugged when they want to be and given freedom to move about when they want to be. Certainly, most babies appear most tranquil and contented when they are held for most of the day, but in order to be responsive to the baby, we need to be flexible and attuned to the baby's communications.

To have loving eye contact

Most parents are already aware of their infants' need to be stroked, handled gently, and spoken to with tenderness. A less talked about but equally essential need is for infants to have frequent, affectionate eye contact with their carers. (This needs to be done according to the baby's need – they will soon protest if they feel over-stimulated.) In fact, it's not so much the eye contact in and of itself that satisfies a baby's longing for connection, but the way the parent's facial and eye expression is visibly responsive. If a baby watches a smiling image of her mother on a TV monitor, he is likely to become distressed, because her smile is not related to the baby's communications. The baby soon realises he is irrelevant, he has no impact on her mother. The baby is only contented when his mother's face is responding to him.

To be free of imposed routines

It is vitally important, around the dawn of life, that the child's few and simple physical and emotional needs be met on his terms, according to his own organic rhythms, rather than according to the parent's (and society's) needs for routine. He does not have adequate psychological resources to cope with the delayed gratification that imposed feeding and sleeping schedules demand of him. The most up-to-date advice given by the World Health Organization (WHO),[25] lactation specialists and a growing number of paediatricians and child psychologists is that babies must be fed as soon as they show hunger cues, and their emotional and physical needs should be responded to without delay. This will also be dealt with in more detail in Chapter 26.

To be responded to promptly

A commonly held belief among socialising mode parents is that if we meet our babies' needs on their terms, this will make them overly dependent. This is the exact opposite of the truth. Our transition to the helping mode comes from the growing realisation that it is categorically not possible to 'spoil' a baby by responding faithfully and immediately to his needs.

Margot Sunderland's (British psychologist) review of child development research adds weight to the idea that we should not leave crying babies unattended, and that parental responsiveness is the key to healthy attachment in babyhood.

A distressed, crying baby's nervous system is dependent on the parents' comforting to bring it back into balance. 'The more responsive you are to your infant,' explains Sunderland, 'the greater your regulation of her body arousal systems will be, and the more long-lasting the effects'[26]. Babies left to cry unattended show elevated levels of cortisol, and after six hours of separation from the mother, a baby's stress hormone levels can be twice as high as that of a baby whose mother is close[27]. Over time, these neurotoxic levels of cortisol cause damage to brain cells and upset the balance of brain chemistry.

Joining a growing, international chorus of expert voices, Sunderland warns that babies' nervous systems can become permanently 'wired' for hyper-arousal, if they are not consistently comforted by their parents. Emotional neglect leads not only to long-term psychological vulnerabilities, but also to a range of physical ailments. On the other hand, a parent's soothing ministrations activate the vagus nerve in the child's brain stem, which regulates the function of major organs, the digestive system, the heart rate, breathing and the immune system.

When parents are responsive to their children's emotions, there are a multiple and profound health benefits that last a lifetime. In fact, millions of years of evolution have fine-tuned the human organism in such a way that a baby's cry (and his many other need-cues), always signal a legitimate need for some kind of attention. It can be very stressful for a crying baby "if the mother is not there and does not respond quickly" – and for a baby, stress may "even have the quality of trauma".[28] The emotional equanimity and vitality of the infant rests in the parents' responsiveness to these needs.

What baby is learning at this time
The most primal emotional competencies are learned earliest in life. The foundations of emotional wellbeing at this first rite of passage are related to the infant's core sense that he has a right to exist in this world, to take up space, to be recognised as an important member of his family, and of humanity. The 'right to exist', is a deeply ingrained, unconscious conviction that underwrites all of our attitudes and behaviours. If our personality (our way of relating) is to be strongly rooted in this assumption, this hinges on the following experiences predominating at this stage:

- Getting a strong sense of being wanted and welcomed by both parents – in the womb, at birth and thereafter.
- Feeling secure that our bodily and emotional needs will be heard and fulfilled.
- Feeling essentially safe in the world, and safe with other humans. This bottom-line feeling of safety is possible if our early infancy is free from neglect, harshness, coldness, roughness, violence or excess, unresolved conflict in our families.

No parent provides a perfect environment for their infant, and every child born will be exposed to 'positive' and 'negative' feelings from both parents. What is important is that joy be the predominant feeling that greets the child as he awakens to consciousness, and that the parents have healthy means for processing any ambivalent or negative feelings toward parenthood as these feelings arise, so that the child is not lumbered with the parents' unresolved emotional baggage (it is normal, and safe, to feel unloving towards your children sometimes).

The emotional cornerstone of inner security is positioned at this time. A strong and secure emotional core is what enables us to make our presence felt in the world, and to command attention. The basic building blocks of healthy self-assertion are thus provided at this stage. The right conditions here help us to live our lives based on deep feelings of belonging, of being intrinsically connected to community, humanity and nature, and that this world is essentially a safe, friendly and nourishing place.

The most wounding experiences

Emotional wounding begins in the womb if the foetus gets a pervasive feeling of being unwanted or rejected. The foetus is also disturbed if his mother is beset with anxiety or depression, if she abuses drugs or other noxious substances, if she is emotionally unsupported or lives in an atmosphere of conflict or violence. How she feels about herself becomes etched into the foetal consciousness.

Most adults living in the developed world today experienced their own birth as a terrifying, painful, shocking and traumatic ordeal. Some standard obstetric practices are experienced as violent by the baby; including rough and insensitive handling, severing the umbilical cord before it stops pulsating, the separation from the mother immediately after birth, and other emergency medical measures that are sometimes of debatable benefit. For instance, it was not uncommon around one generation ago for mothers to be placed under general anaesthetic, while forceps were used to deliver the baby. Besides the pain and temporary deformity brought to the infant's head, the critical first moments of mother–infant bonding would be destroyed by the anaesthetic blackout. A difficult forceps delivery raises the baby's cortisol levels more than other types of delivery, indicating how stressful this procedure can be.[29] Since in some hospitals this

286

was a routine procedure rather than a response to complications, it seems worth keeping an open mind about what orthodox obstetric practices are absolutely necessary. Similarly, the soaring rate of elective caesarean delivery poses serious questions about conventional practice. Why, for instance, are 25–30 per cent of babies born in Australian private hospitals delivered by caesarean section[30] – when this is roughly twice the rate recommended by the World Health Organization?[31]

Though birth is never a picnic, much of the birth trauma we and our children have suffered is avoidable. Babies record every detail of their birth, and this has profound and long lasting emotional consequences.

The newborn is injured if he is met with rejection, hostility, coldness, detachment or neglect. He is wounded if his mother is ill or seriously depressed, if there is violence in his family, if his family is surrounded by war or other kinds of social strife. How his parents feel toward him, as reflected in their behaviour, deeply influences how he feels towards himself. If he is hated, he is likely to end up hating himself. If he is neglected, he is likely to end up neglecting himself. If he is controlled and regimented, he is likely to become mechanical towards himself.

Enforced and imposed routines disconnect the baby from his organic, natural rhythms long before he is ready for self-containment. This brings about an early interruption to the flow of feeling. Though his physical survival may be assured, scheduled feeding and strict sleeping routines are un-natural, out of tune with the baby's needs, and emotionally wounding.

Poor responsiveness to his needs, cold or mechanical handling, insufficient holding or frequent abandonment, are all shocks to the crystalline sensitivity of the baby. Such is the importance of tender touch that, as neuroscientist Bruce Perry says "a newborn infant that is not touched for 2 weeks will be severely traumatised".[32] An insensitive, rough or violent environment is experienced by the baby as utterly shattering – it even feels annihilating.

Our culture (backed, until not so long ago, by mainstream paediatrics and psychology) has tended to deny the emotional acuity and receptivity of infants under two, which has given rise to their tragic isolation in cots, pens and incubators, and the disregarding of their cries for touch and nurturing. Deep feelings of alienation, separateness, unworthiness and even hostility can result from these earliest and most primal needs for near-constant contact not being met. Later in life, these feelings manifest in disturbances of relationships or intimacy, even when masked by superficial functionality.

To the great disservice of babies, many doctors and nurses still tell us that sometimes babies cry for no particular reason. Nothing could be further from the truth; all cries are a legitimate expression of need. Even when a baby's cry is purely cathartic – that is, he cries not to ask for something but to relieve his stress – he still needs to be held. When a baby is left to cry untouched, even for a few minutes, this causes him to feel abandoned and frightened.

How experiences shape emotional make-up and beliefs

Our 'core beliefs' are the most deeply held beliefs about ourselves, about human relationships, and about the nature of the world around us. These beliefs usually remain unconscious (until we choose to acquaint ourselves with the depths of our minds), but they form a basis for many of our feelings, attitudes and behaviours. Core beliefs colour the way we perceive ourselves and each other.

Children are very prone to drawing false and narcissistic conclusions about themselves, and highly generalised conclusions about life, based on their experiences. For instance, when parents are absent, even if due to unforeseeable circumstances, many little children conclude that this is because they are unlovable. Core beliefs such as these tend to remain with us well into adulthood.

The following are some core beliefs held by adults, which arose from injurious experiences at this time.

Negative core beliefs:

I don't belong
I am worthless or loathsome
There is something wrong with me
Life is dangerous or terrifying
I am alone in the world
I have no right to exist, to be here, to take up space
Life on the physical plane does not matter – what is important
    is 'spiritual', in another world, after death
The world of flesh is evil, tarnished, worthless

The following are some core beliefs held by adults, which arose from positive experiences at this time.

Positive core beliefs:
Life is good
It is safe to be me
I belong here
I have the right to be here
I have the right to show the way I feel
It is safe and OK to feel my feelings
I can accept conflict as part of life
Life is essentially safe and nurturing

The greatest fears that motivate the interpersonal defences that are constructed at this time are: the fear of death, the fear of falling apart or going crazy, the fear of attack. These fears produce in individuals a tendency to be overly anxious, perhaps even paranoid.

How emotional wounds affect adult behaviour

There are two categories of response to stress and trauma: they are fight-or-flight and freezing. The set of responses known as fight-or-flight are characterised by an increase in blood pressure, heart rate and muscle tone, and a hyper-vigilant demeanour. At the opposite end of the response spectrum are the freezing responses; which happen when neither 'fight' nor 'flight' are possible. So the earlier the trauma, the more vulnerable the child, the more it is likely that 'freezing' will be the adaptive response.

The first rite of passage is when a baby is most vulnerable. There are no real interpersonal defences available, no escape from painful emotional states other than through passive responses such as freezing, defeat, surrender or giving up. The infant has no conscious and intentional capacity to ask for help and expect it. There is insufficient neuro-muscular tone in his body to armour him and shield him against the flow of unpleasant or painful emotions. Consequently, painful emotions are most overwhelming and unbearable at this time.

Trauma causes the infant to freeze or go numb emotionally, to dissociate from his feelings and his environment. These dissociative defences involve a withdrawal of the self; a disengagement from the world. There may be a fall in heart rate and blood pressure, and a loss of muscle tone, as the baby splits-off from his pain, his despair and his fear; and he becomes detached and unresponsive.[33] These types of defences are mediated by the release of brain chemicals called endogenous opioids that numb us to pain, both physical and emotional. This is a normal and healthy response to an overwhelming threat, but if a baby remains in the freezing response long enough (meaning that the threatening situation is not fleeting but pervasive or recurring), this will alter the balance of his brain chemistry. He becomes predisposed to dissociative defences as his answer to life's stresses. The dissociative or freezing 'state' thus becomes a 'trait'. When trauma is severe at this stage, this predisposes the child to dissociative disorders later.[34]

What follows are examples of the kinds of relating styles (our characteristic ways of relating to one another) and personality traits that arise from emotional injuries occurring during this rite of passage. It is very hard to predict exactly which result will ensue for each child, or how his genetic profile will interact with the experiences he meets. To some degree, the way psychological defences manifest also depends on the kind of nurturance and support that benefit the baby in later stages. In other words, if the child's emotional needs are well met at later stages, this would help to soften the impact of any psychological injury sustained at this time. The more serious manifestations of emotional wounds listed below usually materialise if the child's emotional support is also shaky or inadequate at subsequent stages.

Since withdrawal is the only psychological defence available to the baby at this time, shocks experienced here can lead to a demeanour of remoteness or aloofness. Some of these babies may grow to be day-dreamers, under stress they might feel depersonalised or unreal. Others grow to be overly passive, compliant and obedient. The movement is away from contact with others, taking refuge in excessive intellectualisation; a state of analytical detachment from life, or a tendency to reverie. The adult becomes uneasy in the unpredictable world of feelings and emotion, and therefore over-emphasises the 'reasonable', the 'rational', the 'logical' – or the 'abstract' and the 'philosophical'. He may even look down upon emotions, and avoid strong emotional encounters with others. A fragile countenance or hyper-sensitivity to hurts and slights are also legacies of wounding during the first rite of passage.

When an individual's core sense of a 'right to exist' has been violated, this can lead to difficulties with self-assertion. He grows to be inhibited about making his presence felt in social situations. He finds it hard to command attention when interacting with others. His interpersonal communication tends towards the cerebral; he speaks with little connection to his feelings, as if he is not really there.

Usually, underneath this timidity or lack of assertiveness, there lurks a powerful rage. The difficulty with appropriate self-assertion produces feelings of helplessness and frustration that accumulate over time. Withdrawn individuals tend to deny this pent-up frustration, or have difficulty contacting it, but when provocation overwhelms their defences, their rage can be explosive. Periodically, these feelings can burst through destructively.

Social impact of wounds

Since terror is a principal feature of a difficult passage through this stage, this can make individuals unusually prone to anxiety, even anxiety-related disorders. When trauma is extreme, and this is not compensated for later with restorative warmth, the results can be serious. Unresolved trauma at this time has been associated with a number of severe disorders, including borderline schizophrenia, and alcohol or drug dependency.[35] Prenatal and perinatal traumas have also been associated with delinquency and violence.[36]

Severe and/or ongoing emotional shocks at this stage produce a profound schism from feeling; the connection to emotions is cut off. When a foetus or infant experiences violence, or an acute lack of human warmth, he can grow to become unable to empathise with others. Some may also be prone to bouts of explosive, even murderous rage. To a significant degree, the very thing that enables us to kill, maim or torture other human beings – in other words, to lose our humanness – is severe (and unhealed) trauma beginning at this time, and compacted at later stages. The deepest rage, sadism and hostility that humans are capable of spring from extreme and sustained trauma that starts as early as the first rite of passage.

Individuals who have sustained less extreme first-stage trauma can be highly sensitive – even hypersensitive – but they can also appear to be detached or remote. Because they find it difficult to connect to or sustain emotions, this interferes with their ability to form close bonds with others. They may even be hostile or cynical about emotionality and human intimacy.

Divorced from the real world, and haunted by a sense of not belonging, some of these individuals may be drawn towards cults where they can reclaim at least an awkward sense of family and belonging, and lose themselves in otherworldly pursuits. No amount of intellectual sophistication can ground us in reality, when our emotional wounds are serious enough.

In Part V, we saw how early trauma can profoundly disrupt brain development and brain chemistry, potentially leading to a lifetime of disturbed emotionality, violence or dissociation from feeling. Since trauma at the dawn of life is so widespread, it is no wonder that the world suffers from such recurring random acts of mass violence. We lose our sanity and our reason too easily, and explode into irrational vengeance for the pain we have suffered – though we have long forgotten the real source of our pain. The innate ability to feel our intrinsic oneness with all of humanity has been destroyed – we fear and distrust those who are culturally or ethnically different, they become the enemy, the cause of our woes. The choice to make war is not rationally made; it is driven by the hidden – but not forgotten – rage of a wounded child.

Since our capacity for feeling and for empathy has been compromised, we are content to feather our own nests and let the less fortunate perish. Though much of the world's population exists as the tormented slaves of oppressive and brutal regimes, many of us in the developed world brush this off as '*their* problem, for *them to sort out amongst themselves*'.

Perhaps an even greater danger to our collective survival is our pathological disconnection from the natural world. Since we have lost touch with this vital, inner sense of kinship with life, we permit ourselves to remorselessly ravage our planet, to the extent that we now flirt with self-annihilation. Collectively, the unhealed wounds to our 'right to exist' are posing a threat to our existence.

Positive changes

The growing recognition of foetal and infantile awareness is slowly bringing about a much more compassionate approach to prenatal and perinatal care, as we move into the helping mode era. This development is likely to bring about some desperately needed planetary healing.

Unless there is a clear and present need for intervention more people now insist that labour should be treated naturally.

The psychological wellbeing of mother and baby are starting to be given more value, and we have begun to make the birthing process less violent. The natural, non-interventionist births that take place in birthing rooms or at home have gone a long way towards reducing birth trauma and its long term psychological repercussions.

In Australia, the Coalition for Improving Maternity Services (CIMS)[37] has devised a programme called the Mother-Friendly Childbirth Initiative, in order to promote more natural and less traumatic birthing. In the UK, consumer-led organizations and midwifery organizations campaign to ensure mothers are at the heart of decisions about where to give birth and that they get support for normal birth, free of unnecessary medical interventions. [38] The idea that birth is, for babies and mothers, a moment of profound psychological as well as physical vulnerability has slowly begun to catch on – with some reassuring results. The medical profession is beginning to realise, for instance, that complications at labour can be caused by the mother's emotional stress. When mothers are supported by companions at labour, this reduces the incidence of a host of medical complications, and shortens labour.[39]

The Baby Friendly Hospital Initiative (BFHI)[40] is an international project produced jointly by the World Health Organization (WHO)[41] and the United Nations Children's Fund (UNICEF) to promote breastfeeding, and protect the process of mother–infant bonding and attachment. Hospitals or birthing centres that meet the BFHI criteria are awarded a BFHI designation. Some of these criteria include: having newborn babies latched on and breastfeeding within an hour after birth, encouraging 'rooming in' (mother and newborn are not to be separated), discouraging the use of formula or pacifiers unless medically required, and supporting 'on-demand' breastfeeding. There are now roughly 15,000 designated BFHIs around the world.

Recommended further reading

There are probably few choices parents can make that are as significant as the way in which the earliest moments of their newborn's life – and the mother's labour – will be managed. It is every family's right to be thoroughly informed in advance, and I would urge new parents to compare the record of physical *and* psychological safety of a number of approaches to birthing, at hospitals, birthing rooms and at home. Although I cannot vouch for the accuracy of all the information within them, I found the following websites to be informative.[42]

Coalition for Improving Maternity Services (CIMS)
motherfriendly.org

The Maternity Coalition Inc
www.maternitycoalition.org.au

Birth International
www.birthinternational.com.au/articles/wagner03.html

Home Birth Reference Site
www.homebirth.org.uk

Global Maternal/Child Health Association, Inc
www.geocities.com/HotSprings/2840/about.htm

The following books look closely at the pros and cons of a broad range of gentle approaches to childbirth.

- Harper B and Arms S (2005) *Gentle Birth Choices* Healing Arts Press.
- Kitzinger S (1996) *The Complete Book of Pregnancy and Childbirth* Alfred A Knopf.
- Leboyer F (2002) *Birth Without Violence* Inner Traditions.
- Odent M (1994) *Birth Reborn* Birth Works.
- Wagner M (1994) *Pursuing the Birth Machine* ACE Graphics.

Endnotes

1   Please note, although I have used the male and female pronouns alternatively across the next five chapters, what I have written here applies to both genders. There are definitely some very important gender differences in psychological development, but all I have room to cover here are the aspects of the developmental journey that are common to both genders.
2   Verny (1981).
3   De Mause (2002c).
4   Righetti (1996).
5   Van den Bergh (1990); de Mause (2002c).
6   Monk, Fifer, Myers, Sloan, Trien and Hurtado (2000).

7   De Mause (2002c).
8   DiPietro (2002).
9   De Mause (2002c); Gerhardt (2004) p 172.
10 Laibow (1986); Cheek (1986); Chamberlain (1999).
11 Johnson (1994) p 22; Easterbrook, Kisilevsky, Muir and Laplante (1999); Johnson, Dziurawiec, Ellis and Morton (1991).
12 Johnson (1994) p 22; Blum (2002).
13 Klaus, Jerauld, Kreger, McAlpine, Steffa and Kennell (1972).
14 Gerhardt (2004) p 173.
15 Chamberlain (1994).
16 Verny (1981).
17 Leboyer (2002); Harper and Arms (1994); Odent (1994); Kitzinger (1996); Wagner (1994).
18 See for example the work of the Maternity Coalition http://www.maternitycoalition.org.auu and Home Birth Reference Site http://www.homebirth.org.uk (last accessed 1 December 2004).
19 Buckley (2005).
20 Robotham and Glendenning (2001); Feldman, Weller, Sirota and Eidelman (2002).
21 Trevathan and McKenna (1994) p 94.
22 Anisfeld, Casper, Nozyce and Cunningham (1990).
23 Prescott (1996).
24 Liedloff (1986).
25 See the World Health Organization (WHO) 'Child and adolescent rights' http://www.who.int/child-adolescent-health/right.htm (last accessed 1 December 2004).
26 Sunderland (2006).
27 Sunderland (2006)
28 Gerhardt (2004) p 70.
29 Gerhardt (2004) p 68.
30 See Australian Broadcasting Corporation (1999). The rate in the USA is 25 per cent; see Global Maternal/Child Health Association at http://www.geocities.com/HotSprings/2840/about.htm (last accessed 1 December 2004).
31 World Health Organization (1985) 'Appropriate technology for birth' *Lancet* Vol 332 pp 436–437. See also Wagner (2000).
32 Perry and Pollard (1998).
33 Perry, Pollard, Blakley, Baker and Vigilante (1995).
34 Perry, Pollard, Blakley, Baker and Vigilante (1995).
35 Hall (1986).
36 Prescott (1996).

[37] See the Coalition for Improving Maternity Services http://motherfriendly.org (last accessed 1 December 2004).

[38] See 'Ten steps of the mother-friendly childbirth initiative for mother-friendly hospitals, birth centers, and home birth services' in the Coalition for Improving Maternity Services http://motherfriendly.org/MFCI/steps/ (last accessed 1 December 2004); http://www.rcmnormalbirth.org.uk

[39] Klaus, Kennell, Robertson and Sosa (1986).

[40] See UNICEF's UK Baby Friendly Initiative http://www.babyfriendly.org.uk/home.asp (last accessed 1 December 2004).

[41] See World Health Organization (WHO) website on child and adolescent rights at http://www.who.int/child-adolescent-health/right.htm (last accessed 1 December 2004).

[42] All sites were last accessed on 1 December 2004.

26

SECOND RITE OF PASSAGE:
THE RIGHT TO NEED

The baby is at this time looking to have her needs affirmed, to know she can trust others to respond to her when she seeks nurturing. Her sense of security rests on her being affirmed in this way. When her needs for nourishment and comfort are met promptly and consistently, this enables her to feel, at the core of her being, that she has the right to have needs and to reach out to others, and that the world is essentially a friendly place.

What happens at this time
The second rite of passage spans from immediately after birth to roughly 18 months. The baby is still highly vulnerable and dependent, and so it is important that her needs are attended to as they arise, with as little delay a possible. Her emotional wellbeing rests on being breastfed on demand, that is, as soon as she demonstrates signs of hunger.[1] In order to feel secure, she needs to sleep as close as possible to her carers throughout the night, and to remain quite close to them throughout the day, held and carried whenever practicable – until she shows signs of wanting to move about and explore her world. This stage is an extension of the first rite of passage; it entails the founding of secure attachment.

The unfolding drama of this time revolves around the baby's expression of need; her reaching out and taking in of physical and emotional nourishment. The baby's focus for need-gratification and aliveness is centered on her skin: her arms and hands, and most of all, her lips and mouth, which are richly suffused with nerve endings. These are exquisitely alive centers of awareness that pleasurably connect her to a nourishing world. There are therefore huge psychological benefits that exist beyond the mechanical and nutritional advantages of breastfeeding. The pleasure-inducing contact between a mother's breast and her baby's mouth provides an essential emotional sustenance. The baby-bottle cannot replicate the unique mother–child attunement that comes from direct, flesh-and-skin intimacy.

A baby experiences her hunger as a disturbing, hollow feeling that causes her to tense her body; it arouses distressing emotions that soon mount to anger and despair if her need is not gratified.[2] When we force a baby to wait until the clock says it is OK to feed, this is deeply unsettling to her, it is maddening.

On the other hand, when her oral need is satisfied as it arises, this floods her body-mind with a deep, pleasurable calm; a blissful sense of wholeness and completeness. The dense nerve endings around the lips make the powerful reflexive sucking motions intensely pleasurable, particularly when the baby is latched on at the breast. The sucking reflex, when met with its natural object of desire, sends a stream of pleasurable sensations pulsating throughout her body. These experiences of delicious, blissful contentment are critical to healthy brain growth. Oral fulfilment is a fundamental cornerstone for emotional development: it builds a lasting repository of serenity and contentment deep within the mind and body of the infant. When her needs for nourishment and holding are faithfully met, a dense layer of emotional security is installed in her subconscious, leading the child to think of the world as a friendly, nurturing and abundant place, and leading her to think of herself and her needs as good and right. This process lays down the foundation of healthy emotionality, and good social skills.[3]

Baby's emotional needs at this time
There is probably no aspect of child development that is backed by such a formidable body of international research, as the issue of 'attachment'. A child's need to feel securely 'attached' to her carers is particularly pertinent to the first two stages of development. Such is the volume of research substantiating the importance of healthy attachment in early childhood, that I can barely cover a fraction of it in these pages. As a relatively new field of study, attachment theory is now the established body of knowledge regarding early childhood, and it has given rise to the specialty of infant mental health.[4] The promotion of further research, training and education in this field is vital, since we are

still a long way from implementing child health and childcare practices that properly reflect the established tenets of attachment. Decades of research have brought child development experts to the following conclusions:

- Babies are genetically programmed to seek and form a strong attachment or bond to one or more trusted carers, and their healthy emotional development is dependent on this bond.
- Emotional security is based on attachment to carers that are consistent and dependably warm.
- Secure attachment is also dependent on the promptness of carers' responsiveness to babies' needs.
- Disturbances in attachment may have a long-lasting impact on personality, serious gaps in attachment may have serious psychological and social consequences.

Both parents are of prime importance, as babies who are securely attached to both mother and father seem to fare better.[5] Although small babies tend to marginally prefer the mother if both parents are present, the father is a very close second. He is also critical in providing the emotional support that the mother requires if she is to have the capacity to meet the baby's redoubtable emotional needs. Not surprisingly, research shows that the parents' partnership satisfaction is a key factor for the baby's secure attachment.[6]

To be held almost constantly

The baby's almost constant need to be held carries on from the last rite of passage. Babies' behaviour is never random; it is geared toward gaining and maintaining this vital bond. They are born with a repertoire of fixed behavioural patterns; they 'root' with their lips for a nipple, they suck, they grasp, they nestle, their cries are a plea to be closely and tenderly held. These social behaviours have been crucial to our (and our ancestors') survival for millions of years,[7] since during the course of evolution, separation often meant injury or death. The human baby has evolved to require being held close day and night; this is fundamental for the development of emotional security.

Separation is probably the most stressful experience for babies – when they are removed from close physical contact with their carers babies often react with intense alarm. Separation produces higher levels of the stress hormone cortisol, elevated corticotropin-releasing factor (CRF) (the bio-chemical of fear) and elevated heart rates.[8] A baby's abject helplessness causes her to crave the soothing drumbeat of her mother's heart, the rocking and swaying as she is carried upon her mother's body. No matter how safe, warm and well fed a baby is, she is still likely to feel bereft and terrified if left alone in her crib. Most primate infants are carried everywhere by their mothers or allomothers (maternal helpers). Research with humans and primates has shown that when infants are separated from their mothers, they tend to remain more timid or otherwise socially impaired.

Babies that are worn in a sling on their parents' bodies throughout much of the day are helped to feel safe and secure, while their parents enjoy a degree of mobility and activity. Baby-wearing helps to maintain a lovely sense of bonding, and can be quite pleasurable for both parent and child. Typically, babies who are worn on their parents' bodies tend to be more placid and content – as long as the parents are relatively unstressed in their giving.[9]

Babies are highly dependent on regular stroking, warm and tender touch. Skin-to-skin contact helps the baby's body to generate hormones that induce relaxation, and hormones that aid digestion – such as gastrin.

If listened to, the infant will issue very clear indications of her readiness to begin flirting with autonomy. She reaches for the ground so she can feel herself against the earth. She looks away from her mother to the mystery and allure of distant objects. She moves her limbs in early strivings to self-propel; to crawl and to walk. The vigour and confidence with which she moves out toward the larger world is based on how secure she feels about her mother's love. Her exploration rate, as research shows, is related to how emotionally available her mother is.[10] Yet for the most part, she still wants to be inside or near her mother's orbit. Our task as parents is to release our babies according to their need, rather than to expel them according to ours.

Mothers need not be glued to their babies 24 hours a day. Research shows that babies can benefit from secondary attachment to others, as long as these others are regular, consistent, responsive and warm.[11] The ideal scenario is for a baby to be cared for by a small number of kin or close friends, in addition to the parents. When parenting is conducted as part of a group, this protects parents from exhaustion, and adds to the baby's sense of security. What babies cannot tolerate is being left alone and untouched – as often happens when mothers are alone and isolated. A baby's need to be held is virtually unending.[12]

To have her oral needs gratified
It is difficult to replace the wonderful intimacy, sensual pleasure and blissful fulfilment experienced by the baby at the breast. As emotionally nourishing as it is nutritional, breastfeeding is an essential building block of emotional intelligence, imbuing the child with a reservoir of tranquillity, security, connectedness to others and generosity. Breastfeeding affords a vital psychological and immunological sustenance long after it is nutritionally essential. Babies hunger for much more than milk, they hunger for intimacy; to drink-in maternal love. Not surprisingly, some evidence suggests that lack of breastfeeding may be contributing to higher rates of depression.[13]

When a baby is at her mother's breast, the action of her suckling stimulates her mother's body to secrete oxytocin, a mild sedative and hormone associated with feelings of fulfilment, even bliss. This hormone is passed to the baby through the milk, so that, if nature is allowed to take its course, both mother and child are bathed in a pleasurable and peaceful state of union. This delicious experience is an important developmental milestone; it is integral to the baby's emotional health.

Baby will signal her hunger to us quite clearly before she begins to cry. Her cry is usually a late indicator of her hunger. She turns her head toward the breast, extends her lips, becomes agitated, or sucks her hands. A baby's cry and 'rooting reflex' which helps him to find the breast are biological indicators of the right time to feed. These are the kinds of cues that paediatricians now urge mothers to respond to as promptly as possible. If feeding happens according to the baby's cues, she sucks more efficiently, and her emotional needs are satiated as well as her nutritional needs. The American Academy of Pediatrics (AAP) has recently updated their 'Policy Statement on Breastfeeding' [14]. The revised recommendations constitute their strongest endorsement of breastfeeding thus far. Updated advice includes that babies should receive nothing but breast milk for the first six months, and that there is no upper limit to the duration of breastfeeding. Similar guidance comes from the UK Department of Health (http://tinyurl.com/44n9a2).

The World Health Organization (WHO) reports that, around

the world, the average age of weaning (defined as complete cessation of breastfeeding, including occasional comfort suckling) exceeds four years.[15] Professor of paediatrics and lactation specialist, Ruth Lawrence,[16] puts this figure at 4.2 years. These days mothers are encouraged to breastfeed exclusively for up to six months, and if possible to continue enjoying complementary breastfeeding past the child's second birthday.[17] Based on reviews of studies by anthropologists and comparative biologists, the natural age of complete cessation can vary from well over two years, anywhere up to six or seven years.[18] Babies and toddlers long for the emotional sustenance and the deeply fulfilling, oral connection to their mothers long beyond our culturally imposed deadlines. We, the early weaners are certainly an oddity, since only 2 per cent of the world's societies wean their babies at less than one year.[19]

If children are allowed the occasional comfort-suckle at the breast until they naturally self-wean, the next level of psychological independence develops naturally from a stronger base of emotional equanimity. When nature is allowed to run its course, toddlers self-wean with minimal or no sense of conflict. Their longing for the breast becomes less frequent until it gradually falls away.

Some mothers are unable to breastfeed for insurmountable physiological or psychological reasons. Bottle-feeding can be adapted to provide opportunities for tender and loving contact, soft touch, mutual gazing, and gentle rocking. Though the oral intimacy will be missed, it can still be an occasion for pleasurable and peaceful connection, if it is timed in accordance with the baby's indication of need.

To receive loving eye contact
As in the first rite of passage, loving eye contact is a vital, formative experience. To our babies, our eyes communicate far more about how we feel towards them than our words do. What helps them to feel connected is not a stare, but an easy, loving gaze.

Evolution's design is perfect. Infants can only focus their eyes at precisely the distance of their mother's eyes during breastfeeding. A mother's gaze is life-giving sustenance; it is in her eyes that the infant finds love. What babies look for is 'mirroring', that is, to be looked upon with joy, delight and approval. When a baby meets her mother's gaze, she typically revels in the contact, kicking her legs, smiling and gurgling. She signals when she is content, simply by looking away – soon to return for another life-giving dose.

Babies can really read our feelings in our eyes. As we saw earlier in Chapter 21, a 'look of love' cannot be faked: when love is genuinely felt it dilates our pupils. Babies know the difference between a dispassionate look, and a genuinely affectionate look. They are distressed by a sustained lack of expression in the parent's face. In a brief experiment, Ed Tronick, head of paediatric research at Harvard Medical School, instructed mothers to look at their three-month-old babies blankly and without expression.[20] The babies became increasingly agitated, they tried their hardest to elicit a response. When this failed they looked away, trying to self-soothe by thumb-sucking. Over and over again they returned to their mothers' eyes, trying desperately to engage them, smiling and gurgling. The babies were remarkably persistent, but eventually they gave up altogether. Babies simply cannot do without their mother's loving, animated face.

Why is loving eye contact so vital for children's emotional health? At our core, the way we perceive ourselves springs from the way we once saw others perceiving us. It is as if, as babies, we mused 'I see that my mother sees me as loveable, so I see myself as loveable.' Our self-image is being shaped from the moment of birth. Quite literally, images of our mother's loving gaze are stored neurologically in our brains, where they become the unconscious template for our self-esteem. What we say to our children therefore, may have less of an impact than how we feel about them – as is clearly reflected in our eyes.

To receive a timely response to her needs

Babies are not born predisposed to feeling secure or insecure.[21] The key to secure attachment is the parent's warmth, and their sensitive responsiveness to the baby's needs.[22] Studies conducted in the USA, Canada, Germany, Netherlands and Japan have repeatedly shown that babies' emotional security depends on their parents consistently and immediately attempting to soothe their distress, as well as responding to their expressions of joy and pleasure.[23] A baby's emotional security depends on her carers' 'emotional availability', that is, their emotional responsiveness and attunement to the whole range of the baby's emotions.[24]

A fear of infants' dependency seems deeply entrenched in our culture, and the myth of the 'spoiled baby' is pervasive. One

303

of the greatest fallacies of socialising mode parenting is that if we respond to our baby's needs as they arise, she will remain clingy and dependent. Research demonstrates the exact opposite to be true. Researchers have found that a prompt response to a baby's cry is what reduces how much she cries when she is older.[25] In fact, our impatient push to make our babies more independent suppresses their willingness to explore their surroundings, and tends to make them more clingy.[26]

In a study conducted in the Netherlands, a group of mothers were taught how to respond consistently and appropriately to their babies' expressions of need. The goal was not to make mothers feel burdened or overly anxious, but simply to encourage them to regard their babies' cries as undeniably meaningful communications that deserved attention. The results were dramatic. Their children became considerably more secure than those of mothers who had not received this training.[27]

In a recent study[28], researchers observed what happens when mothers did not respond to their babies as they reached out to them. They found some babies tended to react with sadness, others with anger. The saddened babies had elevated residual levels of the stress hormone cortisol, whereas the babies that reacted angrily did not. The babies' brain chemistry showed that their anger at being ignored is potentially healthier. The damaging effects of excess residual cortisol arise when babies 'give up' reaching out for contact.

The results imply that we should perhaps be particularly concerned for babies who cease to reach out when their cries are ignored; the ones who become sad and then give up, such as when practices like 'controlled crying' are used. Training babies to stop reaching out or crying out may be causing psychological and neurological harm.

What most helps a baby to flourish is her parents' 'relaxed responsiveness'.[29] Whereas parents needn't jump anxiously at every sound the baby makes, it is equally undesirable to systematically delay responding to her vocalised needs.

To sleep near Mum and Dad
Contrary to the fast-track trends in modern child rearing in the west, this is not the time for the child to learn about independence. Ideally, the baby should sleep very close to, or in bed with her parents, staying connected to them through

the night, via their scent, their sounds, their touch. Co-sleeping is what babies are born to expect, and it contributes to their emotional security. In this regard, the baby's need carries on from the first rite of passage.

There are many vital physiological and psychological benefits brought by co-sleeping. Since infant breathing is erratic for the first few weeks of life, they can learn to breathe more regularly by sleeping close to their parents. Infants are sensitive to both the sound and the rhythmic rocking of their parents' breathing at night. They respond to these stimuli by regulating their own breath. Additionally, they are directly pacified by the sound of their parents' heartbeat.

James McKenna PhD, Director of the Centre for Behavioural Studies of Mother–Infant Sleep at Notre Dame University, Indiana, says that because of the benefits mentioned above, it is possible that co-sleeping might prevent some kinds of Sudden Infant Death Syndrome (SIDS). He notes that in China and Japan, both co-sleeping cultures, the SIDS rates are comparatively quite low. There is a growing sense that co-sleeping, putting the baby to sleep on her back and night time breastfeeding can reduce the risk of SIDS.[30]

It has been conclusively shown that co-sleeping promotes night time breastfeeding.[31] Night time breastfeeding is a key regulator of ovulation. Surges in prolactin produced by suckling are four to six times greater between 12 am and 4 am, when melatonin (a hormone associated with sleep regulation) levels are highest. This specific, nocturnal hormone-cocktail works as a powerful contraceptive; so that night feeds are more effective than day feeds at delaying ovulation. Nature's wise purpose here is to lengthen birth spacing, because this translates to more emotional security for both siblings, and to the great relief of the whole family, less rivalry. And in their small but delightful way, siblings who are several years older can often be quite helpful in the care – especially the entertainment – of younger children.[32]

There is now a large, fast-growing and international body of paediatricians, psychologists and childcare experts advocating co-sleeping. For some well-substantiated advice on the value of co-sleeping, refer to the work of Thevenin, Sears, Jackson, Granju, Fleiss, Goodavage and Gordon in the 'recommended further reading' section at the end of this chapter.[33]

It must be said that not every parent can safely share a bed with a baby. Bed sharing is not encouraged where parents have overriding medical problems, such as alcoholism, obesity, tobacco or drug dependency. Obviously, babies should sleep separately from parents who do not trust their own behaviour around the baby at night. Some parents feel afraid that if they share a bed with their babies, they might accidentally roll onto them in their sleep. A bassinette next to the parents' bed or a hammock over their bed can be reassuring alternatives.

Our fears and discomforts about co-sleeping are real, but entirely cultural – since this practice has been lost to us westerners for many generations. When healthy parents and their babies share a bed, some basic precautions should be taken. For instance, the mattress must be firm so that the baby cannot roll into where it sags in the middle, and risk suffocation. This means that it is not safe to sleep with a baby on a water-bed. You need to make sure that no object such as a pillow, a cover, or a parent's long hair could obstruct the baby's face; the head must be kept clear. Most parents find that they remain sensitively aware of their baby while asleep, so they could not possibly roll onto them or injure them in any way. For further recommendations regarding safe co-sleeping, refer to the work of Kate Alison Granju.[34]

Many of us have long lost our capacity to tolerate – let alone enjoy – sleeping close to others. For parents who have difficulty relaxing in such a physically intimate space, this may require some commitment to practise, willingness to be creative and to experiment with a variety of sleeping arrangements. Once we re-learn how to be comfortable with it, going to sleep and waking up together can be a bonding, satisfying and fulfilling experience for parents and baby alike.

What would really support both parents and babies to sleep more soundly is to teach them how to sleep close to each other. It's not that parents have to jump at every whimper – over-anxious involvement can be invasive for the baby, as well as stressful for the parents. There are times when it seems enough for a baby to know that her parents are nearby and available if she becomes distressed.

For parents to feel well supported

Natural parenting consists of being guided by the baby's cues, letting her take the lead. This is difficult for any pair of parents, which is why it is so important for babies that their parents feel emotionally supported, and cared for by others. Parents are not meant to raise their children in isolation. I believe that we humans have evolved to nurture our children in groups, and that most parenting problems arise from our misguided efforts to care for our children in a separate, nuclear family. The 'mum–and–dad–in–a–house' idea is simply not enough: it entails compromises that are stressful for parents and potentially wounding for children. The need for group support applies even more to the hands-on, empathic and contact-driven parenting style that is now emerging. Parents who feel generally well supported in their lives, and who have been adequately nurtured themselves, will be more capable of spontaneous and empathic responses to their baby's physical and emotional needs. More will be said in Part VII about the importance of support for parents.

It can be enormously beneficial for new parents to join (or start) one of the rapidly growing number of informal, 'attachment parenting' or 'natural parenting' groups. The Attachment Parenting International (API) website (http://www.attachmentparenting.org) locates these groups around the world, and also offers suggestions on how to start up your own group in your area. The internet resource 'Yahoo Groups' (http://groups.yahoo.com) also lists local parenting groups and is an excellent forum for starting your own.[35] There are around 100 groups registered with API in the USA, and many more around the world. At the time of writing, though there are numerous groups in Australia, only one is registered with API. Groups are springing up everywhere under the banners of natural parenting, continuum parenting, attachment parenting, and possibly other labels for the same thing – without necessarily affiliating themselves to a larger organisation.

What baby is learning at this time
The child is at this time trying to learn that it is OK to need, to reach out interpersonally and to ask for what she wants. At a core level she is also learning about deserving, and the joy of receiving. What can be imprinted during this stage is that satisfaction and fulfilment are a birthright, always worth vigorously and assertively pursuing. Our capacity for interpersonal care, giving, and generosity is likely to be most authentic to the degree that our passage through this time was favourable. True independence, as opposed to defensive self-reliance, can only spring from the satiation of our early dependency needs.

307

The most wounding experiences

Emotional wounds at this stage tend to be associated with non-validation of babies' reaching out to have their needs met, as if their cries have no significance.

Denial of oral needs

In the west, even up until modern times, almost all children have been either denied their mother's breast altogether, or weaned too early.[36] In the modern era, the loss of the instinct and art of breastfeeding have been blamed on the overuse (and over marketing) of artificial formula. (In some countries, after World War II, women were actually given injections to suppress lactation.) This assault on breastfeeding prompted the World Health Organization to publish codes limiting the marketing of formula feeding.[37]

Western women are reclaiming control of this natural process, but since role models have been suppressed, relearning this art has proved to be difficult. Common complications associated with breastfeeding, such as nipple damage or insufficient milk syndrome, are almost entirely due to incorrect positioning, scheduled feeding, other products of ill-advice and lack of role models.

When weaning is traumatic for babies, this is largely because it is imposed upon them long before they are emotionally ready to let go of the maternal breast. As westerners we have not yet completed our collective recovery from the eras of wet-nursing and saturation marketing of artificial formulas.

Health authorities are coming to recognise the importance of returning to nature's way. The American Academy of Pediatrics, the largest association of paediatricians in the world, asserted in 1998 that breastfeeding is the norm against which all alternative feeding methods must be measured.[38] Numerous studies published in medical journals suggest that routine bottle-feeding might increase the baby's risk of developing some kinds of infections, allergies, certain cancers, juvenile diabetes, Crohn's Disease and ulcerative colitis, and a lower IQ.[39] Some research has indicated that artificially-fed babies have lower levels of polyunsaturated fatty acids (PUFA),[40] a substance essential to the healthy development of the brain's emotional centres. Low PUFA levels have been linked to depression in adults.[41] There is also some suggestion that the risk of SIDS (Sudden Infant Death Syndrome) might be a little lower among breastfed babies.[42]

We are quickly coming to the end of an era when infants' nourishment is regimented by fastidious timetables. Many infant health authorities have now recognised that babies are not psychologically or physiologically equipped to wait, and so enforced schedules or delayed gratification can be harmful. In a 1998 media alert, the American Academy of Pediatrics stated that "the best feeding schedules for babies are the ones babies design themselves...Scheduled feedings designed by parents may put babies at risk for poor weight gain and dehydration".[43] There is no reason to deliberately frustrate a hungry baby, and the obsolete custom of scheduled nurturance reflects a common desire to keep babies in check.

Scheduled feeding has been known to disrupt infant sleep patterns and blood sugar levels, and it can interrupt maternal milk production. It is interesting to note that although a number of breastfeeding problems are common among infants and mothers in schedule feeding cultures such as Australia and the USA, they are virtually unknown in cue-feeding cultures.[44]

The fact that so many children develop thumb-sucking habits may be further evidence of our insufficient and over-regulated breastfeeding customs. Species of monkeys and apes who never suck their thumbs in the wild, often become thumb-suckers if bottle-fed in captivity. The children of tribal !Kung, an African culture that is natural in its approach to breastfeeding, are never seen sucking their thumbs.[45]

Denial of her need to be held

Socialising mode child rearing tends to be hesitant about accepting babies' emotional dependency. So many of us are awe-struck by our babies' seemingly unending appetite for attention, we feel imprisoned, we fear becoming engulfed. We fear that we will never escape our voracious babies. We begin as early as possible to train our babies' to quieten their need. We fear that unless babies are taught to wait patiently until the designated feeding hour, and to cry themselves to sleep alone in a separate room, they will grow up to be undisciplined and unable to fend for themselves. Instead of reaching to our families and community for support when we feel overwhelmed, we fight for our freedom – and thus we betray our little ones.

Driven by fear and perhaps exhaustion, we pressure our children to outgrow their infantile needs much too early. Myths abound that create an image of a devouring infant. 'If you let your baby sleep in your bed, you will never get him out.' 'If you breastfeed on demand and wean naturally, you will create a rod for your back.' 'If you pick up your baby when she asks to be held, she'll never grow up.' 'It is OK to leave a baby to cry unattended, because this exercises her lungs.' These superstitions are the vestiges of historical parenting, and have now been dispelled by science.

Cortisol levels in babies' brains can surge to very high levels if their cries are not responded to.[46] Ignoring a baby's cries can be "particularly hazardous" as excess cortisol can be corrosive to the emotional centres of her brain – and this has long-term consequences for her emotional make-up.[47] Babies have no concept of time, and therefore they have "no capacity to anticipate needs being met in 10 minutes' time".[48] This gives the baby the message that she mustn't ask for what she wants or needs. Her impulses to reach out collapse, and she becomes resigned. She is not as yet equipped to cope with delayed gratification, and therefore experiences things such as rigidly scheduled feeding, early weaning and 'controlled crying' as abandonment. Even if a baby is crying to release stress, she still needs to be held.

Night time loneliness

One of the main complaints heard by paediatricians is from parents struggling to get their infants to sleep alone. Few people have thought to question why we make infants sleep alone in separate rooms, since humans have been accustomed to sleeping socially for aeons – we have evolved to sleep that way, for reasons of safety, security and general wellbeing. Most westerners would be surprised to hear that modern advice to make infants sleep alone is culturally driven, and it is based on nothing scientific. In almost every culture around the world, babies share a bed with their parents, or at least sleep in the same room with them.[49] Simply put, the peculiar Anglo-Celtic custom of forcing infants to sleep separately is abnormal, and is at the root of many common sleep disturbances and heart-breaking, night time struggles.

The sleep patterns of infants who are separated from their mothers has been observed to be fitful and restless, with frequent awakening.[50] Babies who are separated tend to suck more on their thumbs or inanimate objects: a sign of increased stress.[51] Their core temperature drops, and they sustain an increase in stress hormones. Separate sleeping is clearly not nature's design for babies. Psychologically, they are unprepared to sleep alone.

The practice of separate sleeping for infants was initiated centuries ago in western Europe. Co-sleeping with infants was legally banned, in order to curb the endemic problem of nocturnal infanticide: parents were deliberately suffocating their infants.[52] It was also a measure to reduce the historically high incidence of incest (see Part III).

In more ways than one, our modern expectation that babies should sleep alone (and that they should sleep through the night), stymies a natural, biological order that took millions of years to evolve. Infants have a naturally shorter sleep cycle. As well as serving the need for night time feeding, shorter sleep cycles enable babies to have more rapid eye movement (REM) sleep, which is vital for healthy brain development. Though some infants might spontaneously sleep for longer periods, it is both un-unrealistic and unhealthy to *expect* infants to sleep through the night. Usually, the things that are emotionally wounding are the things that sabotage nature.

Because sleep deprivation is such a devastating problem in cultures where parents do it alone, 'controlled crying' has become a popular technique employed to train babies to stop crying for the contact they need, and fall asleep alone. In a nutshell, it involves refusing comfort to a crying baby in her crib for progressively longer intervals – the maximum length of time varies from practitioner to practitioner – until she learns to fall asleep alone. There is some evidence[53] that overstressed mothers will feel less depressed if this technique works – though it often doesn't. This is an example of a method that addresses the parents' needs at the expense of the baby's.

The Australian Association for Infant Mental Health has issued a position statement regarding this technique, which is unequivocal and unambiguous. Part of this statement says, "AAIMHI is concerned that the widely practiced technique of 'controlled crying' is not consistent with what infants need for their optimal emotional and psychological health, and may have unintended negative consequences". In the UK, the Association of Infant Mental Health issued a statement in response to a television series called 'Bringing Up Baby', broadcast in 2007, which showed a mentor ordering parents to ignore the screams of their newborns in order to get the babies into a routine. Criticising the broadcaster for presenting this method

311

uncritically, AIMH stated the show was "clearly harmful to those taking part."[54] Babies do not have a concept of time. When you walk away from them and leave them alone in the crib, they cannot reassure themselves that you'll return.[55] As far as they are concerned, you have gone completely – and that's why they cry out for you. If they become distressed in your absence, this distress soon turns to terror and despair. Many adults who have retrieved infant memories recall moments such as these to be devastating, heartbreaking and terrifying. They report that these moments of abandonment are pivotal to the development of emotional difficulties in adulthood.

As we saw earlier, studies show that emotional security in infants is related to a mother's prompt responsiveness to their distress, and maternal warmth.[56] Since controlled crying or controlled comforting involves the systematic delaying of comfort to a crying baby, this erodes their sense of security.

When controlled crying 'succeeds' in teaching a baby to fall asleep alone, it is due to a process that neuro-biologist Bruce Perry calls the "defeat response".[57] When infants are not responded to, they may eventually abandon their crying – the nervous system shuts down the emotional pain and the striving to reach out. This does not mean that they are OK, on the contrary – they are numbed out. This adaptive 'defeat response' has lasting implications, which parents do not tend to notice. Although there are many babies for whom controlled crying fails entirely, who keep on howling until they're hoarse, there are others who learn quickly to switch off. No doubt this brings great relief to the harried parents, and may save the baby from potential abuse. Severe sleep deprivation can drive even loving parents to extreme behaviour. Ultimately, this technique is a tragic compromise.

How experiences shape emotional make-up and core beliefs

The following are some core beliefs held by adults, which arose from injurious experiences at this time.

Negative core beliefs

I must do it alone, I must show that I don't need anyone or anything

I don't deserve love

I am not lovable

I am lovable only if I don't have emotional needs
When I am needy, I am loathsome
I am only lovable when I am 'giving'
Others' needs are more important than mine
My happiness depends on being liked by others
In order to be loved and lovable, I must: perform well sexually,
   be wealthy, be famous, be popular, be fashionable etc
If I don't take care of others' needs, I will be abandoned
If I take care of others, I will be loved
The world owes me…
Since relationships don't nourish me, I get filled up by
   acquiring things. I need more and more and more and
   more things

The following are some core beliefs held by adults, which arose from positive experiences at this time.

Positive core beliefs
I have a right to need, and to express my needs and wants
Life nourishes me
Life is plentiful and abundant, and I deserve life's generosity
Others have a right to their needs too

These positive core beliefs comprise the emotional foundations that underpin our capacity to be appropriately assertive, and to be direct rather than manipulative when expressing our needs.

The fulfilment of the essential developmental needs pertaining to this stage is the font from which we can later draw a natural generosity of spirit. The gratification of infantile need is also what gives us the capacity to be genuinely respectful of others' needs and limits; to gracefully let go when someone says 'no' to us. The emotional strength that enables us to sustain disappointments, and to cope with the fact that we don't always get what we want, springs from early childhood satisfaction, not from premature, enforced 'independence'.

The nourishment and attention we receive during this second rite of passage provides us with a source of initiative, self-motivation, patience, emotional stamina and endurance. True independence, as opposed to defensive self-reliance ('I don't need anyone') is, paradoxically, the product of dependency having been embraced. Emotional independence enables us to

313

care deeply for ourselves, it empowers us to reach out to others for intimate connection yet also to let them go.

The greatest fears that motivate the interpersonal defences that are constructed at this time are: the fear of loss, abandonment and aloneness. These fears produce in individuals a tendency to be either clingy, self-sacrificing, or over-compensating with exaggerated self-reliance.

How emotional wounds affect behaviour

Modern, highly sophisticated observational techniques[58] have enabled attachment researchers to make some fascinating (and sobering) discoveries about the far-reaching social repercussions of early attachment experiences. How securely attached an infant is to her carers can predict much about her social functioning as she grows up.

In toddlers

Much of what is labelled as a 'discipline problem' or a 'behaviour problem' has its genesis in this stage of development.[59] Insecurely attached toddlers tend to be more moody and more attention seeking. Children who have spent a great deal of time in childcare, away from their parents, tend to be less compliant with their parents. On the other hand, a number of studies show that children who are emotionally secure are more co-operative with their parents[60] and they develop a stronger conscience.[61] The best 'discipline' measure is affection,[62] and the kind of parental responsiveness that helps a child to feel heard, seen and emotionally secure, from the dawn of life. The opiates (brain chemicals associated with pleasure) that are secreted in the baby's brain when she experiences her carers' affection nourish her 'prefrontal cortex' and cause it to grow.[63] This is the portion of the brain that regulates behavioural impulses.

Securely attached infants grow to become more enthusiastic, persistent and co-operative as toddlers. They tend to be less oppositional, less angry, less fearful and more joyful.[64] Secure toddlers tend to be more popular among their peers, they are more socially competent,[65] and they are capable of more empathy towards others.[66] Children's moral and social development is a function of how sensitively they were treated as babies; how promptly and consistently their needs were attended to.

Follow-up studies have shown that toddlers who were securely attached as infants are more resilient, and more independent.

Being more assertive, these children are more difficult to bully, and hence they are less likely to be targeted.[67] Conversely, the insecurely attached babies grew to be clingy or avoidant, hypersensitive, or more aggressive and disruptive. They tend to seek attention in oblique or irritating ways.[68]

In older children

The effects of attachment last well beyond toddlerhood. Ten-year-olds who were treated with acceptance and sensitivity as babies, tend to be more self-confident and less hostile.[69] Teenagers with a secure attachment history handle conflict better, they are more assertive, less angry, and they are more admired by their peers.[70] There is an increasing sense that many examples of psychopathology in teenagers – such as depression, or anxiety disorders – may be understood by looking at their attachment history.[71]

Attention deficit and hyperactivity disorder (ADHD) may be an over-diagnosed mental disorder in children and adults. Almost five million Americans use the drug Ritalin to control ADHD. In Australia, one in 40 children is being medicated for an emotional or behavioural problem.[72] This is especially worrying since it remains to be proven that ADHD is an illness, and there are as yet no accepted neurological correlates of ADHD.[73] Frances Thomson Salo, psychoanalyst and senior lecturer at the University of Melbourne, and George Halasz, psychiatrist and senior lecturer at Monash Medical Centre have provided compelling evidence that ADHD may be a behavioural reaction to deep anxiety or depression arising from disturbances in attachment.[74] They argue that it would be more appropriate to treat this behavioural reaction, in many cases, as a deficit in attachment rather than as a disease.

Emotional security is also relevant to the issue of sibling rivalry. Children who are emotionally secure are more likely to comfort distressed younger siblings, and are less likely to get into conflicts with them.[75] This is not surprising: empathy arises out of emotional security. All these findings have forced us to reappraise our views on 'good behaviour'. They imply that that if we want 'good' children, we first of all need to respond thoroughly to their dependency needs.

In adults

Given the child-rearing customs that prevailed in the western world over the last two generations, almost all of us have experienced some wounding at this stage. For this reason, much of the manifestation of second-stage injury is considered in the range of quite 'normal' behaviour. Normal or not, it is a manifestation of deep emotional wounding nonetheless.

Early security of attachment is what most empowers us to create and maintain satisfying, healthy relationships as adults.[76] Since this rite of passage is about nourishment and need, emotional injury tends to manifest as disturbances in the balance of giving and taking.

Some of us tend to compensate for insecure attachment in early childhood by remaining narcissistic and overly demanding. We stay stuck in dependency, living as if waiting for Mother to show up, sub-consciously longing for the lost bliss of unity at her breast. Beneath the veneer of 'competent adult' is the baby screaming for her unresponsive mother's return. Many of our interactions are unconsciously calculated to attract the attention which we were once deprived of as children. We 'suck' at and cling to relationships, food, alcohol, drugs, tobacco, gambling or material goods. All these are substitutes for love and attention we needed but failed to get as infants. Our addictive, ravenous over-consumption, or compulsive behaviour, masks a deep, inner emptiness. We feel as if life owes us, waiting passively for things to change, or impatiently grasping at life.

Our co-dependent relationships have an addictive quality that reflects unresolved, infantile clingyness. We cannot stand to be apart, we possess each other and we are easily provoked to jealousy. Unwittingly we set-up our partners to replace the parent we feel we have lost. This co-dependent clinging provides no contentment, for it places too much emphasis on our partners as the source of our happiness. We fantasise romantic notions of a 'true love' that lasts forever, a fanciful and symbiotic union that will meet all our needs for love and understanding; and thus we harbour unrealistic expectations of one another. Subsequently, we blame each other for our personal dissatisfaction. The unsatiated grow up to become insatiable.

Many of those who were once pressured to outgrow their infant needs prematurely, grow to harbour an exaggerated sense of responsibility for others' needs. They seem over-concerned with nurturing and healing others, to the point that others might experience them as smothering. Although their sacrificial self-denial may earn them some kudos, it can also lead them to emotional break-down. Often, there is seething resentment underneath, which periodically boils over.

Others who, as babies, adapted to deprivation by switching-off to emotional needs, grow to be stoically self-reliant. They might lead somewhat isolated lives, adamant that they must 'do it alone', rejecting the support of others and avoiding intimacy. They cut themselves off from healthy dependency on other humans. This compensatory strategy is a recipe for emotional exhaustion and bitterness.

For many of us, our infant needs were only met under strict conditions. As a result, many of us grew up to be somewhat passive and unassertive, finding it difficult to know – let alone ask for – what we need. We became ashamed of our needs, doubtful of our deservingness, afraid to ask, reach out or receive. Our essential 'right to need' has been disabled. But underneath this passivity there is a festering anger – an anger that we have trouble expressing appropriately, since we have collapsed emotionally.

As the distinguished psychiatrist John Bowlby once said, "There is no experience to which a young child can be subjected that is more prone to elicit intense and violent hatred for the mother than that of separation."[77] Many of us carry this hostility unconsciously, well into adulthood. This deep but impotent rage might be acted-out anti-socially, or turned inward against ourselves through self-sabotage, accident-proneness or illness.

Though they may never acknowledge it to themselves, some individuals carry a particularly strong fear of being alone, and a powerful abandonment-rage. They become frighteningly irrational when a partner leaves them: they threaten suicide, they harass or even stalk the partner who is trying to leave, they may even become uncharacteristically violent. This kind of extreme behaviour is not restricted to marginal or dysfunctional individuals. It is a legacy of early and repeated emotional abandonment, and it is equally likely to ensue among otherwise successful and respected individuals, who fall apart only when facing a new abandonment.

Emotional security in early childhood is the main factor that ensures our resilience as adults. When working with adults who have sustained a traumatic experience, trauma counsellors have found that those who had a stable attachment history were less likely to develop post-traumatic stress disorders.[78] In other words, insecure attachment makes us more vulnerable to stress later.

In more extreme cases, emotional wounding at this stage can be a contributing factor for depression, bipolar disorder, and other mood disorders. A deep emotional insecurity and fear of aloneness can also contribute to anxiety disorders, panic attacks, even agoraphobia.[79] A number of research studies have associated some common eating disorders to a combination of early, insecure attachment and excessive parental control.[80]

Social impact of wounds

Modern understanding about the pivotal role of early attachments casts a new light on the social forces that have driven historical events. For much of our history, few individuals benefited from meaningful attachment to their parents. Few escaped abandonment; at the doors of foundling homes, at the hands of wet-nurses, at monasteries or at apprenticeships. The social chaos, dictatorship, brutality and wholesale human rights abuses that characterise much of human history can be made sense of in terms of severe attachment disorders. This legacy of early attachment wounds continues to have widespread social ramifications, even if these are less extreme now than in bygone days.

An insufficient level of core emotional fulfilment stunts our development. In terms of emotional intelligence we remain child-like, as 'suckers', lacking in healthy scepticism. We tend toward gullibility: we are too easily duped by the seductive wiles of PR machinations, conned by merchandising campaigns and 'charismatic' individuals. All too easily we fall prey to shady sales deals, dazzling advertising, and political stunts – the product of expert image-builders who know precisely how to appeal to our inner emptiness, insecurity and despair. Though we ridicule adolescents who adore rock stars, this is no different to the childish trust that millions of adults invest in popular politicians. The cult-figure, the guru, and the screen legend are parental substitutes. We refuse to see their ordinariness or their human vulnerability. Our gnawing, unresolved need prevents us from seeing the deviousness and cunning of those we are driven to idolise. Unconsciously longing for parenting, we compulsively fantasise that they are larger-than-life, and thus leave ourselves wide-open to exploitation.

The breathless greed that afflicts our civilisation is no more than the cry of the emotionally malnourished baby disguised in adult garb. No amount of material accumulation can feed our emotional hunger, yet we seem powerless to control our need to possess.

In vast numbers, we suffer a desolate barrenness inside – which we desperately try to medicate with excess food, drugs or alcohol. The social problem of addiction is as devastating and widespread as it is because so many of us are emotionally arrested in a state of emotional deprivation. Our hopelessly ineffectual and horrendously costly 'drug-wars' miss the point altogether: addiction is an emotional problem. It can only be effectively addressed through psychological healing, investment in family wellbeing and the continued evolution in child rearing.

Psychologists have presented some compelling evidence that insecure attachment can also contribute to a range of disruptive and anti-social behaviours in children.[81] These effects can last well into adulthood, contributing to violent crime and delinquency.

Fortunately, it is possible for experiences of healthy attachment in late childhood, even in adulthood, to be restorative. Healthy, loving relationships can teach us to be more empathic, sensitive to ourselves and to others, and thus mitigate some of the emotional damage sustained in infancy. Counselling and psychotherapy are also invaluable resources that are proving helpful in promoting emotional development. But the most powerful agent of social change is the continuing evolution in child-rearing customs.

Some positive changes

Our present-day, surprisingly early weaning standards certainly warrant revision – and this revision is gradually underway. Currently, we are experiencing a growing public acceptance of demand feeding (some call it cue-feeding) and child-led weaning, owing to increased professional support from lactation consultants and paediatricians. A growing number of texts recommend exclusive breastfeeding for the first six months,[82] and that it is natural for breastfeeding to continue past the child's second birthday. Mothers are being reassured that breastfeeding can continue for as long as it is an emotionally bonding and nourishing experience for mother and child. It is therefore increasingly common for children to enjoy the psychological benefits of occasional comfort suckles well into their fourth and fifth years. As we continue to learn more about the value of this miraculous aspect of the mother–child connection, it will become culturally acceptable, even unremarkable, to see contented mothers and their toddlers nursing in public.

A large body of research tells us that educating and supporting families to help their children be emotionally secure would cause a significant reduction in a very broad range of social ills.

It would be too simplistic to say that an insecure passage through this stage will render anyone depressive, an addict or a violent delinquent. Not everyone becomes paralysed as a result of insecure attachment at this stage. However, what can be said with certainty, is that if a society helps families to provide emotional security for their infants, through appropriate parenting education, professional support, and government initiatives such as those tested in the Netherlands,[83] social problems such as substance addiction, problem gambling, over-consumption, depression and delinquency would be radically reduced. As we'll see in the final chapter, the social pay-offs would be immense, far outweighing the costs.

Recommended further reading

When shopping for parenting manuals, I would recommend that you favour books whose authors are qualified in a health profession, who are well versed in early childhood physical, mental and emotional development, and – most importantly – who appreciate current and recent understandings about attachment theory and research. This is not an exhaustive list, but they are the most reliable and well-researched early childhood parenting manuals I am aware of:

- Granju KA and Kennedy B (1999) *Attachment Parenting* Pocket Books.
- Fleiss P (2000) *Sweet Dreams: A Paediatrician's Secrets for Baby's Good Night Sleep* McGraw/Hill.
- Goodavage M and Gordon J (2002) *Good Nights: The Happy Parents' Guide to the Family Bed and a Peaceful Night's Sleep* Griffin.
- Hunt J (2001) *The Natural Child* New Society Publishers.
- Jackson D (1999) *Three in a Bed: The Benefits of Sleeping with Your Baby* Bloomsbury.
- Leach P (1997) *Your Baby and Child* Knopf.
- McKay P (2001) *Parenting by Heart* Lothian Books.
- McKay P (2002) *100 Ways to Calm the Crying* Lothian Books.
- Palmer L (2001) *Baby Matters, What Your Doctor May not*

Tell You About Caring for your Baby Lucky Press.
- Sears W (1999) *Night-time Parenting: How to Get Your Baby and Child to Sleep* Plume.
- Sears W (2001) *A Commonsense Guide to Understanding and Nurturing Your Baby* Little, Brown & Co.
- Solter AJ (2001) *The Aware Baby* Shining Star Press.
- Thevenin T (1987) *The Family Bed* Perigee Books.

The following websites[84] are also extremely informative:

- Alliance for Transforming the Lives of Children (aTLC), in particular, read 'Proclamation & blueprint': http://www.atlc.org
- The Natural Child Project: http://www.naturalchild.org/
- Attachment Parenting International (API): http://www.attachmentparenting.org/
- The Leidloff Continuum Concept Network: http://www.continuum-concept.org/

Endnotes

1 As recommended by the World Health Organization, lactation specialists, and paediatricians. More detail will be provided throughout the chapter.
2 Greenspan (1999).
3 Greenspan (1999).
4 World Association for Infant Mental Health (WAIMH) http://www.waimh.org/ (last accessed 1 December 2004); Australian Association for Infant Mental Health (AAIMH) http://www.aaimhi.org/ (last accessed 1 December 2004). The WAIMH in partnership with the AAIMH convened its 2004 annual conference in Melbourne, Australia.
5 Karen (1994).
6 Karen (1994).
7 Hrdy (2000).
8 Gerhardt (2004).
9 See Chapter 25 where we discussed research indicating the biological and psychological benefits of baby-wearing.
10 Belsky and Cassidy (1994) p 376.
11 Belsky and Cassidy (1994) p 377.
12 Hrdy (2000).
13 Allen, Lewinsohn and Seeley (1998).

[14] 'Breastfeeding and the Use of Human Milk.' *Pediatrics Vol 115 pp. 496-506*. The full text of the revised 2005 version can be downloaded at: http://www.pediatrics.org/cgi/content/full/115/2/496.[15] See World Health Organization 'Child and adolescent rights' http://www.who.int/child-adolescent-health/right.htm (last accessed 1 December 2004).

[16] Lawrence (1999).

[17] See the World Health Organization (WHO) 'Child and adolescent rights' and 'Children and nutrition' http://www.who.int/child-adolescent-health/NUTRITION/infant_exclusive.htm (last accessed 1 December 2004). See also United Nations Children's Fund 'Key messages on breastfeeding' http://www.unicef.org/ffl/04/key_messages.htm (last accessed 1 December 2004).

[18] Riordan and Auerbach (1999); Granju (1999); Lawrence (1999).

[19] Broude (1995).

[20] Als, Tronic and Brazelton (1980) in Field pp 181–204.

[21] Belsky (1999).

[22] Karen (1994) p 177; Belsky and Cassidy (1994) p 390.

[23] Belsky (1999).

[24] Easterbrooks and Biringen (2000).

[25] Bell and Ainsworth (1972).

[26] Belsky and Cassidy (1994) p 380.

[27] Van den Boom (1990) in Koops (ed) pp 249–270; Van den Boom (1994) pp 1457–1477. Having reviewed evidence from around the world, one attachment theorist concludes that providing sensitive care "requires the accurate reading of, and timely and empathic responding to, a child's affective and behavioural cues": Belsky (1999) p 265.

[28] Lewis and Ramsay (2005).

[29] Gerhardt (2004) p 197.

[30] Riordan and Auerbach (1999); Granju and Kennedy (1999); Blair, Fleming, Smith, Platt, Young, Nadin, Berry and Golding (1999); Mosko, Richard and McKenna (1997).

[31] Granju and Kennedy (1999).

[32] Hrdy (2000).

[33] Thevenin (1987); Sears (1999); Jackson (1999); Granju and Kennedy (1999); Fleiss (2000); Goodavage and Gordon (2002).

[34] Granju and Kennedy (1999) p 191.

[35] There are currently almost 700 attachment parenting groups on this site. Care, however should be taken. Some groups using the

term 'attachment' are completely different to the attachment parenting described in this book, and prescribed by API. If you witness any form of violence or coercive tactics, then walk away. As has been shown time and again in this book, no violence (be it psychological or physical) is acceptable when it comes to children, and obedience training is not a good idea.

[36] We saw in earlier chapters how negative attitudes to baby care led many parents to send babies out to wet-nurses, or to devise artificial feeding methods.

[37] In Exibit E of the World Health Organization Summary of International Code of Marketing of Breast Milk Substitutes see http://www.i-case.com/newdemo/inffeed/docs/052if.pdf (last accessed 1 December 2004).

[38] Granju and Kennedy (1999) p 90. See American Academy of Pediatrics 'Breastfeeding' http://www.aap.org/healthtopics/breastfeeding.cfm (last accessed 1 December 2004).

[39] Granju and Kennedy (1999) p 90.

[40] Gerhardt (2004) p 119.

[41] Gerhardt (2004) p 119.

[42] See UNICEF UK Baby Friendly Initiative, 'Health benefits of breastfeeding' http://www.babyfriendly.org.uk/health.asp#sids (last accessed 1 December 2004); Alm, Wennergren, Norvenius, Skjaerven, Lagercrantz, Helweg-Larsen and Irgens (2002) pp 400–402; McVea, Turner and Peppler (2000) pp 13–20; and Chen and Rogan (2004) pp 435–439.

[43] Granju (1999) p 90.

[44] Broude (1995).

[45] Lawrence (1999).

[46] Gerhardt (2004) p 65.

[47] Gerhardt (2004) p 65.

[48] Gerhardt (2004) p 210.

[49] Broude (1995).

[50] Trevathan and McKenna (1994).

[51] Hofer (1994).

[52] Trevathan and McKenna (1994).

[53] Hiscock and Wake (2002).

[54] Australian Association for Infant Mental Health see 'Controlled crying' http://www.aaimhi.org/polsSubs.htm (statement issued in November 2002, revised March 2004); Association for Infant Mental Health (UK) press release issued 7 October 2007, re Bringing Up Baby (Channel Four) http://socialbaby.com/shop/page.asp?id=Cvaimh

55   The hippocampus is a part of the brain that organises narrative memory. Up until it is developed, at three years of age, a baby or toddler cannot anticipate the future. They are neurologically unable to soothe themselves with the concept that, once Mummy has left the room, she will come back later: Gerhardt (2004).

56   Fonagy, Target, Steele and Steele (1997) p 155.

57   Perry and Pollard (1998).

58   Hrdy (2000). A child's level of emotional security can now be measured, using methods such as Ainsworth's and Main's "strange situation test", or Waters' and Deane's "attachment Q sort", which have been honed through hundreds of studies worldwide.

59   Belsky, Steinberg and Draper (1991) p 656; Fonagy, Target, Steele and Steele (1997) pp 159–161; Belsky and Cassidy (1994) p 394; Belsky, Fearon (2002).

60   Belsky and Cassidy (1994) p 393; Thompson (1999) p 272.

61   Thompson (1999) pp 270–271.

62   Gerhardt (2004).

63   Gerhardt (2004).

64   Karen (1994); Kochanska (2001).

65   Thompson (1999); Belsky, Steinberg and Draper (1991) p 657; Belsky, Fearon and Pasco (2002).

66   Thompson (1999).

67   Thompson (1999).

68   Thompson (1999).

69   Belsky and Cassidy (1994) p 384; Thompson (1999).

70   Belsky and Cassidy (1994); Thompson (1999); Fraley (2002) pp 123–151.

71   Thompson (1999).

72   Manne (2002).

73   Anaf (2002).

74   Halasz (2002).

75   Belsky and Cassidy (1994) p 394.

76   Thompson (1999).

77   Bowlby (1960) p 24, see also pp 9–-52.

78   Rothschild (2003).

79   Dozier, Stovall and Albus (1999); West and George (2002).

80   Karen (1994); Latzer, Hochdorf, Bachar and Canetti (2002); Orzolek-Kronner (2002).

81   Fonagy, Target, Steele and Steele (1997).

82   See World Health Organization (WHO) 'Child and adolescent

rights' and 'Children and nutrition' http://www.who.int/child-adolescent-health/NUTRITION/infant_exclusive.htm (last accessed 1 December 2004).

83 Van den Boom (1990), (1994).

84 All websites were last accessed 1 December 2004. Although I cannot vouch for the accuracy of all the information within the websites, I found them helpful.

27

THIRD RITE OF PASSAGE:
THE RIGHT
TO HAVE SUPPORT

T he cusp between babyhood and toddlerhood is a fragile time when the child begins the hesitant journey towards autonomy. His emotional health will depend on his parents' support to grow and test his new abilities – at his own pace.

What happens at this time
The third rite of passage spans roughly between 10 months to two years. Until around 18 months, the baby has not fully learned to distinguish his mother as separate from himself, and he experiences himself and mother as part of one continuum. As he takes his first tentative steps, and begins to form his first words, he begins to move away from this symbiosis toward differentiation: an autonomous existence as a separate self. To the extent that his earlier security needs have been met, he begins in earnest to explore the world beyond his mother. He discovers and masters his bodily power to set his own direction, from crawling to climbing and walking.

As his speech begins to develop, he can articulate some of his basic needs with increasing clarity. His steps and his words are the key to re-defining his existence and self-image in terms of autonomy. It begins to dawn on him that he can exert some influence over himself, over his environment, that he can start to exercise choice. This is both a revolutionary and a delicate moment, when the child literally constructs a new sense of self. Standing on his own legs, his view of the world is permanently transformed, and he gains a new view of himself in relation to the world around him.

It is critical to his emotional development that the child be supported to make this momentous transition entirely at his own pace, at his own time, and for his own sake. For some time, his budding attempts at individuation will be hesitant and uncertain, his transformation is both exhilarating and frightening, he swings from elation to helplessness. Consequently, he will repeatedly need to regress to his mother's and, increasingly, his father's side. Being reassuringly received and supported is what re-energises the toddler to make renewed forays out into the world. His emerging sense of autonomy will rest on strong foundations to the extent that he is supported both as a vulnerable baby, and as a magnificent toddler during this rite of passage.

As he explores his new powers and learns to influence his world in novel ways he may feel elated and grandiose. It is at this time that he becomes particularly sensitive to shame. His expanding ego is extremely fragile.

By the end of his first year, the child is able to generate abstract mental images of others' faces, which act as his record of being approved of – or disapproved of. This faculty makes it possible for the child to start absorbing shame and embarrassment for the first time.[1] As a result of his newfound mobility, the child begins to encounter more friction with his parents. They are now starting to restrict his impulses. He in turn is starting to be defiant. The way his parents set boundaries for him has profound ramifications for his self-esteem, and as we saw in Part IV, shaming and corporal punishment are particularly destructive at this stage.

This third stage marks a tenuous threshold of transition from babyhood into childhood, from prostrate helplessness to the boldness of standing. The developmental drama unfolding at this time is about personal power; the power to directly affect his environment and to influence others as the child becomes mobile and articulate. His task is to begin the long-term project of mastering his personal power and autonomy in ways that enhance his experience of himself, and his relationship with others. This includes some difficult but important lessons about interpersonal boundaries. His passage through this stage depends on his parents' sensitivity. Will he be supported to learn these faculties for himself at his own pace? Will he be shamed for his increasing adventurousness and self-assurance? Will he be pressured or manipulated to grow up too quickly?

Child's emotional needs at this time

There needs to be an abundance of support provided at this time. Support is only true support if it meets the child's needs as these emerge. This means supporting the child for his own sake, according to his need. It does not mean 'encouraging' or cajoling him to progress at the rate expected by parents or others. It does not mean enticing him to outdo himself in order to please or impress. The toddler needs his parents behind him as he tentatively steps out to explore. He wants us to share in his wonder as he becomes more agile, but also to hold him when he stumbles, to be his unfailing safety net when he becomes afraid. The child's innate rhythm sets his pace; if allowed to he will come to walk and talk without hurry or push. Appropriate support therefore embraces him both at his strength, as at his frailty.

Now that the toddler is mobile, boundary setting becomes an issue. Realistic safety boundaries can be defined compassionately, clearly and respectfully, without resorting to punishment, shaming or manipulation. Though at times boundaries might frustrate him, ultimately they reassure him and help him feel safely contained – so long as limits are set non-punitively.

He needs his carers' blessing to enjoy his newfound sense of power, his freedom to explore. He needs to be allowed his exuberance free of suffocating or overanxious control. But he equally needs to feel that there are safety boundaries around him. He also needs to feel that he can rely on his carers to hold him when he is afraid or hurt, and to gently contain him when he intrudes upon others.

As we saw in Chapter 18, at this delicate age in particular, parental restriction on a child's behaviour needs to be followed up with some soothing or reassurance that he is loved, so that he does not absorb the message that he is inadequate or unworthy.

What child is learning at this time

At this time, the toddler is learning whether or not he can trust in the support of others. He needs to find that it is OK to reach out for and receive support, as well as rely on his own strength; that it is human to be vulnerable as well as strong. This includes trusting that his vulnerability will evoke care, rather than manipulation or shaming. It also involves the experience that his strength will be respected, and not exploited by others. He needs to distinguish help that is genuine, from help that is manipulative, or bait on a hook. His autonomy and personal power are there to serve his own development, not others' expectations. Hopefully, he will learn by example that true personal power comes through honesty, not through manipulation or domination. Finally, the toddler wants to learn that love is only real if it is love for being himself, not for being what others wish him to be.

The most wounding experiences

The child's growing personal power is a central theme at this time. There are a number of ways in which the wrong kind of support can distort personal power so that instead of being based on honesty, it is based on manipulation or the use of force. Following are some of the ways that this might happen.

Unfulfilled or lonely parents at times seek comfort in their child, exploiting the child's willingness to please. The following scenario is an exceedingly common example. The parents' marital relations are unsatisfactory, perhaps the father is an alcoholic, or chronically absent from home. The mother may not be consciously aware that she is loading her son with her own unfulfilled emotional needs, she inadvertently leans on her son for comfort and intimacy. The boy valiantly but unrealistically – and impotently – tries to meet her need, and in so doing grows up far too quickly. This is the case of 'Mummy's little man'. Having lost a father who passes away or walks out, many young boys are told 'you are the man of the house now'. While some parents in this kind of situation seek comfort through their children overtly, many just tacitly permit the child to be their comforter, without intervening to stop the child from trying to assume the role of absent husband or wife.

The abuse consists of over–empowering the child, who is given (or intuitively 'picks up') the message that the parent is emotionally dependent on him. Even if there are no sexual overtones, this is a kind of emotional incest.

Children are uncannily able to sense their parent's pain, if permitted to they grow prematurely to satisfy the adult's emotional need. Long before they are sufficiently mature they become comforters, they offer solace. Tragically, this entails learning to deny their own frailty and their own need for support. They abandon their true childish selves, and present a false self, scripted to enchant the parents. When a child becomes the counsellor, the rescuer or the hero for his parent, inside he feels deeply betrayed, and becomes suspicious and mistrustful. But he learns to embody the role that is expected of him, he gains control over his parents by pleasing them, by disguising his vulnerability and by becoming indispensable.

It is alarming how a young child can adopt the post of protector, healer or confidant – especially when he is rewarded for his precociousness by the thankful parent. This child becomes astute about other's unspoken needs, and gains control by exuding the promise to meet these needs.

The pay-off for the child who tries to take care of his parent is that he gets to feel special, almost omnipotent. But this 'specialness' and power come at a great expense: he loses his own self. And underneath, he feels small, used, manipulated and unloved. He is no longer loved for who he is; he is loved for what he can do.

It is very tempting, at this stage of the child's development, to manipulate him to exceed his own need for supported growth. Parents who feel inadequate and are starved for praise, sometimes err by deriving their pride through their child: they seduce the child into making Daddy or Mummy proud. They make the child special for being a 'champ', saying to him, 'Come on, you can take another step for Mummy, be a big boy!' They seek an outstanding child who will make them feel like great parents. By rewarding him with fanfare for his brilliance they seduce him to outdo himself. The obliging child quickly learns the part he must play to gain the ovation from his audience. His essence is sacrificed to his image.

This is the time when the flattery of 'big boy!' and 'big girl!' makes its appearance in many homes. When children learn that the approval they depend on may be based on being bigger than themselves, they work hard to outgrow their natural smallness. What they learn to do for the pat on the head is a denial of their natural selves.

This dynamic orients the child toward performance, or showing off: adults become their appreciative spectators, as the child splits off from his authentic self to project an 'image' designed to keep drawing the parents' applause. In the quest to have the 'wonder child' that we can gloat about, 'support' becomes manipulative and exploitative. The seduced child struggles to perform more competently (feats of walking, talking, being 'cute' or 'clever') as he rises up to meet the parental expectation. He trades-in his inner pleasure for the power to entertain, gratify – and thereby control his audience.

What is so confusing about this seductive dynamic is

that on the surface, most people see no more than a doting and indulgent parent, showering their child with praise and encouragement. The more perceptive observer however, would sense when this kind of interaction is not nourishing but exploitative, when the child is the parents' trophy, a focus for their pride. There is nothing wrong with being proud of one's child – until he is expected to or relied upon to bear that role.

As boundary setting becomes increasingly important, punishment, shaming and humiliation rear their heads in authoritarian families. Dismayed by the new exuberant mobility of the toddler, parents try to wrest control by dominating or over-powering the child. Children respond to domineering parents with alternating 'good behaviour' and rebellion. They soon get the impression that relationship is about control, manipulation, about might-is-right; and they begin to act accordingly.

Authoritarian parenting is deeply humiliating to the child. He is not only frustrated by punishment, he also becomes deeply ashamed and feels worthless. He learns that in order to be approved of he must project a false self that suits the shamers. This is another reason why so many children lose track of their authentic selves altogether.

As babyhood wanes, boys in particular are humiliated for their vulnerability; they begin to hear such messages as, 'Boys don't cry, be a man, etc.' Many boys soon learn to puff up their little chests, and be 'tough' for their Dad. Underneath this bravado, however, they harbour a deep sense of shame and inadequacy, and a sense of having been betrayed.

The more the child strives to act out the qualities he feels are expected of him, the more he loses touch with his natural self. The innocent child is metamorphosed into the clever, gifted little grown-up that takes care of his parents, or impresses their friends. Some grow to be the tough little kids who may end up dominating, even bullying their peers. Others become the seducers or actors who, by rising above child-like innocence and vulnerability, reap parental pride and positive strokes.

How experiences shape emotional make-up and core beliefs

The following are some core beliefs held by adults, which arose from supportive experiences at this time.

Positive beliefs
I have the right to be supported
I can reach for support from others without shame, and
     without fear of being used, exploited or manipulated
I have the right to be afraid, to feel vulnerable, to feel weak
It's OK and not shameful to ask for help
Being 'up-front' and honest works better than manipulating,
     scheming or pretending
I am lovable for who I am, not for the 'image' I present

The following are some core beliefs held by adults, which arose
from injurious experiences at this time.

Negative beliefs
Never trust anyone
Always suspect other's motives
Always stay on top, in control, preferably in authority
I am not a worthy person unless I am a 'winner'
If I lose, then I am a worthless, shameful 'loser'
If I let people get close to me, they'll see my weakness, and
     I'll be taken advantage of
Vulnerability is shameful
If I'm really honest, I'll be manipulated
People only love me for what I can give them
I am safe as long as I can manipulate others
People can be easily manipulated, once you figure out what
     they need

The greatest fears that motivate the interpersonal defences that
are constructed at this time are: the fears of being used, being
humiliated, being manipulated, or being betrayed. These fears
produce in individuals a tendency to be suspicious of others.

How emotional wounds affect adult behaviour
When he learns early in life that he has the power to gratify his
parents' hunger for pride, this gives the child an over-expanded
sense of ego. This is particularly disastrous for children who have
already been significantly wounded at the first two stages. The
introduction of harsh 'discipline' or control at this stage begins
a hardening of the personality. The results are either an overly
dominant character, or, an individual who has learned to control
others by making promises and being seductive; through pretense.

Personal power is distorted in meaning, and is exerted through domination, intimidation, threats or manipulation.

Having been exploited very early and manipulated to abandon his real self to become what was wanted of him, he is desensitised to the exploitation of others. In his experience, relationships are about manipulation; so he is capable of remorseless acts of exploitation and abuse.

Much of his drive is based on maneuvering to achieve and maintain a position of power, for he has vowed never to let himself be manipulated or used again. On the surface, he appears to be in control – big, powerful and fearless. Underneath, he is emotionally two years old. But he does not know how to show this part of himself, and may not even know it exists. Quite often, the inner weakness that he has denied manifests in the form of sexual impotency. His proclivity to mistrust others inhibits any show of weakness, and he therefore maintains his poise at all costs, through the denial of his human vulnerability.

The persona he presents to the world can be charming, charismatic, imposing, even 'larger-than-life'. This can make him, at least initially, very attractive to others – particularly those who are gullible, insecure and needy – those who long for a hero or a saviour. But to those who look for his human-ness or his earthy-ness, he will seem unreal and inauthentic.

Underneath the charm and charisma, there is a violent, potentially murderous rage – the product of early shaming and humiliation – and woe be to any who trigger it. As we saw in Chapter 18, few parenting interactions can infuriate a child like shaming or humiliation can. Many bullies, in school or in business, are driven by shame-rage.

Because he learned very early to project a false image of himself, he places an inordinate amount of value on appearances. He is addicted to the 'right' looks, the 'right' car, the 'right' clothes, he may choose a partner as a trophy, based on her outward presentation, in the same way as he was once a trophy to his parents.

He is highly narcissistic, lacking in humility, and untroubled by guilt or remorse. He has an exaggerated sense of entitlement. This combination often empowers him to go very far in leadership roles, in politics, or in business. However, this is disastrous for intimate relationships and inside, he feels devastatingly empty and inadequate.

He has enticed others in his life to admire and adore his image, and thus he is not known as a real person. This leaves him feeling miserably alone. He masks his despair with alcohol, drugs or promiscuity.

He may be generous, and a great leader. He may even be somewhat of a hero or a savior. But his self-worth is dependent on holding this role, without which he crumbles into inadequacy and worthlessness, and he may become depressed. He is just as emotionally dependent on his followers or his audience, as they are emotionally dependent on him. Personality types range from the charmer to the tough-guy, from the actor, the rock-star, the wily salesman, to the dictator.

Micha Popper PhD, lecturer in psychology at Haifa University (Israel) conducted a number of research projects into the motivations that drive charismatic leaders. His research showed that exploitative and unscrupulous leaders are narcissistic personalities whose early attachment relationships had failed them. Even supportive and ethical leaders who are driven to assume leadership positions are very likely to have had a father who was distant or absent. The drive to be in a leadership role is for many individuals the result of emotional wounding. Leaders who are unattached to leadership, and are sincerely motivated for the public good (transformational leaders), are those who benefited from secure attachment as children.[2]

Social impact of wounds

Children who are manipulated or seduced tend to become expert manipulators. Those who are overpowered and humiliated tend to become dominant. The less secure and self-confident individuals become their admirers, their followers, their market or their prey.

To a significant degree, our system of commerce relies on the interplay of gullibility and seduction; a dovetailing of dysfunctions stemming from the second and third rites of passage respectively. The generally credulous attitude to 'image' springs from lack of fulfilment at the second stage, and provides a fertile ground for the work of seductive advertisers, marketeers and PR illusionists. Image builders are extremely adept at tapping into people's unconscious emotional insecurities; they can use this to seduce the more insecure amongst us into buying or believing almost anything. Ironically, this sad state of affairs contributes massively towards our economy. Narcissists at the helm of many corporations gain power by promising an unchallenging and credulous public that they have our best interests at heart. All too often at the expense of public health and the environment, they do what they do – so they tell us – for 'the economy', to 'boost employment', and the like.

Our model of 'strong' and implacable authority breeds submissiveness and hero-cults, and dates back to unresolved issues from this third early-childhood rite of passage. Magnetic leaders and charismatic gurus harbour deep wounds from this stage. Among their avid devotees and susceptible, image-driven voters are those who, having suffered from insecure attachments in the first two stages, are still unconsciously searching for strong parent surrogates, or father figures. The most apocalyptic cults, and the most corrupt and iron-fisted politicians, can count among their disciples some of the most erudite and scholarly individuals. This phenomenon is not a matter of academic intelligence or logic, it is a matter of emotional intelligence.

Wounds sustained during this rite of passage set the stage for a 'winners-and-losers' mentality, and an attitude of exploitative dominion toward the world and its resources. A sense of entitlement allows rapacious captains of industry to irresponsibly exploit both environmental and human resources.

It is not necessarily natural for humanity to be so destructive of its environment, and to be so plagued by material inequality. Our exploitative behaviour has gone out of control to the point of placing our very existence at risk. This pervasive abusiveness is an emotional disturbance that arises out of deficient early childhood attachment and wounding at this third stage. Too many of us are either addicted to power, or too easily – even willingly – at the disposal of the powerful. Too often, those in power that behave abusively can count on the public to provide direct support, tacit approval, or to present little opposition.

When wounding is severe at the first three stages, individuals grow up to be both inhuman and superhuman. Their power over others comes from a combination of charisma, charm, a cunning ability to manipulate others, and an absolute absence of empathy, sensitivity or remorse. This is the profile of the psychopathic personality. Many of history's most brutal dictators and godfathers of crime syndicates suffered exactly this combination of wounds in their upbringing. Having survived by denying their own emotional vulnerability, they are impervious to and utterly unmoved by the suffering of others. But this relating style is not confined to the arenas of tyranny and crime. This particular profile of core emotional wounding is also manifest among covertly corrupt but popular

335

politicians, corporate raiders, and all power-oriented narcissists who operate within the law. According to Kenneth Eisold, president of the International Society for the Psychoanalytic Study of Organisations, many of the world's CEOs should be considered as sociopaths.[3] Similarly, psychologist Dr Robert Hare opines that in their ordinary conduct of business, many actions of renown corporate executives have met the criteria for psychopathy: their determination to destroy competition, their self-interest and their remorseless and wholly unempathic exploitation of labour and the environment.[4] The credo of the wounded narcissist is 'the end justifies the means'. He is known for rationalising his exploitative behaviour by saying such things as 'if I didn't do it, someone else would have'.

Humanity need not be at the mercy of narcissistic, exploitative or psychopathic individuals. Their power is not real, since it is entirely based on the permission, the 'carte blanche' and even the adoration we all give them. We complain bitterly about our leaders, as if oblivious of the fact that we have empowered them in the first place. No individual can wrest control over an organisation, or a nation, without the express permission of an overawed or malleable public. Throughout history, even tyrants who have seized power by force have only managed to do so in cultures that embrace strong-arm rule, 'Big Man' ethics, and obedience training for children. Since we were deprived of secure attachments as infants, we remain child-like and emotionally dependent on 'authorities'; they are our surrogate parents. We seek the comfort of leaders whose authoritarian style feels familiar, reminiscent of our own controlling parents. Therefore, we fail to scrutinise, challenge or question authority. We refuse to believe they are human, fallible, perhaps even self-serving.

As parenting continues to evolve, it will be progressively more difficult for narcissistic and autocratic leaders to gain positions of influence.

Endnotes

1. Schore (1994).
2. Popper (1999), (2000a), (2002); Popper, Mayseless and Castelnovo (2000b).
3. Moore (2003); Recchia (2003) p 15.
4. Bakan (2004) pp 56–57.

28

FOURTH RITE OF PASSAGE:
THE RIGHT TO FREEDOM

The growing toddler has begun to make her move from attachment to separation. Love now encompasses the to-and-fro between parental embrace and freedom. As her will-power emerges she will begin to test the boundaries of relationship, and the boundaries of her world.

What happens at this time
The child is now starting to move beyond the critical bonding stages. Her development now depends as much on healthy differentiation as on secure attachment. The theme of this rite of passage is about the development of 'free will'. Between the ages of two and four approximately, the child is trying to learn that she can be separate and different from her parents. She wants to find that she can have her own will, mind, and body; while retaining a sense of her inner 'goodness', and still being loved by her parents.

Having been nurtured at the earlier stages, the child is now starting to explore the larger world, wandering further and staying longer away from the safety of a parenting presence. To the extent that earlier dependency-needs were fulfilled, the toddler now starts to bring boundless energy to the flight to freedom, as she asserts her separate self-identity. Tentatively, the child is testing the limits of autonomous individuality; her freedom to want and feel differently from Mother. Efforts to differentiate herself from her parents begin in earnest, so the child now needs support in the shape of being let go, yet warmly received when she runs back to the parent's side. The parents act as a safe 'home base' for the exploring child.

At around two years, most children learn to anticipate the

consequence of their behaviour. They learn to comply with requests, but they also build up a natural resistance to the enforcement of another's will. Healthy children fiercely defend themselves against what they experience as intrusive or unfair. They do not easily lend themselves to being subjugated. For authoritarian parents, it takes concerted efforts to crush their will, and the consequences are disastrous.

The assertion of individuality takes many shapes at this time: the child runs away, she yells at her parents to 'go away!' The child is now finding immense pleasure in saying 'no!' and she will want to taste the power of this word over and over. The maddening frustration of childhood powerlessness is momentarily averted through the joy of being contrary. This experiment serves the critical function of strengthening her boundaries and her separate self-identity, which she is now defining through opposition. Flaunting her newly found strength can be delicious; she may occasionally relish defying her parents just for the delectation of feeling her selfhood, and her 'otherness'.

The organic basis of any individual's *will power* comes from having been respectfully allowed, in these early years, one's own rhythm around vital bodily functions such as toileting, feeding and sleeping. If the child is not excessively controlled around these functions, a strong sense of autonomy will be rooted in a healthy trust of her own body and internal biological rhythms. It is fortunate that these days, toilet-training is decreasingly a battle-ground, since paediatricians and psychologists began to advise a later and more self-regulated transition to the toilet.

To the degree that the emotional needs of earlier stages have been fundamentally met, the toddler has now become quite robust. Bliss is now found in freedom, rather than in symbiosis with the parents. This enables the child to withstand a certain measure of conflict. It is of paramount importance that she be given the right to protest her disappointments and not be crushed for speaking out. As long as she isn't cruelly punished or humiliated, her tolerance for disagreement grows stronger and her resilience matures. This allows the parents more space to show their children a broader range of their own feelings, to begin asserting more of their own needs and personal boundaries, and to expect some age-appropriate considerate behaviour. The more the parents are willing to be transparent, authentic and emotionally alive in relating to the child, the more she is empowered to individuate and find her own separate and unique self. As long as parents modulate their self-expression to what the child can safely understand, this kind of interpersonal contact helps the child to mature.

Child's emotional needs at this time

The growing toddler needs to be allowed her to-and-fro forays into independence, at her own pace. She needs to be given the right to self-regulate and thus find her own safety boundaries wherever possible. The challenge for the parent revolves around the imposing of healthy, safe limits, and introducing the expectation of respect for others, without guilt-tripping, shaming or otherwise crushing the child's spirit. (Refer to Chapter 20 for boundary-setting using honest contact as opposed to authoritarian rules.)

It is vital that she be shown boundaries without resort to shame, guilt-tripping or punishment, for this will help her to contain her impulses appropriately whenever necessary. Self-containment is nothing like suppression. It is an act of free choice, motivated by consideration for others rather than by the craving for approval, and it comes at no cost to the child's self-esteem.

Most children develop a tremendous strength of will during this stage. Unless they can exercise their self-assertion liberally, they cannot fully individuate. When a child's strength is allowed and respected, she learns to make and maintain healthy interpersonal boundaries, and to be strong about what she wants in life. Obviously, each child needs to learn that others have personal boundaries also, so she can learn to use her newfound assertiveness appropriately.

As it begins to dawn on her that others have their own needs and limits, there will invariably be moments of disappointment and frustration. As parents, we fall from grace – we frustrate our children by imposing limits on their behaviour. Inevitably our children find that as finite human beings we are not all they would wish us to be. It is essential they be allowed to voice their frustrations and disappointments – guilt-free. This empowers them to develop their own strengths and to rely on a broader range of relationships – with other family members and friends.

Since children are so unrestrained and exuberant at this stage, it is natural that there will be some conflict with their parents. Far from having to be harmful, this stage-appropriate conflict is both a necessary and rich learning experience. When parents are able to manage these conflicts sensitively, acting as role models for assertive and respectful self-expression, they prepare for their children a base for lifelong self-confidence and natural negotiation skills. This is an optimal time to learn that when it is expressed honestly and constructively, anger can enhance relationships rather than destroy them. These experiences demonstrate to the child that mature love encompasses all feelings, and it embraces opposing points of view. A child learns an enormous amount about respectful relating at this time.

Notwithstanding the child's occasionally defiant stance, she still deeply needs security and holding. It is important for parents to not get caught up in power struggles, not to contribute to a battle of wills that pits the 'righteous' against the 'misbehaved'. The child has too long been condemned for her powerful emotionality at this age; she stands accused of all sorts of nasty 'attention-seeking' schemes – as if the need for attention is an offence!

Much has been written about how to conquer and defeat the tantrum-throwing child, precious little has been said in support of the powerless child's right to express her rage. Toddlers don't need 'taming', or 'correcting' – as many socialising mode parenting manuals suggest – they need our empathy and respect. Might we instead, as parents, wonder at the astonishing emotional potency of our children – something that for most of us has been buried long ago. When a child defies us, resists and protests, she needs to be given some space to do so. Her self-confidence depends on being allowed this strength. She doesn't need parental capitulation, just her freedom to express her feelings, and to be heard. When the focus is on listening and empathy, neither parent nor child need be the victor.

Temper tantrums are a feature of this stage because the part of the brain concerned with containing raw emotion has not yet fully developed. Even at three years of age, the cortex is relatively disorganised, and so the child has very limited capacity to regulate tantrums, or any strong emotional charge.[1] The punishment of tantrums is therefore unjust. The parents act as the child's emotional container, through their emotional resonance, their reassurance and their holding, until the child can take over healthy self-containment. Each child grows to contain herself in the same way that her parents once contained her. In other words, she will contain herself with reassurance, or censor herself with shame, based on how she was treated. What most helps a child to modulate her own emotional outbursts, are her stored memories of being comforted and reassured.[2]

Permissiveness is not an alternative; it is not OK for the child's behaviour to be damaging to herself or to others. This is the age when kids begin to need to know you through your boundaries. If you can set strong limits non-violently and non-abusively this helps her to feel your strength and your presence. The respect she shows you is proportional to the respect you have for yourself. Without realistic interpersonal boundaries you don't seem 'real' to her. She feels lost, confused and angry. Many children react to a lack of boundaries by becoming highly provocative. This is not, as many mistakenly assess, a call for negative 'strokes' or attention. It is a protest, and a search for her parents' solidity.

This developmental stage can be very confronting for parents. A toddlers' passion can be formidable, both in hate as in love. In order to not respond with punishment or guilt-tripping, parents need to be secure enough in themselves that they do not crumble, or feel wounded by the toddler's rage.

The child will always need copious amounts of affection, but the kind of ongoing attention that helps pre-toddlers to thrive in the earliest three stages could be overindulgent and even smothering at this stage. When we overprotect our children, we stifle their need to discover their own strengths, and to develop their own resources. The toddler asks us to say farewell to the baby, and to welcome the self-regulating child; she adamantly wants to make her own mistakes and thus develop competency. And although she will periodically regress and become baby-like, she wants her parents to gradually begin to let her go, which includes letting her experience her parents as real people: warm and loving, yet sometimes tired and cranky.

The child now gains her strength of will and her sense of self from her freedom to decide when she needs to be in our arms, and when she needs to run free.

What child is learning at this time

The child is now learning much about the pleasure of aloneness, of wandering off and exploring the world unaccompanied. She is also beginning to learn that differences and distance are substantive to healthy relationships. By learning to withstand and survive conflict and disagreement, she learns that love encompasses opposition. She can now begin to articulate her frustrations and her disappointments; a function that will be vital to her wellbeing.

It is now that the seeds are sown for the child's ability to 'follow her bliss'; to become self-regulating and self-directive, to locate and trust her 'inner authority'. She is attempting to relinquish, sometimes forcefully, her identification with her parent's emotional states and attitudes. This disentangling process is essential if she is not to feel overly responsible for others' feelings later in life.

One symptom of excessive enmeshment with others is when we feel guilty after saying 'no'. It is therefore a major goal of this rite of passage for the child to master differentiation, without which close relationships can feel confining. When we remain excessively responsible to or burdened by the feelings of others, this indicates that we have not fully embraced our separateness.

The child's task at this stage is to carry her inner feelings of pleasure, fullness and satiation, which were previously dependent on Mother, into autonomous existence, that is, to begin to master the making of her own destiny.

The opportunity exists here to lay a strong foundation for freedom of thought, which rests upon a non-compulsive response to 'authority'.

The most wounding experiences

Some parents are threatened by their child's growing autonomy and strength of will. They may have been nurturant during earlier, attachment stages, but the wilful and independent toddler presents a whole new challenge. They react by trying to crush the child's spirit, her will and her individuality, through the use of shaming, guilt-tripping, or punishment.

Parents who are themselves burdened with shame and guilt – because they were once punished and humiliated as toddlers – are most likely to feel threatened by the child's freedom. Perhaps they feel unconsciously resentful of their own child's freedom and self-confidence, for these were the qualities they were themselves never allowed to develop. Consequently, they become over-controlling and intrusive at this stage of their child's growth.

Intrusive parents can be meddlesome around their children's behaviour and natural bodily functions. Eating tends to be forced, toileting is over-regulated, sleep times are fastidiously imposed. In times that featured what Lloyd de Mause called 'intrusive mode' child rearing, parents obsessively forced their children to 'finish everything on the plate', they stood over them and expected them to defecate on cue, they subjected them to the humiliation of regular enemas and brutal beatings. To say that parenting was a battle of wills would be an understatement. This level of intrusiveness has dissipated, but not completely died out. Many parents continue to enforce their wills upon children's natural and involuntary bodily functions, instead of trusting the health and rightness of their natural biological rhythms.

Care can be smothering at this stage if we over-protect, or lumber the child with so many rules, 'shoulds' and 'don'ts' that her natural explorative impulses become stifled, and held in. The child's natural exuberance withers under a regime of obsessive interference, over-preoccupation with cleanliness, orderliness, propriety, 'good' manners, or obedience. Consider this option: instead of a perfectly orderly house temporarily accept a small amount of chaos, mess, disorder and lack of punctuality. Instead of a home with breakable goods never touched or explored consider child-proofing. Such modest compromises welcome and encourage the wide-eyed child, instead of stifling her.

As the child's language becomes more sophisticated, words are often used to impose shame on the child. Labels used to scold can create a powerful resonance in the impressionable mind of the child. Her self-identity is being shaped around the things that she hears about herself, and thus words used against her have a profound impact on her behaviour and self-image. Words such as 'bad', 'naughty', 'wrong', all strike a blow at the heart of her self-esteem. Dualities of reward and punishment, or 'good girl' and 'bad girl' admonitions, split her consciousness, and reduce her to an approval seeker. The more the child orients herself toward gaining reward and escaping punishment or shaming, the more she abandons her natural self. Her spirit crushed, she survives by becoming submissive and compliant, and by presenting an outward 'good-little-child' image that conceals an underlying spite and obstinacy.

When a child's will is crushed, she learns to crush herself, in order to escape punishment, humiliation or disapproval. She learns this so well, that eventually she does not even know she is doing it. Thereafter, self-suppression and inhibition become unconscious, automatic, and habitual reflexes.

The premature parroting of 'please' and 'thank you' reflects the child's attempts to meet adult expectations, or to do 'the right thing'. 'Good manners' will therefore rarely have meaning for the 'well behaved' toddler other than in pleasing authority. Social etiquette, when enforced at this stage, will do very little to instil in the child a true empathy for the needs of others.

When a toddler begins to assert her independence, and to move away from the symbiotic intimacy of babyhood, it is not unusual for some parents to feel abandoned or rejected. The powerful toddler is no longer quite the cuddly helpless baby she once was, and parents might feel a sense of loss. They react possessively, attempting to control the child's powerfully expanding sense of self, and her movements toward freedom and self-mastery. Overprotection or overindulgence risks stifling the toddler's thrust towards independence.

Parents who don't assert their own needs and boundaries with their child, who don't express 'negative' feelings and always speak softly disarm the child as a way to avoid conflict. This can disempower the child, whose development now depends on being met with a parent who is a solid individual. Many children react to this frustration by whingeing, complaining or becoming provocative.

The guilt-trip is another form of manipulation aimed at keeping the child from asserting herself. It may come in the form of 'How could you do this to me?' This dynamic creates a child who is excruciatingly aware of her parents' discomforts and hurts. Children are prone to feeling excessively responsible, and they readily accept blame for how their parents feel. Under the pressure of guilt, the child may consent to 'be good' in order to not 'upset Mummy or Daddy'. But underneath this 'good child' veneer, she simmers with spite.

How experiences shape emotional make-up and beliefs

The following are some core beliefs held by adults, which arose from positive experiences at this time.

Positive core beliefs
I have the right to be free, to be autonomous, to make my own decisions

I have the right to be assertive, to be different, to stand out

I have the right to strongly and vigorously express who I am, my feelings

I have the right to be unique and creative

I have the right to my own space and privacy

I can approve of myself even when others don't approve of me

The following are some core beliefs held by adults, which arose from injurious experiences at this time.

Negative core beliefs
It is up to me to take care of others
If people who are close to me are hurting it is my fault
To be free means to be alone
To be intimate means to be trapped
Deep inside, I am shameful
I am safe if I follow suit
Life is a struggle to be toiled at
Love is defined by duty and obligation
Life is a series of 'shoulds'

The greatest fears that motivate the interpersonal defenses that are constructed at this time are the fear of others' expectations and their disapproval, the fear that one will be abandoned if one is self-assertive, and the fear that relationships will entail obligations, confinement or entrapment.

How emotional wounds affect adult behaviour
When our earliest flights towards freedom have been repeatedly subverted, we fear freedom and everything associated with it. Many of us live our lives saddled with statements like 'I should do this' and 'I shouldn't do that', and our relationships are bound by an exaggerated sense of duty or obligation. Pleasure and spontaneity elude us as we battle inner demons of guilt and shame. We do what is 'right', less from a base of care and empathy than in order to seek approval. We groan under a crushing burden of self-imposed responsibility. An excessive preoccupation with 'getting it right' restricts our mobility, our creativity, and our willingness to take risks. This kind of existence leaves us feeling spiteful, resentful, and at times even miserable.

A morbid fear of punishment, disapproval and humiliation paralyses us; we dread initiating new projects. We are able to work very hard, to plod on and endure adversity, but a chronic fear of disapproval prevents us from following our bliss. To those who have suffered emotional arrest at this stage, the idea of enjoyable work is alien, and pleasure itself is suspect.

When we are over-awed by 'authority', we live defensively, as if afraid of 'getting into trouble'. We suffer from hypersensitivity to the expectations of others. Self-protection takes the shape of excessive and unquestioning compliance, as with the servile 'good boy' or 'good girl'. Alternatively, in reaction to others' expectations, we get stuck in compulsive obstinacy – we dig our heels in, saying, 'I will not be moved!'

In our close relationships, an abiding sense of duty may make us extremely loyal. While this is a worthwhile quality, obligation tends to dull emotional expression. This prevents us from experiencing the depths of tenderness, deliciousness and excitement that are possible through intimacy.

A smothering, shaming and punitive environment at the fourth stage can leave us tending toward negativity, pessimism and lack of self-confidence. Socially, we might feel painfully inhibited. When our own natural exuberance has been crushed, the exuberance of others can make us uncomfortable. We put others down, we rain on others' picnics, and we are compulsively cynical.

Fourth stage wounding is discernible in the long-suffering 'martyr'. Since her natural expression of anger or disappointment has been crushed, her hurts and irritations fester and turn to deep bitterness and resentment. Unable to express this, she holds it in, remains outwardly pleasant, but can show her displeasure indirectly, through derisive humour, back-handed and oblique put-downs, or the 'silent treatment'. She is capable of holding grudges interminably. Instead of expressing her displeasure directly, she whines and complains, and she tries to make others feel guilty by broadcasting her martyrdom.

Though they may be highly valued contributors to their community, these individuals' greatest dilemma is their difficulty with experiencing joy, pleasure and spontaneity.

Social impact of wounds

Many individuals who have been wounded at this stage can function extremely well: they are law abiding, they have an enormous endurance for hard work, they are amongst the most loyal individuals, and are able to be highly devoted, protective and loving parents. However, few of society's leading innovators, creative thinkers and drivers of social progress are likely to be characterised by emotional wounds from this developmental stage.

Interestingly, psychotherapists are finding that the more severe neuroses that arise from emotional wounding at this stage have become less prevalent.[3] This is not surprising, since parenting modes have become generally less intrusive over the last century, and collectively, we seem to have matured enough to be able to tolerate more of our children's freedom.

Endnotes
[1] Perry (1997).
[2] Schore (1994).
[3] Johnson (1994).

29

FIFTH RITE OF PASSAGE:
THE RIGHT TO LOVE

The child's capacity for love, passion and sensuality are growing, and infantile sexual feelings begin to emerge now. What children learn about love at this time will reverberate into future loving and sexual relations.

What happens at this time

From around three to six or seven years of age the focus of bio-psychological development moves downward to the genitals, so that the child becomes aware of a full infantile sexual charge permeating his body. Up until this point, nerve endings in the genitals had not provided for so much awareness nor arousal there. As this new consciousness function emerges, it is experienced by the child as integral to his being; his genitals, heart and head are one. The child now develops an exploratory pre-occupation with his genitals. He is delighted by the deeply pleasurable sensations he discovers, and the way these can radiate throughout the rest of his body.

Children are in love with their parents at this stage, and when they reach to embrace their loved ones they bring their infantile sexual energy to the embrace. Loving contact now encompasses the whole, connected, physical self. The infantile sexual longing for the parent is not to be confused with adult sexuality or the adult sexual act of intercourse; it is merely about the sensual energy of love flowing throughout the whole body of the child, for whom affection has become increasingly physical and sensual.

As the fact of gender differences dawns on the child, he is overcome with curiosity about the nature of his own sexuality (as a girl is with hers), and the variances between boys and girls. Enthralled with the new dimensions of himself that he is discovering, and reveling in the newfound aliveness in his body; he may for some time become exhibitionistic. Life brings numerous delights and wondrous pleasures to the developing child at this stage.

The child now begins to grapple with primitive notions of morality and convention. He begins to sense a difference between accidental and intended outcomes, and thus starts to grasp the notion of cause and effect. As he approaches his sixth year, he begins to take rules quite seriously. Juvenile morality is simplistic: it splits the world into 'good' and 'bad', 'right' and 'wrong'. For a while, this two-dimensional vision makes him especially vulnerable to authoritarian adults who moralise and impose rigid rules.

Child's emotional needs at this time

Optimally, the parents are relatively unashamed and unafraid of loving-sexual energy, and they enjoy a fulfilling and active sexual partnership. These conditions enable the parents to remain open, unthreatened and loving in the presence of their child's sensual aliveness, without excessively censuring or turning away from the child. They model boundaries of appropriate behaviour without damaging the child's dignity. Moreover, the sexually healthy and satisfied parent does not over-respond to the child's emerging sexuality with inappropriate, sensually charged advances.

Continued warmth and non-interference support the child to develop the basis for an adult sexual self-identity that is free of shame, guilt, or fear, as well as an inclination to be respectful of his own and other's sexual boundaries. As self-discovery unleashes the child's curiosity and thirst for understanding, his questions need direct, simple and truthful answers.

Healthy children will begin to fondle and stimulate their genitals around this time, and at times they innocently exhibit themselves. If children's masturbation is not interfered with, or met with judgment, they learn in a natural way that they are masters of their own bodies, and thus they avoid developing distorted attitudes to sexuality. It is, after all, the child's right to explore and celebrate the abundant pleasure that the body so generously grants. Children are better protected from violation or interference if they are confident in their right to self-regulation and privacy. It benefits them to learn that they have the right to expect and demand privacy, 'My body is my own, and *I* decide what happens to it!'

What child is learning at this time

This stage of development prepares the foundation for mature sexual love; the seeds are sown here for the child to learn about loving and being loved with his whole being, his whole body. He seeks to acquire and develop the psychological capacity for sexual love that is unencumbered by shame, or by disrespectful attitudes.

If he can become well-grounded in the pleasure function of his body, the child evolves a positive and balanced attitude to pleasure in general. The pleasure principle – not to be confused with self-serving hedonism – is vital to our ability to take in and enjoy life's sweetness, and to share pleasurable experiences with others. Without a healthy grounding in the pleasure principle we lose our balance; we become obsessive, overly task-oriented and dull.

The child wants to cultivate pro-social behaviour that is based on empathy and a genuine interest in the wellbeing of self and others. He does not want to get stuck in abstractions, or the 'letter' of rules and regulations. Moral behaviour springs from care, not from pedantry or piousness. As he becomes a more social being, he naturally seeks to strike a balance between freedom of self-expression and sensitivity towards others.

These years find the child practising healthy self-containment, based on grounded, non-explosive emotional self-expression. He relies, for this learning, on what is role-modelled for him. This aspect of emotional intelligence stands in contrast to rigid armouring against emotion, which results from strict authoritarianism.

The most wounding experiences

Parental responses to the child's exhibitionism are recorded in the orbitofrontal cortex, a structure that regulates the mature sexual drive.[1] This means that the way we regulate our own drives is based on how we were related to as children. One kind of injury to the child's sexual identity can take the form of rejection or condemnation. Many parents become very uncomfortable around infantile sexuality. They punish or shame their children, or turn away from them. Children cannot understand the new parental reserve, they feel personally rejected.

Shaming or moralistic responses to the child's burgeoning sexual exploration can produce an up-tight temperament, or result in rebellious, sexual acting-out later in life. The child defends himself from his parents' or teachers' judgement and disgust with a rigid and inflexible attitudinal armour. He protects his heart by blocking soft and tender feelings. Both direct injunctions against his sexuality, and unspoken parental embarrassment or discomfort, are experienced by the child as a heart-breaking rejection of his expanding self. Fearing punishment, or sensing a withdrawal of parental affection, he blames his emerging sexuality and reacts by suppressing or splitting-off this part of himself. Thus begins the separation of sex from love, genitals from heart. The need for love and for pleasure is sublimated, and substituted by a need to over-achieve, to prove the worth he feels he has lost. Hence he re-diverts his energies toward competitiveness and a high accomplishment-drive.

At the opposite end of the spectrum is the child whose emerging sexuality is exploited or violated. Adults close to him use his innocent, childish arousal and curiosity in the service of their own needs. Some children suffer increased and inappropriate physical embraces at this time, from adults who, without necessarily realising it, are turning to them to satisfy their own unmet physical longings. Many incestuous adults claim – and are convinced – that carnal contact with a child is an act of love. I cannot emphasise strongly enough that this is an absolute delusion. During the act itself, their interest is not in the child as a person, but on what the child can gratify. When the adult perpetrator says, 'I love you', he or she really means 'I need you' – but is unable to tell the difference. This is because he or she is likely to have once been abused in the same way. It is precisely this confusion between love and exploitation that makes sexual abuse so catastrophic. When, in the child's mind, sexual interference becomes associated with love, the consequences are disastrous.

It is not uncommon for abusive adults to blame children for being 'seductive'. In Chapter 5 we examined the history of girl rape-victims who were tried and executed as witches. This tendency to exploit and then blame children has not entirely disappeared. Children who have been insecurely attached are particularly at risk of sexual exploitation. If they are exceptionally starved for affection, their sensuality becomes exaggerated – they may even try to initiate improper kinds of contact. Children's innocent curiosity – or their desperate appeals for comfort – are misconstrued as 'seductive' by adults who have dysfunctional interpersonal boundaries. Many victims of incest or non-familial sexual abuse report that they partly enjoyed the experience, since it brought the secondary payoff of human contact, and it made them feel temporarily 'special'. The offending adult misinterprets the child's confusion as a sign that the abuse is welcome. Nothing could be further from the truth.

Incestuous interference ranges from intercourse, genital play, sexualised hugs or deliberate adult exhibitionism, to intrusive questions and voyeurism. It is hard to know how many children suffer some form of sexual victimisation since research estimates vary considerably, but conservative studies say that at least one in four children are molested,[2] though realistically, the proportion may be higher, since so many people are too afraid or ashamed to disclose, or they have repressed the memory.

Emotional wounding at this stage is not only sexual in nature. Many children are faced with an increase in rigid, disciplinarian interventions from their parents at this time. While their performance is evaluated, then punished or rewarded according to a standard, they feel that they are not seen as persons. Their immense capacity for fun and play eventually withers; it is gradually subverted by the dictates of 'getting it right'.

Authoritarian parenting can arrest the development of more sophisticated and complex thinking processes. It prevents the development of the deeper understanding of human motivation that is so essential to the growth of humility and compassion. The result is a smug, righteous and moralistically bipolar (good versus evil) attitude to human relations.

As we saw in Part IV, children do not learn compassion through the rote-learning of rules. Moral behaviour of this kind is robotic and lacks any spontaneity. Children only learn to be empathic and respectful if they are themselves treated this way.

How experiences shape emotional make-up and beliefs
The following are some core beliefs held by adults, which arose from positive experiences at this time.

Positive core beliefs
I can love with my whole being, and be loved for my whole being
My heart is full, I have much love to give

It is safe to reach out, to be intimate
Sex is an act of love between adults
I am loveable for who I am, not for what I accomplish
Failures and mistakes are an important part of learning and
living.
Life is meant to be pleasurable
Work is meant to be enjoyable, meaningful and fulfilling
A strong mind is a flexible and open mind
It is fine for opinions and points of view to change and
grow
I value friendships with people who see the world differently
from me. We learn from each other
It is safe to feel my feelings
The best decisions come from the heart and head together
When I feel and express my emotions, I feel closer to others

The following are some core beliefs held by adults, which arose
from injurious experiences at this time.

Negative core beliefs
I am unlovable
I am not good enough
I must have done something wrong
If I am sexual, I am dirty or shameful and I'll be rejected
Rightful sex is defined by strict moral codes; things like
masturbation, oral sex, homosexuality, are wrong, kinky
or sinful
Sex is only for procreation
Sex and love are separate
The act of sex is no more than a discharge of energy
I'm only lovable if I am sexually attractive
My worth comes from pleasing others sexually
Sex is about conquest
Good sex is about performance, 'skill', and points on the
score-board
The will must control emotion, passion is bad
Life is a struggle between good and evil
The evil or impure must be punished

The greatest fears that motivate the interpersonal defenses that
are constructed at this time are: the fear of rejection, the fear of
heartbreak and the fear of other's judgments.

How emotional wounds affect adult behaviour

Almost none of us have emerged unscathed from this developmental stage. The immensely rich and diverse range of human sexual behaviour is suffocated by shame, ignorance and rigidity. We think we live in a sexually liberated society, yet much of what passes for 'liberation' is compulsive, exhibitionistic, or based on performance rather than contact. Compulsive, serial promiscuity and moralistic rigidity are two extreme poles, both reflecting a legacy of either repressive or abusive up-bringing.

Wounds from this stage wreak havoc on adult sexual relations. Inner conflicts and tensions surrounding our sexuality keep us from experiencing our full potential for pleasure and fulfilment. The human body is in its entirety capable of integrated orgasm, yet for most people the pleasure of orgasm is restricted to the genitals. Deeply held bodily tensions that defend against childhood hurts inhibit our capacity to fully surrender to the loving ecstasy of total-body release. Since a deep satisfaction eludes us, this gives sex a quality of urgency or compulsivity for some individuals, while others lose their libido altogether.

Much of the pain we suffer in relationships exists because sexuality has been devalued to a mere function of discharge, a release of frustration and tension. This shallow version of sex, the product of a disconnection between the heart and the genitals, affords no intimacy. It accepts the most profound physical embrace when there is no heartfelt connection between two individuals. The act might be titillating and exciting, but it lacks the depth of passion and tenderness that takes place when two souls meet. Sexual liberation may have freed us to enjoy sex, but it has not necessarily taught us to make love. A heartfelt sexual union takes time to develop; it requires mutual emotional transparency and vulnerability. This is not possible in casual encounters.

Human sexuality seems beleaguered by an array of predicaments that reflect the manifold wounds so many of us experience at this stage. Some use sex as a currency to bargain for company, comfort or control, or as a means of 'proving' their personal worth. Any early sexualisation of girls, in particular, is discernible in excessively coquettish or flirtatious affectation, or in promiscuous behaviour. Others find it difficult to be sexual with those they really love. Yet others compensate for deep-seated feelings of inadequacy with an attitude of contempt towards the opposite sex.

Our exaggerated emphasis on looks, tight bodies, washboard

stomachs and fat-less thighs reflects our displaced eroticism: we are disproportionately excited by superficial and transient qualities, rather than by qualities of sensuality, warmth and vitality.

In repressive societies, we view pleasure with suspicion. Instead, we take pride in how 'hard' we can push or drive ourselves. An unbalanced task-orientation gives birth to the workaholic and the compulsive high-achiever for whom the playful poetry of living remains out of reach. Individuals who habitually take refuge in action may accomplish wonders, and achieve positions of respect and notoriety. They contribute much to their organisations and to society, but their work keeps intimacy at bay; they are walled in behind their occupation and cannot be reached. They may seem stiff, formal and humourless. The child that grew up feeling like his performance was under the microscope becomes a performance-based person. His competitive drive and ambition are displaced pleas for love and recognition. He finds it difficult to loosen up and relax. Others may find him somewhat insensitive, and hard to get to know as a person.

A repressive upbringing is also behind some individuals' compulsive adherence to rituals. Terrified of the unpredictability, the intensity and the whimsy of human passion, they seek refuge in the detail and minutiae of formalities, with little or no connection to the meaning and feeling of their actions. They might, for instance, fastidiously enact religious rites with little or no depth of feeling.

Many children compensate for the rejection and judgment they feel at this stage by learning to hold back tender or soft feelings. They armour themselves against further pain by becoming emotionally hardened. They learn to control their emotions through sheer force of will. Consequently, their thinking becomes overly rational and clinical, divorced from feeling.

The mentally rigid cannot cope with complexity or paradox. They see the world two-dimensionally, in terms of good and bad, and they see life as a struggle between 'good' and 'evil'. This defensive rigidity is found in the stickler for living 'by the book', who clings to the letter rather than the spirit of the law. It is possible for people to become so inflexible in their adherence to traditions and values that they are no longer able to grow and be changed through experience. This 'either-or', 'black-or-white' cognitive style makes people controlling, unyielding, unfeeling, and as parents, rigid disciplinarians. Emotional rigidity stifles compassion, understanding, and imagination.

Social impact of wounds

Moral rigidity and legalism are irrational and desperate attempts to cover up for how dirty, 'impure' or shameful we feel deep inside. The cost of this defense mechanism is great. When we hold repressive and puritanical attitudes, we cause considerable grief to all those in our sphere of influence, we strangle their vitality and their pleasure.

These forces are extremely destructive for any society: they drive people to prejudice. In some societies, homosexuals are made to suffer a life of alienation and scorn. In others, being a woman is crime enough. When normal sexual desires are suppressed they are driven underground; where, through frustration, they become monstrous. It is no surprise therefore that sexual abuse is prevalent among puritanically religious families. In fact, rates of incest are higher among patriarchal families where the father is dominant and the wife is submissive.[3]

We cannot possibly overestimate the catastrophic effects of the sexualisation of children. Many survivors of sexual abuse are driven to recurring depression, and finally suicide.[4] By the same token, neither should we underestimate the impact of emotional deprivation and repression. Paedophiles are created, not born. They come from the ranks of those who were emotionally deprived, received a repressive upbringing, and were used as sex objects themselves. Paedophilia is sometimes the dark flip-side of the puritanical.

Historically, the sexual abuse of children was the rule, rather than the exception. Child sexual abuse has never attracted the kind of universal censure it receives today. Its victims have never, until modern times, had access to the kind of professional treatment that prevents them from transferring the abuse to the next generation. Since this kind of sexual deviance seems to have declined somewhat, some of the more severe symptoms suffered by victims – such as 'conversion disorder', previously referred to as 'hysteria' – appear to be less prevalent. Future societies will benefit in myriad ways, if we maintain – and increase – our commitment to reducing the incidence of this crime against children.

A further corollary of authoritarian upbringing through

this stage is mental and emotional rigidity. On a social scale, these traits can be politically disastrous, as recent and current geo-political events attest. Some of the political comments we have heard across the globe of late have been exemplary of this particular arrest in emotional development. The shallow rhetoric of 'good versus evil' espoused by certain politicians, as from some extremist religious leaders, has repeatedly fanned the flames of war. The speeches that mobilised entire nations to bellicose ends have been characterised by simplistic talk of an 'axis of evil', getting the 'bad guy', launching a 'crusade', or wiping out the 'infidel'. This crude view of morality, resulting from early emotional injury, makes meaningful, rational and effective action impossible.

Conclusion to Part VI

As psycho-emotional development continues throughout life, there are additional stage-specific lessons and challenges which we all face, each adding new layers to our personalities. However, psycho-emotional structures formed during these first five stages comprise the core of our emotional make-up, and hence govern our characteristic or pattern-like relationship styles. Some caution is warranted to avoid over-simplification or rigid determinism in the interpretation of how early-childhood emotional injury affects personality.

Our childhood emotional wounds do not always entrap us; we are not forever condemned to act out our developmental arrests. Our past does not define us nor does it inescapably drive our relationships. It is the unconscious, neurally programmed defences that we built up early to protect ourselves from hurt, that impinge on our relationships every day. To some extent, this can be remedied with awareness, willingness to grow, and with the support of counselling or psychotherapy. The enriching experience of psychotherapy can greatly assist us to see beyond old defensive patterns and to develop new and more rewarding ways of relating – making both our relationships and our personal lives much more fulfilling. The gift of psychotherapy is to restore our capacity to feel, to know ourselves in new ways, and to trust once again our connection with others.

Under special circumstances, when healing opportunities are available, some people manage to turn their wounds into gifts. Although most people carry some wounds from childhood, many are able to compensate by creating unique and surprising traits and abilities. It is a common paradox that for some individuals compassion, commitment and devotion to great causes can have its genesis in childhood injury.

What can be said with certainty however, is that significant deviations from meeting the child's stage-specific, basic emotional needs, are hurtful and potentially damaging. On the other hand, the more any society moves towards ensuring that all its children have these core emotional developmental needs met, the more it becomes a peaceful, harmonious, sustainable and productive society.

These chapters have dealt with core developmental issues that are universal. Beyond these basic, common developmental themes, there are many variations in the way children learn and grow, but these variations are beyond the scope of this book. Ultimately, the key to empathic and supportive parenting is to trust our children's messages, to heed their needs and feelings, and to be guided by their cues.

Most parents would find it quite difficult to sustainably meet their children's emotional needs without a plentiful supply of help and support from their families, friends and community. In Part VII, we will look at the kinds of assistance that parents should have, and we will critically examine some of the family support schemes currently available. Finally, we will look at some of the extraordinary social changes that could materialise if child rearing continues to evolve, and if we collectively increase our commitment to the support and protection of families.

Endnotes

1   Schore (1994).
2   See de Mause (2002c) p 359, (1991) pp 130–142. Neville A 'Child sexual abuse: traumatic aspects and associated losses' in Open Doors http://www.opendoors.com.au/ChildSexAbuse/ChildSexAbuse.htm see 'Prevalence studies' (last accessed 1 December 2004).
3   Thorman (1983).
4   Johnson (1994).

WHERE TO FROM HERE?

The wellbeing of our own children can only be secured when the wellbeing of all other peoples' children is also secure.

Lilian Katz[1]

30

WHO PARENTS THE PARENTS?

A person cannot be committed to a child unless other people are committed to that person's commitment to children

Dr Bronfenbrenner[2]

It really takes a village!

Now that we know so much more than we have ever known about healthy emotional development, how do we manage to give our children what they need? If it is difficult – sometimes overwhelmingly so – for a mum and dad to meet their children's developmental needs, that is because nature has not designed us to parent as couples. Some parents seem to be endowed with a bottomless supply of emotional energy; they are able to be consistently and warmly present for their children with little or no stress – while maintaining a healthy interest in their own lives and in their adult relationship. But I think this kind of parent is rare. Our levels of patience and endurance vary naturally from individual to individual. I contend that for most people, the 'mum and dad' model of parenting is insufficient and unrealistic.

Our children need to feel that it is pleasurable for us to look after them. The pleasure of parenting quickly runs out when we become physically and emotionally exhausted. And most of our children's hurts arise when we reach the end of our tether, and there is no one to replace us. For this reason, it was always nature's intention that we parent in groups.

Historically, whenever parents lacked social support and material security, they tended to deny or distort their children's needs. Coping methods ranged from infanticide, to abandonment, to corporal punishment, emotional manipulation

360

and neglect. We have come to accept many false ideas, such as 'it is OK to leave a baby to cry alone for 20 minutes', or 'children under two don't remember anything', or 'a good smack cannot do any harm', because these ideas relieve us of the burden of empathic parenting. Ideas such as these have been damaging to children. When, as parents, we do not have the support we need, the reality of our children's emotional needs can be unbearable. Even if we can stretch ourselves, the moment we begin to feel strained, the joy goes out of parenting.

We are more likely to invent parenting short cuts and compromises when we have entirely unrealistic expectations of ourselves as parents – that is, that we can do it alone, without the supportive and regular input of an extended family, or a social group. When we think of parenting more as a communal endeavour, rather than as a nuclear family enterprise, much of the struggle of child rearing falls away. Parenting is meant to be a much more pleasurable experience than it is for many people today.

So, what are the influences that support us to fulfil our potential as parents?

Our own childhood histories

No experience from our earliest years is lost to us; we saw that in Chapter 23. Perhaps the most powerful influence on how we respond to the many challenges of parenting, are those experiences of our own carers which we have stored as emotional memory, or as implicit, body memory. How many times have you heard yourself, or someone you know, say, 'Oh my goodness, I just sounded exactly like my mother!' or, 'I swore I would never speak to my child like my dad did to me. Now, when I open up my mouth to speak, I hear my dad!' Our childhood experiences are so deeply ingrained in our bodies, that they permeate our thoughts, feelings and behaviours without our realising it. In particular, our automatic responses that erupt under stress are often faithful representations of how we were once treated. Thus, the well-nurtured seem to act kindly towards their children as a matter of reflex. Those who tyrannise their children, on the other hand, are re-enacting their own oppression.

It is our own personal childhood history, with its unique blend of oft-forgotten joys and sorrows, which holds the key to our parenting style. At various times during parenting, we all must confront and heal our own childhood wounds that confound our ability to see our children for who they are.

The link between childhood experience and parenting style has received much attention from social researchers. When parents have suffered a painful loss, either recently or during childhood, any lingering, unresolved grief can compromise the quality of their parenting; their infants may be less securely attached.[3] This is particularly true if they had lost their own attachment figures, and have not fully mourned their loss.

Australians were recently confronted by the publication of the 'Stolen generation' report,[4] which detailed the gratuitous removal of thousands of aboriginal children from their families. Many of these wounded souls, it was told, faced considerable difficulties when the time came to parent their own children.

Our parenting skills are learned through the way our own parents treat us. In fact, a child's quality of attachment to both parents can be predicted, before he is born, on the basis of how secure his parents felt as children.[5] Mothers who have an unresolved history of insecure attachment, may be more at risk of mistreating their own children.[6] There are many more studies suggesting that parents' attachment histories get passed down.[7]

Children of physical or sexual abuse survivors also tend to be less securely attached, if their parents have not sought healing for their traumas. At times, parents' post-traumatic reactions make them behave in ways that frighten their children. Parents that have suffered abuse as children are many times more likely to abuse their own.[8]

When a new baby enters our lives, her presence powerfully evokes from our unconscious memory a plethora of feelings, both positive and negative, that we felt when we were infants. Many parents find themselves overcome by waves of love and tenderness, beyond anything they have known in their adult lives. Emotional memory floods our senses, though we usually cannot link this memory to specific events. My own daughter brought back to me some childhood feelings that had been wiped from my consciousness for decades. I can now distinctly recapture the ineffable sense of magic that permeated all things around me when I was at the age she is now. Each of my toys was much more than a toy; it was a door to a parallel universe, a fantastic story waiting to unfold. At every new stage of our children's lives, some our most deeply buried childhood feelings come wafting to the surface, altering our attitudes and behaviour.

If we felt rejected or abandoned as infants, it is possible that we may find ourselves feeling resentful, even hostile towards our children. If our own childhood emotional needs weren't met, we might find our children's dependency intolerable. It is hard to give what has not been given us, and our babies' cries assail our ears unbearably. These kinds of feelings are not of themselves a danger, if we can recognise where they come from. Abuse or neglect take place when we blame our children for the way we feel – instead of recognising the true source of our feelings.

On the other hand, when parents have had a secure attachment history, their nurturance flows more freely. They are therefore more likely to have children who can express their feelings and find resolution for their emotional difficulties.[9] A Swedish study found that expectant mothers who had experienced more emotional warmth from their own mothers were better able to establish an affectionate relationship with their unborn baby.[10]

So, although we study the manuals, attend the courses and learn new skills, under stress our parenting responses frequently reflect what was done to us. Manuals are not enough. Parenting books tell us a lot about 'what to do when', or 'what to do if'. What they rarely help us with is how to cultivate our emotional capacities; our patience, our endurance, our humour and our playfulness. The ability to be lovingly present, and emotionally responsive, cannot be learned from a book.

Working through personal blocks to parenting

Parents who express anger or disappointment about any mistreatment they received as children are less likely to pass on this mistreatment to their own children.[11] If we can be honest with ourselves about our emotional wounds, and if we allow ourselves our grief, we free ourselves from the tendency to repeat history.

A group of American psychologists who were working with mothers that were indifferent and neglectful towards their babies, invited them to talk about their childhoods. They helped these mothers to connect with their own pain, and to cry. Immediately after this emotional release, these mothers spontaneously cuddled their babies. Their nurturing energies had been walled up behind a layer of frozen, unexpressed grief.[12]

The willingness to reflect upon one's own emotional development is a keystone to our growth as parents. As we develop our capacity for insight, healing experiences are available in many forms. Many people have turned to counselling or psychotherapy, and found these to be extremely helpful. By deepening our self-awareness, psychotherapy can renew and refresh our relationships with our children so we do not pass on to them painful aspects of our own childhood histories. One of the greatest gifts of parenthood lies in the way our children, just by being themselves, can help us to see where our wounds are. The way to transform our relationship with our children is to heal ourselves.

Many people seem to find profound healing through their work or expressive arts, through loving relationships or spiritual pursuits. Our own personal growth is important if we are to offer each successive generation increasing attunement to their emotional needs.

Memory's role in empathy for our children

Real empathy means seeing and feeling the world from a child's point of view. This hinges on our ability to recollect how we ourselves once felt as children. It is when we have lost our connection to our own childhood feelings that we risk passing our hurts on to our children.

When we encounter persistent and recurring difficulties in a specific stage of parenting, this might be a sign that we were wounded at the same stage. It can be enormously fruitful then to ask ourselves, 'What was happening to me at the age that my child is now? How did that make me feel?' This kind of self-inquiry can be extremely helpful in deepening our empathy and understanding, while highlighting that which wants healing inside each of us.

Our children make us better parents, and also better people; and in this regard they give us as much as we give them. Without knowing it, they help to shape our emotional intelligence as we contribute to theirs.

Importance of social support

Early psychoanalysts made a fatal error: they blamed mothers for their children's mental illnesses.[13]

Parents alone should never be blamed, nor be made to feel singularly responsible for neglectful or insufficient parenting. Parents do not exist in a vacuum. As we saw earlier, parenting is deeply influenced and limited by our childhood history. But also as parents we are as good as the supporters we have behind us.

In other words, to give of our best, we depend on back-up. The welfare of children is a wider social responsibility.

In our culture of privacy, social isolation and dislocation, the concept of group or 'tribal' child rearing is difficult to embrace. Parenting could be a joy; it becomes a burden when we are bereft of community. Our culture rewards the stoic trooper who does it alone, we give a pat on the back to the self-sacrificial. You've seen it a dozen times: a magazine awards a struggling single parent a 'Super Mum' or 'Super Dad' tag, because they can hold together a large family while working two jobs. Struggling parents don't need to be made into heroes, and they don't need medals. They need help, and they need community.

Research shows that lack of support from community or from her partner is particularly ruinous to a mother's capacity to be emotionally responsive to her baby. Absence of social support for parents results in insecurely attached infants, because social support affects the quality of parenting directly; it makes parents more responsive to their children's needs.[14]

Most importantly, support for parents needs to address their emotional needs. Mothers who do not feel emotionally supported may be more at risk of committing child abuse.[15] This does not make her a bad mother; every one of us has a breaking point. The most loving individuals can behave monstrously when chronically starved of emotional support. That is why social isolation is known to be a risk factor in child abuse; it deprives parents of one of the most vital enabling factors.

An abundance of research from the USA, Germany, Israel and Japan has demonstrated that good partner support is essential for maternal sensitivity, and consequently for infant security.[16] Marital difficulties, poor emotional support from her partner and her social network are most detrimental to a mother's ability to show affection to her child.[17]

We can now understand why downtrodden women from patriarchal societies find it hard to maintain the kind of emotional responsiveness that is so essential for their children's emotional health. For a mother to be able to mother, she must feel emotionally and materially supported by her partner, her family and her community. Without emotional support she suffers, and her capacity to mother suffers. Gender equality (by this I mean that neither gender dominates the other, not that both genders must have equal roles all the time) is crucial for emotionally healthy children. If history's parents have been cruel and neglectful, as we saw in Part II, that's because most cultures have been heavily patriarchal, men have been neglected, brutalised and manipulated, and women have been devalued and abused.

If low socio-economic status and poverty are risk factors for child abuse,[18] it's because impoverished parents struggle more to survive, and are therefore less likely to feel supported to be the parents they want to be. Community support is therefore particularly urgent among low-income families.

Responsibility for children's wellbeing is as societal and communal as it is parental. A family's commitment to its children requires the backing of conducive social and industrial policy, and quality parenting education.

Role of alloparents

In her book Mother Nature, anthropologist Sarah Blaffer Hrdy[19] underscores the critical importance of 'alloparents' for the success of child rearing. Alloparents are secondary parents who have a special and ongoing relationship to the child, whether they are grandparents, other kin, or close friends of the family.

Since the birth of our species, mothers have depended on others for help with child rearing. The same is true for many other species. Co-operative parenting exists among – to name but a few examples – wolves, tamarinds, marmosets, and elephants. Based on her extensive studies of primates, as well as of traditional and modern cultures around the world, Hrdy concluded that the best predictor of a mother's commitment to her infant is the amount and quality of support available to her. If, over millions of years, women have evolved to reach menopause – and thus become infertile – while they are still so young and able, perhaps it is for a good reason. Nature usually harbours a wonderful method in her madness. With the wisdom and patience that only maturity in age can provide, grandparents and great-grandparents are vital organs of the family body. Our nurturing role does not cease when our children are grown up. In pilot whales, elephants, and in humans, grannies increase breeding success. Even monkey mothers pick up their mothering skills from grandmothers, relying on the elder's assistance along the way. The idea that we humans can raise our children without the help of our elders has led to inevitable and costly compromises. What we offer our children is a downsized version of what they really need.

The role of alloparent is not only open to grandparents. When we think of co-operative parenting, we can include grandparents, other kin, trusted friends, teachers, and individuals with whom we share common values. In foraging societies, allomothers are recognised as essential for the wellbeing of infants. Among the Agta of the Philippines and the Efe of Central Africa, for instance, each newborn is greeted by a community of friends and relatives. Alloparental care is what the human child is born to expect; it is an evolutionary imperative. It also exists among many of our animal cousins.

I strongly suggest to all prospective parents to think, as part of your preparation for your baby: who will be your alloparents? Even if we are separated by distance or disagreement from our biological families, there is no reason why we cannot gather around us a loyal, tribe-like co-operative parenting group. Bonds of friendship, common vision and values can be as strong as biological ties – if we let them be. Modern day mothers' groups, formed by mothers who meet at birthing centres or antenatal classes, are a wonderful step in this direction. The key to their success lies in shared parenting values, and a willingness to give and receive support.

Historically, child abuse and neglect has been related to a lack of co-operative parenting and allomothers. At the 1990 world conference on infanticide sponsored by the National Science Foundation in Erice, Sicily, attendees agreed that infanticide rates were highest in societies that had no contraception, and no access to allomaternal support. As we saw in Chapter 4, the group-mothering approach of 19th century Sardinia, for instance, ensured a far lower infant abandonment rate than for surrounding cultures. That was in spite of the fact that Sardinia was relatively poor.

The strain that many parents suffer in trying to be closely involved with their children comes from their attempt to do what it takes a village to do – without the support of the village. In order to nurture, the parent must be nurtured.

What causes post natal depression?

These days it is popular to assume that all kinds of depression are caused by freak hormonal aberrations. We have a smorgasbord of pharmaceuticals at our disposal – and sometimes, they can be helpful. But since our society became drug-addicted, we have stopped recognising some of the very real situational factors that cause depression, and thus we undervalue the restorative things we can do to feel stronger again.

Post natal depression (PND) is a common and devastating syndrome that can make parenting burdensome, even nightmarish. It robs families of the joy that a new child can bring when circumstances are otherwise favourable.

It seems that there are some genetic predispositions to PND, but these influences are only modest.[20] Studies show that what knocks a mother into depression is the gulf that exists between her emotional needs surrounding the birth of her child, and her actual circumstances. The moment her baby comes, when her need for holding and support is most acute, she finds herself alone for hours at a time, faced with a baby who wails for her attention. Though she may not suspect it, her baby's cries may be triggering her own painful memories of infancy. In modern western cultures, few parents belong to supportive family or tribe-like groups. Furthermore, a mother's social status seems to rank low in our culture. No wonder mothers get depressed!

The fact that PND does not materialise in all societies is a further indicator that it is circumstantial. Among the Kipsigis of Kenya, PND is altogether unknown. Kipsigi mothers receive abundant social support throughout pregnancy and after the baby's birth.[21]

A mother's difficulty relating to babies may predate the birth of her own. Researchers have found that women who are more bothered by the sound of a baby crying are more likely to develop PND once their own baby arrives.[22] The sound of a baby's cry can be quite aversive to those who have unresolved, painful unconscious memories from infancy. Mothers who felt emotionally deprived in their early years find the demands of a baby particularly nerve-racking, and this places them at risk of PND.[23] A new baby acts as an extremely powerful trigger, causing the mother's emotional memories of infancy to resurface. If she had difficulties with attachment to her own mother, her pain may re-emerge, though she may not consciously know why she is crying. The link between childhood experiences and proneness to PND has been borne out by research. Women who feel their own mothers were less than caring enough, or that their fathers were overprotective, are more likely to suffer from PND.[24] An ongoing, emotionally supportive and empathic relationship with her own mother can be the most potent vaccine against PND.

Fathers are vital protectors of their family's emotional welfare, and their lack of support can be costly. Many women who suffer from PND report that their partners are either unsupportive, or controlling.[25]

For some mothers PND may be a mistaken diagnosis: they might in fact be suffering from post-traumatic stress disorder (PTSD). For many women, the experience of labour can be highly traumatic. Around 20 per cent of mothers lose at least some memory of the labour experience: they report being in a 'fog'. This partial amnesia is a kind of dissociation, and a classic symptom of trauma.[26] British psychologists have found that two to five per cent of mothers get full-blown PTSD after a difficult childbirth. A much larger proportion suffer symptoms of PTSD, such as nightmares, intrusive thoughts, problems with breastfeeding, feelings of failure, feelings of estrangement and difficulty bonding to their baby.[27] The cold, clinical atmosphere and the intrusiveness of defensive obstetrics can feel violating for many women. Mothers usually feel extremely vulnerable at this time, and modern obstetric wards place insufficient emphasis on her psychological needs. Some hospital staff trivialise and minimise mothers' emotional ups and downs through this delicate process, their terror, their pain, and their loss of control, as if the only thing that matters is that mother and child have survived the process physically unscathed. Jean Robinson, research officer at the Association for Improvements in the Maternity Services (UK) says that the incidence of PTSD among new mothers has risen along with an increase in interventions such as induced labour and caesarean section. But even after normal births, symptoms of PTSD can arise when mothers are made to feel helpless, disempowered and their right to make birthing decisions is taken away from them.[28] We dismiss these birthing-related emotional traumas and their consequences at a grave cost to mothers and their babies.

As at every other stage of mothering, a raft of emotional support for the mother is extremely important during labour. The sensitive support of a companion has such profound effects, it actually reduces medical complications at labour quite significantly. Mothers who are accompanied by a female supporter (in addition to their male partners) have shorter labour, less incidence of caesarean section, and their babies are less likely to require neonatal intensive care.[29]

Childcare

Why is childcare often not like good alloparental support? As we shall see below, compelling evidence confirms what attachment theory would predict. Institutional childcare is problematic when it does not provide opportunities for children to develop selective attachments to affectionate and dependable adults.[30]

When they examine the research data, child development experts do not have many good things to say about our modern trend for institutionalised childcare. A review of 88 studies conducted around the world, involving over 20,000 children, found that institutionalised care in infancy increases the risk of insecure attachment by 66 per cent.[31] Australian psychiatrist Peter Cook concludes that the childcare trend "overlooks accumulating evidence of risks" and "is contrary to much expert opinion about what is likely to be best for infants".[32]

Some researchers have tried to quantify the level of childcare that might constitute a risk factor. One study found that for children who are less than one year old, over 20 hours per week in childcare can lead to emotional insecurity.[33] Another found that children in long day care tend to have higher levels of the stress hormone cortisol.[34] These alarmingly high levels of cortisol have been detected in long day care children even if they show no outward signs of distress[35] – so that their parents and carers might be unaware of their suffering.

It seems the more time children spend in childcare, the more aggressive they tend to become. Findings such as these have led Jay Belsky – former professor of Human Development at Penn State University, USA, and now director of the Institute for the Study of Children, Families and Social Issues, Birkbeck, University of London, and internationally recognised expert on the effects of childcare – to assert that "extensive non-parental care initiated in the first year is a risk factor for developments such as insecure attachment to the mother, non-compliance, aggressiveness, and possibly withdrawn behaviour".[36]

The overuse of childcare is a modern trend that I believe most parents would prefer to avoid.[37] It is a tragic fact of modern living that an increasing number of parents in affluent nations find themselves with no choice but to tear themselves from their children, just in order to make ends meet. The cost of housing and other basics is getting pumped ever higher, beyond the reach of a growing sector of societies, by an unrestrained 'market economy'. If this wave of separation of children from

370

their families is not arrested – and wound back – very soon, the social results could be catastrophic. The fragmentation of families is perhaps the biggest threat to the social-evolutionary gains we have created in the last five decades.

One research study found that children in childcare had normal cortisol levels only when this vital condition was met: that their carers were highly responsive to their needs and feelings.[38] I would contend that, in the absence of an extended family or alternative alloparental support (by far the preferable options), the use of professional childcare might be safe provided that the following conditions are met:

1. The child needs to be able to form enduring and warm attachments to carers in the institution.

2. The carers must be empathic, warm, responsive and affectionate. They also need to be constant. Staff turnover forces a child to face the loss of important attachment figures, and then to have to go through another bonding process with new staff.

3. Childcare needs to feel like an extended family.

4. A child needs to be kept in childcare for the least amount of time possible. The main thing is to respect each child's limit, and to understand that there will be considerable variation in the age when each child is ready to face separation. When a child can say goodbye to her mother without crying, and when she is obviously enjoying her time with other people, that's when she is ready. Her separation anxiety is a sign that she is not emotionally ready for separation. The child should be the first 'expert' we consult regarding the appropriateness of childcare.

5. Separation needs to be a gradual transition over which the child has control. It needs to be introduced at the child's speed. Many childcare facilities do not permit parents to stay with their child until she feels at home there. This policy is baseless, and is likely to be traumatic for the child.

6. Parents should stay until the child has formed bonds of trust to others at the centre. Swedish 'open' schools, and many 'democratic' pre-schools around the world invite parents to join in classes with their

children. Parents make invaluable contributions to the group, and the children thrive when all of their environments – that is, home, childcare and school – feel safe, nurturing and familiar.

7. The use of childcare needs to be put off at least until the child is partially weaned. This is so that breastfeeding is not interrupted.

8. The carer–infant ratio needs to be small enough to permit copious, individualised attention and personalised bonding.

9. The child needs to feel securely attached to his parents first, before he ventures out to form other attachments. Childcare may be particularly difficult for children who feel insecure at home.

10. Childcare needs to be avoided at least until the child has mastered enough language to be able to tell her parents how she feels about the people there and about the place.

Conclusion

Just as children need to feel securely attached to their parents, it is within the nurturing 'village' experience that the human brain is given its most favourable conditions for growth. It is when families are held within a supportive community that their hearts can open to the greatest love. The kind of support that promotes a family's emotional wellbeing can be provided without imposing on parents and their children a premature and excessive separation during early childhood. Some proven initiatives for community child rearing and family support will be discussed in the next chapter. We will also look at how the most modern and revolutionary approaches to education have done much to further children's emotional development. Finally, we will look at some exciting social changes that have been unfolding around the world – and many more that we can anticipate – if child rearing continues to evolve.

Endnotes

[1] Co-Director, Clearinghouse on Early Education and Parenting, University of Illinois. See Katz (2003).

[2] Cited in Greenleaf (1978) p 144.

[3] Crittenden and Ainsworth (1989); Main and Hesse (1990).

4   The 700-page report of the 'Stolen children' National Inquiry: 'Bringing them Home', was tabled in Federal Parliament on 26 May 1997: see Human Rights and Equal Opportunity Commission http://www.hreoc.gov.au/social_justice/stolen_children/how_to.html (last accessed 1 December 2004).

5   Main and Hesse (1990); Fonagy, Steele, Moran, Steele and Higgitt (1993).

6   Moncher (1996).

7   Karen (1994).

8   Hall, Sachs and Rayens (1998).

9   Steele, Steele and Johansson (2002).

10 Siddiqui, Hagglof and Eiseman (2000).

11 Hunter and Kilstrom (1979).

12 Karen (1994) p 236.

13 Psychologists said, for instance, that schizophrenia was caused by 'cold mothering' – many of us cringe when we remember the term 'schizophrenogenic mothering'. This caused mothers of disturbed individuals enormous hurt and guilt, on top of the pain they were already feeling for their children. It may take years yet for this collective wound to heal, and for society to trust psychologists again. This narrow view of parents precipitated a backlash against psychology that suppressed many of the important innovations from this field. The social cost has been terrible. Psychologists came to be viewed with suspicion, so that now we treat social and emotional problems expeditiously with pills. This regrettable trend has taken us away from healing, and the community. Drugs certainly contain and relax people; they temporarily dull emotional pain – and as such, they serve a purpose. But this truth must be brought sharply into focus: drugs do not heal. Drugs do not teach us how to gain new relating skills and new emotional intelligences, so we can grow, learn to love ourselves better, and overcome our difficulties.

14 Belsky (1999).

15 Moncher (1995).

16 Belsky (1999); Pauli-Pott, Mertesacker, Bade, Bauer and Beckmann (2000).

17 Stein, Gath, Bucher, Bond, Day and Cooper (1991).

18 Crittenden and Ainsworth (1989).

19 Hrdy (2000).

20 Treloar, Martin, Bucholz, Madden and Heath (1999).

21 Edgerton (1992).

22 Little (1982).

23   Boyce, Hickie and Parker (1991).

24   Boyce, Hickie and Parker (1991).

25   Boyce, Hickie and Parker (1991).

26   Gonda (1998).

27   Bailham and Joseph (2003).

28   Hilpern (2003).

29   Klaus (1986).

30   Rutter and O'Connor (1999).

31   Cook (1996).

32   Cook (1999).

33   Belsky and Cassidy (1994) p 391.

34   Manne (2002).

35   Dettling, Gunnar and Donzella (1999) pp 519–536.

36   Cook (1996) p 77.

37   For details of UK government plans for daycare provision visit http://www.daycaretrust.org.uk/mod.php?mod=userpage& menu=2603&page_id=122 and for details of the longitudinal study by Families, Children & Childcare, http://www. familieschildrenchildcare.org/.

38   Dettling, Parker, Lane, Sebanc and Gunnar (2000) pp 819–836.

31

EMOTIONALLY
HEALTHY CHILDREN:
A COMMUNAL RESPONSIBILITY

nothing would serve us better than to pay whatever it costs to help families give their children adequate, loving care

Robert Karen[1]

Since we are all directly affected by the way children are cared for around the world, we should be concerned that all children are nurtured and educated; that both their physical and emotional needs are met. This includes their need for emotional security, affection and empathy, their freedom from violence, and from economic, sexual, or emotional exploitation. I believe the protection, nurturance and education of the world's children needs to become the number one agenda for all communities, governments and the United Nations. Any mass incidence of child abuse or neglect, whether or not it is culturally sanctioned, endangers and impoverishes the entire world community.

There will always be more for us to learn and discover about the wonder of the human child, but much of the knowledge we need is already available. We now know enough about healthy emotional development to enable us to create societies that are far more peaceful, dynamic and sustainable than the world has ever known. Let's take a look at what is possible if we apply this body of knowledge in the practice of raising our children.

Pay-off for funding parenting support

Parents give of their best when their community is behind them. When psychologist Robert Karen[2] proclaims that we should spend whatever it costs to help families care for their children, he is basing his convictions on solid ground. It is inverted logic to think that any society cannot afford the cost of supporting its parents to stay close to their children through their early years. What we cannot afford is the cost of not doing this.

When social services such as support groups, mentoring programmes or therapeutic interventions are provided for parents who are deemed at risk of maltreating their children, the cycle of abuse is broken.[3]

Government-sponsored home visitation ('early intervention') programmes have proven to be highly beneficial. These programmes involve nurses or trained volunteers regularly visiting mothers at home. They foster the mother's sensitivity towards her infant, and teach her how to interpret her baby's cries as an indication of a need, rather than as a burden or a sign of her failure. Mothers who have been receiving these educational, supportive, practical and helpful services tend to report that their babies cry less and are 'less fussy', and their babies display improved cognitive development. Programmes such as these have reduced the incidence of abuse and neglect,[4] and improved babies' emotional security.[5] Even when home visits are conducted by trained volunteer coaches who have no formal qualifications, babies are helped to become more securely attached.[6]

Between 1975 and 1985 in Hawaii, the 'Hana Like Home Visitor Project' and the 'Healthy Start Programme' were launched, with the goal of preventing child abuse and neglect. Paraprofessionals visited at-risk families during pregnancy and after babies were born. Their aim was to help mothers strengthen bonds with their infants, and to provide emotional support and practical information. Support groups were set up to give mothers a break. Home visits were regular and continued up to five years. These programmes significantly reduced child maltreatment among at-risk families.[7] The success and cost-effectiveness of these programmes has convinced the Hawaiian government to continue funding these kinds of projects, and to give them full legislative support. A 1991 Report of the US Advisory Board of Child Abuse and Neglect recommended the funding and establishment of a national volunteer neonatal home visitation programme. The effectiveness of these programmes is now well established.[8]

In cultures as diverse as Latin America, England, Australia and the USA, recipients of home visits interact better with their infants, and they provide more stimulating home environments. Their children have 'easier' temperaments, better cognitive functioning, and suffer less abuse and neglect. The worst that could be said about these programmes, based on the most conservative cost-benefit calculations, is that they are revenue neutral from the standpoint of government spending.[9] In other words, the least successful of these programmes improves children's wellbeing, at no net cost.

In Syracuse, New York, a large group of low income families were given a trial of extra family support measures until their children reached the age of five. When researchers visited those children at 15, they were performing better at school than similar children whose families had not been placed in the programme, and they were four times less likely to have committed offences! Additionally, they ran away less, had fewer sex partners, smoked less, drank less, and had less behavioural problems related to drug use or alcohol use.[10] Among other benefits, home visitation has also helped to reduce maternal substance abuse during pregnancy, family size, incidence of closely spaced pregnancies, conduct disorders in children and antisocial behaviour among youth.[11]

A multi-faceted support and educational program in London, UK that taught parenting skills to disadvantaged families showed, after a five-year evaluation, a 75 per cent success rate at reducing child maltreatment.[12] A similar project in Connecticut USA found that when extra family support services were provided early to low income families, 10 years later this saved the state an average of $3000 annually, per child, in welfare and special education resources.[13]

Prenatal and early childhood home visitation programmes have been refined, tested and improved over the last two decades. They have been particularly helpful when they teach parents to involve other family and friends, instruct partners to support one another, and if necessary, link them with community and health services.[14] These programmes seem to be most successful when visitations commence during pregnancy, and are followed-up for some time through infancy.[15]

Robert McFarland's community parenting centres – set

up to provide all new parents with child-rearing education, practical and emotional support – were instituted throughout several municipalities of Boulder, Colorado (USA).[16] These centres have not only produced a decrease in child abuse,[17] but also a drop in infant mortality, a steady decrease in the number of children and adolescents dying violently, decreasing youth automotive-death rates and decreasing hospital admissions for injury.[18] Fuelled by their remarkable success, programmes such as these have begun to sprout in many places around the USA, and elsewhere. McFarland is even helping to start a parenting centre in Tajikistan! Parenting centres in Vermont saw their teenage pregnancy rate drop by 36 per cent, welfare dependency drop by 57 per cent, new incidents of child abuse drop by 90 per cent, while the rate of adolescent parents completing high school rose by 58 per cent.[19]

The cost–benefit ratio of supporting parents is immensely attractive. An American study calculated that the cost to society from criminal behaviour, drug use, and high school dropouts for a single youth ranges between US$1.7 million to US$2.3 million.[20] Lloyd de Mause estimates that in the USA it would cost US$5 billion a year to run parenting support centres in every municipality. He estimates that this would result in a total yearly saving of US$750 billion through reductions in social violence.[21] According to McFarland's calculations, every community on earth could provide successful parenting centres similar to his in Boulder, funded through a 'children's tax', equivalent to a one-tenth of one percent increase in sales tax.

Although early intervention programmes are only a fraction of the total support needed by families in order to ensure children's emotional health, their contribution is impressive. A recent review of 70 published studies found early intervention programmes to be universally effective, and that improvements in parental sensitivity helped children to become more emotionally secure.[22]

Research into children's emotional needs has already created massive social changes in a relatively short time. For a child these days, a sojourn at the hospital is a radically different experience than it was in the 1960s. In recognition of the trauma caused by separation, parents are encouraged to stay overnight with their hospitalised children. Orphaned or abandoned children are much more likely to be directed toward adoptive or foster parents, so they may be given personalised care. In most developed countries, the Dickensian orphanages of old have all but been abandoned.[23] However, as we learn more about the social ramifications of child rearing, the need for further changes becomes increasingly obvious, and feels increasingly urgent. Following are some further measures that governments at every level and industry groups need to introduce, to ensure that children are given the opportunity for healthy emotional development. Remember, the social and global dividends would outweigh the costs by far.

Following an extensive analysis of the kinds of policies that most powerfully enable nations to progress, McFarland reached this conclusion, "Helping new mothers and young babies is the most cost-effective form of economic development known".[24] His research demonstrates how societies as diverse as Sweden, Switzerland and the Indian state of Kerala, have progressed through child-rearing reform and through the promotion of education for all children. Education for both boys and girls, according to McFarland, can be even more important than industrialisation.[25]

Government and industry sponsored steps to a peaceful world

Based on what we have learned about the value of better child rearing, I would like to propose a few pro-child and pro-family initiatives that I believe will bring about incalculable social rewards.

1. Grant appropriate maternity and paternity leave provisions. Most European countries have now introduced reasonable maternity leave. Sweden leads the world with almost two years' paid leave. Denmark, Italy and Finland allow for almost a year with pay. Australia, New Zealand, and Canada offer a year, though Australian mothers receive no more than a modest government allowance. While there are State-by-State variations, the American government offers only 12 weeks' leave, without pay. For the richest country on earth, this is a disgrace. Contrast this with Brazil, a far less wealthy nation that gives mothers four months' off on full pay.[26]

2. For mothers who are unable to stop work, make work-places more child-friendly: extend attachment-oriented,

workplace-based childcare, and factor-in breastfeeding breaks.[27]

3. Ensure that a basic education about childhood emotional development is available to all, through programmes in high school, and public education campaigns.

4. Provide regular prenatal and neonatal parenting support home visits such as those mentioned above for all first-time parents and all parents at risk.

5. Ensure that all child health workers are brought up-to-date with new findings from child development research.

6. Encourage group support networks for parents.

7. Help to institute, coordinate and promote volunteer-based community groups that provide caring attachment figures for the children of families in need.[28]

8. Legislate against the use of corporal punishment in the home, as well as at school.

9. Financial incentives for retirees and for grandparents to care for their own grandchildren in-house – perhaps even for others' grandchildren if some training and certification is provided. Our governments should reward pensioners for home-based, family-centred care of their grandchildren.

An education revolution

Most education systems benefit children, provided that they help children feel empowered, independent, less vulnerable to exploitation, and more able to think for themselves. When education is freely available to all girls and boys, this is a considerable step towards social progress.

The spread of universal education over the last 200 years has certainly had a civilising effect on humanity. However, a further leap in social evolution will come as schools around the world renounce the shaming and punishment of children, and learn to truly respect each individual child for his or her uniqueness, and his or her individual interests.

Innovative applications based on attachment theory are revolutionising the way we educate our young. Teachers are learning to better manage children's 'behavioural problems' without recourse to punishment, while protecting the child's dignity and self-esteem. A project conducted in an Australian pre-school[29] demonstrated that children's inappropriate or disruptive behaviour could be dramatically reduced – and teacher satisfaction sharply increased – once they were helped to feel personally connected to an emotionally available teacher. A secure emotional base, established through empathic relationships with teachers, was demonstrably a highly effective method of 'discipline'. The predilection for punishing 'bad' behaviour is being relegated to the annals of history, while we learn instead to understand and address the hurt that underlies children's disruptiveness.

As we step into the age of 'helping mode' child rearing, we find ourselves dropping the old – and utterly invalid – idea that children must be coerced in order to learn. Coercive education has brought a lot of humiliation, and needless suffering into children's lives at school – while creating unnecessary headaches for teachers. New educational methods that emphasise trusting children, respecting rather than patronising them, and allowing them greater liberty in how they tackle their learning journeys, are burgeoning around the world. Educators are discovering that every child has a unique learning profile, and that when children are allowed to follow their natural interests at their own pace, they learn with incredible efficiency, and without the need for enforcement. This method raises the level of respect between teacher and pupil.

Helping mode educators recognise that schooling can be an instrument for peace; if the teaching style models tolerance, compassion, and a commitment to appreciate individual differences – rather than measuring children against statistical norms. In varying degrees, this kind of philosophy is evidenced in a range of new trends that are too numerous to mention here in depth (for example, the 'Reggio Emilia' system, the Sudbury system, the Rudolf Steiner and Montessori systems (see related websites below)). One of the most rapidly growing of these movements is that of 'democratic education', a system that is expressly devoted to teaching children how to be socially responsible, self-motivated individuals who live democratically and sustainably. Democratically run schools have joined forces to create a dynamic and expanding international network.

In 2002, an International Democratic Education Conference (IDEC) was held in Christchurch, New Zealand. It was attended by around 200 teachers and school principals from 10 countries. The IDEC conference is held annually, to facilitate the exchange of research and development. The 2003 conference, held in New York, attested to the speedy growth of this movement. This time, there were 500 educators, students, and parents in attendance from over 90 schools throughout the United States, and from 25 other countries.[30]

IDEC members agreed that Article 26(2) of the International Declaration of Children's Rights, which is directed toward freedom, tolerance and understanding, constitutes a working framework for the day-to-day practice in democratic learning environments. In a nutshell, this means that students are given a vote over curricular and administrative decisions that affect their lives.

In Japan, what they call the 'free school system' now claims nearly 100 schools. There are at least 250 similar schools in the USA, and many more throughout Europe and Asia. But this movement is most advanced in Israel, where it is spearheaded by visionary educator Yaacov Hecht. Having founded over 26 democratic schools in Israel, Hecht is now the head of the Israeli Institute for Democratic Education. He has established a Faculty of Democratic Education at the Hakibbutzim College in Tel Aviv, which conducts research and development, trains new teachers in democratic methods, and publishes four books a year in the field. What propels Hecht is his conviction that the democratisation of schools will create individuals that are more self-directed, socially responsible, and more embracing of human diversity − a vital insurance for the future of humankind. In keeping with this larger social-ecological purpose, the Institute operates an ambitious project called 'education for peace' which is currently democratising 200 regular public schools in Israel.[31]

In England, dozens of schools embrace principles of democratic education to varying degrees. The oldest one, Summerhill, has been operating successfully for over 80 years, and serves as a model for hundreds of schools worldwide.[32] As the trend toward more democratic education gathers momentum, more such schools have opened in 30 countries around the world.[33]

In a seminar that took place in Sydney in 2003, Hecht recounted how not long ago, the mayor of Tel Aviv contacted Hecht to ask for his help. A school that was rated the most violent in Tel Aviv, was about to be closed down. Hecht was invited to democratise the educational method in this school to see if this would lower the rate of violence. A couple of years later, this school had been turned around dramatically: it earned the rating of the least violent in the city, and its students were rated as the most satisfied with their school. Hecht states that the measure of success of democratic schools is the rate of violence between students. This rate is consistently low among Israel's democratic schools. Why? When a child feels that his or her uniqueness is honoured and valued, he or she is in a position to appreciate every other child's uniqueness. The same experience has been reported in Japan, where the 'free school' system has proved to be a powerful antidote to the school bullying epidemic that plagues their mainstream schools. Hecht does not hesitate to declare that democratic education is the way of the future, and it is an extremely effective inoculation against social and international violence.[34]

Close by, a Palestinian refugee named Hussein Issa dreamed of educating children non-traditionally, in the principles of peace, democracy and tolerance. He formed a democratic school with Israeli Eyal Bloch, near Bethlehem. Children from these two otherwise antagonistic cultures were bussed weekly to shared grounds, where they learned each other's language, prayers, customs, heard each others' traditional songs, and forged deep bonds of friendship, through the vehicle of a co-operative agricultural project. They called it the Hope Flower Project.[35] In a world that is riven by ethnic hatred, dictatorship and cataclysmic weaponry, one can hardly imagine a more vital educational emphasis. This is a perfect example of the way in which better child rearing can break the cycle of violence created by religious extremism and tribalism.

Do the goals of fostering children's emotional intelligence and social responsibility undermine academic performance? Far from it. Research from the US, UK, and Japan shows that students attending democratic schools are academically and socially on par with or better off than those from conventional schools.[36]

Another developing trend, that of home schooling, has been inspired by eminent educators such as John Holt, author of *How Children Learn* (1983), and *Teach Your Own* (1981), and John Gatto, author of *Dumbing Us Down: the Hidden Curriculum of Compulsory Schooling* (1991). Home schooling is another viable and dynamic alternative to regimented schooling, and it mainly involves parents helping children to follow an approved curriculum at home. Home schooling seems to be most highly developed in the USA, where estimates of the number of registered home schoolers range up to 2 million, a figure that is growing annually at a rate of seven to 15 per cent.[37] A number of other developed nations such as the UK, Germany, Switzerland and Japan have thriving home schooling movements. By some estimates, Australian home-schoolers could number as high as 60,000.[38] Home schooling families have joined together to create highly organised networks, making home schooling another fast growing trend. Numerous studies have shown that home schoolers rate above average on academic achievement tests, while enjoying better self-esteem and less behavioural problems than their peers.[39]

To learn more about some of these evolutionary changes in education, see these websites:

The Institute for Democratic Education:
www.democratic-edu.org

The Education Revolution:
www.educationrevolution.org

Spirit of Learning:
www.spiritoflearning.com

The Sudbury Valley School:
www.sudval.org

The Reggio Emilia system:
www.cmu.edu/cyert-center/rea.htm

The Rudolph Steiner system:
www.freedom-in-education.co.uk/Steiner.htm

The Montessori system:
www.montessori.edu

Family Unschoolers Network:
www.unschooling.org
Home Education Association Inc:
www.hea.asn.au

These new, non-authoritarian approaches to education will bring inestimable contributions toward world peace and sustainable living.

Is the world becoming a better place?

In the new millennium, humanity has come face-to-face with threats that exceed anything we have ever known. Recently released documents reveal just how close the world came to an apocalyptic nuclear war around 40 years ago.[40] Nevertheless, I believe that the principles of social justice and human rights are far more established now in many places around the world, than they have been at any other time in history.[41] Social improvements will continue to grow apace, wherever child rearing continues to evolve.

Over the last century, we have benefited from a considerable number of new developments in the area of social justice that have no precedent in the history of nation states. These include the criminalisation of war atrocities, and the capture and prosecution of perpetrators at an international court. Concerted, multinational interventions have helped to limit civil conflicts and injustice in hot-spots as diverse as South Africa, Rwanda, East Timor, and Liberia. Though this restorative measure is insufficient, the negotiated partial return of lands to some dispossessed indigenous peoples, such as in parts of Canada, Australia and New Zealand, has no parallel in human history. As we saw in Parts II and III, political activism is increasingly non-violent, and mass protests against war and racism attract millions of supporters around the world.

Modern societies have taken formidable strides towards gender equality, freedom of self-expression and tolerance of diversity. Often these advancements are enshrined in legislation.

In 1990, only 10 per cent of countries had ratified all six of the world's major human rights instruments, but by 2000, nearly half of all countries had.

Further, there has never been a moment in history when such a large proportion of humanity has had access to democratic processes. In 1985, there were only 44 democratic countries and 67 dictatorships. Tyrants were way out in front. By 2000, there were 82 democratic countries, and only 26 with authoritarian governments.[42]

During the 1980s and 1990s, UN Human Development Reports [43] stated that 81 countries took significant steps toward democracy, and today, 140 countries hold multi-party elections.

Although democracy is severely compromised when special-interest lobbies dominate government through campaign donations, world democratisation is progressing with remarkable velocity. At this rate of change, it is not unrealistic to expect that within the lifetimes of most of us, almost every country on earth will become – to varying degrees – 'democratised'. This is good news for many reasons, not the least of which is that, as history demonstrates, democratic nations are extremely unlikely to make war against each other.[44] Globalisation of democracy is one of the most reliable guarantees of world peace – and this is the predestined outcome of the democratisation of child rearing.

In social evolutionary time-scale terms, we are today experiencing a very rapid march towards a peaceful, integrated and just global society, the pace and scope of which is entirely unprecedented.

Based on recent world events, and the saturation of media with images of global atrocities, one could be forgiven for thinking that the world is becoming more and more hopelessly violent. And yet, believe it or not, human violence is actually declining. Over the 20th century, combat deaths exceeded 100 million people, and over 170 million people died at the hands of governments, thanks to technologies for destruction that have grown to monstrous proportions. However, as a ratio of total populations, adult war deaths have plummeted for modern democracies. Archaeological evidence tells us that with very few exceptions, most foraging societies and early agricultural civilisations were at war almost incessantly – or at least far more frequently than modern societies.[45] Whereas among foraging and early agricultural societies an average of 25 per cent of adults would die at war,[46] this average fell to less than 10 per cent in early modernity. Among modern democratic nations, an average of less than one percent of adult deaths are war casualties.[47] In fact, in 2002, the World Health Organization estimated that around the world only 0.3 per cent of deaths were caused by war[48]. Considering the high-tech weaponry that abounds today, this suggests that humanity has made considerable progress in finding non-violent means of dispute resolution.

Most of us are appalled by modern rates of gun and knife ownership and violent crime, yet our past is even more grim. Homicide rates in Mediaeval and early modern history, when most people carried knives or swords, were about 10 times higher than they are now for most modern, democratic nations.[49] We are much better equipped to kill, and yet we are murdering each other less. No amount of social violence will ever be less than horrific – but it is important to note that there has been a steady decline in violence over the ages. Even though we still live in a violent world, the average citizen of a modern democracy knows more peace than our forebears could have dreamed of.

The impact of economic growth in its present form is causing devastating environmental harm, bringing the planet perilously close to a catastrophic decline in viability. Climate change is the greatest challenge facing humanity at the start of the twenty first century [50]. But there are signs that humanity is undergoing a seismic shift in consciousness in relation to our natural environment. Populations are awakening to these environmental, economic and social challenges, and rallying in waves of socially responsible action that span the globe.

Consider this: when in 1787, the abolitionist (anti-slavery) movement began in London, it was the first time in history that a citizen group was formed to defend the rights of people that they didn't even know, and to file grievances on behalf of others. Contrast that to the contemporary world with its myriad social justice groups, and we discover a prodigious growth in human compassion.

Today, almost two million organisations exist worldwide promoting social justice, indigenous rights and environmental sustainability – striving for a common purpose despite the fact that most are unaware of each other, that there is no stand-out leader, no figurehead and no single unifying manifesto[51].

This is suggestive of a collective shift in human consciousness: we seem to be poised on the threshold of a more empathic, 'we-centred' rather than 'me-centred' social ecology.

These reassuringly positive trends are, I believe, a direct result of the continued evolution in child rearing. From 1960–2001, the world mortality rate for children under five dropped from 197 per thousand births to 82 per thousand births. Literacy and education rates are slowly increasing, and the gender gap for education is slowly closing. In 1990, world literacy for boys was 82 per cent, and 69 per cent for girls. In 2000, boys are up to 85 per cent, and girls up to 74 per cent.[52]

Tolerance and justice are not entirely unknown to history – they have surfaced from time to time, in less authoritarian and less patriarchal societies. What is radically new is the scale, scope and endurance of the human commitment to universal human rights.

Current impediments to further social evolution

Global poverty represents one area of social-evolutionary inertia. UN reports have found that progress on poverty has ground to a halt, and 54 countries are poorer now than they were in 1990. This is certainly one of the bigger threats to advancements in parenting. History has shown when parents are placed under dire stress, their capacity to be emotionally attuned to their children suffers, and even collapses.

While humanity slowly moves away from overt violence, we seem to be finding new ways to be exploitative. Economic globalisation has been sold worldwide as a golden egg, full of promise. Ostensibly, 'free trade' and 'free market' reforms have been imposed to help poor nations to develop, and undoubtedly, some of the intended benefits have materialised. But when 'help' masks exploitation, a 'gift' turns out to be a Trojan Horse. Some aspects of economic globalisation have brought about an explosion of poverty and social chaos for many developing nations. A detailed and authoritative analysis of the social effects of globalisation was presented by Nobel Prize winning economist Joseph Stiglitz, who was vice president of the World Bank and chief economic advisor to a US president. His report shows that some of the economic reforms imposed on developing nations by the world's chief lending institutions (such as the International Monetary Fund (IMF)) have lined the pockets of western corporations while undermining the social and economic frameworks of the nations they are supposed to be helping.[53]

Thanks to globalisation, while world income increased by 2.5 per cent annually in the last decade of the 20th century, an extra 100 million people plunged into poverty.[54] In fact, since the inception of the World Bank and the IMF, the wealth gap existing between the world's richest 20 per cent and the poorest 20 per cent has more than doubled.[55] Some 'free trade' agreements have caused a drop in incomes, and an increase in unemployment in poor countries, as the cost of essential services soared due to enforced privatisation and monopolisation. We should all, even the wealthiest and most selfish among us, be extremely worried about this trend. The World Health Organization recognises that poverty and the inequitable distribution of wealth is one of the principal conditions that breed endemic social violence.[56] How can anyone who is struggling to survive give their children the time and emotional nurturance they need? Extreme poverty sabotages children's emotional development.

The World Trade Organization has repeatedly intruded upon sovereign governance, preventing countries from enacting laws to protect the environment, and forcing them to rescind fair labour laws, on the pretext that these laws interfere with 'free trade'.[57] As a condition for qualifying for desperately needed loans, many developing countries have been explicitly forced to slash spending on education and health.[55] This aspect of globalisation is systematically dismantling the very structures that move societies towards peace and sustainability, and it is ravaging the lives of millions of children. In its current and exploitative form, globalisation is sowing the seeds of a disastrous social devolution that will, if unchecked, haul us back toward a more violent and inequitable world. There is nothing wrong with globalisation per se, and there are many benefits to be gained. But as Stiglitz points out, economic measures that compromise social development will eventually backfire. Economic and social gains are scuttled if we don't put children and their families first.

Of further concern is the fact that the global arms trade has arrested its downward slide since the end of the Cold War, and has begun to climb again, quite steeply. The technology of war remains the largest sector of expenditure in the world, at over one trillion dollars annually, and it has been rising in recent years. World military expenditure in 2005 was estimated to comprise 2.5 per cent of world GDP, or an average spending of $173 per person. In 2005 it had increased by 3.4 per cent in one year, and 34 per cent over 10 years. [58]

One can barely imagine the miracles that could be achieved if military spending was diverted towards education, poverty eradication, development of renewable energy, and environmental restoration. A peaceful, just and sustainable global society rests on childrearing reforms and the improved human relations that would follow.

Are there alternatives to war?
So far, the so-called 'War Against Terror' seems to have caused as many problems as it has solved. Australian intelligence analysts repeatedly warned the federal government, before it joined the US-led coalition, that invading Iraq would inflame extremism and increase terrorist recruitment. Britain's joint intelligence

committee also advised that the threat of international terrorism would be "heightened by military action against Iraq".[58] These warnings proved to have been well founded. The London-based International Institute of Strategic Studies has declared that far from dealing a blow to al-Qaeda and making the USA and its allies safer, the American-led Iraq invasion has substantially strengthened Osama bin Laden's al-Qaeda network, increased their fundraising and recruitment drives, while placing the west in further danger of attack.[59] It should come as no surprise that military action in Iraq has helped to make violent extremists more popular. War is not the answer to terrorism, because this is a policy that fails to take into account the childhood causes of violence. Unless measures are taken to eliminate violence toward children in the strongholds of terrorist organisations, bombing can only serve to shift the problem from one place to another.

A social disinterest in violence will only be secured via respectful, non-punitive child rearing. This can be brought about through international reforms to gender relations, and reforms to child rearing and education in societies where religious or political extremism dominate government policy.

Far less costly and a great deal more effective than a 'War Against Terror', would be an international effort to sponsor free, non-partisan education for every boy and girl around the world. While the US defence budget exceeded US$360 billion in 2002, the Bush administration spent only US$25 million on fostering political reform in the Arab world. This is a ratio of 400:1 between military and political effort.[60] Meanwhile, it was recently estimated that it would cost as little as US$10 billion to bring education to the 180 million children in the world who don't have access to schools. This is 40 times less than what the world spends on cigarettes, 300 times less than what the world spends on military, and 16 times less than what the world spends on beer.[61] The quest for peace through better child rearing is many times cheaper – not to mention infinitely less traumatic – than answering violence with more violence.

Lasting and worthwhile change can only happen at the level of culture, that is, in the domains of family relations, child rearing and education. Gender egalitarian societies raise their children less violently, and until such societies become the norm, international disputes will be managed via the gun. An international resolve to sponsor free and non-partisan education for all boys and girls, enactment – and policing – of laws protecting women and children; these are the kinds of measures that will ultimately bring about the end of terrorism and war. The spread of democratic processes and press freedom are indisputably preconditions for a peaceful world. However, I believe history has demonstrated – as we saw in Part III – that democracy cannot be imposed upon a culture from above. Nations produce their own grassroots democratic movements as their cultures evolve away from authoritarianism, and as family relationships become more democratic.

What's in store for the future?

This book has brought together the findings of many disciplines: of psychohistory, neuroscience, child psychology and social psychology. On this subject, these diverse arts and sciences speak with one voice: we can be assured that any society that invests in its families, and in its children's emotional development, will see a huge proportion of its costly social problems dissolve. Since social progress rests on child-rearing reform, it is not guaranteed, and it is therefore possible for societies to devolve and become more violent. If we are to reap the benefits of a continuing child-rearing evolution, our collective, deliberate efforts will be required.

We saw in earlier chapters that social changes that would have been considered utopian and unrealistic 200 years ago have come to pass. If more cultures continue to move towards helping mode child rearing we can expect this evolutionary process to continue.

When we realise the range of social problems that are caused by entirely remediable and avoidable child-rearing practices, some of our more utopian ideals about the future begin to appear realistic, perhaps even inevitable. I would like to propose a number of social improvements that we can reasonably expect as an outcome of the evolution of child rearing, based on what we have come to know about core emotional development.

Since governments mirror family types, the spread of democratic family structures, and democratic education, will fuel the spread of democracy around the world. As families become less patriarchal, less authoritarian, and as schools continue to become less repressive and coercive, individuals will forcefully demand more democratic processes as well as contribute more responsibly to their societies. We can also expect existing democracies to become more advanced, with more diversified and independent media, more transparent administration, less collusion between powerful vested interests and government, and more use of referenda and other consultative processes.

The right to vote and freely express opinion will increasingly be considered an indivisible and universal human right. Therefore dictatorship and autocracy will itself be considered illegal; a crime against humanity. Nations will act in concert to pressure any remaining autocratic governments to surrender to their people's will; through verifiable free elections and evidence of an analytical and critical press.

If democratic processes continue to improve and spread, armed conflict between nations will become a thing of the past. Since war is an organised, collective expression of severe childhood trauma, the continued evolution of child rearing will eliminate it. International disputes will increasingly be resolved through recourse to international law. This will bring about an enormous reduction in military expenditure, freeing-up mountains of global capital for development, combating poverty, and environmental repair. As a further spin-off of democratisation, a code of Universal Human Rights and Children's Rights will finally be ratified, adopted and policed by all nations.

The research we examined in the chapters on emotional development demonstrated that to a large extent, anti-social behaviour, domestic violence, delinquency, drug and alcohol abuse are the results of insecure attachment, and other accumulated emotional wounds from childhood. We can look forward to a considerable diminution in all of these social problems as children's lives become less traumatic.

It is also made quite clear by the research that a sharp fall in mental health problems such as depression, personality disorders and ADHD is in store for us if we keep improving the emotional lives of children. The return to breastfeeding and natural weaning will reduce the incidence of obesity, diabetes, and generally enhance our natural resistance to disease.

As family relationships become more sustainable, we will live more sustainably. Our almost limitless human capacity for inventiveness will be geared towards sustainable technologies that operate in harmony with nature, rather than in competition with it.

However, these results are certainly not guaranteed. They are to a considerable extent dependent on wise allocation of resources by governments on behalf of the communities they serve. The proliferation of educational and supportive services for families, as we know from state-of-the-art research, is pivotal to social evolution.

Our liberation from a long history of brutality, and possibly the survival of our species, are at stake. Surely there cannot be a more urgent need than to secure all children's emotional wellbeing as a matter of top international priority.

In our endeavours to nurture our children's emotional health, our dependence on government services varies according to our affluence. Those who struggle to make ends meet don't need all-day childcare services; what they need is adequate assistance so that their babies and toddlers can remain where they need to be; with their families. Nevertheless, when we cannot rely upon government co-operation, we should join together into communities and groups that nurture parents, so they in turn can give of their best. A community's responsibility is not only towards its children. We are also all responsible for helping and supporting parents. The best that is in each parent comes forth when they feel emotionally and practically supported, when they feel like they are not doing it alone.

It is, as Stiglitz so lucidly argues, social reforms – and not the enriching of a few at the expense of the many – that will create the conditions in which children can be brought up non-violently. Therein lies the keystone of societies that can prosper in peace. Economic progress does not come from slashing spending on health, education, and other vital social services – that only leads to disaster. Governments are not immune to public opinion. If we want them to put children's wellbeing, and families first, we need to insist upon it.

World peace is not only an entirely attainable goal, it is a modest one. The conditions that would bring it about require but a small fraction of the effort and expense we devote to fighting wars and fighting crime. A continued social evolution is quite possible, but it depends entirely on our collected efforts to keep improving the emotional lives of children. Our commitment to children's emotional health will ensure our rapid evolution toward a peaceful, just, sustainable and enjoyable existence for all of humanity.

Endnotes

1   Karen (1994) p 425.
2   Karen (1994) p 425.
3   Hunter and Kilstrom (1979); Hall, Sachs and Rayens (1998).
4   Olds and Henderson (1989).
5   Van den Boom (1990) in Koops (ed) pp 249–270, Van den Boom (1994) pp 1457–1477.
6   Jacobson and Frye (1991).
7   Murphey and Braner (2000).
8   Frenza (1993).
9   Olds and Kitzman (1993).
10 Olds, Henderson, Cole, Eckenrode, Kitzman, Luckey, Pettitt, Sidora, Morris and Powers (1998b).
11 Olds, Pettitt, Robinson, Henderson, Eckenrode, Kitzman, Cole and Powers (1998a).
12 Naughton and Heath (2001).
13 Karen (1994) p 421.
14 Olds, Kitzman, Cole and Robinson (1997).
15 Eckenrode, Ganzel, Henderson, Smith, Olds, Powers, Cole, Kitzman, Sidora (2000).
16 Linden and McFarland (1993) pp 7–20.
17 De Mause (2002a).
18 McFarland and Fanton (1997).
19 Brown and Jenski (1997).
20 De Mause (2002a) p 285.
21 De Mause (1996) pp 344–392.
22 Bakermans-Kranenburg, Van Ijzendoorn and Juffer (2003).
23 Rutter and O'Connor (1999). However other countries, such as Romania, still struggle with this issue. See for example, http://news.bbc.co.uk/2/hi/europe/4629589.stm
24 McFarland (1999) p 209.
25 McFarland (1999) pp 200–211.
26 See for example, Human Rights and Equal Opportunity Commission (2002a); Baird (2002); O'Halloran (2003); Illinois State Laboratory for Integrated Learning and Technology (2003).
27 A report by the United States Breastfeeding Committee, entitled 'Workplace breastfeeding support' outlines the numerous benefits generated for the employer, as well as for mothers and their babies of such a workplace system: United States Breastfeeding Committee see 'Publications' then 'Workplace breastfeeding support' http://www.usbreastfeeding.org (last

accessed 1 December 2004).

[28] A good example of this kind of volunteer-based organisation is the Sydney-based 'Aunties and Uncles'. Visit their website http://www.auntiesanduncles.com.au/ (last accessed 1 December 2004).

[29] Dolby and Swan (2003).

[30] See The Education Revolution, the website of the Alternative Education Resource Organization (AERO) http://www.educationrevolution.org/idec20032.html (last accessed 1 December 2004) for more information.

[31] See the Institute for Democratic Education http://www.democratic-edu.org/ (last accessed 1 December 2004).

[32] See the website of Summerhill School http://www.summerhillschool.co.uk/ (last accessed 1 December 2004).

[33] The Education Revolution, the website of the Alternative Education Resource Organization (AERO) http://www.educationrevolution.org/idec20032.html (last accessed 1 December 2004).

[34] See the Institute for Democratic Education http://www.democratic-edu.org/ (last accessed 1 December 2004).

[35] See MidEast Web, 'The Peace Education Directory' http://www.mideastweb.org/educdir.htm (last accessed 10 July 2008).

[36] Grille (2003).

[37] Hill (2000); Jahns (2003); and personal correspondence from Janelle Hardy, spokesperson for the Home Education Association, 26 September 2003.

[38] Jahns (2003).

[39] Hill (2000); Jahns (2003).

[40] Chomsky (2003).

[41] This proposition may tend to be more applicable among the more developed nations.

[42] http://homepages.nyu.edu/~mrg217/es.pdf

[43] http://hdr.undp.org/en/reports/

[44] De Mause (2000).

[45] Keeley (1996); LeBlanc (2003).

[46] LeBlanc (2003).

[47] De Mause (2000).

[48] http://www.who.int/whr/2004/annex/topic/en/annex_2_en.pdf

[49] De Mause (2000).

[50] Human Development Report 2007/2008 Fighting climate

change: Human solidarity in a divided world
http://hdr.undp.org/en/reports/global/hdr2007-2008/
[51] Hawken (2007).
[52] United Nations Children's Fund (2003) http://www.unicef.org/sowc03/tables/table4.html (last accessed 10 July 2008); United Nations Children's Fund (2004).
[53] Stiglitz (2002).
[54] Stiglitz (2002).
[55] Pilger (2002).
[56] See World Health Organization http://www.who.int/violence_injury_prevention/violence/world_report/wrvheng/ (last accessed 10 July 2008).
[57] Stiglitz (2002); Klein (2002).
[58] http://www.globalissues.org/Geopolitics/ArmsTrade/Spending.asp#WorldMilitarySpending (last accessed 7th August 2008)
[59] Allard (2004) p 1.
[60] Zakaria (2002).
[61] Kielburger (2001) p 12.

Bibliography

For additions or corrections to the Bibliography see
www.our-emotional-health.com

A

AAP (2004) 'Child detention is legal: High Court' *The Age* 7 October 2004 http://www.theage.com.au/articles/2004/10/07/1097089466449.html

Ackerman P and Du Vall J (2000) *A Force More Powerful* Palgrave, New York

Afkhami M, Mahnaz G, Hofmann N and Haleh V (1998) *Safe and Secure: Eliminating Violence Against Women and Girls in Muslim Societies* SIGI, Bethesda, USA

AFP (2002) 'Hindu right threatens to strike Islam' *The Australian* 23 October 2002

Ahmad W (1999) *The State of Pakistan's Children – 1998* SPARC, Islamabad, Pakistan

Ali T (2002) *The Clash of Fundamentalisms* Verso, London

'Alive and kicking – the facts' (2004) *New Internationalist* August 2004 Vol 370 p 18

Allard T (2004) 'PM was told war would spur terrorism' *The Sydney Morning Herald* 23 August 2004 p 1

Allen NB, Lewinsohn PM and Seeley JR (1998) 'Prenatal and perinatal influences on risk for psychopathology in childhood and adolescence' *Development and Psychopathology* Vol 10 pp 513–529

Alm B, Wennergren G, Norvenius SG, Skjaerven R, Lagercrantz H, Helweg-Larsen K and Irgens LM (2002) 'Breastfeeding and Sudden Infant Death Syndrome in Scandinavia 1992–5' *Archives of Disease in Childhood* Vol 86(6) pp 400–402

AlMunajjed M (1997) *Women in Saudi Arabia Today* Macmillan Press, London

Als H, Tronic E and Brazelton TB (1980) 'Stages of early behavioural organization: the study of a sighted infant and a blind infant in interaction with their mothers' in Field T (ed) (1980) *High-Risk Infants and Children* Academic Press, New York pp 181–204

Altorki S (1986) *Women in Saudi Arabia – Ideology and Behaviour Among the Elite* Colombia University Press, New York

Anaf G (2002) 'ADHD and the subversion of meaning' in Halasz G (2002) *Cries Unheard – A New Look at Attention Deficit Hyperactivity Disorder* Common Ground Publishing, Altona, VIC

Andrews B and Hunter E (1997) 'Shame, early abuse, and course of depression in a clinical sample: a preliminary study' *Cognition and Emotion* Vol 11(4) pp 373–381

Anisfeld E, Casper V, Nozyce M and Cunningham N (1990) 'Does infant carrying promote attachment? An experimental study of the effects of increased physical contact on the development of attachment' *Child Development* Vol 61 pp 1617–1627

Armstrong MK (2001) 'The myth of the happy childhood' *The Journal of Psychohistory* Vol 29(1) pp 47–49

Atapur AP (2002) 'Killing for mother Kali' *Time Australia* 29 July 2002 p 30

Atlas J (2001) 'The central paradigm: child-rearing as the fulcrum of psychohistorical explanation' *The Journal of Psychohistory* Vol 29(1) pp 9–36

Australian Association for Infant Mental Health (2002) 'Controlled crying – AAIMHI position paper' November 2002

Australian Broadcasting Corporation (1999) 'Special delivery' Lateline 16 September 1999 http://www.abc.net.au/lateline/stories/s52576.htm

Australian Institute for Health and Welfare (2002) 'Trends in long day care services for children in Australia, 1991-99' Children's Services Series No 4 http://www.aihw.gov.au/publications/index.cfm/title/8107

B

Baartman H (1994) 'Child suicide and harsh punishment in Germany at the turn of the century' *Pedagogica Historica – International Journal of the History of Education* Vol 30 pp 849–864

Badinter E (1981) *Mother Love: Myth and Reality* Macmillan, New York

Bailham D and Joseph S (2003) 'Post-traumatic stress following childbirth: a review of emerging literature and directions for research and practice' *Psychology, Health and Medicine* Vol 8(2) pp 159–168

Baird J and Verghis S (2000) 'It's the cane mutiny as schools fight to do it with love and care' *The Sydney Morning Herald* 25 October 2000 see World Corporal Punishment Research http://www.corpun.com/aus00010.htm

Baird M (2002) 'Paid maternity leave in Australia: HREOC's valuing parenthood' *Australian Review of Public Affairs* 14 June 2002 http://www.australianreview.net/ see 'Digest archive'

Baird V (2003) 'The big switch' *New Internationalist* June 2003 Vol 357 pp 9–12

Bakan J (2004) *The Corporation – The Pathological Pursuit of Profit and Power* The Free Press, New York

Bakermans-Kranenburg MJ, Van Ijzendoorn MH and Juffer F (2003) 'Less is more: meta-analyses of sensitivity and attachment interventions in early childhood' *Psychological Bulletin* Vol 129(2) pp 195–215

Baldry AC and Farrington DP (1998) 'Parenting influences on bullying and victimisation' *Journal of Legal and Criminological Psychology* Vol 3(2) pp 237–254

Bandura A (1973) *Aggression: A Social Learning Analysis* Prentice-Hall, New Jersey

Barkun M (1995) 'Militias, Christian identity and the radical right' *The Christian Century* 2–9 August 1995 pp 738–740

Baron RA (1977) *Human Aggression* Plenum Press, New York

Baron-Cohen S, Wheelwright S, Hill J, Raste Y and Plumb I (2001) 'The "reading the mind in the eyes" test: revised version' *Journal of Child Psychology and Psychiatry* Vol 42(2) pp 241–251

Baumrind D (1967) 'Childcare practices anteceding three patterns of preschool behaviour' *Genetic Psychology Monographs* Vol 76 pp 43–88

Baumrind D (1996) 'The discipline controversy revisited' *Family Relations* Vol 45 pp 405–414

Baumrind D, Larzelere R and Cowan P (2002) 'Ordinary physical punishment: is it harmful? Comment on Gershoff' *Psychological Bulletin* Vol 128(4) pp 580–589

Beisel D (1994) 'Looking for enemies 1990–1994' *The Journal of Psychohistory* Vol 22(1) pp 1–38

Bell SM and Ainsworth MD (1972) 'Infant crying and maternal responsiveness' *Child Development* Vol 43 pp 1171–1790

Belsky J (1999) 'Interactional and contextual determinants of attachment security' in Cassidy J and Shaver PR (eds) (1999) *Handbook of Attachment* The Guilford Press, New York

Belsky J and Cassidy J (1994) 'Attachment: theory and evidence' in Rutter M and Hay DF (eds) (1994) *Development Through Life: A Handbook for Clinicians* Blackwell Scientific Publications, Boston

Belsky J and Fearon RM (2002) 'Early attachment security, subsequent maternal sensitivity, and later child development: does continuity in development depend upon continuity of caregiving?' *Attachment and Human Development* December 2002 Vol 4(3) pp 361–387

Belsky J, Steinberg L and Draper P (1991) 'Childhood experience, interpersonal development, and reproductive strategy: an evolutionary theory of socialisation' *Child Development* Vol 62 pp 647–670

Ben Cramer R (2004) *How Israel Lost the Four Questions* Simon & Schuster, New York

Berger AM, Knutson JF, Mehm JG and Perkins KA (1988) 'The self-report of punitive childhood experiences of young adults and adolescents' *Child Abuse and Neglect* Vol 12 pp 251–262

Berkowitz L (1993) *Aggression, Its Causes, Consequences and Control* McGraw-Hill, New York

Berman D (1995) 'From continuity to renewal' *New Menorah* Fall 1995

Berman P (2003) 'The philosopher of Islamic terror' *The New York Times* 23 March 2003 Section 6 p 24

Biddulph S (1993) *The Secret of Happy Children* Angus & Robertson, Sydney

Blair PS, Fleming PJ, Smith IJ, Platt MW, Young J, Nadin P, Berry PJ and Golding J (1999) 'Babies sleeping with parents: case control study of factors influencing the risk of Sudden Infant Death Syndrome' *British Medical Journal* Vol 319 pp 1457–1462

Blatchford C (2002) 'Judge backs CAS seizure of spanked children – St Thomas parents used the scriptures to defend discipline' *National Post (Canada)* 12 October 2002 – see Project No Spank http://www.nospank.net/n-j62.htm

Blum D (2002) 'Love lessons – new insights into the biology and chemistry of connection reveal love's pure power' *Science and Spirit Magazine* http://www.science-spirit.org/articles/printerfriendly.cfm?article_id=329

Bone J (2003) 'Childhood wounds of the butcher of Baghdad' *The Weekend Australian* 1–2 March 2003 p 14

Boswell J (1988) *The Kindness of Strangers – The Abandonment of Children in Western Europe from Late Antiquity to the Renaissance* Pantheon Books, New York

Bounds A (2000) 'Bull by the horns: Costa Rica abandoned its national army half a century ago – and hasn't look back since …' *New Internationalist* December 2000 – search http://www.findarticles.com

Bowlby J (1960) 'Grief and mourning in infancy and early childhood' *Psychoanalytic Study of the Child* Vol 15 pp 9–52

Boyce P, Hickie I and Parker G (1991) 'Parents, partners or personality?

Risk factors for post-natal depression' *Journal of Affective Disorders* Vol 21 pp 245–255

Bradshaw J (1988) *Healing The Shame That Binds You* Health Communications, Florida

Breiner S (1990) *Slaughter of the Innocents – Child Abuse through the Ages and Today* Plenum Press, New York

Breitman R (1998) *Official Secrets: What the Nazis Planned, What the British and Americans Knew* Penguin Books, London

Brennan BA (1993) *Hands of Light: A Guide to Healing Through the Human Energy Field* Bantam Doubleday Dell, New York

Broude GJ (1995) *Growing-up: A Cross-Cultural Encyclopaedia* ABC-CLIO, California

Brown GW and Jenski J (1997) 'Two modes of child nurturing: local paradigm shifting in Alaska and Vermont' *Journal of Psychohistory* Vol 24(4) pp 339–352

Brownlee S (1996) 'The biology of soul murder – fear can harm a child's brain. Is it reversible?' *US News and World Report* 11 November 1996 – see Project No Spank http://www.nospank.net/trau.htm

Buckley S (2005) *Gentle Birth, Gentle Mothering* One Moon Press, Brisbane

Burleigh M (2001) *The Third Reich: A New History* Pan Macmillan, London

Burleigh M and Wippermann W (1991) *The Racial State: Germany 1933-1945* Cambridge University Press, Cambridge

C

Cantor CH, Neulinger K and De Leo D 'Australian suicide trends 1964–1997 – youth and beyond?' *Medical Journal of Australia* – search http://www.mja.com.au

Campbell C (1980) 'Yin yang: A holistic approach to viewing and integrating the seven body regions' Doctoral dissertation, International College, Los Angeles CA

Campbell C (1990) 'Course notes on character structure' Verosa College of Interactive Psychotherapy

CBC News Online staff (2002) 'Lawyer wants light sentence for beatings with heavy stick' CBC 26 October 2002 – see Project No Spank http://www.nospank.net/n-j68.htm

Chamberlain D (1994) 'The sentient prenate: What every parent should know' *Journal of Prenatal and Perinatal Psychology and Health* Vol 9(1) pp 9–32

Chamberlain D (1999) 'Reliability of birth memory: Observations from mother and child pairs in hypnosis' *Journal of Prenatal and*

Perinatal Psychology and Health Vol 14(1–2) pp 19–30

Chamberlain S (2004) 'The nurture and care of the future master race' *The Journal of Psychohistory* Vol 31(3) pp 367–394

'Charges faced by Milosevic' CNN 24 April 2002 http://www.cnn.com/2002/WORLD/europe/02/12/milosevic.charges/index.html

Cheek DB (1986) 'Prenatal and perinatal imprints: Apparent prenatal consciousness as revealed by hypnosis' *Journal of Prenatal and Perinatal Psychology* Vol 1(2) pp 97–110

Chen A and Rogan WJ (2004) 'Breastfeeding and the risk of postneonatal death in the United States' *Pediatrics* Vol 113(5) pp e435–439

Chiclet C (2001) 'Otpor: the youths who booted Milosevic' *The Courier UNESCO* March 2001 http://www.unesco.org/courier/2001_03/uk/droits.htm

Chomsky N (2003) *Hegemony or Survival* Allen & Unwin, Sydney

Clairbourne W (2001) 'Canadians from sect flee to US over right to spank' *The Washington Post* and *Houston Chronicle* 2 August 2001 – see Project No Spank http://www.nospank.net/n-i27.htm

Clendinnen I (1999) *Reading The Holocaust* Cambridge University Press, Cambridge, UK

Cohn-Sherbok D and el-Alami D (2002) *The Palestine-Israeli Conflict* One World, Oxford

Coleman M (1993) 'Human sacrifice in Bosnia' *The Journal of Psychohistory* Vol 21(2) pp 157–169

Colloff P (2001) 'Remember the Christian Alamo' *Texas Monthly* December 2001 – see Project No Spank http://www.nospank.net/colloff.htm

Conger JP (1994) *The Body in Recovery – Somatic Psychotherapy and the Self* Frog Ltd, Berkeley, California

Connolly E (2001) 'Man sues teacher and Catholic Church over 1984 strapping' *The Sydney Morning Herald* 30 January 2001 – see Project No Spank http://nospank.net/n-h25.htm

Cook P (1996) *Early Childcare – Infants and Nations at Risk* News Weekly Books, Melbourne

Cook P (1999) 'Rethinking the early childcare agenda' *Medical Journal of Australia* Vol 170(1) pp 29–31

Cooper J (1996) *The Child in Jewish History* Jason Aronson, Northvale, New Jersey, London

Cornelius H and Faire S (1999) *Everyone Can Win* Simon & Schuster, NSW, Australia

Costello A and Sachdev H (1998) 'Protecting breastfeeding from breastmilk substitutes' *British Medical Journal* Vol 316 pp 104–105

Cox K (2002) 'She said a prayer, then hit the children' *Globe and Mail* 1 October 2002 – see Project No Spank http://www.nospank. net/n-j51.htm

Crittenden PM and Ainsworth M (1989) 'Child maltreatment and attachment theory' in Cicchettti D and Carlson V (eds) (1989) *Child Maltreatment: Theory and Research on the Causes and Consequences of Child Abuse and Neglect* Cambridge University Press, New York

Crockenberg S and Litman C (1990) 'Autonomy as competence in 2-year-olds: Maternal correlates of child defiance, compliance, and self-assertion' *Developmental Psychology* Vol 26(6) pp 961–971

Crum T (1998) *The Magic of Conflict* Touchstone Press, New York

D

Damasio A (2000) *The Feeling of What Happens – Body Emotion, and the Making of Consciousness* Vintage, London

De Bellis M, Keshavan MS, Clark DB, Casey BJ, Giedd JN, Boring AM, Frustaci K and Ryan ND (1999) 'Developmental traumatology Part II' *Biological Psychiatry* Vol 45 pp 1271–1284

De Mause L (ed) (1974) *The History of Childhood – The Untold Story of Child Abuse* Peter Bedrick Books, New York

De Mause L (1982) *Foundations of Psychohistory* Creative Roots Inc, New York

De Mause L (1990) 'The gentle revolution: Childhood origins of Soviet and east European democratic movements' *The Journal of Psychohistory* Vol 17(4) pp 341–352

De Mause L (1991) 'The universality of incest' *The Journal of Psychohistory* Vol 19(2) pp 123–164

De Mause L (1996) 'Restaging early traumas in war and social violence' *Journal of Psychohistory* Vol 23(4) pp 344–392

De Mause L (1997) 'The psychogenic theory of history' *The Journal of Psychohistory* Vol 25(2) pp 112–183

De Mause L (1998) 'The history of child abuse' *The Journal of Psychohistory Vol 25(3) pp 216–236*

De Mause L (1999) 'Childhood and cultural evolution' *Journal of Psychohistory* Vol (26)3 pp 642–723

De Mause L (2000) 'War as righteous rape and purification' *The Journal of Psychohistory* Vol 27(4) pp 356–445

De Mause L (2001) 'The evolution of childrearing' *The Journal of Psychohistory* Vol 28(4) pp 362–451

De Mause L (2002a) 'The evolution of the psyche and society' *The Journal and Psychohistory* Vol 29(3) pp 238–285

De Mause L (2002b) 'The childhood origins of terrorism' *The Journal of Psychohistory* Vol 29(4) pp 340–348

De Mause L (2002c) *The Emotional Life of Nations* Karnac, New York

De Meo J (2006) *Saharasia – The 4000BCE Origins of Child Abuse, Sex-Repression, Warfare and Social Violence in the Deserts of the Old World* Natural Energy Works, Oregon

Dettling A, Gunnar M and Donzella B (1999) 'Cortisol levels of young children in full-day care centres' *Psychoneuroendocrinology Vol 24 pp 519–536*

Dettling A, Parker S, Lane S, Sebanc A and Gunnar M (2000) 'Quality of care and temperament determine changes in cortisol concentrations over the day for young children in childcare' *Psychoneuroendocrinology* Vol 25 pp 819–836

Diamond J (1991) *The Rise and Fall of the Third Chimpanzee* Vintage, London

Diamond J (2005) *Collapse – How Societies Choose to Fail or Survive* Allen Lane, London

Dietz TL (2000) 'Disciplining children: Characteristics associated with the use of corporal punishment' *Child Abuse & Neglect* Vol 24 pp 1529–1536

DiPietro JA (2002) 'Prenatal/perinatal stress and its impact on psychosocial child development' *Encyclopedia on Early Childhood Development* 3 June 2002 http://www.excellence-jeunesenfants. ca/ documents/DiPietroANGxp.pdf

DiPietro JA, Hilton SC, Hawkins M, Costigan KA and Pressman EK (2002) 'Maternal stress and affect influence foetal neurobehavioural development' *Developmental Psychology* Vol 38(5) pp 659–668

Dolby R and Swan B (2003) 'Strengthening relationships between early childhood staff, high needs children and their families in the preschool setting' *Developing Practice – The Child, Youth and Family Work Journal* Vol 6 pp 18–23

Dover G (2000) 'Anti-Dawkins' in Rose H and Rose S *Alas Poor Darwin – Arguments Against Evolutionary Psychology* Vintage p 47

Dozier M, Stovall KC and Albus KE (1999) 'Attachment and Psychopathology in Adulthood' in Cassidy J and Shaver PR (eds) *Handbook of Attachment* The Guilford Press, New York

Dubow EF, Huesmann LR and Eron LD (1987) 'Childhood correlates of adult ego development' *Child Development* Vol 58 pp 859–869

Dunn PP (1988) 'That enemy is the baby: Childhood in imperial Russia' in de Mause (ed) *The History of Childhood – The Untold Story of Child Abuse* Peter Bedrick Books, New York pp 383–406

Durrant JE (1999a) *A Generation Without Smacking: The Impact of*

Sweden's Ban on Physical Punishment Save The Children, London

Durrant JE (1999b) 'Evaluating the success of Sweden's corporal punishment ban' *Child Abuse and Neglect* Vol 23(5) pp 435–448

Durrant JE (2000) 'Trends in youth-crime and wellbeing since the abolition of corporal punishment in Sweden' *Youth & Society* Vol 31(4) pp 437–455

E

Easterbrook MA, Kisilevsky BS, Muir DW and Laplante DP (1999) 'Newborns discriminate schematic faces from scrambled faces' *Canadian Journal of Experimental Psychology* Vol 53(3) pp 231–241

Easterbrook MA and Biringen Z (2000) 'Mapping the terrain of emotional availability and attachment' *Attachment and Human Development* September 2000 Vol 2000 2(2) pp 123–129

Eckenrode J, Ganzel B, Henderson CR, Smith E, Olds DL, Powers J, Cole R, Kitzman H and Sidora K (2000) 'Preventing child abuse and neglect with a program of nurse home visitation – The limiting effects of domestic violence' *Journal of the American Medical Association* Vol 284(11) pp 1385–1391 http://jama.ama-assn.org/cgi/content/abstract/284/11/1385

Eckersley R (2004) *Well and Good – morality, meaning and happiness* Text Publishing, Melbourne

Edgerton RB (1992) *Sick Societies: Challenging the Myth of Primitive Harmony* The Free Press, New York

Eisler R (1995) *The Chalice and the Blade – Our History, Our Future* Harper Collins, New York

ElBaradei M (2004) cited in 'UN atomic energy chief warns that terrorists could go nuclear' 19 March 2004 – search http://www.spacewar.com

Ellingsen P (2002) 'Making mind matter' in Halasz G (2002) *Cries Unheard* Common Ground Publishing, Altona, Vic

Ellis MH (1999) *O, Jerusalem! – The Contested Future of The Jewish Covenant* Augsburg Fortress, Minneapolis

Ellison CG, Bartkowski JP and Segal ML (1996) 'Do conservative Protestant parents spank more often? Further evidence from the National Survey of Families and Households' *Social Science Quarterly Vol 77(3) pp 663–673*

Ellison CG and Sherkat DE (1993) 'Conservative Protestantism and support for corporal punishment' *American Sociological Review* Vol 58(1) pp 131–144

Engfer A and Schneewind KA (1982) 'Causes and consequences of harsh punishment – An empirical investigation in a representative sample of 570 German families' *Child Abuse & Neglect* Vol 6 pp 129–139

Erlich V (1966) *Family in Transition – A Study of 300 Yugoslav Villages* Princeton University Press, New Jersey

Evangelical Sisterhood of Mary (2001) 'Changing the future by confronting the past – Talks and testimonies, Jerusalem Convention, April 17–20' Darmstadt-Eberstadt, Germany

EzerT (2003) 'Children's rights in Israel: an end to corporal punishment?' *Oregon Review of International Law* Vol 5 Spring 2003 p 139

F

Farrell W (1994) *The Myth of Male Power* Simon & Schuster

Feldman R, Weller A, Sirota L and Eidelman AI (2002) 'Skin-to-skin contact (kangaroo care) promotes self-regulation in premature infants: sleep-wake cyclicity, arousal modulation, and sustained exploration' *Developmental Psychology Vol 38(2) pp 194–207*

Fleiss P (2000) *Sweet Dreams: A Paediatrician's Secrets for Baby's Good Night Sleep* McGraw Hill/Lowell House, Los Angeles

Firestone D (2001) 'Child abuse at a church creates a stir in Atlanta' *The NewYork Times* 30 March 2001 – see Project No Spank http://www.nospank.net/revalen6.htm

Fiske-McFarlin I, Nelson MR and Sherman A (1993) 'Free the kids! And Quarry Hill Community' *The Journal of Psychohistory* Vol 21(1) pp 21–27

Flannery T (2005) *The Weather Makers – The History and Future Impact of Climate Change* Text Publishing, Melbourne

FloryV (2004) 'A Novel Clinical Intervention for Severe Childhood Depression and Anxiety' *Clinical Child Psychology and Psychiatry*, Vol 9(1) pp: 9-23

Fonagy P, Steele M, Moran G, Steele H and Higgitt A (1993) 'Measuring the ghost in the nursery: An empirical study of the relation between parents' mental representations of childhood experiences and their infants' security of attachment' *Journal of the American Psychoanalytic Association* Vol 41(4) pp 957–989

Fonagy P, Target M, Steele M and Steele H (1997) 'The development of violence and crime as it relates to security of attachment' in Osofsky JD *Children in a Violent Society* The Guilford Press, New York

'Food and farming – the facts' *New Internationalist* January/February 2003 Vol 353 p 20 – search http://www.findarticles.com/

Fraley RC (2002) 'Attachment stability from infancy to adulthood: Meta-analysis and dynamic modelling of developmental mechanisms' *Personality & Social Psychology Review* May 2002 Vol 6(2) pp 123–151

Frenza L (1993) 'An early intervention approach to ending child abuse and neglect: *Hana Like* Home Visitor Program' *Journal of Psychohistory* Vol 21(1) pp 29–36

G

Gardner H (1993) *Frames of Mind* Basic Books, New York

Gathorne-Hardy J (1972) *The Rise and Fall of the British Nanny* Hodder and Stoughton, London

Gellately R (2001) *Backing Hitler: Consent and Coercion in Nazi Germany* Oxford University Press, Oxford

Gelles R J and Straus MA (1987) 'Is violence toward children increasing?' *Journal of Interpersonal Violence Vol 2(2) pp 212–222*

Gerhardt S (2004) *Why Love Matters – How Affection Shapes a Baby's Brain* Brunner–Routledge, Hove and New York

Gershoff E (2002a) 'Corporal punishment by parents and associated child behaviours and experiences: A meta-analytic and theoretical review' *Psychological Bulletin* Vol 128(4) pp 539–579

Gershoff E (2002b) 'Corporal punishment, physical abuse, and the burden of proof: Reply to Baumrind, Larzelere and Cowan, Holden, and Parke' *Psychological Bulletin* Vol 128(4) pp 602–611

Gershoff ET, Miller PC and Holden GW (1999) 'Parenting influences from the pulpit: Religious affiliation as a determinant of parental corporal punishment' *Journal of Family Psychology* Vol 13(3) pp 307–320

Gilbert P and Gerlsma C (1999) 'Recall of shame and favouritism in relation to psychopathology' *The British Journal of Clinical Psychology* Vol 38 pp 357–373

Glazov J (2001) 'The sexual rage behind Islamic terror' *Front Page Magazine* 4 October 2001 – see Project No Spank http://nospank. net/glazov.htm

Glazov J (2001) 'Atta's rage rooted in Islam's misogyny' *Front Page Magazine* 12 October 2001 – see Project No Spankhttp://nospank. net/glazov2.htm

Goldhagen DJ (1996) *Hitler's Willing Executioners – Ordinary Germans and the Holocaust* Abacus, London

Goleman D (1995) *Emotional Intelligence – Why It Can Matter More than IQ* Bantam Books, New York

Goleman D (2006) *Social Intelligence – the New Science of Human Relationships* Hutchinson, London

Gonda B (1998) 'Postnatal depression or childbirth trauma?'

Psychotherapy in Australia Vol 4(4) pp 36–41

Goodavage M and Gordon J (2002) *Good Nights: The Happy Parents' Guide to the Family Bed and a Peaceful Night's Sleep* St Martins Griffin, New York

Gordon T (1975) *Parent Effectiveness Training* Penguin Books, New York

Granju KA and Kennedy B (1999) *Attachment Parenting* Pocket Books, New York

Grant G (1998) *The Rhythm of Life* Doubleday, Sydney–Auckland

Grasmick HG, Bursik RJ and Kimpel M (1991) 'Protestant fundamentalism and attitudes toward corporal punishment of children' *Violence & Victims* Vol 6(4) pp 283–298

Grasmick HG, Morgan CS and Kennedy MB (1992) 'Support for corporal punishment in schools' *Social Science Quarterly* Vol 73(1) pp 177–187

Greenleaf BK (1978) *Children Through the Ages: A History of Childhood* McGraw Hill, New York

Greenspan S (1999) *Building Healthy Minds* Perseus Books, Cambridge, Massachusetts

Grille R (2003) 'Democracy begins at school' *Sydney's Child* April 2003

Gruen A (1999) 'The need to punish: The political consequences of identifying with the aggressor' *The Journal of Psychohistory* Vol 27(2) pp 136–154

Guthrow J (1998) 'Correlation between high rates of corporal punishment in schools and social pathologies' – see Project No Spank http://www.nospank.net/guthrow.htm

H

Haj-Yahia MM and Tamish S (2001) 'The rates of child sexual abuse and its psychological consequences as revealed by a study among Palestinian university students' *Child Abuse and Neglect* Vol 25 pp 1303–1327

Halasz G (2002) 'Smartening up or dumbing down? A look behind the symptoms, at over-prescribing and re-conceptualising ADHD' in Halasz G (2002) *Cries Unheard – A New Look at Attention Deficit Hyperactivity Disorder* Common Ground Publishing, Altona, Vic

Hall LA, Sachs B and Rayens MK (1998) 'Mother's potential for child abuse: The roles of childhood abuse and social resources' *Nursing Research* Vol 47(2) pp 87–94

Hall WF (1986) 'Psychological treatment of birth trauma with age regression and its relation to chemical dependency' *Journal of*

Prenatal and Perinatal Psychology and Health Vol 1(2) pp 111–134

Halley L (1980) 'Old country survivals in the new: An essay on some aspects of Yugoslav–American family structure and dynamics' *The Journal of Psychological Anthropology* Vol 3(2) Spring 1980

Harkabi Y (1988) *Israel's Fateful Hour* Harper & Row, New York

Harper B and Arms S (1994) *Gentle Birth Choices* Inner Traditions, Healing Arts Press, Rochester, Vermont

Harris J (1988) *The Nurture Assumption – Why Children Turn Out The Way They Do* Bloomsbury, London

Hart J, Gunnar M and Cicchetti D (1996) 'Altered Neuroendocrine Activity in Maltreated Children Related to Symptoms of Depression' *Development and Psychopathology* Vol 8 pp 201–214

Hawken P (1997) 'Resource waste' *Mother Jones* March/April 1997 – search http://www.mindfully.org/

Hawken P (2007) 'Blessed Unrest – how the largest movement in the world came into being and why no one saw it coming' Viking, NY

Hendrix H and Hunt H (1997) *Giving the Love that Heals* Pocket Books, New York

Henry BR, Houston S and Mooney GH (2004) 'Institutional racism in Australian healthcare: a plea for decency' *Medical Journal of Australia* Vol 180(10) pp 517–520 – search http://www.mja.com.au

Hertsgaard M (2004) 'World bank on horns of dilemma' *San Francisco Chronicle* 6 June 2004 http://www.markhertsgaard.com/Articles/2004/WorldBank-Dilemma

Hewitt WF (2003) 'Women, democracy and violence in the Arab world' *The Journal of Psychohistory* Vol 31(1) pp 65–73

Hill PT (2000) 'How home-schooling will change public education' *Hoover Digest* 2000 (2)

Hilpern (2003) 'The unspeakable trauma of childbirth' *The Sydney Morning Herald* 5 June 2003 – search http://www.smh.com.au

Hiscock H and Wake M (2002) 'Randomised controlled trial of behavioural infant sleep intervention to improve infant sleep and maternal mood' *British Medical Journal* May 2002 Vol 324(7345) pp 1062–1065

Hodge A (2003) 'Time we trimmed national waste line' *The Australian* 1 August 2003

Hofer MA (1994) 'Early relationships as regulators of infant physiology and behaviour' *Acta Paediatrica* Vol 397 pp 9–18

Hoffman H (1990) *Struwwelpeter* (English version) Forum Books, Surrey

Hoffman P (1988) *German Resistance to Hitler* Harvard University Press,

Cambridge

Holden GW (2002) 'Perspectives on the effects of corporal punishment – Comment on Gershoff' *Psychological Bulletin* Vol 128(4) pp 590–595

Holden R (1999) *Orphans of History – The Forgotten Children of the First Fleet* Text Publishing, Melbourne

Hopkin M (2004) 'Human populations are tightly interwoven' *Nature. com* 29 September 2004 – search http://www.nature.com

Hrdy Sarah Blaffer (2000) *Mother Nature – Maternal Instincts and the Shaping of the Species* Vintage, London

'HREOC inquiry into children in immigration report tabled' Joint media release VPS 68/2004 Attorney-General the Hon Philip Ruddock MP http://www.minister.immi.gov.au/media_releases/media04/v04068.htm

Hughes R (1996) *The Fatal Shore* The Harvill Press, London

Human Rights and Equal Opportunity Commission (1997) 'Stolen children' National inquiry *Bringing them home* – search http://www.hreoc.gov.au

Human Rights and Equal Opportunity Commission (2004) 'A last resort? The report of the national inquiry into children in immigration detention 2004' – search http://www.humanrights.gov.au

Human Rights and Equal Opportunity Commission (2002a) 'Valuing parenthood, options for paid maternity leave: Interim Paper 2002' – search http://www.hreoc.gov.au

Human Rights and Equal Opportunity Commission (2002b) 'A time to value: proposal for a national paid maternity leave scheme' Appendix B – search http://www.hreoc.gov.au

Human Rights and Equal Opportunity Commission (2001) 'National inquiry into children in immigration detention' Press releases 28 November 2001 – search http://www.hreoc.gov.au

Human Rights and Equal Opportunity Commission (2002) Media releases 21 January 2002 – search http://www.hreoc.gov.au

Human Rights and Equal Opportunity Commission (2004) 'Not one child should remain in detention, says Human Rights Commissioner' Press release 6 July 2004 – search http://www.humanrights.gov.au

Human Rights Watch (2004) 'Worldwide use of child soldiers continues unabated' 16 January 2004 – search http://hrw.org

Humphreys M (1994) *Empty Cradles* Corgi Books, London

Hunt J (2001) *The Natural Child – Parenting from the Heart* New Society Publishers, Gabriola Island, BC

Hunter RS and Kilstrom N (1979) 'Breaking the cycle in abusive families' *American Journal of Orthopsychiatry* Vol 136 pp 1320–1322

Ihanus J (1994) 'Zhirinovsky and the swaddled Russian personality' *Journal of Psychohistory Vol 22(2) pp 187–198*

I

Ihanus J (1996) 'Shame, revenge and glory: On Russian child rearing and politics' *Journal of Psychohistory* Vol 23(3) pp 260–268

Ihanus J (1998) 'Transformations of Eros: Sexuality and the family in Russia' *Journal of Psychohistory* Vol 25(3) pp 240–261

Ihanus J (1999) 'Water, birth and Stalin's thirst for power: Psychohistorical roots of terror' *The Journal of Psychohistory* Vol 27(1) pp 67–84

Illick J (1988) 'Child-rearing in seventeenth-century England and America' in de Mause (ed) *The History of Childhood – The Untold Story of Child Abuse* pp 303–350 Peter Bedrick Books, New York

Illinois State Laboratory for Integrated Learning and Technology (2003) 'Worldwide study exposes wide variations in maternity benefits' 16 January 2003 – search http://lilt.ilstu.edu

International Labour Organization (2002) 'World day against child labour' ILO Office for China and Mongolia 12 June 2002 http://www.ilo.org/public/english/region/asro/beijing/childlab.htm

Itim (2004) 'Haifa court sentences rabbi to 4 years for abusing students' in *Haaretz* 27 August 2004 http://www.theawarenesscenter.org/Weisfeld_Nachman.html

J

Jackson D (1999) *Three in a Bed: The Benefits of Sleeping with Your Baby* Bloomsbury, London

Jacobson SW and Frye KF (1991) 'Effect of maternal social support on attachment: Experimental evidence' *Child Development* Vol 62 pp 572–582

Jahns A (2003) 'Research on home-schooling: What does it say' *Byron Child* Vol 7 September–November 2003 pp 20–21

Johnson MH, Dziurawiec S, Ellis H and Morton J (1991) 'Newborns' preferential tracking of face-like stimuli and its subsequent decline' *Cognition Vol 40 pp 1–19*

Johnson SM (1994) *Character Styles* WW Norton & Co, New York

Kahr B (1991) 'The sexual molestation of children: Historical perspectives' *The Journal of Psychohistory* Vol 19(2) pp 191–214

K

Karen R (1994) *Becoming Attached* Oxford University Press, Oxford

Karon T (2004) 'Why al-Qaeda thrives' *Time* 26 May 2004 http://www.time.com/time/world/article/0,8599,642825,00.html

Karmiloff-Smith A (2000) 'Why babies' brains are not Swiss army knives' in Rose H and Rose S (eds) (2000) *Alas Poor Darwin – Arguments Against Evolutionary Psychology* Vintage, London p 144

Katz LG (2003) 'Tomorrow begins today' Opening Ceremony of the Second Caribbean Conference on Early Childhood Education 1 April 1997 University of West Indies http://www.uwi.edu/caribecd see 'Conferences' and see '2nd Caribbean Conference'

Kaufman G (1989) *The Psychology of Shame – Theory and Treatment of Shame-based Syndromes* Springer Publishing Co, New York

Keeley LH (1996) *War Before Civilization – The Myth of the Peaceful Savage* Oxford University Press, New York

Kempe CH, Silverman FN, Steele BF, Droegemueller W and Silver HK (1962) 'The battered child syndrome' *The Journal of the American Medical Association* Vol 181 pp 105–112

Kielburger C (2001) 'Inspiring a generation' *Sydney's Child* August 2001 p 12

Kilzer L (1998) 'Harsh detention centres for kids run by preacher' *Rocky Mountain News* 6 December 1998 – see Project No Spank http://www.nospank.net/grise5.htm

Kitzinger S (1996) *The Complete Book of Pregnancy and Childbirth* Alfred A Knopf, New York

Klaus MH, Jerauld R, Kreger NC, McAlpine W, Steffa M and Kennell JH (1972) 'Maternal attachment: Importance of the first post-partum days' *New England Journal of Medicine* Vol 286 pp 460–463

Klaus MH, Kennell JL, Robertson SS, Sosa R (1986) 'Effects of social support during parturition on maternal and infant morbidity' *British Medical Journal* Vol 293 pp 585–587

Klein N (2000) *No Logo* Flamingo, London

Klein N (2002) *Fences and Windows* Flamingo, London

Knode H (2001) 'The school for violence – A conversation with Riane Eisler' *La Weekly* – see Project No Spank http://nospank.net/eisler.htm

Knutson JF and Selner MB (1994) 'Punitive childhood experiences reported by young adults over a 10-year period' *Child Abuse and Neglect* Vol 18(2) pp 155–166

Kochanska G (2001) 'Emotional development in children with different attachment histories: the first three years' *Child Development* March–April 2001 Vol 72(2) pp 474–490

Kohn A (1996) *Punished by Rewards – The Trouble with Gold Stars, Incentive Plans, As, Praise, and other Bribes* Houghton Mifflin, Boston

Kohn A (1996) *Beyond Discipline – From Compliance to Community* ASCD, Alexandria, Virginia

Kurtz R and Pestrera H (1976) *The Body Reveals – An Illustrated Guide to the Psychology of the Body* Harper & Row, New York

Kurtz R (1990) Body-Centred Psychotherapy – The Hakomi Method Life Rhythm, Mendocino, California

L

Laibow RE (1986) 'Birth recall: A clinical report' *Journal of Prenatal and Perinatal Psychology* Vol 1(1) pp 78–81

Lamprecht F, Eichelman B, Thoa NB, Williams RB and Kopin IJ (1972) 'Rat fighting behaviour' *Science* Vol 177 September pp 1214–1215

Lamprecht F, Eichelman B, Thoa NB, Williams RB and Kopin IJ (1990) 'Rat fighting behaviour' *Brain Research* Vol 525 pp 285–293

Lansford, et al (2005) 'Physical Discipline and Children's Adjustment: Cultural Normativeness as a moderator' *Child Development* Vol 76(6) Nov/Dec 2005

Lateline (2001) 'Concerns over children in detention centres lead to inquiry' 28 November 2001 http://www.abc.net.au/lateline/content/2001/s428172.htm

Latzer Y, Hochdorf Z, Bachar E and Canetti L (2002) 'Attachment style and family functioning as discriminating factors in eating disorders' *Contemporary Family Therapy: An International Journal* December 2002 Vol 24(4) pp 581–599

Lawrence R (1999) *Breastfeeding: A Guide for the Medical Profession* Mosby, St Louis, Missouri

Leach P (1997) *Your Baby and Child* Knopf, New York

LeBlanc, SA (2003) *Constant Battles – The Myth of the Peaceful, Noble Savage* St Martin's Press, New York

Leboyer F (2002) *Birth Without Violence* Inner Traditions/Healing Arts Press, Rochester, Vermont Lewis HB (1987) 'Introduction: Shame – the 'sleeper' in psychopathology' in Lewis HB (ed) (1987) *The Role of Shame in Symptom Formation* Lawrence Erlbaum Associates, Hillsdale, New Jersey

Lewis M (1992) *Shame: The Exposed Self* The Free Press, New York

Lewis M and Ramsay D (2005) 'Infant Emotional and Cortisol Responses to Goal Blockage' *Child Development,* Volume 76(2)

Lewis T, Amini F, Lannon R (2000) *A General Theory of Love* Vintage Books, New York

Lewit D (2002) 'Participatory democracy in Porto Alegre' 27 February 2002 – search the Alliance for Democracy http://www.thealliancefordemocracy.org

Lewontin RC, Rose S and Kamin LJ (1984) *Not In Our Genes* Pantheon Books, New York

Liedloff J (1986) *The Continuum Concept* Perseus Publishing, New York

Linden K and MacFarland RB (1993) 'Community parenting centres in Colorado' *The Journal of Psychohistory* Vol 21(1) pp 7–19

Lipton BH (1997) 'Adaptive mutation: A new look at biology: the impact of maternal emotions on genetic development' *Touch the Future* Spring 1997 pp 4–6

Lipton EL, Steinschneider A and Richmond JB (1965) 'Swaddling, a child care practice: Historical, cultural, and experimental observations' *Paediatrics* March Part II pp 521–567

Little BC, Hayworth J, Benson P, Bridge LR, Dewhurst J and Priest RG (1982) 'Psychophysiological ante-natal predictors of post-natal depressive mood' *Journal of Psychosomatic Research* Vol 26(4) pp 419–428

Loader P (1998) 'Such a shame – A consideration of shame and shaming mechanisms in families' *Child Abuse Review* Vol 7 pp 44–57

Lowen A (1969) *The Betrayal of the Body* MacMillan Publishing, New York

Lowen A (1975) *Bioenergetics* Penguin Books, New York

Lowen A (1980) *Fear of Life* Collier Macmillan, New York

Lowen A (1997) *Narcissism* Touchstone Books, New York

M

Main M and Hesse E (1990) 'Parents' unresolved traumatic experiences are related to infant disorganised attachment status' in Greenberg MT, Cicchetti D and Cummings EM (eds) *Attachment in the Pre-School Years – Theory, Research and Intervention* The University of Chicago Press, Chicago

Manji, I (2003) 'The Trouble with Islam' Random House, Sydney

Manne A (2002) 'Cries unheard: Children, ADHD and the contemporary conditions of childhood' in Halasz G (2002) *Cries Unheard – A New Look at Attention Deficit Hyperactivity Disorder* Common Ground Publishing, Altona, Vic

Mascolo MF and Griffin S (eds) (1998) *What Develops in Emotional Development – Emotions, Personality & Psychopathology* Plenum Press, New York

Masson J (1999) *The Emperor's Embrace – Fatherhood in Evolution* Vintage, London

Masson J and McCarthy S (1996) *When Elephants Weep* Vintage, London

Maurel O (2001) *La Fessee* Editions La Plage (French Language), Tressan

Maurer A and Wallerstein JS (1987) 'The influence of corporal punishment on crime' – see Project No Spank http://www.nospank.net/maurer1.htm

McAdams M (1998) *Croatia: Myth and Reality* CIS Monographs Arcadia, CA http://mirror.veus.hr/myth/index.html

McConahy SA and JB (1977) 'Sexual permissiveness, sex-role rigidity, and violence across cultures' *Journal of Social Issues* Vol 33(2) pp 134–143

McCord J (1979) 'Some child rearing antecedents of criminal behaviour in adult men' *Journal of Personality and Social Psychology* Vol 37(9) pp 1477–1486

McFarland R (1999) 'Peace on earth, goodwill toward children' *Journal of Psychohistory* Vol 27(2) pp 200–211

McFarland R and Fanton J (1997) 'Moving toward utopia: Prevention of child abuse' *Journal of Psychohistory* Vol 24(4) pp 320–331

McKay P (2001) *Parenting by Heart* Lothian Books, Melbourne

McKay P (2002) *100 ways to Calm the Crying* Lothian Books, Melbourne

McKenna J (1995) 'Is sleeping with my baby safe? Can it reduce the risk of SIDS?' *Horizons* Vol 1(4)

McVea K, Turner PD and Peppler DK (2000) 'The role of breastfeeding in sudden infant death syndrome' *Journal of Human Lactation* Vol 16(1) pp 13–20

Melicharova M (2001–2002) 'Good deeds' *Peace Matters* Issue 36 Winter 2001–2002

http://www.ppu.org.uk/peacematters/pm2001/pm2001_x12_3.html

Milburn MA and Conrad SE (1996) *The Politics of Denial* MIT Press, Cambridge

Miller A (1990) *The Untouched Key – Tracing Childhood Trauma in Creativity and Destructiveness* Virago Press, London

Miller A (1990) *Breaking Down the Wall of Silence – To Join the Waiting Child* Virago Press, London

Miller A (1998) 'The political consequences of child abuse' *The Journal of Psychohistory* Vol 26(2) pp 573–585

Miller A (2001) *The Truth Will Set You Free – Overcoming Emotional Blindness and Finding Your True Adult Self* Basic Books, New York

Miller A (2001) 'The wellsprings of horror in the cradle' – see Project No Spank http://nospank.net/miller17.htm

Minchin M (1985) *Breastfeeding Matters: What we Need to Know about Infant Feeding* Allen and Unwin, Alfredton, Vic

Moncher FJ (1995) 'Social isolation and child–abuse risk' Families in Society: *The Journal of Contemporary Human Services* Vol 76(7) pp 421–433

Moncher FJ (1996) 'The relationship of maternal adult attachment style and risk of physical child abuse' *Journal of Interpersonal Violence* Vol 11(3) pp 335–350

Monk C, Fifer WP, Myers MM, Sloan RP, Trien L and Hurtado A (2000) 'Maternal stress responses and anxiety during pregnancy: Effects on foetal heart rate' *Developmental Psychobiology* Vol 36(1) pp 67–77

Moore M (2003) *Dude, Where's my Country?* Allen Lane, London

Morrock R (1999) 'The genocidal impulse: Why nations kill other nations' *The Journal of Psychohistory* Vol 27(2) pp 155–164

Mosko S, Richard C and McKenna J (1997) 'Infant arousals during mother–infant bed sharing: Implications for infant sleep and sudden infant death syndrome research' *Pediatrics* Vol 100(5) pp 841–849

Muller RT, Hunter JE and Stollak G (1995) 'The interpersonal transmission of corporal punishment: A comparison of social learning and temperament models' *Child Abuse and Neglect* Vol 19(11) pp 1323–1335

Murphey DA and Braner M (2000) 'Linking child maltreatment retrospectively to birth and home visit records: An initial examination' *Child Welfare* Vol 79(6) pp 711–728

Mydans S (2002) 'In Pakistan, rape victims are the 'criminals'' *The New York Times* 17 May 2002

N

National Council of Churches in Australia (2004) 'Churches back calls for release of abused detainee children' Media release 13 May 2004 http://www.chilout.org/files/hr/NCC%2013%20May%202004.html

National Health and Medical Research Council (2003) Media releases 21 November 2003 – search http://www.nhmrc.gov.au

Naughton A and Heath A (2001) 'Developing an early intervention programme to prevent child maltreatment' *Child Abuse Review* Vol 10 pp 85–96

Neville A 'Child sexual abuse: traumatic aspects and associated losses' Open Doors http://www.opendoors.com.au/ChildSexAbuse/ChildSexAbuse.htm see 'Prevalence studies'

Newton D (1990) *Germany 1918-1945: From Days of Hope to Years of Horror* Harper Collins, Sydney

Newton M (1996) 'Written in blood: A history of human sacrifice' *The*

Journal of Psychohistory Vol 24(2) pp 104–131

Noonan G (2000) 'School fighting for right to cane hits at 'politics''
The Sydney Morning Herald 28 October 2000 see World Corporal
Punishment Research http://www.corpun.com/aus00010.htm

Norden P (2004) 'Australia's system of institutionalised child abuse:
life behind razor ribbon wire for children' Address to the World
Congress of OMEP (World Organisation for Early Childhood
Education, 0–8 years) 24 July 2004, Melbourne in Jesuit Social
Services http://www.jss.org.au/research/index.html

O

Oddy WH (2002) 'The impact of breastmilk on infant and child health'
Breastfeeding Review Vol 10(3) pp 5–18

Odent M (1994) *Birth Reborn* Birth Works Press, Medford New
Jersey

O'Halloran D (2003) 'Maternity entitlements' Roller Coaster
February 2003 http://www.rollercoaster.ie see 'Pregnancy' then
see 'Entitlements'

'Oil, the facts' *New Internationalist* June 2001 Vol 335 p 19 – search
http://www.findarticles.com

Olds DL and Henderson CR (1989) 'The Prevention of Maltreatment'
in Cicchetti D and Carlson V (eds) (1989) *Child Maltreatment:
Theory and Research on the Causes and Consequences of Child Abuse
and Neglect* Cambridge University Press, Cambridge

Olds D, Henderson CR, Cole R, Eckenrode J, Kitzman H, Luckey D,
Pettitt L, Sidora K, Morris P and Powers J (1998b) 'Long term-
effects of nurse home visitation on children's criminal and antisocial
behaviour' *Journal of the American Medical Association* Vol 280(14) pp
1238–1244

Olds DL and Kitzman H (1993) 'Review of research on home visiting
for pregnant women and parents of young children' *The Future of
Children* Vol 3(3)

Olds D, Kitzman H, Cole R and Robinson J (1997) 'Theoretical
foundations of home visitation for pregnant women and parents of
young children' *Journal of Community Psychology* Vol 25(1) pp 9–25

Olds D, Pettitt LM, Robinson J, Henderson C, Eckenrode J, Kitzman
H, Cole B and Powers J (1998a) 'Reducing risks for antisocial
behaviour with a program of prenatal and early childhood home
visitation' *Journal of Community Psychology* Vol 26(1) pp 65–83

Oliner SP and Oliner PM (1988) *The Altruistic Personality – Rescuers
of Jews in Nazi Europe* The Free Press, New York http://www.
humboldt.edu/~altruism/home.html

Orzolek-Kronner C (2002) 'The effect of attachment theory in the development of eating disorders: Can symptoms be proximity-seeking?' *Child & Adolescent Social Work Journal* December 2002 Vol 19(6) pp 421–435

P

Palmer G (1988) *The Politics of Breastfeeding* Pandora Press, London

Palmer L (2001) *Baby Matters, What Your Doctor May not Tell You About Caring for your Baby* Lucky Press, Lancaster, Ohio

Patten-Hitt E (2000) 'Childhood abuse changes the developing brain' *Cerebrum* Fall 2000 pp 50–67

Pauli-Pott U, Mertesacker B, Bade U, Bauer C and Beckmann D (2000) 'Contexts of relations of infant negative emotionality to caregiver's reactivity/sensitivity' *Infant Behaviour and Development* Vol 23 pp 23–39

Pearce JC (2002) *The Biology of Transcendence* Park Street Press, Rochester, Vermont

Perry A (2003) 'India's great divide' *Time* 11 August 2003 pp 36–40

Perry BD (1997) 'Incubated in terror: Neurodevelopmental factors in the cycle of violence' in Osofsky JD (1997) *Children in a Violent Society* The Guilford Press, New York

Perry BD (1999) 'Memories of fear: How the brain stores and retrieves physiologic states' in Goodwin J and Attias R (eds) (1999) *Splintered Reflections: Images of the Body in Trauma* Basic Books, New York

Perry BD and Pollard R (1998) 'Homeostasis, stress, trauma and adaptation: A neurodevelopmental view of childhood trauma' *Stress in Children* Vol 7(1) pp 33–51

Perry BD, Pollard RA, Blakley TL, Baker WL and Vigilante D (1995) 'Childhood trauma, the neurobiology of adaptation, and use-dependent development of the brain: How states become traits' *Infant Mental Health Journal* Vol 16(4) pp 271–291

Perry BD and Szalavitz, M (2006). *The Boy Who was Raised as a Dog; and other stories from a child psychiatrist's notebook* Basic Books, New York

Piers M (1978) *Infanticide, Past and Present* WW Norton, New York

Pilger J (2002) *The New Rulers of the World* Verso, London

Popper M (1999) 'The sources of motivation of personalized and socialized charismatic leaders' *Psychoanalysis & Contemporary Thought Vol 22(2) pp 231–246*

Popper M (2000a) 'The development of charismatic leaders' *Political Psychology* Vol 21(4) pp 729–744

Popper M, Mayseless O and Castelnovo O (2000b) 'Transformational leadership and attachment' *Leadership Quarterly* Vol 11(2) pp 267–289

Popper M (2002) 'Narcissism and attachment patterns of personalized and socialized charismatic leaders' *Journal of Social & Personal Relationships* Vol 19(6) pp 797–809

Porter L (2001) *Children Are People Too* 'Small Poppies, McLaren Vale, South Australia

Powell S (2002) 'Teaching Allah's boys' *The Australian* 23 October 2002 p 13

Power TG and Chapieski ML (1986) 'Child-rearing and impulse control in toddlers: A naturalistic investigation' *Developmental Psychology* Vol 22(2) pp 271–275

Prescott JW (1996) 'The origins of human love and violence' *Pre- and Perinatal Psychology Journal* Vol 10(3) pp 143–188

Prince P (2004) 'The High Court and indefinite detention: towards a national bill of rights?' Research brief no 1 2004–05, Parliament of Australia, Parliamentary library, 16 November 2004 http://www.aph.gov.au/library/pubs/RB/2004-05/05rb01.htm#conflict

Puhar A (1993a) 'Childhood origins of the war in Yugoslavia: 1. Infant mortality' *The Journal of Psychohistory Vol 20(4) pp 373–379*

Puhar A (1993b) 'On childhood origins of violence in Yugoslavia: II. The zadruga' *The Journal of Psychohistory* Vol 21(2) pp 171–197

Puhar A (1994) 'Childhood nightmares and dreams of revenge' *The Journal of Psychohistory* Vol 22(2) pp 131–170

R

Radbill SX (1974) 'A history of child abuse and infanticide' in Helfer RE and Kempe CH (eds) *The Battered Child* The University of Chicago Press, Chicago

Rajan J (2004) 'Will India's ban on prenatal sex determination slow abortion of girls?' Hindu Womens' Universe http://www.hinduwomen.org see 'Issues' and 'Female infanticide'

Rampton S and Stauber J (2001) *Trust Us:We're Experts! – How Industry Manipulates Science and Gambles with your Future* Penguin/Putnam, New York

Rancour-Laferriere D (1999) 'Russians react to the idea of Russian masochism' *The Journal of Psychohistory* Vol 27(1) pp 59–66

Raphaeli N (2003) 'The failure to establish a 'knowledge society' in Arab nations: Arab Human Development Report' Economic studies: The Middle East Media Research Institute *Inquiry and Analysis Series – No 151* 6 November 2003 http://www.memri.org see 'Economics'

Recchia P (2003) 'CEOs don't sweat their unethical behaviour: shrink' *New York Post* 26 January 2003 p 15

ReliefWeb (2004) 'Report shows child soldier use continues unabated' 16 January 2004 – search http://www.reliefweb.int

Reynolds K (2004) Speeches and questions 'Asylum seekers: children in detention: Parliamentary motion' 22 July 2004 – search http://www.sa.democrats.org.au

Rhodes E (1997) 'Origins of a tragedy: Joseph Stalin's cycle of abuse' *The Journal of Psychohistory* Vol 24(4) pp 377–389

Rigby K (1994) 'Psychological functioning in families of Australian adolescent schoolchildren involved in bully-victim problems' *Journal of Family Therapy* Vol 16(2) pp 173–187

Righetti PL (1996) 'The emotional experience of the foetus: A preliminary report' *Journal of Prenatal and Perinatal Psychology and Health* Vol 11(1) pp 55–65

Riordan J and Auerbach K (1999) *Breastfeeding and Human Lactation* Jones and Bartlett Publishers, London

Robertson G (2000) *Crimes Against Humanity The Struggle for Global Justice* Penguin Books, Ringwood, Vic

Robertson P (1988) 'Home as a nest: Middle class childhood in nineteenth-century Europe' in de Mause L (ed) (1988) *The History of Childhood – The Untold Story of Child Abuse* pp 407–431 Peter Bedrick Books, New York

Robotham J and Glendinning L (2001) 'It's so touching: this baby knows love is skin deep' *The Sydney Morning Herald* 15 November 2001

Rohde DLT, Olson S and Chang JT (2004) 'Modelling the recent common ancestry of all living humans' *Nature* Vol 431 pp 562–565

Rosenblum LA, Coplan JD, Friedman S, Bassoff T, Gorman JM and Andrews MW (1994) 'Adverse early experiences affect noradrenergic and serotonergic functioning in adult primates' *Biological Psychiatry* Vol 35(4) pp 221–227

Rousselle R (2001) 'If it is a girl, cast it out: Infanticide/exposure in ancient Greece' *The Journal of Psychohistory* Vol 28(3) pp 281–302

Rothschild B (2000) *The Body Remembers – The Psychophysiology of Trauma and Trauma Treatment* WW Norton & Co, New York

Rothschild B (2003) 'Making trauma therapy safer' Two-day seminar, Sydney, Australia

Ruggi S (2004) 'Commodifying honor in female sexuality: Honor killings in Palestine' *Middle East Report* Spring 1998 – search The Middle East Research and Information Project http://www.merip.

org

Rush F (1980) *The Best Kept Secret: The Sexual Abuse of Children* Prentice Hall, New Jersey

Rushdie S (2001) 'Yes this is about Islam' *The New York Times* 2 November 2001 – see Project No Spank http://nospank.net/rushdie.htm

Rutter M and O'Connor TG (1999) 'Implications of attachment theory for child care policies' in Cassidy J and Shaver PR (eds) *Handbook of Attachment Theory, Research and Clinical Implications* The Guilford Press, New York

S

Sabbah FA (1984) *Woman in the Muslim unconscious* Pergamon Press, New York

Sardar Z (2002) 'Islam – resistance and reform' *New Internationalist* May 2002 pp 9–13

Scharf R (2001) 'Pedophobia, the gynarchy, and the androcracy' *Journal of Psychohistory* Vol 28(3) pp 281–302

Scheer C, Scheer R and Chaudry L (2003) *The Five Biggest Lies Bush Told us About Iraq* Allen & Unwin, Crows Nest, NSW

Scheff TJ (1987) 'The shame-rage spiral: A case study of an interminable quarrel' in Lewis HB (ed) (1987) *The Role of Shame in Symptom Formation* Lawrence Erlbaum, Hillsdale, New Jersey

Schore A (1994) *Affect Regulation and the Origin of the Self: The Neurobiology of Emotional Development* Lawrence Erlbaum Assoc, Hillsdale, New Jersey

Schwarz GS (1973) 'Devices to prevent masturbation' *Medical Aspects of Human Sexuality* May 1973 pp 141–153

Sears W (1999) *Night-time Parenting: How to Get Your Baby and Child to Sleep* Plume, New York

Sears W (2001) *The Attachment Parenting Book: A Commonsense Guide to Understanding and Nurturing Your Baby* Little, Brown & Co, Boston

Shahak I (1994) *Jewish History, Jewish Religion* Pluto Press, London

Shahak I and Mezvinsky N (1999) *Jewish Fundamentalism in Israel* Pluto Press, London

Sharma K (2002) 'Rooted custom' India Together Gendercide Watch http://www.gendercide.org/case_infanticide.html

Sheline JL, Skipper BJ and Broadhead WE (1994) 'Risk factors for violent behaviour in elementary school boys: Have you hugged your child today? *American Journal of Public Health* Vol 84(4) pp 661–663

Siddiqui A, Hagglof B and Eiseman M (2000) 'Own memories of

upbringing as a determinant of prenatal attachment in expectant women' *Journal of Reproductive and Infant Psychology* Vol 18(1) pp 67–74

Sigman, A (2005) *Remotely Controlled – How Television is Damaging our Lives* Vermillion, London

Smibert J (1988) 'A history of breastfeeding – with particular reference to the influence of NMAA in Victoria' *Breastfeeding Review* 12 May 1988 pp 14–19

Smith J, Thompson JF and Ellwood DA (2002) 'Hospital system costs of artificial infant feeding: estimates for the Australian Capital Territory' *Australian and New Zealand Journal of Public Health* Vol 26 pp 543–551 – search http://www.phaa.net.au/anzjph/anzjph.htm

Solomon CR and Serres F (1999) 'Effects of parental verbal aggression on children's self-esteem and school marks' *Child Abuse & Neglect* Vol 23(4) pp 339–351

Solter AJ (1998) *The Aware Baby: A New Approach to Parenting* Shining Star Press, Goleta, California

Spatz Widom C (1989) 'Does violence beget violence? A critical examination of the literature' *Psychological Bulletin* Vol 106(1) pp 3–28

Spock B (1946) *The Common-Sense Book of Baby and Child Care* Duell, Sloan and Pearce, New York

Steel Z and Silove DM (2001) 'The mental health implications of detaining asylum seekers' *Medical Journal of Australia* 175 pp 596–599 http://www.mja.com.au/public/issues/175_12_171201/steel/steel.html

Steele M, Steele H and Johansson M (2002) 'Maternal predictors of children's social cognition: An attachment perspective' *Journal of Child Psychology and Child Psychiatry* Vol 43(7) pp 861–872

Stein A, Gath DH, Bucher J, Bond A, Day A and Cooper PJ (1991) 'The relationship between post-natal depression and mother–child interaction' *British Journal of Psychiatry* Vol 158 pp 46–52

Stein R (2004) 'Breastfed babies less likely to die: Study finds overall risk fell 20 percent during an infant's first year' *The Washington Post* 3 May 2004 p A03

Steiner C (1997) *Achieving Emotional Literacy* Bloomsbury, London

Stevenson G (1967) 'Psychopathology of international behaviour' *American Journal of Psychiatry* Vol 124 pp 166–167

Stiglitz J (2002) *Globalisation and its Discontents* Penguin Books, London

St Louis Post-Dispatch (2002) 'Acting on faith: Desperate parents – unregulated reform schools in Missouri' 19 November 2002 – see

Project No Spank http://www.nospank.net/n-j70.htm

Strassberg Z, Dodge KA, Pettit GS and Bates JE (1994) 'Spanking in the home and children's subsequent aggression towards kindergarten peers' *Development and Psychopathology* Vol 6 pp 445–461

Straus M and Kaufman G (1994) 'Corporal punishment of adolescents by parents: A risk factor in the epidemiology of depression, suicide, alcohol abuse, and wife beating' *Adolescence Vol 29(115) pp 543–562*

Straus M and Mathur AK (1996) 'Social change and the trends in approval of corporal punishment by parents from 1968 to 1994' in Frehsee D, Horn W and Bussman KD (eds) *Family Violence Against Children: A Challenge for Society* Walter de Gruyter, New York

Straus M and Paschall MJ (1997) 'Corporal punishment by mothers and child's cognitive development – A longitudinal study' *Archives of Paediatric Adolescent Medicine* Vol 151 pp 761–767

Straus MA and Mouradian VE (1998) 'Impulsive corporal punishment by mothers and antisocial behaviour and impulsiveness of children' *Behavioural Sciences and the Law* Vol 16(3) pp 353–374

Sunderland, M (2006) *What Every Parent Needs To Know* 2006 DK Publishing, London (was *The Science of Parenting*)

T

Tal U (1985) 'Foundations of a political, messianic trend in Israel' *The Jerusalem Quarterly* Vol 35 Spring 1985

Tangney JP and Fischer KW (1995) *The Self-Conscious Emotions – The Psychology of Guilt, Embarrassment, and Pride* The Guilford Press, New York

Tangney JP, Wagner P and Gramzov R (1992) 'Proneness to shame, proneness to guilt, and psychopathology' *Journal of Abnormal Psychology* Vol 101(3) pp 469–478

Teicher MH (2002) 'The neurobiology of child abuse' *Scientific American* March 2002 pp 68–75

Terzieff J (2004) 'In Pakistan, those who cry rape face jail' *WeNews 16 May 2004 – see Women's e-News* http://www.womensenews.org see 'Search the archives'

The Baby-Friendly Hospital Initiative Newsletter (1994) 'What the world's religions teach about child nutrition and breastfeeding' December 1994

'The good oil for Exxon is having a buddy in the White House' *The Sydney Morning Herald* 18 April 2001 p 10

Theobald R (1997) *Reworking Success – New Communities at the Millennium* New Society Publishers, Gabriola Island, BC

Thevenin T (1987) *The Family Bed* Perigee Books, New York

Thompson RA (1999) 'Early attachment and later development' in Cassidy J and Shaver PR (eds) (1999) *Handbook of Attachment* The Guilford Press, New York

Thomson Salo F (2002) 'The trauma of depression in infants: A link with attention deficit hyperactivity disorder?' in Halasz G (2002) *Cries Unheard – A New Look at Attention Deficit Hyperactivity Disorder* Common Ground Publishing, Altona, Vic

Thorman G (1983) *Incestuous Families* Charles C Thomas, Springfield

Time Magazine (Australian Edition) (2002) 'World-watch section' 1 April 2002

Time Magazine (Australian Edition) (2002) 'Killing for mother Kali' 29 July 2002 p 30

'Timeline: the Milosevic years' CNN 31 August 2004 http://www.cnn.com/2004/WORLD/europe/08/31/milosevic.timeline/index.html

Tomazin F (2004) 'Review may ban strap in schools' *The Age* 8 September 2004

Totton N and Edmondson E (1988) *Reichian Growth Work* Nature & Health Books, Bridport, Dorset, UK

Treloar SA, Martin NG, Bucholz KK, Madden PA and Heath AC (1999) 'Genetic influences on post-natal depressive symptoms: Findings from an Australian twin sample' *Psychological Medicine* Vol 29(3) pp 645–654

Trevathan WR and McKenna JJ (1994) 'Evolutionary environments of human birth and infancy: Insights to apply to contemporary life' *Children's Environments* Vol 11(2) pp 88–104

U

United Nations Children's Fund (1998) 'The state of the world's children 1998' http://www.unicef.org/sowc98/foreword.htm

United Nations Children's Fund (2003) 'The state of the world's children 2003' http://www.unicef.org/sowc03/tables/table4.html

United Nations Children's Fund (2004) 'The state of the world's children 2004' http://www.unicef.org/sowc04/sowc04_contents.html

United Nations Foundation (2003) '"Honor Killings" in Pakistan reach 631 this year, group says' *United Nations Foundation* 15 September 2003 http://www.unwire.org/UNWire/20030915/449_8405.asp

V

Van den Bergh BR (1990) 'The influence of maternal emotions during pregnancy on fetal and neonatal behaviour' *Journal of Prenatal and Perinatal Psychology and Health* Vol 5(2) pp 119–130

Van den Boom DC (1990) 'Preventive intervention and the quality of mother–infant interaction and infant exploration in irritable infants' in Koops W (ed) (1990) *Developmental Psychology Behind the Dikes* Eburon, Amsterdam pp 249–270

Van den Boom DC (1994) 'The influence of temperament and mothering on attachment and exploration: An experimental manipulation of sensitive responsiveness among lower-class mothers with irritable infants' *Child Development Vol 65 pp 1457–1477*

Van der Kolk B (1994) 'The body keeps the score: Memory and the evolving psychobiology of posttraumatic stress' *Harvard Review of Psychiatry* Vol 1 pp 253–265

Verny T and Kelly J (1981) *The Secret Life of the Unborn Child* Delta Books, New York

Villanueva Siasoco R (2001) 'Slavery: Human bondage in Africa, Asia, and the Dominican Republic' 18 April 2001 – search http://www. infoplease.com/spot/slavery1.html

Vincent P (2003) 'Global warming – the debate heats up' *The Sydney Morning Herald* 30 October 2003

Vissing YM, Strauss M, Gelles RJ and Harrop JW (1991) 'Verbal aggression by parents and psychological problems of children' *Child Abuse and Neglect* Vol 15(3) pp 223–238

W

Wadud A (2002) 'A'isha's legacy' *New Internationalist* May 2002 pp 16–17

Wagner M (1994) *Pursuing the Birth Machine* ACE Graphics, Camperdown, NSW

Wagner M (2000) 'Fish can't see water: The need to humanize birth in Australia' Birth International http://www.acegraphics.com.au/ articles/wagner03.html

Walters GC and Grusec JE (1977) *Punishment* WH Freeman, San Francisco California

Watson L (1995) *Dark Nature* Sceptre, London

West M and George C (2002) 'Attachment and dysthymia: The contributions of preoccupied attachment and agency of self to depression in women' *Attachment and Human Development* December 2002 Vol 4(3) pp 278–293

White RK (ed) (1986) *Psychology and the Prevention of Nuclear War* NYU Press, New York

Wiehe VR (1990) 'Religious influence on parental attitudes toward the use of corporal punishment' *Journal of Family Violence* Vol 5(2) pp 173–187

'Women and the United Nations – Directory' (Autumn 2002) p 5 – search http://www.findarticles.com

Y

Youssef RM, Attia MS and Kamel MI (1998) 'Children experiencing violence I: Parental use of corporal punishment' *Child Abuse & Neglect* Vol 22(10) pp 959–973

Z

Zakaria F (2002) 'Ideology the only way to beat fanatics' *The Weekend Herald (New Zealand)* 28–29 December 2002 p A23

Zeanah CH and Scheeringa MS (1997) 'The experience and effects of violence in infancy' in Osofsky JD *Children in a Violent Society'* The Guilford Press, New York

Index

Index

P

Parenting, 19, 142, 167, 176
  alloparents, role of, 366–7
  childcare, 370
  assertive, 176, 213–15
  empathy, role of, 219, 225, 375
  'instinct', 19
  need for support, 329–30
  own childhood histories, affect of, 361, 364
  working through personal blocks to, 363
  see also Abandoning mode, Ambivalent mode, Authoritarian parenting, Authoritative parenting, Community, Core Emotional development, Emotional intelligence, Helping mode, Intrusive mode, Infanticidal mode, Religious extremism, Socialising mode
Patriarchy, 101, 144
  see also Child–rearing
Perry, Bruce, 228, 262–3, 287, 312
Piaget, Jean, 73, 75, 252
Piers, Maria, 46, 122
Pinochet, Augusto, 169
Plato, 28, 35
Politicians, 2, 6, 43, 137, 143, 171, 335, 357
  see also Policy–makers
Policy-makers, 107
Popper, Micha, 334
Porter, Louise, 179, 191, 207, 213
Positive core beliefs, 289, 313, 344, 352
Post natal depression (PND), 368
Post-traumatic stress disorder (PTSD), 317, 369
Prescott, James W, 283
Psychohistory, 24, 100, 391
Psychotherapy, 74, 85, 252, 259–60, 278, 319, 357, 364
Psychology, 4, 73, 85, 96, 173, 201, 204, 254, 287, 391
Puhar, Alenka, 107
Punishment, *see* Child battery, Discipline

R

Rape, *see* Sexual abuse
Religious extremism, 142–3
Rewards, *see* Manipulation
Robertson, Geoffrey, 169
Robinson, Jean, 369
Robinson, Mary, 169
Rousseau, Jean-Jacques, 62, 160, 221
Rumsfeld, Donald, 6
Rush, Florence, 51
Russian child-rearing, 114

S

Sabbah, Fatna A, 144
Sardar, Ziauddin, 146
Scharf, Robert, 4
Scheff, Thomas, 199
Schreber, Daniel Gottlieb Moritz, 122
Sewall, Samuel, 162
Sexual abuse, 50, 56, 59, 66, 81
  see also Child abuse
Shahak, Israel, 153–154
Shaming, 194–7, 351
  adulthood, carried to, 199
  brain development, and, 236
  children, damage to, 198
  mental illness, and, 200
  psychological study of, 197
  relationships, damage to, 198–9
Social evolution, 3, 24, 388
  Socialising mode, 69–70, 72, 76, 172, 176, 179–180, 194, 309
  dividends of, 167
  passing of, the, 176

Acknowledgments

Many friends, colleagues and family members have blessed me with their warmth, support and helpful contributions to this project. Your energies have enriched this book immeasurably, and made my writing journey more joyous and fulfilling. I am deeply grateful to the following people.

Linda, for your belief in me and in this project, for your love and support through the years of work, and for the pleasure of a passion shared. Your insightful feedback has knocked rough-edges off every page. I cannot imagine a better mate with whom to share a vision.

Barry, without whose support this book might not have been written, and Rosmarie, for your steadfast prayers and encouragement.

There is much to thank my parents for, but in relation to this book there are two main things: your immense courage in risking everything — time and again — to find and settle in this world's most democratic societies. I thank you also for your commitment to my education.

Chris Campbell, for your friendship and for the profound and life-changing influence you have had on my relationships, on my practice and on my worldview.

Beth McGregor, who dared me to write my first article, who was the initial spark behind the ideas in Chapter 18, and who co-authored with me the original article on which that chapter was closely based.

This book owes much to the visionary works of Lloyd de Mause, who has accomplished a formidable task in unearthing the historical evolution of parenting, and alerting the world to its weighty implications. And to Stephen Juan, whose courageous writings first awakened my interest in psychohistory, and who shepherded me towards the works of other psychohistorians.

Tanya West of Mona Vale library, for your bubbly nature and your relentless pursuit of every book and journal article that I ever asked for.

W.E., for your diligent translation of ancient texts and John Kot, for your generosity and your photographic skill.

Mitch Hall, for the enormous enthusiasm you have generously shown me, you have often helped to put the wind back in my sails. Jan Hunt, John Travis, Victor Evatt, Kali Wendorf, Pinky McKay, Sue Williamson and John Cunningham; you have each helped me so much to trust in this book, and you have each with your invaluable suggestions left your personal imprint upon it.

This book has been blessed with gifted editors whom, beyond providing invaluable challenges in matters of style and dogma, also share a deep commitment to the betterment of children's lives. Jessica Perini, not only have you empowered every chapter with your editorial advice, you have added more through your own research, and with your expertise in historical matters, than I could have dreamed of. For daring to sift through and transform the inchoate mass that was my first four chapters, I thank Carol Witt, David Witt and Joanna Pagan.

David Longfield of Longueville Media, thanks for your professionalism, your integrity and your wizardry in helping to bring this project to fruition.

When I close my eyes I see a procession of faces, the many friends who have in so many ways, with supportive words, curiosity, excitement and encouragement, provided so much of the fuel that kept me going with this large project. To all of you, my heartfelt thanks.

Updates to this book are available from
www.socialbaby.com/shop/page.asp?id=PPWup

and extra information about Robin Grille and his work are available
from **www.our-emotional-health.com**

THE CHILDREN'S PROJECT
STARTING FROM DAY ONE TO MAKE THE DIFFERENCE™

Outstanding books from the Children's Project

THE SOCIAL BABY
Understanding Babies' Communication from Birth
Lynne Murray and Liz Andrews
Clear text and hundreds of pictures show how new babies are able to communicate their strengths and vulnerabilities. By understanding this unique communication, parents and carer's can respond sensitively to their baby's needs during the first important months.

Available in paperback and on DVD

THE SOCIAL TODDLER
Promoting Positive Behaviour
Helen and Clive Dorman
Toddler behaviour explained in clear, simple text and over 1700 pictures. Covering the period from 12 months to 4 years, the book offers a remarkable insight to how toddlers view their ever expanding world from *their* point of view.

Available in paperback, DVD and Professional Edition DVD

The Children's Project produces and sells a range of books, DVDs and products that help parents and carers of babies and pre-school children better understand and respond sensitively to the needs of children.

For more information, or to buy online visit

www.socialbaby.com